Mission and Catechesis

Figure 1. Portrait of Alexandre de Rhodes, S.J. Preserved in Paris at the Musée de la France d'Outre-mer. According to L. Cadière, "Iconographie du Père de Rhodes" (1938), it is probably a copy of an old portrait preserved at the Seminary of the Paris Foreign Mission Society. The portrait reproduced here was executed by Sarut for the Colonial Exposition of Marseille in 1922.

FAITH AND CULTURES SERIES

Mission and Catechesis

Alexandre de Rhodes and Inculturation
in Seventeenth-Century Vietnam

Peter C. Phan

ORBIS BOOKS

Maryknoll, New York 10545

Text of Part One, "Mission and Catechesis in Seventeenth-Century Vietnam," copyright © 1998 by Peter C. Phan.

Translation of Part Two, "The *Cathechismus* of Alexandre de Rhodes, S.J.," originally published as *Cathechismus pro iis, qui volunt suscipere baptismum in octo dies divisus* (Roma: Typis Sacrae Congregationis de Propaganda Fide, 1651), copyright © by Peter C. Phan.

Published by Orbis Books, Maryknoll, New York, U.S.A.

Manufactured in the United States of America

Library of Congress Cataloging-in-Publication Data
Phan, Peter C., 1943-
    Mission and catechesis : Alexandre de Rhodes and inculturation in
  seventeenth-century Vietnam / Peter C. Phan.
      p.   cm. – (Faith and cultures series)
    Includes bibliographical references and index.
    ISBN 1-57075-166-8 (cloth)
    1. Rhodes, Alexandre de, 1591-1660. 2. Jesuits – Missions –
  Vietnam – History – 17th century. 3. Missionaries – Vietnam –
  History – 17th century. 4. Rhodes, Alexandre de, 1591-1660.
  Cathechismus pro iis qui volunt suscipere baptismum. 5. Catholic
  Church – Catechisms – History and criticism. 6. Vietnam – Church
  history – 17th century. I. Rhodes, Alexandre de, 1591-1660.
  Cathechismus pro iis qui volunt suscipere baptismum. English.
  II. Title.   III. Series.
  BV3311.2.R48P48 1998
  266'.2'092 – dc21
    [B]   97-42447
                                                   CIP

For my mother, Anna Le Thi So,
who taught me, among other things, the proverb
Ta ve ta tam ao ta; du trong du duc, ao nha cung hon,
Come back and bathe in your own pond;
clear or muddy, the home pond is always better

Contents

Part One
MISSION AND CATECHESIS
IN SEVENTEENTH-CENTURY VIETNAM

THE SEVENTH DAY:
The Passion, Death, Resurrection, and Ascension of Jesus –
Pentecost and the Church

THE EIGHTH DAY:
Eschatology – The Decalogue – Preparation for Baptism

Illustrations and Maps

Foreword

Robert J. Schreiter, C.P.P.S.

This book carries the deceptively simple title *Mission and Catechesis*, but holds a remarkable trove of information and reflection. It is about the seventeenth-century apostle to Vietnam, Alexandre de Rhodes, S.J., who built upon initial efforts of sixteenth-century missionaries to establish the church in that region. De Rhodes the man is of intrinsic interest. Not only can he be considered the founder of the church in what is now Vietnam; he also carried on missionary efforts later in Armenia and Persia. This is the first book-length study of his life and work to appear in any language.

But de Rhodes is of interest not only as one of the remarkable missionaries of the sixteenth and seventeenth centuries, along with his fellow Jesuits Francis Xavier, Roberto de Nobili, and Matteo Ricci. He adapted the form of the Christian message to Vietnamese culture in such a way that Christianity was able to enter more fully into Vietnamese culture. Indeed some of the Vietnamese words he proposed to translate Western theological concepts remain part of the Vietnamese theological vocabulary to this day. In the process, the European Christianity de Rhodes brought was amplified by encounter with a culture already three millennia old.

For this contribution alone, de Rhodes deserves to stand alongside his better-known confreres de Nobili and Ricci. In addition, though, the heritage of de Rhodes as a seventeenth-century interpreter of what now would be called inculturation and his contribution to Vietnamese culture as a whole cannot be underestimated. The *Cathechismus* he wrote to evangelize the Vietnamese people was the first Vietnamese-language book to be published in the West. And the Roman alphabet with a diacritical marking system he devised became the basis for the alphabet used to this day in the Vietnamese language. In many ways he remains an example of what genuine inculturation should be: a presentation of the Christian message in forms that are appropriate to the culture and that contribute further to the building up of that culture, even as they raise questions for those who evangelize.

Peter Phan has done us all a service by presenting the life and work of this man, delving into archival resources hitherto unmined for this intriguing story. He presents an important figure about whom little has been written up to this time. Alongside this important historical presentation, he gives us also the first translation of de Rhodes's most important work, the *Cathechismus,* through which he evangelized Vietnam. This makes accessible an important text not only for scholars, but also for the many contemporary Vietnamese who would be able to read this three-century-old cultural monument only with great difficulty and limited understanding.

Phan augments this historical work — significant in itself — with an examination of de Rhodes's central work from a theological and pastoral point of view. He begins by looking at the sixteenth-century genre of the catechism itself, as used by both sides of the European Reformation. He notes its significance as adapted for first evangelization in lands and among peoples new to the European missionaries, rather than as means for instructing the ignorant in their faith, as had been its use in Europe. He goes on to show how the genre was adapted in Asia and traces especially Ricci's influence on de Rhodes's work. In view of the renewed discussion of the catechism genre prompted by the publication of the *Catechism of the Catholic Church,* Phan's reflections are both revelatory of the past and instructive for the present.

Pioneering as de Rhodes's work was, Peter Phan's study is by no means anachronistic. He refuses to glide over what would now be seen as shortcomings in a process of inculturation. Phan concludes his study with a look at the achievement of de Rhodes in light of contemporary discussions of inculturation. De Rhodes, of course, does not measure up completely to them. But this should not obscure his importance for contemporary students of faith and culture. He offers a marvelous study of an evangelizer who enters a completely different culture and works to give the Christian message a form that is more than superficially understandable to those whom he wishes to reach. The inculturated message works not only to bring the Gospel, but to deepen the encounter between Gospel and culture. It shapes the future directions of the culture itself and raises significant questions about the form in which the Gospel is presented in any place.

Peter Phan has done a tremendous service to many readers by this book. For historians, he has presented the life and work of a missionary who deserves to be better known. For theologians he offers significant insights into the presentation of Christian faith, the strengths and limitations of the catechism genre, and the challenges of authentic inculturation. For students of Vietnamese history and culture he makes available a significant text that has influenced the development of Vietnam in many different ways. All in all, this work is exemplary of what missiological study can be at its best: allowing a greater appreciation of the past, raising important questions for missionary practice in the present, and enhancing the cultural sphere in which missionary activity takes place.

Preface

Cristoforo Borri reports that one day Francesco Buzomi, an Italian missionary, who had arrived in Indochina in 1615 and who was superior of the Jesuit mission there, was a spectator at a popular comedy in which a Vietnamese actor, dressed as a Portuguese, came onto the stage, carrying a bag in which a child was hidden. He pulled the child out of the bag and asked: "Child, do you want to enter into the belly of the Portuguese?" To which the child answered affirmatively. Then, the comedian pushed the child into his belly, then pulled him out again, and again asked him the same question. He repeated this sketch a number of times, and each time the crowd roared with laughter.[1]

Then it dawned on Buzomi that the question that was repeated by the comedian was the same question the missionaries' interpreters asked someone if he or she wanted to be baptized. Buzomi realized to his horror that the Vietnamese had misunderstood that to become a Christian he or she must renounce being a Vietnamese and become a Portuguese. To correct this fatal error, he tried to devise another formula to replace the one used by the interpreters. Buzomi finally settled on the formula: "Muon vao dao christian chang?"[2]

The question of the relationship between the Christian faith and local cultures is as old as Christianity. It became the subject of intense theological debate as Christianity moved out of its Jewish matrix into the Greek, Roman, Germanic and other cultural contexts. If this question has become more acute in this century, it is certainly not because it is entirely novel, but because, in addition to the disappearance of Western colonialism and the subsequent emergence of national and cultural independence, our times have witnessed a more lively sense of the universal presence of Christ and his Spirit in all peoples and their cultures and therefore of the intrinsic worth of each people's cultural heritage.

In this book I explore the achievements of one missionary to Vietnam in the seventeenth century, the French Jesuit Alexandre de Rhodes, who attempted to inculturate the Christian faith into the Vietnamese society. As a result, both the Christian faith and the Vietnamese culture were enriched and transformed.

In more ways than one this book is my homecoming. To research on its theme I came back to my native country after two decades of enforced absence to gather necessary materials, often under most difficult circumstances.

---

1. Borri, 102. Borri reports the question in Vietnamese: "Con gnoc muon bau tlong laom Hoalaom chiam?"

2. Literally, this formula means: "Do you want to enter the Christian way?" In the old spelling it reads: "Muon bau dau Christiam chiam?" See Borri, 103.

But more than a physical return, the work afforded me the opportunity to immerse myself in the cultural, religious, and spiritual streams that have fed and refreshed the minds and hearts of my people for thousands of years before the coming of Christianity and have continued to nourish them ever since the Good News was preached to them.

It is for me a great pleasure to record here my deepest gratitude to the various people who assisted me in this research. To be mentioned first and foremost is Dr. Do Quang Chinh, S.J., whose scholarly studies on de Rhodes have been of immense help to me. Concern for Dr. Chinh's personal safety does not permit me to relate the circumstances in which I met him in Vietnam and received from him literature on de Rhodes, both archival materials and his own writings, since he himself had suffered years of imprisonment for his scholarly research. I am profoundly grateful to him for his gracious welcome to his humble lodgings, his generous scholarly assistance, and his faithful witness to the Christian way of life amidst plenteous suffering.

Two friends in Vietnam, Mark Nguyen Duc Huynh and Amélie Nguyen Thi Sang, were of great help in procuring indispensable materials on de Rhodes.

My cousin André Ta Dinh Chung and his family have efficiently helped me locate other sources on de Rhodes in Paris, France. From Rome, Italy, Professor Achille Triacca was also helpful in obtaining for me sources on seventeenth-century catechesis. In this country, Professors William Cenkner, Monika Hellwig, Berard Marthaler, and Robert Schreiter were willing to lend their academic reputation in support of my applications for grants, and to them go my sincere thanks.

Funding for research leading to this publication was provided by the Research Enablement Program, a grant program for mission scholarship supported by the Pew Charitable Trusts, Philadelphia, Pennsylvania, U.S.A., and administered by the Overseas Ministries Study Center, New Haven, Connecticut, U.S.A. I am grateful to the Director of the Research Enablement Program, Dr. Gerald H. Anderson, and its Coordinator, Rev. Geoffrey A. Little, for their kindness, especially during the colloquium in Nashville in June 1996. I am thankful to the members of the colloquium who have made very helpful comments on my work, especially Drs. Andrew Walls, Dana Robert, Daniel H. Bays, Andrew Thornley, Gail O. King, Richard Pierard, and Robert Frykenberg.

To Gerard Austin, David Granfield, Patrick Granfield, and John Ford, who occasionally removed me from my sabbatical hiding with invitations to culinary delights, my heartfelt thank-you.

My thanks are also directed to Dr. William Burrows, editor at Orbis Books, and Catherine Costello, for their careful work on the manuscript, and to Susan Perry, also editor at Orbis Books, for her continued support and encouragement. I also thank Roland Jacques for his invaluable comments on the earliest stages of Catholic mission in Vietnam. Last but not least, my deepest thanks are owed to Dr. Linda L. Stinson for sharing with me her insights into the psycho-sociological aspects of inculturation.

Finally, three notes on the text itself. First, it has not been possible to append diacritical marks to the Vietnamese words. As is well known, the same Vietnamese word, when marked with different diacritical marks (five in all, plus the unaccented tone), has entirely different meanings. Those who know Vietnamese can easily guess the appropriate marks for these words; for those who do not know the language, those diacritical marks do not mean anything and are therefore unnecessary. Second, with rare exceptions, I have not cited Vietnamese scholarly works, mainly because they are not accessible, and have limited myself to works in Western languages. Third, all translations of de Rhodes's works, which aim more at accuracy than literary elegance, are mine. For reason of space, it is not possible to quote the original texts in the footnotes to allow verification of the accuracy of the translations.

With this modest book I hope not only to enable Western readers to get better acquainted with one of the most glorious chapters of the history of Christian mission, catechesis, and inculturation in the seventeenth century but also to encourage Vietnamese expatriates, especially the young ones, to return and bathe in their own cultural pond and discover therein refreshing waters for their cultural enrichment and faith.

PETER C. PHAN
The Catholic University of America

Abbreviations

I. ALEXANDRE DE RHODES'S WORKS

Relazione   *Relazione de' felici successi della Santa Fede Predicata*... (1650).

Dictionarium   *Dictionarium annamiticum, lusitanum, et latinum*... (1651).

Linguae annamiticae   *Linguae annamiticae seu Tunchinensis brevis declaratio* (1651).

Cathechismus   *Cathechismus pro iis, qui volunt suscipere Baptismum*... (1651).

Histoire du Royaume   *Histoire du Royaume de Tunquin, et des grands progrez que la prédication*... (1651).

Tunchinensis historiae   *Tunchinensis historiae libri duo*... (1652).

Relation des progrez   *Relation des progrez de la Foy au Royaume de la Cochinchine*... (1652).

La glorieuse mort   *La glorieuse mort d'André Catéchiste de la Cochinchine*... (1653).

Divers voyages   *Divers voyages et missions du P. Alexandre de Rhodes en la Chine*... (1653).

Sommaire   *Sommaire des divers voyages, et Missions apostoliques*... (1653).

Histoire de la vie   *Histoire de la vie et de la glorieuse mort, de cinq Pères de la Compagnie de Jésus*... (1653).

Relation de la mission   *Relation de la Mission des Pères de la Compagnie de Jésus*... (1659).

II. OTHER WORKS

AHSI   *Archivum Historicum Societatis Jesu.*

ARSI, JS   *Archivum Romanum Societatis Jesu, Jap.-Sin.*

BAVH   *Bulletin des Amis du Vieux-Hué.*

BEFEO	*Bulletin de l'École française d'Extrême-Orient.*
Borri	Cristoforo Borri, *Relation de la nouvelle Mission des Pères de la Compagnie de Jésus...* (1631).
Cadière I	Léopold Cadière, *Croyances et pratiques religieuses des Vietnamiens*, vol. I (1944).
Cadière II	Léopold Cadière, *Croyances et pratiques religieuses des Vietnamiens*, vol. II (1955).
Cadière III	Léopold Cadière, *Croyances et pratiques religieuses des Vietnamiens*, vol. III (1956).
Cardim	António Francisco Cardim and Francesco Barreto, *Relation de ce qui s'est passé depuis quelques années...* (1646).
Chappoulie I	Henri Chappoulie, *Aux origines d'une Eglise*, vol. I (1943).
Chappoulie II	Henri Chappoulie, *Aux origines d'une Eglise*, vol. II (1948).
Do Quang Chinh	Do Quang Chinh, "La Mission au Viet-Nam 1624–30 et 1640–45 d'Alexandre de Rhodes" (1969).
Machault	Jacques de Machault, *Relation des Missions des Pères de la Compagnie de Jésus...* (1659).
Marini	Giovanni Filippo de Marini, *Relation nouvelle et curieuse des Royaumes de Tunquin et de Lao...* (1666).
Nguyen Chi Thiet	Nguyen Chi Thiet, "Le Catéchisme du Père Alexandre de Rhodes" (1970).
Nguyen Khac Xuyen	"Le Catéchisme en langue vietnamienne romanisée du P. Alexandre de Rhodes" (1956).
Pub. EFEO	*Publications de l'École française d'Extrême-Orient.*
Saccano	Metello Saccano, *Relation des progrez de la Foy au Royaume de la Cochinchine és années 1646 & 1647...* (1653).
Tan Phat	Placide Tan Phat, "Méthodes de catéchèse et de conversion du Père Alexandre de Rhodes" (1963).
Tissanier	Joseph Tissanier, *Relation du voyage du P. Joseph Tissanier de la Compagnie de Jésus...* (1663).

Chronology of Alexandre de Rhodes

AVIGNON – ROME

March 15, 1593	Birth of Alexandre de Rhodes in Avignon.
April 14, 1612	Entrance into the Jesuit novitiate in Rome.
April 15, 1614	First vows in the Company of Jesus.
1614–18	Theological studies in Rome.
1618	Ordained to the priesthood.

ROME – MACAO

October 1618	Departure from Rome – Loretta – Milan – Avignon – Barcelona – Toledo – Lisbon.
January 1619	Arrival in Lisbon.
April 4, 1619	Departure from Lisbon for Goa.
October 9, 1619	Arrival in Goa.
April 12, 1622	Departure from Goa – Cochin – Comorin Cape – The Fisheries Coast – Ceylon (Sri Lanka) – Megapatam.
June 24, 1622	Departure from Megapatam for Malacca (Malaysia).
July 27, 1622	Arrival in Malacca.
April 1623	Departure for Macao.
May 29, 1623	Arrival in Macao.

FIRST MISSION IN COCHINCHINA

December 1624	Departure from Macao for Cochinchina.
1624–26	Language study in Thanh Chiem (Quang Nam).
July 1626	Return to Macao to prepare for mission in Tonkin.

MISSION IN TONKIN

March 12, 1627	Departure for Tonkin.
March 19, 1627	Arrival in Cua Bang (Thanh Hoa).
April 1627	First meeting with Lord Trinh Trang.
May 3, 1627	Construction of the first church in Tonkin at An Vuc.
June 1627	Departure from An Vuc for the capital of Tonkin.
July 2, 1627	Arrival in Thang Long, the capital.
November 1627	First Jesuit residence in Tonkin built at the order of Lord Trinh Trang.
May 28, 1628	Edict of expulsion. De Rhodes under surveillance.
March 1629	Exiled to Bo Chinh and Nghe An.
November 1629	Return to the capital of Tonkin.
May 1630	Establishment of the institution of catechists in Tonkin. (Between March 1627 and May 1630, de Rhodes baptized some 5,602 people.)
May 1630	De Rhodes expelled definitively from Tonkin.
1630–40	Professor of Theology at the Jesuit College in Macao.

SECOND MISSION IN COCHINCHINA

February 1640	Arrival in Cua Han (Da Nang). First meeting with Lord Nguyen Phuoc Lan, "king" of Cochinchina.
September 1640	Expelled from Cochinchina. Return to Macao.
December 17, 1640	Arrival in Cua Han. Missionary work in Thanh Chiem, Ha Lam, Cat Lam, Bau Goc, Dinh Phu Yen.
July 2, 1641	Return to Macao by way of Manila.
July 20, 1641	Arrival in Bolibao.
August 15, 1641	Arrival in Manila.
September 21, 1641	Departure from Manila for Macao.
January 1642	Return to Cochinchina. Arrival in Cua Han.
July 31, 1643	Establishment of the institution of catechists in Cochinchina.

July 31, 1643	Return to Macao.
March 1644	Return to Cochinchina. Arrival in Cua Han.
July 26, 1644	Witnesses the martyrdom of Catechist Andrew.
June 11, 1645	Imprisoned in Hue, the capital of Cochinchina. Condemned to death, but penalty commuted to expulsion.
June 17, 1645	De Rhodes brought from Hue to Hoi An. In prison in Hoi An for twenty-two days.
July 9, 1645	Definitive expulsion from Cochinchina. (From February 1640 to July 1645, de Rhodes baptized some 3,400 people.)
July 23, 1645	Arrival in Macao. Participation in a discussion with Jesuits regarding the baptismal formula adapted by de Rhodes for the Vietnamese.

MACAO – DJAKARTA – ISFAHAN – ROME

December 20, 1645	Leaves Macao for Rome.
January 14, 1646	Arrival in Malacca (Malaysia).
February 22, 1646	Leaves Malacca for Djakarta (Indonesia).
July 29, 1646	Imprisoned for three months in Djakarta (July–October 1646).
October 21, 1646	Leaves Djakarta for Bantam.
October 25, 1646	Leaves Bantam for Macassar (Celebes). Meeting with Carim Patingaloa, the "king" of Macassar.
June 15, 1647	Leaves Macassar for Bantam.
June 30, 1647	Arrival in Bantam.
July 31, 1647	Leaves Bantam for Surat.
September 30, 1747	Arrival in Surat. Four months in Surat.
February 3, 1648	Departure for Persia.
April 13, 1648	Arrival in Isfahan, the capital of Persia. Three months in Isfahan.
June 28, 1648	Departure from Isfahan.
August 1648	Arrival in Julfa, the ancient capital of Armenia.

September 1648	Arrival in Erivan, a city of upper Armenia. Three months in Erivan because of illness.
December 10, 1648	Leaves Erivan for Erzurum, a city of lower Armenia.
December 18, 1648	Arrival in Erzurum.
January 11, 1649	Departure from Erzurum.
February 21, 1649	Arrival in Tokat.
March 17, 1649	Arrival in Smyrna.
June 27, 1649	Arrival in Rome.

ROME – PARIS – ISFAHAN

1649–52	Work in Rome to establish a hierarchy in Vietnam.
1652–54	Work in Marseille, Lyon, and Paris for the church in Vietnam.
November 16, 1654	Leaves Marseille for Persia. Stopover in Malta.
December 2, 1654	Leaves Malta for Syria.
December 12, 1654	Arrival in Seyde (Syria). Christmas in the Holy Land.
November 1655	Arrival in Isfahan. Superior of the Jesuit mission in Persia. Study of the language.
November 5, 1660	Death in Isfahan.

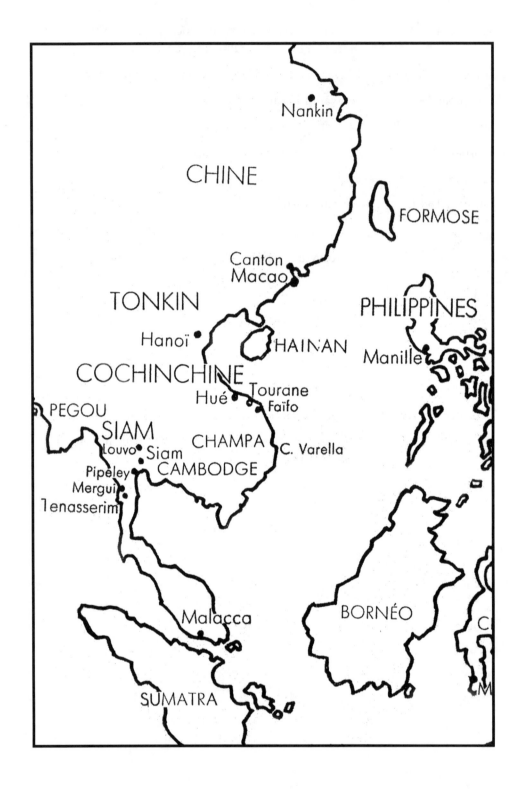

Figure 2. Important locations in the life of Alexandre de Rhodes.

Part One

Mission and Catechesis in Seventeenth-Century Vietnam

1

Vietnam in the Seventeenth Century

The Context of Christian Mission

The Vietnam which Alexandre de Rhodes came to evangelize is of course not identical with the Vietnam of today, officially known as the Socialist Republic of Vietnam. With the current population at about 75 million and with an area of 128,000 square miles, contemporary Vietnam, whose thousand-mile-long, narrow, and elongated shape resembles an *S*, lies in Southeast Asia, between the Tropic of Cancer and the Equator. It is bounded on the west by Laos and Kampuchea (named once again as Cambodia in May 1989), on the north by China; to the northeast it is bathed by the Gulf of Tonkin, to the east by the Pacific Ocean, to the south by the Gulf of Thailand.

To understand the challenges facing de Rhodes in his missionary activities and the magnitude of his manifold accomplishments, it is necessary to make a leap over the three hundred and seventy-odd years that separated de Rhodes's first arrival to Vietnam in 1624 from our times and to acquire some basic knowledge of the cultural, political, and religious situation of seventeenth-century Vietnam in which he labored as a missionary.[1]

---

1. Besides innumerable works in Vietnamese (among which the most useful is Pham Van Son, *Viet Su Tan Bien*, in seven volumes), the following works in European languages are especially helpful: Charles Maybon, *Histoire moderne du pays d'Annam: 1592–1820* (Paris: Plon, 1920); idem, *Lectures sur l'histoire moderne et contemporaine de l'Annam: 1428–1926* (Hanoi, 1930); idem, *Histoire du Viet-Nam* (Paris: Larose, 1931); Lieutenant Colonel Bonifacy, *Les débuts de Christianisme en Annam: Des origines au commencement du XVIIIè siècle* (Hanoi, 1930); Adrien Launay, *Histoire de la Mission de Cochinchine (1658–1823): Documents historiques,* vol. 1 (Paris, 1920); idem, *Histoire ancienne et moderne de l'Annam* (Paris, 1884); Manuel Teixeira, *As Missões Portuguesas no Vietnam* [*Macau e a sua diocese,* vol. 14] (Macau: Imprensa Nacional, 1977); Josef Metzler, *Die Synoden in Indochina: 1625–1934* (Paderborn: Ferdinand Schöningh); Le Thanh Khoi, *Le Viet-Nam, Histoire et Civilisation* (Paris, 1955); idem, *Histoire du Viet-Nam des origines à 1858* (Paris: Sudestasie, 1982); Pierre Huard and Maurice Durand, *Connaissance du Viet-Nam* (Paris-Hanoi, 1954); Nguyen Van Huyen, *La civilisation ancienne du VietNam* (Hanoi: Editions The Gioi, 1994; this is an abridged reprint of *La civilisation annamite,* published in 1944); Henri Bernard, *Pour la compréhension de l'Indochine et de l'Occident*

ANNAM: ONE COUNTRY IN TWO PARTS, TONKIN AND COCHINCHINA

As with most other peoples' beginnings, the dawn of Vietnamese history is shrouded in the mist of mythology. According to the *National Annals,* King Lac Long, of the Hong Bang or Hung dynasty and grandson of the sea god, married Au Co, a mountain goddess. From this union a hundred boys were hatched from a hundred eggs carried in a pouch by Au Co. Half of the children followed their father to his sea domain, and the other half joined their mother in the mountains. From this separation the kingdom of One Hundred Principalities (Bach Viet) came into being, the most powerful of which was the Lac Viet or Van Lang, literally, the country of the cultured, whom the Vietnamese claim as their first ancestors.

The Hong Bang dynasty is said to have lasted from 2879 B.C.E. to 258 B.C.E., with eighteen kings. It was brought to an end by Thuc Vuong Phan, a member of the Thuc dynasty, who changed the name of the country to Au Lac and ruled under the name of An Duong Vuong. King An Duong sought to protect his country by building a fortressed city in the form of a three-story conch, the remains of which can be seen today in Co Loa, some ten miles from Hanoi. In 208 B.C.E. a Chinese general, Trieu Da, vanquished An Duong Vuong, renamed the country Nam Viet, and ruled until his death in 137 B.C.E. The Trieu dynasty was brought to end in 111 B.C.E. by the invasion of the Chinese Han dynasty.

The Chinese ruled over Vietnam off and on for ten centuries (111 B.C.E.–39 C.E., 43–544, 602–918, 1414–27), from the occupation by the Han dynasty to that by the Ming dynasty. Sporadic insurrections by the Vietnamese (of which two were led by women: the sisters Trung Trac and Trung Nhi in 40 C.E. and Trieu Au in 248) occurred, and periods of national independence took

(Paris: Cathasia, 1950); L. E. Louvet, *La Cochinchine religieuse,* 2 vols. (Paris, 1885); Edouard Digues, *Les Annamites: société, coutumes, religions* (Paris: Challamel, 1906); Tran Van Trung, *Le Viet-Nam et sa civilisation* (Paris: Ed. Belle page, 1956); Joseph Buttinger, *The Smaller Dragon: A Political History of Vietnam* (New York: Praeger, 1958); Chappoulie I, 3–21; Tan Phat, 10–23; Nguyen Huu Trong, *Les Origines du clergé vietnamien* (Saigon: Tinh Viet, 1959), 41–56.

Besides these modern authors, the writings of seventeenth-century missionaries provide an extremely valuable mine of information not only on the situation of Christianity but also on the sociopolitical and cultural aspects of both Tonkin and Cochinchina. Most of these writings are yet unpublished manuscripts located principally in the archives of the Jesuit order (ARSI), section *Jap.-Sin.,* and *Fondo Gesuitico,* and to a lesser extent, at the Biblioteca Nazionale Centrale in Rome, *Fondo Gesuitico,* and in the archives of the Propagande Fide.

De Rhodes himself gives us lengthy and amazingly accurate information on Tonkin (see the first part of his *Histoire du Royaume,* entitled *De l'Estat temporel du Royaume de Tunquin,* and the second part, chaps. 6 and 7 of his *Divers voyages*) and on Cochinchina (see the second part, chap. 1 of his *Divers voyages*). See also Borri, Cardim, Machault, Marini, and Tissanier.

For bibliographies on Vietnam, see Nguyen The Anh, *Bibliographie critique sur les relations entre Viet Nam et Occident en langues occidentales* (Paris: Maisonneuve et Larose, 1967); Chantal Descours-Gatin and Hugues Villiers, *Guide de recherches sur le Viet Nam: bibliographies, archives et bibliothèques de France* (Paris: L'Harmattan, 1983); and Kennedy G. Tregonning, *Southeast Asia: A Critical Bibliography* (Tucson: University of Arizona Press, 1969).

place with various dynasties, especially the Ngo (919–65), the Dinh (968–80), the Le (980–1009), the Ly (1010–1225), and the Tran (1225–1400, 1409–13) dynasties.

This millennium of Chinese domination unavoidably left indelible marks on the course of Vietnamese history, not only in political and economic arenas but also in cultural and religious spheres. With regard to culture and religion in particular, the Chinese practiced a systematic policy of assimilation. Chinese, with its ideogrammatic characters, was made the official language, and under the Ming occupation, the "five *Ching*," which the Vietnamese call *ngu kinh*, and the "four *Shu*," which are called *tu thu* in Vietnamese, were made obligatory textbooks at all educational levels. All existing important Vietnamese documents such as historical, legal, and military writings were taken off to China, and no traces of them are left today. Chinese customs were imposed, especially rituals of marriage and funerals. Men were forced to keep long hair, and women to wear short dresses. Even the widespread Vietnamese customs of blackening teeth and chewing betel (a combination of betel leaf, slivers of the areca palm nut, and a lime paste) were proscribed.

With regard to religion, of which we will speak at greater length, the three religions of China, i.e., Taoism, Confucianism, and Buddhism, were already introduced to Vietnam during the occupation by the Han dynasty, especially during the third century of our era. As we will see, of the three religions, which the Vietnamese call *tam giao*, Confucianism and Buddhism were given official support, especially under the Ly (1010–1225) and Tran (1225–1413) dynasties.

From the perspective of Christianity, the most important dynasty is the Le dynasty, often referred to as the Hau Le dynasty (literally, the Later Le) to distinguish it from the Tien Le dynasty (literally, the Early Le, of 980–1009). In 1427, after a ten-year struggle for independence, Le Loi overthrew the Ming occupation and founded the Le dynasty which lasted until 1788. In addition to social, agricultural, and educational reforms, such as the establishment of the College of National Sons (Quoc Tu Giam), this almost four-century-long dynasty is celebrated for two significant achievements. The first is the creation of the most advanced legal code known in Southeast Asia at that time, called the Hong Duc Code, the title of Emperor Le Thanh Ton (1460–97), who promulgated it. The second is the southward expansion of the kingdom (*nam tien*, literally, southward march) during which the southern kingdom of Champa (whose culture was practically obliterated) and parts of Cambodia were gradually annexed to Vietnam.

The Le dynasty reached its apogee in the second half of the fifteenth century, but by the beginning of the sixteenth it suffered decline. In 1527 Mac Dang Dung murdered King Le Chieu Ton, usurped the throne, and established the Mac dynasty. In 1532 Nguyen Kim and his son-in-law Trinh Kiem, who remained faithful to the Le dynasty, defeated the Mac, and restored the Le dynasty.

The country was subsequently divided into two kingdoms: the tiny kingdom of the Mac dynasty (called Bac Trieu, i.e., the northern kingdom), and the larger kingdom of the Le dynasty (called the Nam Trieu, i.e., the southern kingdom) from Thanh Hoa to the southernmost city of Phu Yen.

However, in the southern kingdom, the Le kings were only puppets. Real power rested in the hands of Trinh Kiem who, after his father-in-law's death, attempted to seize total power. Fearing opposition from his father-in-law's two sons, he had the elder (Nguyen Uong) killed, and the younger (Nguyen Hoang) sent to Thuan Hoa, the southern part of the country, in 1558. In 1592, Trinh Tung, who had succeeded his father Trinh Kiem, invaded the Mac's territory, defeated King Mac Mau Hop, and reunited the country. The surviving Mac family withdrew to the northernmost part of the country called Cao Bang, and with the help of the Ming and Ch'ing dynasties, survived until 1667.

In the meantime, Nguyen Hoang (1502–1613) succeeded in building his own independent domain in the southern part of the country where he had been exiled. His son, Nguyen Phuoc Nguyen, who ruled from 1613 to 1635, declared independence from the Trinh in the north.

At the beginning of the seventeenth century, then, the country known to the West as Annam[2] was divided into two major parts:[3] the northern part, called the Dang Ngoai, literally, the external region, under the rule of the Trinh clan, was made up of Tonkin, Thanh Hoa, Nghe An, Ha Tinh, and the northern part of Quang Binh, with Thang Long (today Hanoi) as the capital. To the West it was known as Tonkin.[4] The southern part, called the Dang Trong, literally,

---

2. As with most countries, Vietnam was known under many different names in the course of its history, some of which were adopted by native rulers, others imposed by the Chinese. Altogether, it has had twelve names: Van Lang under the Hong Bang dynasty (2879 B.C.E.–257 B.C.E.), Au Lac under the Thuc (257 B.C.E.–207 B.C.E.), Nam Viet under the Trieu (207 B.C.E.–111 B.C.E.), Giao Chi under the Chinese Early Han (111 B.C.E.–203 C.E.), Giao Chau under the Chinese Later Han (203–544), Van Xuan under the Early Ly (544–603), An Nam under the Chinese Tang (603–939), Dai Co Viet under the Tran (969–1054), Dai Viet under the Ly and the Tran (1054–1400), Dai Ngu under the Ho (1400–1407), again, An Nam under the Chinese Ming (1407–27), again, Dai Viet under the Le (1428–1802), Viet Nam under Emperor Gia Long (1802–20), Dai Nam under Emperor Minh Mang and his successors (1820–1945), and again Viet Nam after 1945. In almost all of these names, there is the word "Viet," which indicates the ethnic origin of the people, as distinct from that of the Han of the Yellow River in China. The word "Nam" means south, that is, south of China.

3. Strictly speaking, there were three parts, the third being Cao Bang, the northernmost region where the Mac dynasty withdrew after it had been defeated by the Trinh in 1592. It was called Dang Tren, literally, upper region. The Mac dynasty vanished in 1667, and Cao Bang was absorbed into the Chinese Ch'ing dynasty.

4. The name Tonkin (in Vietnamese: Dong Kinh) was originally used for the capital of the country, Thang Long, under the Ho Dynasty (1400–1407) and means "the eastern capital," as opposed to the site where the Ho had moved, namely, Tay Do (literally, the western capital). The name Thang Long, however, remained the official name of the capital until the reign of Minh Mang (1820–40) who changed it to Ha Noi. When Western merchants and missionaries first came to Vietnam in the seventeenth century, they transcribed Dong Kinh into "Tonkin" and used it to designate the region ruled by the Trinh. Other spellings of Tonkin include: Tunkin, Tunquin, Tunquim, Tunchin, Tungking, Tum Kinh, Tonquim, Tonquin, Toncquin, Tonchin, Tong-King, etc. In the seventeenth and eighteenth centuries, the Vietnamese called it "Dang Ngoai," that is, the external region. See Do Quang Chinh, 62–63. In this work I will refer to it as Tonkin or North Vietnam.

Both Tonkin and Cochinchina, about which see the next note, were well administered. Tonkin was divided into seven provinces, in addition to the province of the capital called the court or province of the

the internal region, under the rule of the Nguyen clan, comprised the southern part of Quang Binh, Quang Tri, Thua Thien, Quang Nam, Quang Ngai, and the provinces of ancient Champa (especially Qui Nhon and Phu Yen), with the capital in Hue. To the West it was known as Cochinchina.[5]

The border dividing the two parts is located at the river Gianh situated slightly above the 17th parallel.[6] Officially, there was only one king (Vietnamese: *vua*) of the Le dynasty, whose functions were exclusively ceremonial. Both the Trinh and the Nguyen, who called themselves lords (Vietnamese: *chua*), professed loyalty to the Le kings. In fact, however, they were independent and rival rulers with dynastic ambitions.

In 1620 the Trinh attempted to destroy the Nguyen who thereafter ceased paying tribute to the northern lords. When Lord Nguyen Phuoc Nguyen twice refused to obey Lord Trinh Trang's summons to go to Thang Long to explain his actions, the latter led a military expedition against the south in 1627. In fact, on his way to Tonkin de Rhodes met Lord Trinh Trang as the latter was going

---

court: Bo Chinh, Nghe An, Thanh Hoa, Ke Nam (southern province), Ke Tay (western province), Ke Bac (northern province), Ke Dong (eastern province). See de Rhodes's map of seventeenth-century Vietnam, reading from south to north, given in his *Divers voyages*.

5. The name "Cochinchina" seems to have derived from the old name of the country "Giao Chi," which, as we have seen, was given to the country under the Chinese Early Han Dynasty (111 B.C.E.–203 C.E.). Giao Chi means "people with separated toes." Toward the end of the sixteenth century, when the Japanese merchants arrived at Hoi An (Faifo) and Cua Hang (Da Nang), they called the natives "Coci" (from Giao Chi. Subsequently, the Portuguese merchants also called them "Cochi" and sometimes "Cochin." To avoid confusion with Cochin in India, they added the word "Cina" at the end to indicate nearness to China. Hence, Cochinchina. Other spellings include: Cochimchina, Chochimchina, Cocinchine, Caucicina, Cauchichina, Cauchj China, Cauchinchina, Coccincina, Concincina, Cauchenchina, Cachenchina, Cocamchina, Canchimchyna, Quachymchyna, Quamcymchyna, Eochijchina, etc. In the seventeenth and eighteenth centuries the Vietnamese referred to this region under the Nguyen officially as Dang Trong, literally "internal region." Other names for it are "Xu Quang" (country of the Quang provinces: Quang Binh, Quang Nam, Quang Nghia), "Xu Nam" (country of the south), "Nam Ha" (country to the south of river Gianh), "Mien Nam" (southern region). In this work I will refer to it as Cochinchina and as central Vietnam.

According to de Rhodes (although his information has been recently challenged by Yang Baoyun in his *Contribution à l'histoire de la Principauté des Nguyên au Vietnam méridional (1600–1775)* [Geneva: Olizane/Études Orientales, 1992]) Cochinchina was divided into six provinces: Ranran (Phu Yen), Qui Nhon, Quang Nghia, Ciam (Quang Nam), Thoa Noa, and Quang Binh. See de Rhodes's map, reading from south to north.

It is most important to note that both Tonkin and Cochinchina of the seventeenth and eighteenth centuries are not identical with those of the nineteenth century. Under French domination, Vietnam was divided into three parts by the June 6, 1884, Franco-Vietnamese treaty: Tonkin, Annam, and Cochinchine. In the seventeenth century, Cochinchina was part of Annam and stretched from the river Gianh to Phan Thiet, whereas the Cochinchine of the French occupation extended from Phan Thiet to Ha Tien. See Do Quang Chinh, 42–43.

6. In 1630 Lord Nguyen Phuoc Nguyen had a six-mile-long fortification, stretching from the mountain to the sea, built to prevent penetration by the Tonkinese army. The following year, another much more important wall was constructed at Dong Hoi, a little to the north of the first line of defense, by Dao Duy Tu, extending from Nhat Le port to Dong Hoi mountain. It was called "Luy Thay," literally, ramparts of the master, i.e., Dao Duy Tu. Thanks to this double rampart Cochinchina was able to repel several attacks by the north (1643, 1648, 1659, 1661, 1672). About the wall of Dong Hoi, see Léopold Cadière, "Le Mur de Dong Hoi au point de vue religieux," *Annales de la Société des Missions Étrangères* VIII (1905): 43–49, 107–18, 158–68; idem, "Le Mur de Dong Hoi: Étude sur l'établissement des Nguyen en Cochinchine," *BEFEO* VI, 1–2 (1906): 87–254.

to war against Lord Nguyen Phuoc Nguyen. Between 1627 and 1672, the Trinh waged seven unsuccessful wars against the Nguyen. After almost half a century of warfare, the two sides declared truce and agreed to be two independent parts of one country.

The unification of the two regions did not happen until 1802 when Nguyen Anh, one of the descendants of the Nguyen clan, wrested both the north and the south from the Tay Son Dynasty (1788–1802). He declared himself emperor under the name of Gia Long, and founded the Nguyen dynasty which ended on August 25, 1945, when the last emperor, Bao Dai, handed his imperial seal and sword over to the Communist delegate.

Emperor Gia Long renamed the country Vietnam and divided it into three parts (*ky*): Bac Ky (north), Trung Ky (center), and Nam Ky (south), with the capital in Hue. One of Gia Long's lasting achievements was the promulgation of a new code, called Gia Long Code, in 1815, replacing the fifteenth-century Hong Duc Code.[7]

THE BEGINNINGS OF THE CHRISTIAN MISSION

Christianity seems to have made its first appearance in Vietnam in the sixteenth century.[8] An edict of 1663 mentions that in 1533 there had been a prohibition of the diffusion of "the false doctrine of Gia To [Jesus] preached by a man of the sea [*duong nhan*] by the name of I Ne Khu (possibly Ignatius) in the villages of Ninh Cuong and Quan Anh of the district of Nam Chan and in the village of Tra Lu, of the district of Giao Thuy, in the province of Son Nam."[9] I Ne Khu was probably a Christian (priest?) who was sailing from Malacca to Macao along the coast of Vietnam and decided to enter the country to preach the Gospel.

---

7. For a study of the Gia Long Code, see Raymond Deloustal, *La justice dans l'ancien Annam, traduction, commentaire du code des Le* (Hanoi: École française d'Extrême-Orient, 1912–19).

8. It is to be noted that in the history of Portuguese expansion into the East, Portugal's interest in Vietnam came rather late. It was only when Japan closed its doors to Portuguese merchants that the Portuguese began its contact with Vietnam. Toward 1616, at the invitation of Cochinchina, viceroy Jerónimo de Azevedo, with the support of the Portuguese crown, planned the establishment of Portuguese colonies in the country, but the opposition of viceroys João Coutinho and Francisco da Gama scuttled these plans. In spite of this failure, there would later be regular commercial exchanges between Macao and the two Vietnamese states. See the studies of Pierre-Yves Manguin, *Les Portugais sur les côtes du Viet-Nam et du Campa: Études sur les routes maritimes et les relations commerciales, d'après les sources portugaises des XVIè, XVIIè et XVIIIè siècles* (Paris: E.F.E.O., 1972); Roderich Ptak, ed., *Portuguese Asia: Aspects in History and Economic History [16th–17th Centuries]* (Stuttgart: F. Steiner, 1987); Anthony Reid, *Southeast Asia in the Age of Commerce (1450–1680)*, vol. 1: *The Lands Below the Winds* (New Haven: Yale University Press, 1988); and George Bryan Souza, *The Survival of Empire: Portuguese Trade and Society in China and the South China Sea, 1630–1754* (Cambridge: Cambridge University Press, 1986).

9. See *Kham Dinh Viet Su Thong Giam Cuong Muc* (Text and commentary of the complete mirror of the history of Vietnam, established on imperial order), principal part, vol. 33, plate 6b. This important history was written in 1859 under the direction of Phan Thanh Gian and published in 1884.

The first missionaries to Cochinchina were no doubt the Portuguese Dominicans of the Province of the Holy Cross of the East Indies founded at Malacca. According to Marcos Gispert,[10] Gaspar de Santa Cruz was sent to Cambodia in 1550, and on his way there he stopped at Ha Tien and worked in this location, later a Vietnamese town, for five years (under the reign of King Le Trung Tong).[11]

In 1583 a group of Spanish Franciscans of the Province of the Holy Rosary in Manila came to Da Nang to preach but left after fifteen days because they did not know the language. One of them, Bartolomé Ruiz, came back the following year with a companion and was well received by King Mac Mau Hiep, but was able to baptize only a dying infant during his entire stay. He had to leave the country in 1586 following the decision of the superior general of the Franciscans, Francesco Gonzaga, in 1584. Later Pope Sixtus V decided to assign the mission of Indochina to the Portuguese.[12]

According to his own memoir, Ordonnez de Cevallos, an adventurous traveler and a priest from Andalusia, landed in Tonkin in 1590. He claimed to have found two Portuguese priests, Alfonso da Costa and Juan Gonsalvez de Sa, who had been sent there by the bishop of Macao. He reported that he himself had converted a sister of King Le The Tong, the princess of Champa. Again, according to his memoir, the princess fell in love with him and wanted to marry him, but he explained his inability to accept her offer of marriage on account of his vow of celibacy. He then went to preach in the south and boasted of having baptized the governor of Hue, Nguyen Hoang, one of his sons, Nguyen Kim, and numerous mandarins.[13] Historians do not give much credence to Ordonnez de Cevallos's memoir and believe that much of it, especially his claim to have converted Nguyen Hoang and his family, was simply the concoction of an overheated imagination.

On June 24, 1596, two Dominicans from Manila, Diego Aduarte and Alonso Ximénez, arrived at Da Nang and found there two Augustinians, Miguel los Santos and Rafael da Madre de Deus. These were serving the Japanese and Portuguese Christians and were not allowed to preach to the natives. Ximénez stayed for a while and then returned to the Philippines.[14]

---

10. See Marcos Gispert, *Historia de las Misiones Dominicanas en el Tunkin* (Avila, 1929).

11. Gaspar de Santa Cruz, a Portuguese, was the first Dominican missionary to the Far East. See his book *Tractado em que se cõtam muito por extěso as cousas da China, cõ suas particularidades, & assi do reyno dormuz. Cõpuesto por el R. padre frey Gaspar da Cruz da ordĕ de sam Domingos [...]* (André de Burgos: Évora, 1569). There is no historical evidence that Gaspar da Cruz carried out missionary activities in Vietnam.

12. See Marcello de Ribadeneyra, *Historia de las Islas del Archipelago y regios de la gran China, Tartaria, Cochinchina, Malacca, Siam, Cambogia y Japon, y de lo sucedido en ellas a los religiosos descalzos de la Orden de San Francisco* (Barcelona, 1601).

13. See his *El trattado de las relaciones verdaderas de los reinos de la China, Cochinchina y Champa y otras cosas notables y varios sucesos sacados de sus originales por el licenciado don Pedro Ordonnez de Cevallos Presbytero que dio la vuelta al mundo. Provisor, Juez y Vicario general de aquellos reinos, Chantre de la Santa Iglesia de la ciudad de Guamariya en el Peru y Canonigo de la Astorga* (Jaen, 1628).

14. See Diego Aduarte, *Historia de la provincia de santo Rosario de Filipinas, Japon, y China de la sagrada Orden de Predicadores* (Zaragossa, 1693).

In sum, Christian mission in Vietnam by the end of the sixteenth century was insignificant. Despite sporadic attempts by Dominican and Franciscan missionaries, no lasting imprints were left on the country. It was only with the arrival of the Jesuits in Cochinchina in 1615 that Christianity began to take root.

THE FIRST JESUIT MISSION AND THE POLITICAL SITUATION BETWEEN TONKIN AND COCHINCHINA

The Jesuit mission to Vietnam was not a planned enterprise as the Jesuit missions to India, Macao, China, Malacca, and Japan had been. Vietnam was still thought of by Westerners as a part of China.[15] Rather, the Jesuit mission in Vietnam was begun as a response to a request of Fernandes de Costa, a captain of a Portuguese merchant ship. De Costa had come back from Cochinchina and proposed to the Jesuits to set up a mission there. Valentim de Carvalho, then the provincial of Japan, agreed with de Costa's proposal, and on January 6, 1615, he sent three Jesuits, Fathers Francesco Buzomi and Diego Carvalho, and Brother António Dias, to Cochinchina.[16] Central Vietnam was then under the rule of Lord Nguyen Phuoc Nguyen (1613–35), also known as Sai Vuong.

The three Jesuits arrived at Cua Han (near Da Nang) on January 15, 1615, where they celebrated that year's Easter in a small, recently built chapel. On that occasion ten Vietnamese received baptism, the first fruits of evangelization. In 1618 there were already three hundred Christians at Cua Han, Hoi An (Faifo), and Thanh Chiem. Between 1616 and 1623 six more Jesuits arrived. They were stationed at three locations: Hoi An, Nuoc Man, and Thanh Chiem.[17]

---

15. The goal of Christian missionaries in the sixteenth century was to convert the Chinese emperor. Once China was converted, it was thought, the other dependent countries such as Tonkin and Siam would follow suit. Such thinking was endorsed by Francis Xavier. Later, Alessandro Valignano, who had been a visitor of the Jesuit missions in the Orient since 1573, thought that Japan should be the target of the missionary efforts of his order. During the persecutions in Japan, his focus shifted to China where he sent Ruggieri and Ricci. Of course, Augustinians, Franciscans, and Dominicans were also interested in China and Japan.

16. See V. Carvalho's letter to Nuno Mascarenhas, the Assistant for Portugal, written in Macao on February 9, 1615: *ARSI, JS* 16 II, f. 174. Buzomi, a Neapolitan, was superior of the mission in central Vietnam, left the country in 1639, and died in Macao in the same year. Of Buzomi de Rhodes writes: "He was a saintly man, tireless in his efforts, courageous in the face of any danger, firm in all decisions. He spent himself entirely in founding and increasing that Christian community. He succeeded so well that although he found very few Christians on first arriving in Cochinchina, he left at least 12,000 when he went to heaven to receive as many crowns as he had made new Christians" (*Divers voyages*, 116–17). Carvalho was martyred in Japan on February 12, 1624. Dias left Vietnam in 1639; it is not known where and when he died.

It is to be noted that the Jesuit Province of Japan was under the Portuguese jurisdiction and was financially underwritten by the Portuguese crown. The majority of its members were Portuguese, though there was a significant contingent of Italians. Toward the end of the sixteenth century, Japanese were admitted to the province but only to secondary positions. When the province extended its activities to China, its headquarters were located in Macao.

17. Hoi An, also known as Hai Pho (which Westerners call Faifo), was a town by the sea where many Chinese and Japanese merchants congregated. During the seventeenth century, many Japanese Christians took refuge there to escape from persecution in their homeland by the three shoguns of the Tokugawa

Meanwhile persecutions in Japan directed the attention of Jesuit missionaries to other parts of the Far East such as Siam (Thailand), Cambodia, and Vietnam. In 1626 Jerónimo Rodrigues, visitor of the two Jesuit provinces of Japan and China, sent Father Giuliano Baldinotti, an Italian, and Brother Julius Piani, a Japanese, to Tonkin to explore the possibility of establishing a mission there.

The two missionaries arrived in Tonkin on March 7, 1626, and were presented to Lord Trinh Trang who was then the real ruler of the country (1620–57). The lord welcomed them most graciously, giving them sumptuous banquets, numerous gifts, and comfortable lodgings. Baldinotti entertained the lord with conversations on astronomy and other celestial sciences. He also discussed religious subjects with one of the chief Buddhist monks of the capital. The lord invited him to prolong his stay, but Baldinotti said that he could not do so without the permission of his superior in Macao.

Buoyed by the lord's hospitality, Baldinotti thought that a mission could be established in Tonkin. He therefore wrote directly to Gabriele de Mattos, the Jesuit visitor in Cochinchina, requesting him to send to Tonkin a Jesuit with a knowledge of the language. Baldinotti's secret correspondence was intercepted by Lord Trinh Trang, who began suspecting him of espionage for the rival lord in Cochinchina. To prove his innocence, Baldinotti swore a public oath of loyalty to Lord Trinh Trang, but he did so in front of a picture of Jesus rather than in the Vietnamese way, which might have given the impression that he had compromised his Christian faith.

Baldinotti and his companion Piani left Tonkin for Macao on August 18, 1626, and presented a report to Andrea Palmiero, the successor of Jerónimo Rodrigues.[18] It was his report, as we shall see, that prompted Palmiero to recall de Rhodes from Cochinchina back to Macao and to send him to Tonkin in 1627.

The Baldinotti incident illustrates well the political situation between Tonkin and Cochinchina and the web of complex and intricate relations in which the Jesuit missionaries, and, as we shall see, especially de Rhodes, were tangled. As we have mentioned above, since 1600, Tonkin and Cochinchina, though two parts of the same country under the Le dynasty, were ruled independently by two clans with a consuming ambition for total and absolute power. Direct con-

---

family: Ieyasu (1598–1616), Hidetada (1605–23), and Iemitsu (1623–51). Nuoc Man, now extinct, was about six miles northwest of today's Qui Nhon. De Rhodes speaks of Nuoc Man and Qui Nhon in one word: Pulocambi. Thanh Chiem, also known as Dinh Cham, was located about three miles northwest of Hoi An.

The Jesuit residence at Hoi An was founded in 1615, that at Nuoc Man in 1618, and that at Thanh Chiem in 1623. In 1620 there were four Jesuits at Hoi An, three at Nuoc Man, and four at Thanh Chiem (including de Rhodes after 1623). See the annual reports of João Roiz, "Annua de Cochinchina do anno 1620," ARSI, *JS* 72, ff. 2–17; of Gaspar Luís, "Cocincinensis Missionis annuae litterae, anni 1620," *ARSI, JS* 71, ff. 23–27.

18. See Giuliano Baldinotti, "Relation du voyage fait au Royaume de Tunquin nouvellement découvert," in Gaspar Paes, *Histoire de ce qui s'est passé es royaumes d'Éthiopie, en l'année 1626 jusqu'au mois de mars 1627. Et de la Chine, en l'année 1625 jusques en février de 1626. Avec une brève narration du voyage qui s'est fait au Royaume de Tunquim nouvellement découvert* (Paris, 1629), 191–210.

tact between the two territories was strictly forbidden. Suspicions of espionage and collaboration with the enemy were rampant.[19]

One may be surprised by the fact that foreign missionaries were warmly welcomed, at least at first, by both lords. The reason for this is not hard to understand. Even Baldinotti understood the motive of Lord Trinh Trang's largesse: "The motive inducing the king [more exactly, lord] to extend to us such generosities seems to be his desire to obtain our alliance and to exchange commerce with the Portuguese, since he has heard the news, well known throughout the kingdom, that their ships have brought much profit."[20] Not rarely the lord's decision to allow missionaries to stay depended on the prospect of the arrival of Portuguese trade ships. For instance, in 1630, when Lord Trinh Trang realized that de Rhodes and Pêro Marques, whom he had warmly welcomed to Tonkin, were no longer useful intermediaries between him and the Portuguese merchants, he decided to expel them.[21]

Of course, foreign merchants were more than happy to trade with the newly discovered country. Already in the sixteenth century, the Portuguese, well established in India, Macao, and Malacca, had visited Vietnam. But only in the seventeenth century did they come regularly to do business at Faifo where there was a large colony of Chinese and Japanese. The Spaniards, situated in the Philippines, made several abortive attempts at trading with the peninsula.[22] The Dutch from Batavia (Djakarta) made the first contacts with Cochinchina in 1633 but were turned off by the haughtiness of Lord Nguyen Phuoc Nguyen. They then turned toward Tonkin and offered it their support against its rival.[23] In general, though the relationships were never clear-cut, the Dutch tended to side with Tonkin, and the Portuguese with Cochinchina.

In addition to and perhaps even more important than economic advantages, there were military benefits that both lords were seeking to reap. Lord Trinh Trang nurtured the ambition to establish his own dynasty by crushing Cao Bang and especially Cochinchina. To achieve his dream, he needed powerful military weaponry that only foreigners, especially the Portuguese, could supply.

Cochinchina, on the other hand, not only had to ward off frequent attacks

---

19. Even de Rhodes was accused of espionage. In 1628, when King Mac Kinh Khoan of the Mac dynasty in Cao Bang was captured by Lord Trinh Trang and condemned to death, he tried to save himself by promising to reveal de Rhodes's secret collaboration with Cao Bang and Cochinchina against Tonkin! See *Tunchensis historiae*, II, 91–92.

20. See Baldinotti, "Relation," 194. As to the attitude of Lord Nguyen Phuoc Nguyen toward the Portuguese merchants, Borri reports: "Le Roy de la Cochinchine a toujours témoigné d'aymer extraordinairement les Portugais, qui viennent pour trafiquer dans son Royaume." See Borri, 95.

21. See *Histoire du Royaume*, 221–25. De Rhodes was well aware of the motives of Lord Trinh Trang: "We have discovered that the main motive of the Lord in keeping us in his kingdom was to attract through our presence business with the Portuguese merchants. . . . " (221).

22. On the presence of the Spaniards in the East, see A. Gallego, "España en Indochina, Expediciones religio-militares," *España misionera* 7 (1951): 298–310, and Benno Biermann, "Die Missionsversuche des Dominikaner in Kambodscha," *Zeitschrift für Missionswissenschaft und Religionswissenschaft* 23 (1933): 108–32.

23. For a history of the dealings of the Dutch from Batavia with Vietnam, see W. J. M. Buch, "La Compagnie des Indes néerlandaises et l'Indochine," *BEFEO* (1936): 97–196 and (1937): 121–237.

from the north but also wanted to enlarge its territory by annexing Champa and Cambodia.[24] To achieve both tasks, it too needed firearms of every kind. It is known that about 1631–40 a Christian Portuguese by the name of João da Cruz directed a cannon foundry for the lord of Cochinchina at Tho Duc, near today's Hue.[25]

The relationship among missionaries, merchants, and militaries was at best ambiguous. Though the missionary enterprise was guided exclusively by spiritual motives, early missionaries in Vietnam were not reluctant to lean on the economic and military power of the Portuguese crown to gain a foothold in the country. Carried into the country by Portuguese ships and presented by the Portuguese authorities to the Vietnamese rulers with great pomp and respect, missionaries cut an impressive figure with the native rulers. Lords and mandarins were eager to entertain them and converse with them about the culture and sciences of the West.

On the other hand, to obtain trade and armament, the Vietnamese rulers shrewdly exploited the missionaries' desire to remain in the country and to evangelize the Vietnamese. As we will see, de Rhodes's opportunities for evangelization, both in Tonkin and in Cochinchina, were tightly connected with the ruling lords' goodwill, which was in turn conditioned by the prospects of commercial and military gains. It was difficult, for both the Vietnamese and the Europeans, to distinguish between the "souls" and the "pepper" that the West was seeking.

THE THREE IMPORTED RELIGIONS: *TAM GIAO*

Christianity was a latecomer to the Vietnamese religious scene. When the Jesuits came to Vietnam in the seventeenth century, they found, besides the indigenous religion, the *tam giao* — literally, three religions — imported from China, already well established: Taoism, Confucianism, and Buddhism.

De Rhodes twice gives us an exposition of these three religions, which he calls superstitious "sects."[26] We will discuss the accuracy of de Rhodes's description later on in our study of his catechism. Here it will be helpful to obtain an overview of these three religions in Vietnam as well as of the native Vietnamese

---

24. When de Rhodes arrived in Cochinchina in 1624, the country extended as far as Phu Yen. In a relentless southward march (*nam tien*), Vietnam gradually annexed Nha Trang (1653), Binh Thuan (1663), Bien Hoa (1668), Saigon (1671), and Ha Tien (1708) to the end of the peninsula. These regions formed the whole of ancient Champa and parts of Cambodia.

25. In 1666 there was a meeting between this João da Cruz and Antoine Hainques, a member of the Missions étrangères de Paris, who referred to him as "Officier & Fondeur des Canons du Roy." See his letter to François Pallu, the first bishop of Tonkin, in François Pallu, *Relation abrégée des Missions et des voyages des évêques français, envoyés aux royaumes de la Chine, Cochinchine, Tonquin, et Siam* (Paris, 1668), 82–84.

26. See *Histoire du Royaume*, 61–77; *Cathechismus*, 104–16.

religion so as to be able to grasp the challenges facing de Rhodes's missionary work and his evangelizing method.[27]

VIETNAMESE BUDDHISM

Buddhism, with its doctrine of the Four Noble Truths and the Eightfold Path, came to Vietnam from India, its birthplace, and through China.[28] As is well known, of the two branches of Buddhism, *mahayana* (the "great vehicle") and *hinayana* (the "lesser vehicle") or *theravada,* it is the former, with its Sanskrit canon, that penetrated Tibet, China, Korea, Japan, and Vietnam. Chinese Buddhism, known as *Ch'an* (Japanese: *Zen*) Buddhism, which emphasizes meditation (*dhyana*) as an everyday activity and locates it in the ordinary tasks of the present moment ("drawing water and carrying firewood"), is a synthesis between India's doctrines of emptiness (*sunyata*) and enlightenment (*bodhi*) and China's practicality and Taoist tradition.

In spite of its antischolastic bias, Chinese Buddhism was influenced by the sutras of Bodhidharma (the twenty-eighth patriarch who was reputed to have carried the "lamp of enlightenment" to China) and of Vimalakirti. During the T'ang dynasty (618–906), Buddhist masters sought to extend the enlightenment opportunities of formal seated meditation (*zazen*) and formal interviews (*sanzen*) to every aspect of daily life by utilizing shouts, slaps, questions, *koans,* and parabolic acts to trigger enlightenment.

Another important development of Chinese Buddhism is the emergence of the Pure Land sect, which emphasizes certain elements of Mahayana Buddhism such as faith in Amida (Amitabha), meditation on and recitation of his name, and the religious goal of being reborn in his "Pure Land," or "Western Paradise." Among the Avalokitesvaras or bodhisattvas, the female figure of Kuan-yin (Vietnamese: Quan Am) as the Buddha of compassion is the most popular.

Buddhism entered Vietnam first from India and then from China, especially toward the second century of the common era. At the beginning of the Later Han dynasty (203–544), a number of Chinese Buddhists came to settle in Tonkin, then known as Giao Chau. But it is only in the sixth century that Buddhism began to take root. The first *dhyana* (Vietnamese: *thien*) school was established by an Indian brahman converted to Buddhism, Vinitaruci (Vietnamese: Ti Ni Da Lu), who on his way to China stopped in Tonkin in 580 and erected a pagoda named Phap Van in the province of Bac Ninh. In 820 a second *dhyana* school

---

27. It is of course not necessary to give here the immense bibliography on these three religions. For an overview of these religions in Vietnam, see Joseph Nguyen Huy Lai, *La tradition religieuse, spirituelle et sociale au Vietnam* (Paris: Beauchesne, 1981); Nguyen Van Huyen, *La civilisation annamite* (Hanoi, 1944), and Tran Van Giap, "Le Bouddhisme en Annam: Des origines au XIIIè siècle," *BEFEO XXXII* (1932): 191–269.

28. For a history of Buddhism in Vietnam, see Minh Chi, Ha Van Tan, and Nguyen Tai Thu, *Buddhism in Vietnam* (Hanoi: The Gioi Publishers, 1993).

was created by a Chinese monk whose Vietnamese name is Vo Ngon Thong and who erected a pagoda named Kien Son in the village of Phu Dong in the province of Bac Ninh.

Under the Dinh dynasty (968–80) Buddhism experienced another spurt of growth. It began spreading among the common people; pagodas were built in many villages. One monk by the name of Ngo Chau Luu of the monastery of Phat Da, renowned for his learning, was called to the court by King Dinh Tien Hoang to explain the Buddhist doctrines and was appointed imperial counselor. Buddhism also enjoyed royal support under the following dynasty, that of the Early Le (980–1009).

It was, however, under the dynasties of Ly (1010–1225) and Tran (1225–1400), that is, between the eleventh and the fourteenth centuries, that Buddhism reached its apogee, never to be attained again. The founder of the Ly dynasty, Ly Thai To (1010–28), a fervent Buddhist, had the monastery of Thai Thanh and the pagodas of Thang Nghiem and Van Tue built near the capital. He sent emissaries to China to bring back Buddhist writings (the *Tripitaka*). During his reign, there were many famous monks such as Bao Tinh, Dao Hanh, Giac Hai, Long Tan, Minh Khong, and Van Hanh. His son, Ly Thai Tong (1028–54), built many pagodas (among which the famous Chua Mot Cot, literally, the pagoda with one column, is still extant in Hanoi), restored statues of the Buddha, founded monasteries, and exempted monks from taxes and military service. Under his successor, Ly Thanh Tong (1054–72), a third *dhyana* school was founded by a Chinese monk named Thao Duong. The last king of the Ly dynasty, Ly Hue Tong (1211–25), abdicated in favor of his seven-year-old daughter Ly Chieu Hoang and retired to a Buddhist monastery.

Arrangements were made for Ly Chieu Hoang to marry eight-year-old Tran Canh, who became king under the name of Tran Thai Tong (1225–58) and founded the Tran dynasty (1225–1400). Under the Tran dynasty, Buddhism again enjoyed an expansive growth. King Tran Thai Tong composed two works, one on Buddhist doctrines, the other on *dhyana*. His son, Tran Thanh Tong (1258–79), and his grandson, Tran Nhon Tong (1279–93), were both devout Buddhists. The latter, after having ruled for fifteen years, abdicated at the age of thirty-nine, and withdrew to a monastery on Mount Yen Tu, in the province of Quang Yen. There he founded the sect Truc Lam Dai Si (The Bamboo Forest). Until the Second World War the great pagodas of Ba Da, Tu Tram, Vinh Nghiem, and Phuc Trinh, all in the north, belonged to this sect.

After the Tran dynasty, Vietnamese Buddhism suffered a long decline during the Ho dynasty (1400–1407), the Ming domination (1407–28), and the Later Le dynasty (1428–1788). The Ming rulers confiscated Buddhist books, closed pagodas, and imposed Confucian doctrines and practices on the country. King Le Thai To, the founder of the Later Le dynasty, forbade the construction of new pagodas, restricted subsidies to monasteries, and required Buddhist monks to undergo examinations on Buddhist books, allowing only those who passed the examinations to continue and dismissing those who failed. That Buddhism was in serious decline in the seventeenth century must be kept in mind when we read de Rhodes's highly negative assessment of this religion in his *Cathechismus*.

Despite these setbacks, Buddhism continued to survive. In the sixteenth century, a Chinese monk, Thuy Nguyet, and his disciple, Ton Dien, founded a *dhyana* sect in Tonkin named Tao Dong. In the seventeenth century, despite the constant warfare between the Trinh and the Nguyen, new *dhyana* sects were established, e.g., the "Lien Ton" sect with the Lien Phai pagoda near Hanoi. In Cochinchina, the pagodas of Quynh Lam and Sung Nghien were restored, and the famous pagoda of Thien Mu, whose bell and seven-storied stupa were much admired, was built near Hue.[29]

VIETNAMESE TAOISM

It is customary to distinguish between Taoism as a philosophical system and Taoism as a religious practice. The former is rational, contemplative, nonsectarian, and accepts death as a natural event, whereas the latter is magical, cultic, esoteric, sectarian, and resists death by means of alchemy. However, in the wake of studies by scholars such as Marcel Granet and Henri Maspéro,[30] it is recognized that these two groups must be viewed as belonging to the same tradition.

The scriptures from which both groups derive their doctrine and practices are the extant Taoist classics: the Tao Te Ching or Lao Tzu (300–250 B.C.E.), Chuang Tzu (300 B.C.E.), and Huai Nan Tzu (122 B.C.E.). What these books have in common is their reaction against Confucianism's preoccupation with the acquisition of knowledge and the ordering of a civilized state. Taoism attempts to go back to the primordial conditions of ancient China where people were thought to live in a natural state in the tranquility of pastoral villages.

Central to philosophical Taoism is the concept of Tao ("The Way"), which is considered to be the source and reality of humanity and nature. Tao is the "creator" (*tsao wu chu;* Vietnamese: *tao vu tru*), though it is impersonal and inseparable from creation. As the source of creation, it is called nonbeing (*wu;* Vietnamese: *vo,* literally, nothing); and as creation, it is called being (*yu;* Vietnamese: *huu,* literally, existence). These two aspects, nonbeing and being, are inseparable in the Tao. Tao is the equivalent of chaos (*hun tun;* Vietnamese: *hon don*) in the archaic creation myth. Cosmologically, Tao, nonbeing, and chaos are identical.

Tao is also considered as a material reality (*Ch'i;* Vietnamese: *khi,* literally, breath, air, ether); it is composed of *yin* (Vietnamese: *am*) and *yang*

---

29. Buddhism did not experience a strong revival until 1951 when the General Association of Vietnamese Buddhists (Tong Hoi Phat Giao) was founded. Later, in 1963, the Buddhist Institute for the Promotion of the Faith (Vien Hoa Dao) was established.

30. See, for instance, Henri Maspéro, *Le Taoisme et les religions chinoises,* rev. ed. (Paris: P.U.F., 1971).

(Vietnamese: *duong*) forces. *Yin* and *Yang* theory was first taught by Tsu Yen (*ca.* 305–*ca.* 240 B.C.E.) and was later incorporated into the Confucian classic *I Ching* and Neo-Confucianism. The *yang* refers to the active, male, hard, and expansive pole; and the *yin* to the passive, female, soft, and contracting pole.

Together with this double pole, there are five cosmic elements (*wu hsing;* Vietnamese: *ngu hanh*): wood and fire belonging to *yang;* water and metal to *yin;* and earth belonging to both. The ebb and flow between the two poles, called "reversal" (*fan;* Vietnamese: *phan*), is used to explain the creation of the cosmos. The combination of the five elements accounts for the variety of things.

Philosophical Taoism uses the theory of *yin* and *yang* to explain not only the reciprocal movement in nature and humanity but also the relation between nonbeing and being. Religious Taoism uses the same theory to symbolize the different forces and focuses on the human body which is regarded as the miniature cosmos.

Coherent with this metaphysics is the Taoist ethics of "noncontrivance" (*wu wei;* Vietnamese: *vo vi*). The Tao is nonpurposive, nondeliberate, and continuously transforming. Hence, noncontrivance ethics, in opposition to Confucian ethics, maintains that human conduct should not be contrary to the spontaneity (*tzu jan;* Vietnamese: *tu nhien*) of the Tao. Rather it should flow naturally from "intuition," not from acquired "knowledge," just as naturally as water flows downward and fire rises upward. Individuals, society, and the state should keep a close touch with the simple, primitive, and undifferentiated source of creativity, which is like the "uncarved block," capable of being made into any instrument.

Religious Taoism (*tao chao;* Vietnamese: *dao giao* or *dao Lao*) came to Vietnam in about the first century of the common era, at the same time as Confucianism. It brought to the country a complex of cultic practices by which Taoist adepts worship the Tao and its numerous emanations, and observe magical, physical, alchemical, and meditative rituals with the purpose of achieving longevity and immortality.

Because Taoists conceive matter and spirit not as discontinuous, much less as antithetical, immortality is attained not by liberating spirit from matter but by conserving, harmonizing, and transforming the body-mind's reservoir of energies. It is done by a series of techniques designed to nourish the vital force. These include hygienic and dietary practices such as eating foods (e.g., avoidance of certain grains), consuming medicinal herbs containing the energies corresponding to the five principal organs (lungs, heart, spleen, liver, and kidneys), and engaging in gymnastic exercises to assist the circulation of the energies.

Other practices are deep and controlled breathing, circulation of the "inner breath" (a vital energy no longer associated with the air of the atmosphere), sexual techniques (e.g., the retention of the seminal essence by suppressing orgasm), and alchemical practices (both external by producing elixirs and internal by producing the "immortal embryo"). Finally, moral actions and attitudes such as humility, impartiality, and control over the passions are considered to contribute to the preservation of the vital energies and to restore harmony with the Tao.

Besides these practices Taoism also imported to Vietnam a host of deities and spirits that were added to the already well-populated pantheon of the Vietnamese indigenous religion. For Taoist philosophers, the goal of life is union with the Tao, the primordial and impersonal principle, by means of noncontrivance, detachment, and meditation, and esoteric practices of diet, breathing, sexual self-control, and alchemy.

But for the average Vietnamese, the intricacies of Taoist metaphysics and the Taoist esoteric practices to procure immortality are beyond their ken and ability. They do not possess the requisite intellectual acumen to grasp the subtleties of Taoist doctrines. Nor do they have the physical stamina or the financial means to undertake the Taoist physico-spiritual discipline. Desiring longevity and immortality themselves but unable to attain them on their own, most Vietnamese had to have recourse to the assistance of deities and spirits.

Foremost among the Taoist deities is the Emperor of Jade (Vietnamese: *Ngoc Hoang*) who dwells in the middle of heaven, flanked by his two ministers: Nam Tao (constellation of the south) and Bac Dau (constellation of the north), the former in charge of the birth of humans and the latter their death. The Emperor of Jade and his two ministers exert their influence over the earth through a multitude of intermediaries, namely, heavenly and earthly spirits.

Besides deities and spirits, the Taoist pantheon includes immortals, that is, humans who have achieved the Taoist ideal of immortality and whose protection against evil spirits can be obtained through worship and sacrifices. Vietnamese Taoists worship immortals of both Chinese and Vietnamese origin. Among the Chinese immortals, most venerated are the "Eight Immortals" (*Bat Tien*) and especially Tran Vu or Huyen Vu, the spirit in charge of the northern part of the sky. In Vietnamese Taoism, he has been transformed into a national deity, the god of war, and a protector of Vietnam. There is a huge statue of him, improperly called "the Great Buddha of Hanoi," in the temple dedicated to him north of Hanoi. King Ly Thanh Ton (1054–72) erected a temple in his honor in the capital Thang Long.

Among the immortals of Vietnamese origin, notable are the *Chu Vi* (great spirits), that is, spirits of the three worlds: heavenly, earthly, and aquatic. At the highest rank of these spirits are four female immortals called *Thanh Mau* (holy mothers): Lieu Hanh (mother of the heaven), Thuong Ngan (mother of the earth), Mau Thoai (mother of the sea), and Mau Nhac Phu (mother of the forest). Below them are the five *Duc Ong* (venerable lords) with a multitude of other inferior spirits.

Besides the immortals, Vietnamese Taoists worship with great veneration Tran Hung Dao, the national hero who saved the country from the Mongols (1284–85, 1287–88). Vietnamese Taoists also cultivate a great devotion to a legendary magician by the name of Toan and his three sons (called *tam thanh,* i.e., the three saints) who, so the story goes, lived in the seventeenth century and who were granted supernatural powers by the immortals to relieve people's miseries and sufferings. This cult is known as *noi dao,* that is, the interior way, the name given by King Le Than Ton (1619–43) who was allegedly healed of a skin disease by Magician Toan.[31]

Taoist priests who serve the cult of the *Chu Vi* are exclusively female mediums (*ba dong*). These women are selected by the immortals themselves, often by means of some psychic signs, and have to undergo a careful ritualistic testing before being recognized as *ba dong.* After a woman has been installed as medium, she would organize seances during which she goes into a trance, incarnates the immortal who has chosen her, and reveals ways to obtain peace, happiness, and success and to avoid sickness, accidents, and misfortunes.

In the cult of Tran Hung Dao, however, the priests are male mediums (*ong dong*). They too use trance to speak in the name of Tran Hung Dao, indicating ways to obtain happiness and avoid misfortune.

Besides participating in seances, Taoist adepts worship at their *den* (temples) and make pilgrimages to famous *den* such as the Temple of Tran Vu, built by King Ly Thanh Ton (1054–72) in Hanoi and the Temple of Bich Cau dedicated to the immortal Tu Uyen and built by the people of the village of An Trach (north of Hanoi) under the reign of Le Thanh Ton (1460–97).[32]

What is distinctive of Vietnamese Taoism then is the presence of intermediaries between humans and the gods whose role is to receive the wills of spirits and deities and communicate them to the people who come to implore their aid. These intermediaries perform different functions for the Taoist adepts. We have already seen the *dong nhan* (mediums) in whom the immortals incarnate during seances. There are others such as *Thay Phu Thuy* (magicians) who possess the power to perform prodigious acts in the name of the gods whose favors the faithful seek to obtain; *Thay Cung* (sacrificer) who officiates at rituals, especially at funerals; *Thay Bua* (maker of amulets and charms) who writes formulas on pieces of paper which will be worn or consumed to ward off misfortunes; and *thay boi* (soothsayer) who interprets horoscopes and dreams and predicts the future.

Needless to say, there is no lack of superstition and credulity on the part of the people who seek the services of these specialists or masters (*thay*). On the other hand, some of these masters are not beyond exploiting the people's faith for financial or other gains. One can understand the harsh words of de Rhodes when he speaks of these "superstitious sects" in his *Cathechismus.*

---

31. For the Vietnamese cult of immortals, see Nguyen Van Huyen, *Le Culte des Immortels en Annam* (Hanoi, 1944).

32. Note that in Vietnamese there are different words to indicate places of worship of each religion: *chua* (pagoda) for Buddhism, *den* (temple) for Taoism, *mieu* (shrine) for Confucianism, *nha tho* (church) for Christianity.

VIETNAMESE CONFUCIANISM

By Confucianism is meant the social, political, ethical, philosophical, and re-ligious system based on the teachings of Confucius (551–479 B.C.E.) and his successors.[33] Known in Chinese as *ju chia* (Vietnamese: *nho giao*) or "School of the Literati," i.e., scholars and teachers of the ancient literature, especially of the "Five *Ching*" (Vietnamese: *ngu kinh*),[34] Confucianism is conventionally divided into (1) classical Confucianism, as embodied in the "Four *Shu*" (Viet-namese: *tu thu*);[35] (2) Han Confucianism, that is, Confucianism which was established as state orthodoxy during the Han dynasty (206 B.C.E.–220 C.E.); it was during this time that the Confucian canon was established and the cult of Confucius emerged as part of the state religion; and (3) Neo-Confucianism as it was revived from the Sung dynasty (960–1279) through the Ming dynasty (1368–1644) until the present day.

As was mentioned above, Vietnam was under the domination of China for a total of ten centuries, from 111 B.C.E. to 1427 C.E. Chinese rulers attempted to assimilate the Vietnamese by imposing their culture and customs, especially dur-ing the Ming dynasty's occupation. Confucianism, along with Taoism, began to strike root in Vietnam in the first century of the common era.[36] In 42 C.E., Gen-eral Ma Vien disseminated Chinese literature, sciences, arts, and ideogrammatic characters.

It was, however, only at the beginning of the third century, under the gov-ernorship of Si Nhiep, that Confucianism began to exercise a widespread influence on the Vietnamese with the introduction of the "Five *Ching*" and "Four *Shu*." Since the eleventh century, with the establishment of schools and especially of the state examinations whose purpose was to select government functionaries (mandarins), Confucianism achieved a prodigious expansion and penetrated into every level of Vietnamese life, from the family to the village to the state, the three basic social units of the Vietnamese society.

In contrast to Buddhist and Taoist religions which prescribe certain cultic acts, Confucianism, except for the cult of Confucius of which we will speak

---

33. It is well known that there are many portraits of Confucius or K'ung Ch'iu (his real name): he has been portrayed as a moral teacher, a wise man, an answerer of conundrums, an itinerant tutor, a successful statesman, a diplomat, and even a magician. Some biographers (e.g., Ssu-ma Ch'ien) endowed him with supernatural powers. The most authentic sources for the life and teachings of Confucius are the *Analects* and *Mencius*. It is widely acknowledged today that Confucius did not write any book (he is said to have "edited" the Five Classics) and was not the founder of the religion called Confucianism. Confucius described himself not as an originator of novel ideas but as a transmitter of the ways of the "Ancients." See *The Analects of Confucius*, translated and edited by Arthur Waley (New York: Vintage Books, 1939), VII, 1: "The Master said: 'I have transmitted what was taught to me without making up anything of my own. I have been faithful to and loved the Ancients.'"

34. The "Five *Ching*" are: *Book of Poetry, Book of Rites, Book of History, Spring and Autumn Annals,* and *Book of Changes.*

35. The "Four *Shu*" are: *The Analects, The Great Learning, The Doctrine of the Mean,* and *Mencius.*

36. For studies on Vietnamese Confucianism, see Yuzō Mizoguchi and Léon Vandermeersch, eds., *Confucianisme et Sociétés Asiatiques* (Paris: Éditions L'Harmattan, 1991), and Le Huu Khoa, ed., *Confucianisme: Permanence et Renouveau* (Nice: Université de Nice–Sophia Antipolis, 1996).

shortly, is more an ethico-political system than a religion, and it is in this respect that its influence on the Vietnamese culture is pervasive and enduring. Indeed, the central concepts of Confucian ethics lie at the basis of Vietnamese morality.

There is first of all the emphasis on the personal cultivation of virtue (*te*; Vietnamese: *duc*) as the first step toward and the sine qua non condition for public service. There is a progression from personal self-cultivation (*tu than*) to governing the family (*te gia*) to ruling the country (*tri nuoc*) and finally, to pacifying the world (*binh thien ha*).[37]

The central virtue is *nhan* (Chinese: *jen*), variously translated as humaneness, humanity, benevolence, virtue, kindness, and goodness. *Nhan* is not a single virtue but a complex of moral dispositions. It makes one practice "reciprocity" which is encapsulated in Confucius's famous saying: "Never do to others what you would not like them do to you."[38]

In practicing *nhan* one will become what Confucius regards as the ideal person, *quan tu* (Chinese: *chun tzu*), best translated as the gentleman or superior man (French: *honnête homme*), that is, one who in all things does what is right and not for profit. One effective way to become the *quan tu* is to use words correctly (the "rectification of names"), and more importantly, to act out correctly the manifold relationships one has with others (*chinh danh*; Chinese: *cheng minh*).

For Confucius, there are three basic relationships or bonds (*tam cuong*): between king and subject, between husband and wife, and between parents and children. Elsewhere he adds two more relationships: between elder brother and younger brother, and between friends. The most fundamental obligation in these relationships is filial piety (*hieu thao*; Chinese: *hsiao*), the all-encompassing virtue in Vietnamese morality.

Did Confucius believe in God and by implication, does Confucianism as a religion prescribe acts of worship to God? It is well known that in the *Book of History* and the *Book of Poetry* the expressions *Ti* (Vietnamese: *De*) and *Shang Ti* (Vietnamese: *Thuong De*) are used to refer to God. God appears therein as a personal and transcendent being, ruling in heaven and on earth, the author of morality, the governor of nations, by whom kings reign and princes decree justice, the remunerator of the good and the punisher of the evil.

By contrast, Confucius prefers to speak of Heaven. In the *Analects*, Heaven is referred to some twenty times. Besides indicating the sky, Heaven has the meaning of Providence, Nature, God, the dispenser of life and death, wealth, and

---

37. On this understanding of the essential link among these various activities, see *The Great Learning*, 5: "Things being investigated, knowledge became complete. Their knowledge being complete, their thoughts were sincere. Their thoughts being sincere, their hearts were then rectified. Their hearts being rectified, their persons were cultivated. Their persons being cultivated, their families were regulated. Their families being regulated, their states were rightly governed. Their states being governed, the whole kingdom was made tranquil and happy." See *Confucius*, trans. James Legge (Oxford: Clarendon Press, 1893), 358–59.

38. See *Analects*, XV, 23.

rank.[39] Confucius himself was unwilling to discourse about Heaven[40], though he admitted that Heaven produced the virtue that was in him[41] and that he did not know the "decrees of Heaven" until the age of fifty.[42] He believed that he was known by Heaven,[43] that Heaven's will is always efficacious,[44] and that the *quan tu* must submit himself patiently to it, because "he who has put himself in the wrong with Heaven has no means of expiation left."[45]

Nevertheless, Confucius never explicitly recommended either prayer to or worship of Heaven as a worthy and dutiful practice. Among the five universal obligations which he says are incumbent upon humans, there is no mention of those that relate them to the transcendent being.

Moreover, with regard to the worship of other spiritual beings, and especially the worship of departed ancestors, Confucius, though appreciative of these practices,[46] tended to be evasive about them. "Chi Lu asked about serving the spirits of the dead, and the master said: 'While you are not able to serve people, how can you serve their spirits?' The disciple added: 'I venture to ask about death,' and he was answered: 'While you do not know life, how can you know about death?' "[47]

As was mentioned above, during the Han dynasty, the cult of Confucius was imposed as part of the state religion. This cult, however, has a history of conflicting interpretations of its own. Whereas during the Han dynasty Confucius was regarded as a divinity, and a corresponding religious cult was rendered to him, in later centuries, especially under the influence of a more rationalist interpretation of Chu Hsi (1130–1200) of the School of Principle during the Sung dynasty (960–1279), Confucius was considered simply as a teacher of wisdom, and the cult to Confucius had an essentially civic function.[48]

In Vietnam during the Ly dynasty, King Ly Nhan Ton (1054–72) erected a *van mieu* (the temple of literature) in the capital in honor of Confucius. In most villages, besides the common building (*dinh*) where all official activities are performed, there is a *van chi* (literary shrine) where the cult of Confucius is carried out. Candidates of the three state examinations rendered a cult to Confucius before the examinations to ask for assistance, and after the successful performance, would go to the *van mieu* to offer thanks to the master of wisdom.

Finally, a brief word should be said about the three state examinations in

---

39. *Analects*, XII, 5.
40. *Analects*, V, 12.
41. *Analects*, VII, 22.
42. *Analects*, II, 4.
43. *Analects*, XIV, 37.
44. *Analects*, XIV, 38.
45. *Analects*, III, 13.
46. *Analects*, III, 12.
47. *Analects*, XI, 11.
48. The history of the controversies that pitted the early Jesuit missionaries to China against the Dominicans, Franciscans, and members of the Missions étrangères de Paris is well known. For a history of this *querelle des rites*, see George Minamiki, *The Chinese Rites Controversy from Its Beginning to Modern Times* (Chicago: Loyola University Press, 1985).

order to grasp the extent to which Confucianism has shaped the ancient educational system of Vietnam, and through it, the entire ethos of the Vietnamese people.[49] In the seventeenth century, there was no national organization for elementary education. It was given in the village in the home of the teacher. Children at the age of eight were taught to read and write Chinese characters; the focus of the education was mainly moral.

At the age of fifteen, there was an eliminatory examination (*hach*) to determine whether the student would qualify as a candidate to the first state examination. The successful candidate would undertake the *dai hoc* (great studies). The subject of study was the Confucian "Five *Ching*" (*ngu kinh*) and the "Four *Shu*" (*tu thu*). At the age of twenty-five or thereabout, most often later, the student would take the examinations at the district level (*phu, huyen*) which were held twice a year. These examinations, which lasted an entire day, did not confer any degree nor grant access to public offices. Those who passed with highest honors were dispensed from military service and statutory labor for one year.

Next, there were literary examinations.[50] These were first organized under the Tran dynasty (1225–1400) and evolved slightly with different names for various degrees. Essentially, however, there were three levels of examination in the seventeenth century: *thi huong* (at the provincial level, once every three years), *thi hoi* (at the capital level, once every six years), and *thi den* or *thi dinh* (at the imperial palace level, a month after the *thi hoi*).

Examinations at all three levels lasted four days, each day devoted to a different subject. The first day required a commentary on the Confucian classics (*ngay kinh*); the second day composition of a poem (*ngay luc*); the third day prose composition (*ngay phu*); and the fourth day a philosophical or political or historical essay (*ngay sach*). Difficulties, of course, increased with each higher level.

At the provincial level, candidates who passed the first three days with highest honors were given the degree of *sinh do*, later changed to *tu tai* (bachelor). Candidates who passed the fourth day with highest honors were given the degree of *huong cong*, later changed to *cu nhan* (licentiate). Candidates who passed the four tests of the *thi hoi*, presided over by the lord himself, were given the degree of *tien si* (doctor).[51] A month later, all newly minted doctors would

---

49. De Rhodes himself has given us some information on the educational system and the examinations current in the seventeenth century which remained unchanged during the following two centuries. See *Tunchensis historiae*, I, 27–29; *Histoire du Royaume*, 40–43. Besides de Rhodes, other missionaries have described Vietnamese education. See Tissanier, 121–28; Marini, 175–82. A seventeenth-century Vietnamese priest, Bento Thien, has also left us an account of the examination system. See his short history of Vietnam in *ARSI, JS* 81, f. 258rv. Among modern authors, see Pierre Huard and Maurice Durand, *Connaissance du Viet-Nam* (Paris, 1954), 83–88, and Louis-Eugène Louvet, *La Cochinchine religieuse*, vol. I (Paris, 1885), 76–90.

50. Note that besides these literary examinations, there were also *military* examinations from which officers were selected. There were two classes of mandarins (*quan*), literary (*van*) and military (*vo*). As expected, the literary mandarins were held in greater esteem.

51. In 1631 several missionaries, António Francisco Cardim and his confreres, were invited by Lord

sit for the examination at the imperial palace (*thi den* or *thi dinh*), presided over by the king himself. The successful candidates would be classified into six categories in descending order of honor: (1) *trang nguyen,* (2) *bang nhan,* (3) *tham hoa,* (4) *hoang giap,* (5) *chinh tien si,* and the rest were called (6) *dong tien si.*

Benefits for degrees were enormous. For the bachelor's degree: dispensation from military service and payment of only half of the taxes. For the licentiate: dispensation from military service, exemption from all taxes, and opportunities for public office at the district level (*phu* and *huyen*). For the doctorate: exemption from all taxes not only for themselves but also for their families, sometimes for several generations, and opportunities for public office at the national level. As a rule, the licentiate and especially the doctorate were awarded very sparingly, given the limited number of public offices available at the national and provincial levels.

It is clear from these examinations, from which all the administrators of the country (mandarins) were selected, that Confucianism reigned supreme in Vietnam. Even after the official abolition of these literary examinations, in 1915 in Tonkin, and in 1919 in Cochinchina, Confucianism continues to permeate the Vietnamese way of thinking and living. It is interesting to note that among the people de Rhodes converted to the Christian faith there were two doctors, Dr. Joachim and Dr. Peter in Tonkin and Dr. Philip in Cochinchina, not counting several *licenciés* and bachelors. Of the three religions, not surprisingly, Confucianism receives the most favorable treatment at the hands of de Rhodes.

VIETNAMESE INDIGENOUS RELIGION:
THE CULT OF HEAVEN AND SPIRITS

When the three foreign religions came to Vietnam, they did not of course enter into a religious vacuum. There was already a deep and pervasive body of religious beliefs and practices as ancient as the Vietnamese people themselves. This indigenous religion is often referred to as animism or the cult of spirits. This cult of spirits, as Léopold Cadière has rightly maintained, is the original religion of the Vietnamese into which elements of Buddhism, Confucianism, and Taoism were amalgamated.[52]

At the head of the hierarchy of spirits, the Vietnamese place *Ong Troi* (Mr. Heaven)[53] above all deities, immortals, spirits, and genies. In this "Mr. Heaven" the Vietnamese see the personal, transcendent, benevolent, and

---

Trinh Trang to witness a *thi hoi.* See Cardim, 91–92. On this occasion the lord came to the examination hall in a golden litter, carried by twelve men, followed by mandarins on horseback and ten thousand armed soldiers.

52. Studies by Léopold Cadière (1869–1955) on Vietnamese religion remain unsurpassed. See in particular his three volumes of *Croyances et pratiques religieuses des Vietnamiens.* Of great interest are Cadière I, 1–84; Cadière II, 9–197; and Cadière III, 42–70. Cadière came to Vietnam in 1892 as a missionary of the Missions étrangères de Paris and remained there until his death in 1955. His voluminous writings constitute a veritable mine of information on Vietnamese religions and culture.

53. The word *troi* in Vietnamese has the same function as the word *thien* in Chinese. It is central in

just God, the creator of the universe, source of all life, and supreme judge. The rendering of cult to this God is reserved to the emperor, the "Son of God" (*thien tu*), who has received a mandate of heaven (*thien minh*), to be carried out by him during the solemn sacrifice (*te*) of *Nam Giao*.[54]

The people themselves do not practice a regular cult to *Ong Troi;* there is no specific temple in which sacrifices would be offered to him. Nevertheless, as Cadière rightly remarks, "people have recourse to him everyday in ordinary language. They recognize him as the principle and providence of humanity, as the immanent cause of all that occurs here below, of life and death, of happiness and misfortune, of wealth and poverty. They call upon Heaven as witness, since Heaven is not far from us; he sees everything; he witnesses all our doings, all our most secret thoughts. They call out toward him since Heaven is good and merciful. They ask him for help, since Heaven is all-powerful. They have recourse to his judgment, because Heaven is not a blind power, but scrutinizes, reflects, and judges. Heaven is just, punishing sins and rewarding good deeds."[55]

Besides the cult to Heaven, the Vietnamese people believe in the existence of an almost infinite number of spirits who can be classified in three categories: *than* (genius loci), *ma* (spirit), and *qui* (demon). In general, *than* are "patron saints" or guardian spirits of the village or district or nation. These may be past heroes, immortals, kings, or mandarins who have made a great contribution to the village or district or nation. Or they may be benevolent spirits dwelling in rocks (sometimes called *but*), tall trees, rivers and forests, and other natural forces.[56]

Ma refers first of all to human cadavers and above all to the souls of those who have not been properly buried and who have no one to offer sacrifices to them (and not to the souls of the ancestors who receive due worship from

---

popular cosmology. Literally, it means "everything that is above us." Its first meaning is the material sky but it also refers explicitly to a transcendent being; in the latter case, it is often preceded by the word *ong*, literally, Mr. Fortunately. In Vietnam there have been no controversies, as in China, regarding the use of the word *troi* to designate God. As we will see, de Rhodes used the expression *Duc Chua Troi*, which is the equivalent of the Chinese *T'ien Chu* (Vietnamese: *Thien Chua*) preceded by the honorific title *duc* meaning the Venerable, the High Lord, the Master. See Cadière III, 43–50.

54. The Vietnamese language has different words for acts of worship. *Khan* refers to praying for a favor, often with a vow. *Cung* refers to offering sacrifices with gifts, most often to deceased ancestors. *Te* refers to offering of sacrifices in solemn rituals, most often carried out by representatives of the village or of the nation. Hence, the expression *te nam giao.* Formerly once a year, and since the nineteenth century once every three years, the emperor, in the most solemn and sublime ceremony of the Vietnamese religion, surrounded by his ministers and mandarins, all clothed in resplendent ceremonial robes, offered sacrifices (*te*) to Heaven, Earth, the spirits, and imperial ancestors in elaborate and precisely dictated rubrics. The sacrifice took place during spring in the open air, on top of a three-storied mound, on a hill south of the imperial city. Accordingly, the sacrifice is called *nam giao*, literally, encounter in the south. For a classic description of *te nam giao,* see Cadière, I, 85–129.

55. Cadière I, 22–23. For a study on the cult of Heaven, see Dominique Tran Thai Hiep, "Le Culte du Ciel au Vietnam: Étude positive et comparative pour un essai d'adaptation missionnaire" (diss., Pontifical University de Propaganda Fide, Rome, 1954).

56. Contemporary Christians have appropriated this term *than* to designate the angels (*thien than*, literally, genies of heaven) and the Holy Spirit (*Duc Chua Thanh Than*, literally, the Most High Lord Holy Genie).

their descendants). *Ma* also designate legions of malevolent spirits whom the Vietnamese seek to control through offerings or by using the help of soothsayers (*they boi*) and magicians (*thay phu thuy*).

Qui are *ma* who have become especially evil and malevolent, the abandoned souls who seek to harm people. In popular parlance, it has become a term of abuse.[57]

Finally, central to Vietnamese popular religion is the cult of ancestors.[58] Vietnamese anthropology maintains that humans have three superior or rational souls called *hon* and inferior or sensitive souls called *phach* or *via,* seven for men and nine for women. These latter, deriving from the *yin* principle, enter the body at conception and do not survive death; the former, deriving from the *yang* principle, enter the body at birth and are immortal. After the funeral, a wooden tablet which bears on the one side the name of the deceased, the family status, and the person's rank in society, and on the other side, the dates of birth and death of the deceased, is placed on the ancestral altar in the home. The soul of the deceased is believed to reside in the tablet.

The ancestors are said to be present and to have needs such as those they had when they were alive. One of the most sacred duties of filial piety is to provide the ancestors with things such as foods to satisfy their needs. On the anniversaries of their deaths, sacrifices are offered to them. They are welcomed (*ruoc*) on New Year's Eve into the family's celebrations and bidden farewell (*dua*) on the third day with great respect and solemnity. Indeed, there is not a single important event in the life of the Vietnamese family to which the ancestors are not invited as witnesses, from the celebrations of the New Year to the birth of a child, the death of a member of the family, the celebration of longevity (when a person reaches seventy), the earning of an academic degree, engagement, and wedding.

The Vietnamese respect and venerate (*tho,* at times wrongly translated as adore) their ancestors with great devotion. A common gesture of veneration is *vai* or *lay:* one joins both hands in front of the chest, often holding incense sticks, then kneels, raises both hands upwards above the head, then lowers them, while bending the head three or four times to the ground.[59]

Before concluding the exposition of Vietnamese religions, three further questions need to be answered to help us understand the challenges seventeenth-

---

57. The two terms *ma* and *qui* have been adopted by Christians to refer to demons, fallen angels and enemies of God and humanity.

58. For studies on the Vietnamese cult of ancestors, see Émile Tavernier, *Le Culte des ancêtres précédé d'un exposé sur le Buddhisme, le Taoisme et le Confucianisme* (Saigon: Albert Portail, 1926) and Joseph Vu Quang Tuyen, "La piété filiale chez les Vietnamiens" (diss., Pontifical University de Propagande Fide, Rome, 1954).

59. No doubt these gestures of extreme veneration shown toward humans must have seemed excessive to the early missionaries. Furthermore, the terms *tho,* used in the expression *tho ong ba* (ancestor worship), is misleading when translated into European languages as *adore* or *adoration.* The word *tho* is rather fluid and does not have the technical meaning of *latreia* as opposed to *duleia.* De Rhodes was already careful to distinguish between *latreia* on the one hand and *duleia* and *hyperduleia* on the other in his *Cathechismus,* 285.

century Vietnam presented to missionaries. The first regards the relationship of the *tam giao* with native religion. It is true that Buddhism, Confucianism, and to a lesser extent Taoism were sponsored by the state. They were so to speak the official religions of Vietnam. As has been shown, they have penetrated into the Vietnamese soul and permanently shaped the educational, political, social, and religious structures of the country.

Nevertheless, as Cadière has convincingly argued, the "true religion of the Vietnamese is the cult of the spirits,"[60] including that of Heaven. This religion is not organized; it has no sacred books, no official ministers, no public houses of worship (except the *te nam giao*), and no formalized rituals. Yet it is the most pervasive and transforming cult, because it is rooted in the family with ancestor worship as its most sacred practice. Every Vietnamese worthy of the name, because of the sacred duties of filial piety, is a minister of this religion.

The *tam giao,* precisely because they are foreign and imported (especially Buddhism which has its origin in India), are Vietnamese religions only to the extent they have been assimilated into the cult of spirits. In fact, these three religions have been so enmeshed with the cult of spirits that their philosophical elements have been combined with popular beliefs that are prima facie contradictory to them. Thus, for instance, Buddhism, which denies the permanence of the self, accepts veneration of ancestors; Confucianism, which in later times has become areligious, welcomes the *te nam giao;* and Taoism, which emphasizes noncontrivance, incorporates sacrificial worship and other cultic acts.

In sum, in the words of Cadière, the Vietnamese "have two religions: one principal, the religion of the spirits, which has a double object: its cult is addressed both to the personified forces of nature and to the souls of the dead (by the latter are included the cult of heroes, the cult of abandoned souls, and the cult of ancestors). This religion also has a double mode of exercise: religious in Confucianism, and magical in Taoism. Beside this principal religion, there is a secondary religion, and that is Buddhism."[61]

The second question regards whether the Vietnamese are "religious." This question may sound odd, in light of what has been said above. Nevertheless, European historians of religion used to raise the issue of whether the Vietnamese are religious in the strict sense of the term. If by religion is meant a social organization with a well-defined creed (especially with clear-cut dogmas on the nature of God and a corresponding personal worship of God), sacred books, rituals, and legal structures, then the great majority of Vietnamese are not religious. But if by religion is meant a worldview in which the invisible is present, the supernatural is efficacious, the spiritual is dominant, then one must say that the Vietnamese are obsessed with religion. There is nothing, literally nothing, in the personal life of the Vietnamese, in their family relationships, and in their

---

60. Cadière I, 6.
61. Cadière I, 31–32.

sociopolitical organization that escapes the presence and influence of *ong Troi* and of the *than,* the *ma,* the *qui,* and the ancestors.

The third question concerns the nature of ancestor worship. It is well known that Matteo Ricci and his fellow Jesuits have maintained that ancestor worship (in particular, the cult of Confucius) is political and civic in nature. The instruction of the Propagande Fide, *Plane compertum est* of 1939, settled the issue after repeated condemnations of the "Chinese rites" by various popes (especially Benedict XIV's *Ex quo singulari* of 1742). Whatever may be said about the advantages of the decisions of *Plane compertum est* for missionary work and about the correctness of the Jesuits' judgment on the nature of ancestor worship from the point of view of the intellectual elite, there is no denying that for the great masses, ancestor worship is a *religious* act, indeed, the most religious act of their religion.

As Cadière, who wrote on the basis of his fifty-odd years of careful observation of the daily life of the common Vietnamese people, correctly affirms, "It is impossible to hold that the Vietnamese, at this moment in time, do not believe in the survival and real presence of the ancestors in the tablets, that they do not attribute supernatural powers to these ancestors, and that, therefore, the cult they render to them is not, properly speaking, a religion. Such a theory is in total contradiction with what can be seen every single day in Vietnam....For the immense majority of the Vietnamese, the ancestors continue to be part of the family and the cult rendered them is clearly religious."[62] It is interesting to note that for once a Jesuit, Alexandre de Rhodes, would agree wholeheartedly with a member of the Missions étrangères de Paris, Léopold Cadière.

THE VIETNAMESE LANGUAGE AND ITS SCRIPTS

An introduction to the background of de Rhodes's achievements must address, however briefly, the question of the Vietnamese language and its writing systems since it was he who published the first two printed books in the "national script" (*chu quoc ngu*), that is, the *Cathechismus* and the *Dictionarium.*[63]

The Vietnamese language is said by some linguists (e.g., E. Souvignet) to have its origins in the family of Malay languages and by others (e.g., Henri Maspéro) in the family of Thai languages, whose most characteristic feature is the system of tones. Of course, whatever the ultimate origin of the Vietnamese language might have been, it has undoubtedly received significant modifications, as successive waves of ethnic groups invaded and settled in the country and as the Vietnamese carried out their southward march to annex the kingdom of Champa and parts of Cambodia.

---

62. Cadière I, 39.

63. It is of course beyond the scope of this work to study the contribution of de Rhodes to the formation of the national script. Most of the writings on the subject are in Vietnamese. Among the foremost scholars in this field are Nguyen Khac Xuyen, Thanh Lang, Vo Long Te, and Do Quang Chinh.

In the formation of contemporary Vietnamese then there are contributions not only of Malay and Thai languages but also of Tai-Kadai, Austro-Asiatic, Mon-Khmer, and most importantly, Sino-Tibetan languages.

CHINESE LANGUAGE AS THE LANGUAGE OF SCHOLARS: *CHU NHO*

As has been mentioned above, even before the Chinese rulers attempted to impose their culture as well as their system of ideogrammatic writing on the Vietnamese, Chinese and its characters had been the official language of Vietnam. Even after throwing off the yoke of Chinese domination, the Vietnamese kings still maintained Chinese as the official language of the country because of necessities of international diplomacy and with a view to promote culture. In this respect, Buddhist monks deserve special commendation for having made an important contribution to the diffusion of the study of Chinese characters.

The study of Chinese characters flourished under the Ly and Le dynasties, especially with the establishment of the three literary examinations and the foundation of Quoc Tu Giam (College of National Sons), Han Lam Vien (Academy of letters), and Van Mieu (shrine in honor of Confucius). Under King Minh Mang (1820–40), the study of Chinese enjoyed another significant revival.

Chinese remained until the beginning of our century the official language of Vietnam. Though still the language of scholars (that is why it is called *chu nho*, literally, script of the learned), it lost its official status with the abolition of the literary examinations in 1915 in Tonkin and in 1918 in central Vietnam.

This multisecular contact with the Chinese literature produced a set of vocabularies parallel to the native Vietnamese language, which are not quite Chinese, but rooted in Chinese and different from the everyday Vietnamese. These words, called Sino-Vietnamese, are mostly used in literary, philosophical, and scientific disciplines. For example, for heaven, the "authentic" Vietnamese word is *troi* (hence, *Duc Chua Troi*, meaning the noble Lord of Heaven), whereas the Sino-Vietnamese word is *thien* (from Chinese *t'ien*), and we have the Sino-Vietnamese word *Thien Chua* for God.[64] Both words are currently in use, though the former is considered less learned than the latter.

DEMOTIC SCRIPT: *CHU NOM*

Though Chinese remained the learned and official language, Vietnamese writers wanted a writing of their own. This system of writing is known as *chu nom*, literally, popular or demotic script.[65] Two characters of this demotic script appeared at the end of the seventh century in the words *Bo* and *Cai* of the title of

---

64. Of course, in English we have a parallel phenomenon: we have words of Anglo-Saxon origin and words of Greco-Latin derivation designating the same thing, e.g., godly and divine.

65. On the *Nom* script, see Nguyen Dinh Hoa, "Chu Nom, the Demotic System of Writing in Vietnam," *Journal of the American Oriental Society* (1959); Tran Nghia, "Le Legs du 'Hán Nôm' — Recherche, Traduction, Étude," in Nguyen Trong Bau and Bertrand de Hartingh, eds., *90 ans de recherches sur la culture et l'histoire du Vietnam* (Hanoi: Éditions des Sciences Sociales, 1995), 400–409;

Bo Cai Dai Vuong (*bo* means father, and *cai* means mother; *dai vuong* means great king) given to a man by the name of Phung Hung who in 791 led an insurrection against the Chinese occupation. There is also the demotic script of Co in the name of *Dai Co Viet* given by the Dinh dynasty to the country in the tenth century.

But the earliest and most important document written in *chu nom* is *Van te ca sau* (the Ode to the Crocodile) composed by Nguyen Thuyen in 1282 under the Tran dynasty. This poet is said to have composed a poem in *chu nom* on a piece of paper and used it as a charm to chase away a crocodile that had appeared in the Red River. Another important document in *chu nom* is a poem on family education (*Gia huan ca*) traditionally attributed to the poet-statesman Nguyen Trai in the fifteenth century. In the sixteenth century, there were attempts to transcribe Chinese classics in this demotic script.[66]

Most Vietnamese ancient literature, including the masterpiece *Kim Van Kieu*, a 3,254-verse poem by Nguyen Du (1765–1820), is written in this script. *Chu nom* was strongly encouraged by King Quang Trung (1788–92) as a way to develop an independent national writing; he had official acts composed in this script and founded the Sung chinh thu vien, charged with creating works of literature in *chu nom*.

Essentially, the *chu nom* is a script in which Chinese characters are borrowed and altered to render the meaning of Vietnamese words. Generally, two Chinese characters are combined, one of which indicates the meaning of the Vietnamese word, while the other indicates its pronunciation. Sometimes the Chinese character is left unchanged but is pronounced in the Vietnamese way. At other times, some new characters are created from scratch out of Chinese characters to represent symbolically the object referred to.

Chu nom was never accepted as the official script, both because it is complicated and somewhat arbitrary (at any rate, it presupposes a knowledge of Chinese!) and because it was perceived as a threat to classical education.

It is very interesting that the first missionaries made use of *chu nom* rather than the Chinese characters in composing catechisms and prayer books. One of them, Gerolamo Maiorica, an Italian Jesuit, wrote some forty-eight books in this script.[67] One reason for its use is that *chu nom*, being more widely known, would permit a more extensive communication with the Vietnamese. More significantly, the missionaries' preference for *chu nom* signaled their decision, in

---

Ho Hai Thuy, "Réflexions préliminaires sur un essai de traitement informatique des textes en nôm," in Nguyen Trong Bau and Bertrand de Hartingh, eds., *90 ans de recherches,* 410–14; and Tran Nghia, "Introduction générale," in Tran Nghia and François Gros, eds., *Catalogue des livres en Hannôm/Di San Han Nom Viet Nam Thu Muc De Yeu* (Hanoi: Éditions des Sciences Sociales, 1993), 1:15–47.

66. For a general history of Vietnamese literature, in particular of Vietnamese literature in *chu nom,* see Pham The Ngu, *Viet Nam Van Hoc Su Tan Bien,* 3 vols. (Saigon: Anh Phuong, n.d.), especially vol. 2.

67. In 1659 Francisco Rangel mentioned that Maiorica had left behind a large library of forty-eight volumes which he wrote in the script of the country. See his annual report about Tonkin in *ARSI, JS* 64, 366v. On the works of Maiorica, see Hoang Xuan Han, "Girolamo Maiorica: Ses oeuvres en langue vietnamienne conservées à la Bibliothèque Nationale de Paris," *Archivum Historicum Societatis Iesu* 22 (1953): 203–14.

line with the Jesuits' policy of inculturation, to keep the nascent Vietnamese Christian Church rooted in the native culture rather than in the foreign culture of which the Chinese characters were a potent symbol.

CHU QUOC NGU: THE ACHIEVEMENT OF JESUIT MISSIONARIES

When the Jesuit missionaries came to Vietnam in the seventeenth century, some of them (e.g., Francisco de Pina, Cristoforo Borri, Gaspar do Amaral, António Barbosa, Gerolamo Maiorica, and Alexandre de Rhodes) learned and mastered the language, while others (e.g., Francesco Buzomi and Manoel Fernandes) preached through interpreters.[68] Thanks to their knowledge of the language, in 1620 the Jesuits in residence at Hoi An (in particular Francisco de Pina) prepared a catechism in *chu nom,* with the collaboration of Vietnamese converts.[69] It is highly likely that the text was written in *chu nom* for the use of the Vietnamese, whereas the foreign missionaries had it written in Roman alphabets for their use.

The use of Roman alphabets to transcribe phonetically languages written in characters was not new. Indeed, missionaries in Japan had already made use of such a device and published Japanese books using the Roman alphabets (*romaji*).[70] It is very likely that Jesuit missionaries who were ministering to the Japanese in Faifo made use of Romanized books published by the Japanese Jesuit Press. In China, Michele Ruggieri and Matteo Ricci had composed a Portuguese-Chinese dictionary,[71] and Nicholas Trigault had published in 1626 a remarkable seven-hundred-page study on the tones of the Chinese language transcribing the Chinese characters in Roman alphabets.[72]

It is very probable that missionaries such as Francisco de Pina and Cristoforo Borri had attempted sometime in 1620 the Romanization of the Vietnamese language.[73] At any rate, by 1632 Gaspar do Amaral (1592–1645) had shown

---

68. Francisco de Pina (1585–1625), a Portuguese, came to Cochinchina in 1617. It was he who baptized Minh Duc Vuong Thai Phi, the last concubine of Nguyen Hoang (1502–1613), the founder of the Nguyen dynasty and the first lord of Cochinchina. He drowned on December 15, 1613, near Hoi An at the age of forty on his way back from a visit to a Portuguese ship. It is said that he was caught in his cassock and could not swim to shore after the boat overturned. He was solemnly buried in Hoi An. See *Divers voyages,* 75–76; Gaspar Luís, "Missio Cocincinae. Anno 1625," in *ARSI, JS* 71, f. 63v–64v; António de Fontes, "Annua de Missam de Annam. Anno 1626," in *ARSI, JS* 72, f. 79r.

69. About this catechism, see the reports of João Roiz, "Annua de Cochichina do anno 1620," in *ARSI, JS* 72 f. 6r, and Gaspar Luís, "Cocincinensis missionis annuae Litterae, anni 1620," in *ARSI, JS* 17, f. 24r. This catechism in manuscript is now lost.

70. See, for instance, *Vocabulario da Lingoa de Japam com a declaração em Portuguez feito por alguns Padres, e Irmaõs da Companhia de Jesu* (Nagasaki: Collegio de Japam da Companhia de Jesu, 1603), João Rodrigues, *Arte da Lingoa de Japam: Composta pello Padre João Rodrigues de Cõpanhia de Jesu. Divida em tres livros* (Nagasaki: Collegio de Japam da Companhia de Jesu, 1604), and the works of Didaco Collado, *Modus confitendi et examinandi paenitentem Japonensem* (Rome, 1632); *Dictionarium sive Thesauri linguae japonicae compendium* (Rome, 1632); *Ars gramaticae japonicae linguae* (Rome, 1632).

71. See *Vocabulario Portughese, ARSI, Sin.* 1, 45.

72. See *ARSI, JS* 127.

73. Cristoforo Borri (1583–1632), an Italian from Milan, entered the Company of Jesus in 1601,

a remarkable mastery of the alphabetization of Vietnamese, better than de Rhodes's, in his annual reports to his superiors.[74] We are informed by de Rhodes that do Amaral had composed a *Diccionário anamita-português-latim,* now unfortunately lost, upon which de Rhodes relied to prepare his own dictionary. In addition, de Rhodes also mentioned a dictionary prepared by another Jesuit, António Barbosa (1594–1647), *Diccionário português-anamita,* on which he also relied and which too is now lost.[75]

These early achievements were significant, but they would not have made the alphabetization of the Vietnamese language a lasting success without the works of Alexandre de Rhodes, especially his *Dictionarium* and *Cathechismus.* We will speak of the *Cathechismus* in detail later on. Here a few words should be said about the *Dictionarium* and about the alphabetization of the Vietnamese language.

Vietnamese is a monosyllabic language with six tones, which give it a sing-song effect. De Rhodes noted this in despair when he first arrived in Vietnam: "We met Fr. de Pina there, who had thoroughly mastered the native language. . . . As for me, I confess to you that when I first arrived in Cochinchina and heard the natives speak, especially the women, it seemed to me I was listening to birds twittering, and I lost all hope of ever being able to learn it. All the words are monosyllables, and their meaning is discerned only by the different tones given them as they are pronounced. One single syllable, for instance *dai,* denotes twenty-three entirely different things depending on the various ways of pronouncing it, which means one can speak only by singing."[76]

---

came to Cochinchina in 1618 and left in 1621. He then returned to the University of Coimbra to teach mathematics. He was also well versed in astronomy and navigation. Because of his controversial theory of three heavens, he was recalled to Rome by the general Mutio Vitelleschi. He then left the Jesuit order and joined first the Bernardines of the Holy Cross, then the Cistercians in Rome. After he had been expelled by the Cistercians, he sued them, and won. As he was going to tell the good news to his friend, he died on the way on May 24, 1632. Borri wrote an informative report on the Jesuit mission in Cochinchina in the early part of the seventeenth century in Italian which was translated into French, Latin, Dutch, German, and English: *Relatione della nuova missione delli PP. de'la Compagnia di Giesu, al regno della Cocincina, scritta dal Padre Christoforo Bori Milanese della medesima Compagnia* (Rome, 1631). On Borri, see Charles B. Maybon, "Notice sur Cristoforo Borri et sur les éditions de sa 'Relation'," *BAVH* (1931): 269–76.

74. See his 1632 handwritten report "Annua do reino de Annam do anno de 1632 pera o Pe André Palmiero da Compa de Jesu, Visitador das Provincias de Japam, e Cina," in *ARSI, JS* 85, f. 125r–174r, and his "Relaçam dos catequistas da Christamdade de Tunk. e seu modo de proceder pera o Pe Manoel Dias, Visitador de Jappao e China," in *Real Academia de la Historia de Madrid, Jesuitas,* Legajo 21 bis, Fasc. 16, 31–37r. Gaspar do Amaral, a Portuguese, was born in 1592, joined the Jesuits in 1608, taught Latin, philosophy, and theology at Evora, Braga, and Coimbra before going to the missions. He came to Tonkin in 1631 with three other Jesuits (Andrea Palmiero, António de Fontes, and António F. Cardim), and was warmly received by Lord Trinh Trang. Do Amaral worked in Tonkin for seven years, then was recalled to Macao to be made rector of the Madre de Deus College. In 1645 he went back to Tonkin but drowned near Hai Nam on December 23, 1645. On do Amaral, see C. Sommervogel, *Bibliothèque de la Compagnie de Jésus,* new edition (Louvain, 1960) under "d'Amaral." Sommervogel dates do Amaral's death to February 24, 1646.

75. See *Dictionarium,* ad lectorem.

76. *Divers voyages,* 72. The difficulty and melodious effect of the Vietnamese language have been noted by other missionaries, e.g., Marini, 171; Tissanier, 200; and Borri, 74–75.

There are six tones: (1) mid-level or flat, (2) high-rising (*sac*), (3) low-falling (*huyen*), (4) falling-rising and constricted (*hoi*), (5) high-rising and broken (*nga*), and (6) low-falling and short and constricted (*nang*). The same word pronounced in six different tones has six different meanings. For instance, the word *ma* may mean ghost, cheek, but, tomb, horse, and rice seedling, if pronounced in the order of the tones indicated above.

Hence, the extreme danger of mispronouncing the tones. De Rhodes delights in telling stories of misunderstanding caused by mispronunciation. Once a priest friend of his told the cook to go to the market and buy some *ca* (the word, with the high-rising tone, means fish). When he came into the kitchen to see what kind of fish the man had bought, he was surprised to see a basket of eggplants (the same word with the low-falling tone means eggplant). Realizing that he had mispronounced the tone, the good father apologized for the error (and probably had to settle for a different menu for that day). Another priest once told the housekeeper to cut down the *tre*. Hearing his order, the children scattered away in terror. The word, with the mid-level tone, means bamboo, whereas he had pronounced with the fall-rising and constricted tone, which means children. Needless to say, it took the good priest a while to reassure the children that he had not meant to have their heads chopped off.[77]

To differentiate these different tones, following the example of others, de Rhodes made use of various diacritical marks found in French, Portuguese, Spanish, and Greek. Thus, leaving the mid-level or flat tone unmarked, the following marks are placed above the vowels: ´ for the high-rising tone, ` for the low-falling, ' for the falling-rising and constricted, ˜ for the high-rising and broken, and . placed at the bottom of the word for the low-falling and short and constricted.

The alphabetization system was perfected by later missionaries such as Bishop Pigneau de Béhaine (1741–99) and Bishop Jean Louis Taberd (1794–1840) with their dictionaries.[78]

With the assistance of the Propaganda Fide, de Rhodes's *Dictionarium* (as well as *Cathechismus*) was published in 1651.[79] The book is composed of three parts: the first part, with a separate pagination (thirty-one pages) is an essay on Vietnamese grammar, entitled *Linguae Annamiticae seu Tunchinensis brevis*

---

77. See "De tonis seu accentibus linguae Annamitae," in *ARSI, JS* 83 and 84, f. 62v; *Histoire du Royaume*, 111–12; *Tunchensis historiae*, I, 86; *Relazione*, 117.

78. De Béhaine prepared a Vietnamese-Latin dictionary but did not publish it. Bishop Taberd made use of de Béhaine's work and composed two dictionaries: *Dictionarium Annamitico Latinum* and *Dictionarium Latino Annamiticum*, both published in Serampore, India, in 1838. Taberd's dictionaries were improved by Bishop J. S. Theurel (1829–59) and republished in Vietnam in 1877.

79. It is likely that de Rhodes worked on his dictionary between 1636 and 1645. The reasons for assigning this date are that his knowledge of Vietnamese, especially of the use of diacritical marks, before 1636 was still imperfect and that after 1645 he was engaged in his travel to Rome to help establish a hierarchy in Vietnam. Of special help to him were the dictionaries of do Amaral and Barbosa and the assistance of catechists such as Ignatius who had been a mandarin learned in Chinese literature and philosophy before becoming a Christian.

declaratio.[80]   The second part is the dictionary proper, entitled *Dictionarium Annamiticum seu Tunchinense cum Lusitana, et Latina declaratione.*[81] And the last part, unpaginated, entitled *Index Latini sermonis,* is an index of Latin words followed by the numbers of the pages in which they occur in the second part. In fact, this part functions as a Latin-Vietnamese dictionary, without the Vietnamese words explicitly given.

The Romanization of the Vietnamese language, facilitated by the European printing system, remained for two centuries a script used almost exclusively by and for Christians.[82] It was still ignored by the majority of the people for whom the knowledge of Chinese remained a condition for professional advancement. It became widespread only under the French domination (1864–1954). In 1898 French Governor Paul Doumer signed the decree, which definitively went into effect only in 1909, mandating the use of *chu quoc ngu* in civil service examinations. In 1917 an imperial decree abolished traditional forms of education in favor of those based on the *chu quoc ngu* and French.[83] Thus, when the three state literary examinations were abolished at the beginning of this century, the Romanized script became the *chu quoc ngu* (national script), replacing both *chu nho* and *chu nom.*[84]

Though the *chu quoc ngu* was the fruit of a collective work of Portuguese missionaries,[85] de Rhodes was its most prominent promoter and the main in-

---

80. It is composed of eight chapters: 1. De literis et syllabis quibus haec lingua constat; 2. De accentibus et aliis signis in vocalibus; 3. De nominibus; 4. De pronominibus; 5. De aliis pronominibus; 6. De verbis; 7. De reliquis orationis partibus indeclinabilibus; 8. Praecepta quaedam ad syntaxim pertinentia.

81. The reason why Portuguese was chosen is that most missionaries to the Far East in the seventeenth century knew this language (on account of the *padroado*). Latin was added because it was hoped that the Vietnamese would use it to learn Latin.

82. The expression "Romanization," though in current use to refer to the alphabetical transcription of the Vietnamese language, is misleading inasmuch as it suggests that it was the work of people in Rome, whereas the creation of *chu quoc ngu* was essentially the collective work of Portuguese missionaries and of de Rhodes.

83. See Nguyen Thi Chan Quynh, "Concours de mandarins," *La Jaune et la rouge* 525, 5 (1997): 36–37.

84. Perhaps it must be said that the replacement of the Chinese script and in particular *chu nom* by *chu quoc ngu* is not an unmixed boon for the Vietnamese. Most Vietnamese today, unable to read the Chinese script and *chu nom,* are cut off from the most important documents of their cultural and religious history. Obviously, de Rhodes cannot be blamed for this ignorance.

85. Roland Jacques has been vocal in asserting the collective nature of the work of alphabetization of the Vietnamese language and the important contribution of Portuguese (and not French) missionaries, especially Gaspar do Amaral and António Barbosa. See his dissertation "L'oeuvre de quelques pionniers portugais dans le domaine de la linguistique vietnamienne jusqu'en 1650" (Paris: INALCO, 1995), and his essay "Le Portugal et la romanisation de la langue vietnamienne: Faut-il récrire l'histoire" forthcoming in *Revue française d'Histoire d'Outre-Mer* (1998).

While Jacques has made some valid points, especially with reference to the contribution of Portuguese missionaries, he went overboard in minimizing the contribution of de Rhodes himself. Without any evidence, he asserts that the dictionaries by do Amaral and Barbosa were not really lost but rather incorporated whole and entire by de Rhodes into his *Dictionarium,* thus rendering the preservation of these two dictionaries unnecessary. Thus, he says, de Rhodes was not the sole "author" nor even the "principal redactor" of *Dictionarium.*

strument of its popularization.[86] Vietnam is grateful to him for this immense cultural achievement. In 1941 a stone monument was erected in Hanoi to commemorate his work which reads:

ALEXANDRE DE RHODES

Born in Avignon on the fifteenth of March MDXCI, entered the Company of Jesus in MDCXII. Leaving Lisbon for the Indies on the fourth of April MDCXIX, he arrived in Macao on the twenty-ninth of May MDCXXIII. He was destined for the missions in Japan, but this country having been closed to evangelization, he was sent to Vietnam. Between MDCXXIV and MDCXLVI he made several sojourns in Annam of the Nguyen and Tonkin of the Trinh, two of which in Ke Cho (Hanoi) (MDCXXVII–MDCXXX).

The success of his preaching was considerable. In order to preserve its fruits and establish the Vietnamese Church on a solid foundation, he obtained from the Holy See the appointment of bishops who were chosen among the French (MDCLII).

He did not leave Vietnam without regret: "I left Cochinchina in my body, but certainly not in my heart; and so it is with Tonkin. My heart is in both countries, and I don't think it will ever be able to leave them."

Sent to the mission in Persia, he died in Isphan on the sixteenth of November MDCLX, at the age of seventy.

He has left many reports which have been translated into many languages, and with the publication of his *Cathechismus* and his *Dictionarium annamiticum, lusitanum et latinum,* the first books in Romanized Vietnamese, his name remains for ever connected with the invention of the *quoc ngu* (national script).[87]

Furthermore, with reference to the *Cathechismus,* Jacques believes that though the final redaction of the Vietnamese text in the Romanized script was de Rhodes's (of course, de Rhodes's Latin translation is his own), the text itself is a collective work. Again, as will be made clear subsequently, it is certain that de Rhodes depended on many persons, not least the Vietnamese converts, in composing his catechism, but it is going beyond historical evidence to say that the *Cathechismus* is an "oeuvre collective." The fact that Metello Saccano refers in 1646 (that is, some six years before the publication of the *Cathechismus*) to "our catechism...in which our mysteries are clearly expounded and the fantasies of the religious sects of these people are effectively refuted, the whole work divided into eight sermons to be taught in so many days" (Saccano, 129) does not mean that this "our catechism" was some catechism different from the one by de Rhodes. Furthermore, "our" does not necessarily mean "collectively written" by the missionaries of that time, but only that de Rhodes's yet to be published catechism was being used by other missionaries.

86. Of course, not in the sense that de Rhodes caused the acceptance of the Romanized script as the official script of the Vietnamese language. That was to be one of the effects of the pressure of French colonial power. Nevertheless, there is no gainsaying that de Rhodes's two landmark works, the *Cathechismus* and the *Dictionarium,* remained the major instruments for the perpetuation of the Romanized script.

87. See Do Quang Chinh, 101–2. In about 1956, the Communist government ordered this memorial destroyed so as to erase the achievements of de Rhodes from the people's memory.

In Saigon (now Ho Chi Minh City) a street was named after him in 1955. The Vietnamese Jesuits also founded a cultural and university center in Saigon and named it after de Rhodes.

In the aftermath of the independence war, anticolonialist sentiments, which unfairly linked de Rhodes with French domination, have led some historians to attack de Rhodes's work.[88] Recently, however, de Rhodes has been rehabilitated by none other than the Communist government itself. His works were allowed to be republished in Ho Chi Minh City, the *Dictionarium* in 1991 and the *Cathechismus* in 1993. In 1995 his 1941 commemorative plaque, which had been removed, was placed in the garden of the National Library in Hanoi. A conference on his life and work was organized by the Ministry of Culture and the National Center of Social and Human Sciences in Hanoi on December 22, 1995, and the acts of the conference were later published.[89]

Such was in brief the sociopolitical, cultural, and religious world in which Alexandre de Rhodes carried out his missionary and catechetical work. We now turn to the man himself and his activities.

---

88. See, for instance, The Hung, "L'Église catholique et la colonisation française," *Les Catholiques et le mouvement national: Études Vietnamiennes* 53 (1979): 9–81; Tran Tam Tinh, *Dieu et César: les Catholiques dans l'histoire du Viet Nam* (Paris: Sudestasie, 1978); and the conference on Catholicism and the history of Vietnam organized by the Institute of Social Sciences in collaboration with the Government Commission on Religious Affairs in Ho Chi Minh City, March 11–12, 1988.

89. The height of de Rhodes's rehabilitation occurred when the vice prime minister Nguyen Khanh declared on that occasion that de Rhodes was "an initiator of cultural activities who has contributed to the development of Vietnamese culture and language." See the text of his discourse in *Xua va Nay* 1 (1996): 19–20.

Figure 3. Map of Indochina designed by early Jesuit missionaries.

2

Alexandre de Rhodes

Founder of Vietnamese Christianity

It is one of life's little ironies that the one who would be called the founder of Vietnamese Christianity did not first choose Vietnam but Japan and China as the countries for his missionary vocation.[1] It was only by default that he was sent by his superiors in 1624 to the mission the order had started almost by chance a decade earlier at the request of Fernandes de Costa, a Portuguese merchant. Japan, for which de Rhodes was destined and had prepared himself by studying the language in Macao, was judged too dangerous for a new dispatch of missionaries after the bloody persecutions by the shoguns of the Tokugawa family, Ieyasu (1598–1616) and Hidetada (1605–23).[2]

In this chapter we will follow de Rhodes's journey from Rome to Vietnam, his activities in Vietnam, and his travel from Macao back to Rome. It is as it were a journey in a circle, the center of which was de Rhodes's missionary heart burning with zeal for the Kingdom of God. De Rhodes himself uses this image of a circle to organize the narrative of his many and long voyages: "Because I went by way of Rome to China, remaining there several years and returning to Europe by a different route, this little work will have three parts: the voyage, the sojourn, and the return."[3] We will not narrate all the details of de Rhodes's life

---

1. In calling de Rhodes the "founder of Vietnamese Christianity" I do not intend to minimize the work of other missionaries, mostly Portuguese, who had come to Vietnam before him. Certainly de Rhodes deserves this title as far as the Vietnamese Church in Tonkin is concerned. As for Cochinchina, though he was not the first one to arrive in this country nor did he found the church there, his long and hard labor during his second sojourn there (1640–45) contributed enormously to the growth and well-being of the church in this part of Vietnam.

2. For the history of Christianity in Japan, see, for instance, Joseph Jennes, *A History of the Catholic Church in Japan from Its Beginning to the Early Meiji Era: A Short Handbook* (Tokyo: Oriens Institute for Religious Research, 1973); Charles Ralph Boxer, *The Christian Century in Japan 1549–1650* (London: Cambridge University Press, 1951); George Elison, *Deus Destroyed: The Image of Christianity in Early Modern Japan* (Cambridge: Harvard University Press, 1988); and Léon Pages, *Histoire de la religion chrétienne au Japon depuis 1598 jusqu'à 1651*, 2 vols. (Paris, 1869–70).

3. *Divers voyages*, 4. For a detailed chronology of de Rhodes's life, see "Chronology of Alexandre de Rhodes."

but will only highlight those events that will help us understand his catechetical work and his *Cathechismus*.[4]

FROM AVIGNON TO ROME:
A MISSIONARY VOCATION (1593–1618)

Born in Avignon, then a papal state, on March 15, 1593,[5] into a family of Jewish origin,[6] Alexandre de Rhodes was the son of Bernardin de Rhodes II and Françoise de Rafaélis.[7] The de Rhodes family enjoyed a friendly relation with the Jesuits in Avignon and was a benefactor of the local Jesuit college.[8] It was there that Alexandre did his high school studies.[9]

Wishing to pursue his missionary vocation, Alexandre joined the Society of Jesus and requested to be admitted into the Roman province rather than that of Lyon because its members were better placed to obtain the permission of the king of Portugal to go to the mission in India.[10] On April 14, 1612, he entered the novitiate of San Andrea on the Quirinal where Matteo Ricci had preceded him in 1571 and John Adam Schall in 1611.

---

4. The most thorough account of de Rhodes's life and activities between 1624–30 and 1640–45 is Do Quang Chinh's unpublished dissertation entitled "La mission au Viet-Nam: 1624–30 et 1640–45. Alexandre de Rhodes, S.J. avignonnais," presented at the École des Hautes Études, Sorbonne, in 1969. For a recent biography of de Rhodes, see Jean Lacouture, "Un Avignonnais dans la rizière," in *Jésuites: Une multibiographie*, vol. 1, *Les conquérants* (Paris: Seuil, 1991), 297–324.

5. In his letter to the superior general Mutio Vitelleschi written in the fall of 1617, requesting to be sent to the Japanese or Chinese mission, de Rhodes wrote: "25. Jam coepi aetatis annum, quartumque Theologici cursus," which means he was born in 1593. See *ARSI, Fondo gesuitico*, n. 732. Again, the register of postulants entering the novitiate of San Andrea in Rome in 1612 notes: "Alessandro Rhodes, francese d'anni 19 incirca," which implies that his year of birth is 1593. See also Edouard Torralba, "La date de naissance du Père de Rhodes, 15 mars 1591, est-elle exacte?" *Bulletin de la Société des Études Indochinoises* 35 (1960): 683–89.

6. The de Rhodes family was from Calatayud in Aragon. Probably the family left the city towards the end of the fifteenth century when the Spanish Inquisition was getting very harsh against "converted" Jews. The family's original name was *Rueda*, written as *Rode* in provençal. "Rode" or "rouelle" means a small wheel, which the Jews were required to wear on their clothes during the Middle Ages. The "de" was added to the name as an elegant way to hide the true ethnic origin of the family. See H. Brenier, "Le Père A. RHODES, un grand missionnaire provençal au XVIIè siècle," *Les Missions Catholiques* 74 (1942): 105, and Michel Barnouin, "La parenté vauclusienne d'Alexandre de Rhodes (1593–1660)," in *Mémoires de l'Académie de Vaucluse*, 8th series, 4 (Avignon, 1995), 9–40.

7. Bernardin de Rhodes II was the son of Jean de Rhodes. See "Testament de Noble Bernardin RHODES, fils de feu Sieur Jean Rhodes, citoyen d'Avignon." Made in Avignon on December 18, 1610. *Archives départementales de Vaucluse. Vincenti 1587*, ff. 259–75r. Françoise de Rafaélis, of Italian origin, was Bernardin's second wife, whom he married in 1590 after the death of his first wife, Marie Giraud. See the marriage contract between Bernardin and Marie Giraud made on April 19, 1588, available at the Museum of Calvet of Avignon, *Manuscripts*, vol. 3806, ff. 42–45v. See L. Gaide, "Quelques renseignements sur la famille du P. Alexandre de Rhodes," *BAVH* (July–December 1927): 225–28.

8. The college was founded in 1565. In 1571 the great grandfather of Alexandre de Rhodes, Bernardin de Rhodes I, gave the Jesuit college forty-two *écus*; in 1588, his father did the same thing. At his death (1615) he left his two Jesuit sons, i.e., Alexandre and Georges, two thousand *écus* each.

9. See Augustine Canron, *Les Jésuites à Avignon: Esquisse historique* (Avignon, 1875), 40–41.

10. Alexandre's younger brother, Georges (1597–1661), also became a Jesuit. He was a professor of philosophy and theology and authored one book on philosophy and two books on theology.

During the novitiate, de Rhodes very probably had the chance to meet Nicholas Trigault, procurator of the province of Japan, who had come to Rome towards the end of 1614 to recruit missionaries.[11] On the day of his first profession of vows (April 15, 1614), probably with Trigault's encouragement, de Rhodes wrote a letter to the superior general Claudius Aquaviva (1543–1615) expressing his desire to go to the missions.

After completing the novitiate, de Rhodes commenced his theological studies at the Roman College, having already done his philosophy with the Jesuits in Avignon. On May 15, 1617, he wrote to Aquaviva's successor, Mutio Vitelleschi (1563–1645), renewing his request to be sent to the missions, this time specifying his choice of Japan and China. During the fourth year of his theology, he again wrote to Vitelleschi, applying to be sent to the missions.[12]

On Easter Sunday, 1618, shortly after de Rhodes's ordination to the priesthood, Vitelleschi granted him his request. Filled with joy, he immediately started preparing for the mission, studying mathematics and astronomy, which later stood him in good stead. Before his departure, he met Pope Paul V to receive his blessing. In October 1618, he left for Lisbon by way of Loretta, Milan, Avignon, and Toledo.[13]

FROM LISBON TO MACAO (1618–25)

During the sixteenth and seventeenth centuries all missionaries to the East Indies, except to the Philippines, had to embark at Lisbon on Portuguese ships bound for Goa from where they would head off to different parts of Asia. This was the arrangement made between the Holy See and Portugal under the system known as *padroado*. A few words on this system would be helpful.[14]

THE *PADROADO* SYSTEM

In 1418 Pope Martin V granted the king of Portugal the right of "ownership" of all the lands he would discover in Africa. Seven years later the same Pope forbade anyone, under pain of excommunication, to enter these lands without previous authorization of the Portuguese crown.[15] With this arrangement Portugal acquired new territories and new wealth thanks to its monopoly

---

11. Trigault has left an account of the Chinese mission: *De Christiana Expeditione apud Sinas* (Augsburg, 1615).

12. De Rhodes's three letters are found in *ARSI, Fondo Gesuitico*, nos. 732, 734, 735.

13. For all this period, see *Divers voyages*, 5–10.

14. On the *padroado* system, see Chappoulie I, 42–54; António da Silva Rego, *Le Patronage portuguais de l'Orient, aperçu historique* (Lisbon: Agência Geral do Ultramar, 1957); and Adelhelm Jann, *Die katholischen Missionen in Indien, China und Japan: Ihre Organisation und das portugiesische Patronat, vom 15. bis ins 18. Jahrhundert* (Paderborn: Ferdinand Schöningh, 1915).

15. See *Bullarium patronatus Portugalliae regum in Ecclesiis Africae, Asiae atque Oceaniae, bullas, brevia, epistolas, decreta actaque Sanctae Sedis ab Alexandro III ad hoc usque tempus amplectens (1171–1600)*, vol. I (Lisbon, 1868), 8, 31–34.

of commerce in these lands. At the same time, its neighbor, the kingdom of Spain, was also gaining in strength, especially after Christopher Columbus's discovery of America.

To put an end to the territorial disputes between these two powers, in 1492 Pope Alexander VI arbitrarily divided the world into two parts by drawing a line running from north to south about one hundred miles to the west of the Azores islands, assigning the lands on the east of the line to Portugal and those on the west to Spain. On June 7, 1494, a treaty between Spain and Portugal at Tordesillas moved the dividing line to 270 miles west of the Azores islands, assigning a bigger portion to Portugal.

The Portuguese appeared in Macao in 1557; nineteen years later, it was placed under the *padroado* of Portugal. Though Japan was not discovered by the Portuguese, the diocese of Funay (today Oita), established in 1588, was also placed under the Portuguese crown.[16] Thus, at the end of the sixteenth century, Portuguese domination stretched from Brazil to Japan.

The *padroado* system gave Portuguese and Spanish kings the right to nominate bishops in their lands and to oversee the development of future churches. In exchange, their ships would carry missionaries, their arms protect them, and their new wealth provide them with living expenses and pay for the construction and maintenance of churches.

Such a system, though not unusual when kings were thought to be obliged to promote the Christian faith, was bound to produce mixed fruits. In such a mixture of the spiritual and the temporal, more often than not the church came out the loser. The spiritual nature of its mission was obscured and its temporal fortunes went up and down together with a waxing and waning of the political powers.[17] In the sixteenth century, whereas Spain was able to maintain its power in South America and the Philippines, Portugal suffered a steady decline in India and the Far East. In particular, since 1493, Protestant Holland succeeded in carving out for itself new lands off Catholic Portugal.

Rome realized that it could no longer rely on Portugal for help to carry out its mission of evangelization. In 1622 Pope Gregory XV founded the congregation of the Propaganda Fide with the express purpose of strengthening the mission in countries assigned to the Portuguese crown, especially India and the Far East. Under the twenty-seven-year leadership of Francesco Ingoli, the congregation attempted to regain control of the missionaries, especially by appointing bishops as "apostolic vicars" under its jurisdiction, thus bypassing the authority

---

16. For a history of the relations between Japan and Portugal, see Kiichi Matsuda, *The Relations between Portugal and Japan* (Lisbon: Centro de Estudios Históricos Ultramarinos, 1965).

17. As an example of how the *padroado* system harmed the mission of the church, especially by interfering with the appointment of bishops, consider that in 1649 Pope Innocent X could not appoint bishops to the many vacant dioceses in Portugal. There was only one bishop in the metropolis, and he lived at the court. In Brazil and Africa, there was only one bishop left. In India, there were bishops in Goa and Cranganor, but the dioceses of Cochin, Malacca, Meliapur, Macao, and Japan were vacant. Missionaries were then complaining that many dioceses in India had been vacant for twenty years.

of Portugal.[18] It is in this context that one can appreciate the difficulties that confronted de Rhodes in his attempt to have Rome establish a hierarchy in Vietnam in the 1650s.

FROM LISBON TO GOA

On July 20, 1619, de Rhodes boarded the ship *Saint Theresa* in Lisbon, and after six months and ten days arrived in Goa. Because of persecutions in Japan, he did not immediately set out for Macao and from there for Japan. He was told to wait in Goa for a while, which turned out to be three and a half years.

During his sojourn in Goa he noticed two things which pained him deeply and which would have profound effects on his later missionary work. First, the missionaries had been very kind and generous to pagans and catechumens, but abandoned them after their baptism. Their previous acts of charity seemed not genuine and disinterested; rather they appeared to be gimmicks for conversion.[19] Second, Indians who had become Christians were forced to abandon their ancient customs, whereas their fellow citizens observed them. For instance, they were dressed in Portuguese clothes, so that in public places one could tell who was a Christian and who was not. This practice created a group of pro-Portuguese Indians and de facto segregated them from the rest of the population. De Rhodes asked himself: "I don't know why they are asked to do things that the Lord himself would not have asked of them, things that would deter them from receiving baptism and being saved."[20] Then he went on to say: "For my part, I well know that in China I vigorously opposed those who wanted to compel new Christians to cut their long hair, which the men all wear as long as the women's, and without which they would not be able to move around the country freely nor be part of the society. I used to tell them that the Gospel obliged them to lop off their spiritual errors but not their long hair."[21] These two lessons de Rhodes did not forget in his later mission to the Vietnamese.

There was a third lesson which was deeply impressed upon de Rhodes. It happened almost by chance. After three months in Goa he fell seriously ill. For convalescence he was sent to Salsette, a town three miles south of the old city of Goa, where the Jesuits had a college. There he met a compatriot by the name of Etienne Crucius. What impressed de Rhodes greatly, besides this man's holiness, was his knowledge of the local languages: "He had learned the two native languages so perfectly — Kanarese, the common people's tongue, and Mahrati, that he spoke them even better than the natives and published several books in both languages that are highly appreciated by all. I also saw an exceedingly

---

18. On the work of the Propaganda Fide under Francesco Ingoli, see Chappoulie I, 71–101.
19. *Divers voyages*, 21.
20. *Divers voyages*, 21.
21. *Divers voyages*, 21. It is interesting to note that from the various portraits of de Rhodes, it is clear that he wore, besides a beard which was de rigueur, long hair, letting it fall on his shoulders. See Léopold Cadière, "Iconographie du Père de Rhodes," *BAVH* XXV (1938): 27–61.

fine poem on our Lord's Passion that the Christians sang in church every Friday evening during Lent."[22] In fact, inspired by him, de Rhodes learned Kanarese so well that soon he was able to hear confessions and preach in that language. Mastery of the native language and liturgical adaptation — to these things de Rhodes would devote his energies in Vietnam.

While de Rhodes was working in Goa, he and his confreres were engaged in a practice which would be objectionable by our contemporary standards but which betrayed a widespread theology of original sin and baptism of their times. De Rhodes reported that "the worthiest project we engaged in was hunting up pagan children who had lost their fathers."[23] The purpose of this "hunt" (de Rhodes used the word *chasse*) was to baptize these children and instruct them in the Christian religion for fear that they would be damned were they left unbaptized. These children were often hidden, so the fathers had to "ferret out the quarry being concealed" from them.

One year, on the feast of the Conversion of Saint Paul, six hundred children were baptized, which de Rhodes declared to be "a fairly successful hunting" (*une assez heureuse chasse*). This belief in the impossibility of salvation without baptism is largely questioned today, but whatever may be said against its validity, it clearly provided a strong impetus for mission in de Rhodes's times.[24]

FROM GOA TO MACAO

De Rhodes's unexpected and long delay in Goa was happily brought to an end when on April 12, 1622, he resumed his journey to Macao, since news had arrived that it was safe to send missionaries to Japan again. The ship stopped at Cochin. There the captain died, so de Rhodes had to board another ship headed for Malacca. On the way the ship rounded Cape Comorin and passed along the Fisheries Coast, renowned for pearls. Next, the ship stopped at the island of Ceylon (today Sri Lanka), famous for cinnamon, and the kingdom of Negapatam. From there de Rhodes wanted to visit Mylapore, where the tomb of St. Thomas was allegedly located and where Francis Xavier, after prolonged prayers, reached the decision to go to Japan. But de Rhodes was prevented from

---

22. *Divers voyages*, 24–25.

23. *Divers voyages*, 22.

24. That de Rhodes firmly believed that people who die unbaptized are damned is clear from the following episode. When de Rhodes went to Tonkin in 1627, he met one of the sisters of Lord Trinh Trang. He had just conducted a funeral of a Christian soldier, and the noble lady was deeply impressed by the solemnity of the burial ritual and the solidarity of the Christians. She invited him to her palace to explain to her the meaning of the ritual. De Rhodes replied that "the solemn ceremony has the purpose to invite people to pray together for the deceased and to manifest God's love shown in his holy death." Thereupon the lady asked him to pray for her recently departed husband, to which de Rhodes replied: "Madam, we are not sent by the Lord of heaven and earth to announce the Gospel to the dead but to the living. We are powerless in giving any help to those who have died in faithlessness" (*Histoire du Royaume*, 141; see also *Divers voyages*, 88). De Rhodes's negative reply brought her to tears and extinguished her desire to become a Christian, though she did arrange for her aged mother-in-law to be baptized.

making a pilgrimage in honor of the two apostles to the Indies because the eight-day trip to Mylapore would make him miss the favorable weather for sailing to Malacca.

On June 24, 1622, the ship headed for Malacca and arrived there on July 28. Because of inclement weather, de Rhodes had to stay in Malacca for nine months. During this time he worked with a Portuguese Jesuit, Gaspar Ferreira, and both of them succeeded in baptizing two thousand people. While there, he heard that the Portuguese in Macao had defeated the Dutch who had come to attack the island. The news, de Rhodes reports with delight, "marvelously cheered the whole Indies. Large bonfires were lit for the occasion and general processions held in thanksgiving for so great a blessing."[25]

One can understand de Rhodes's less than ecumenical attitude towards the Dutch, not only because they were Protestant (whom he considered as "the great enemies of the faith in the Orient") but also because they were competing against the Portuguese for land and commerce. Portuguese and Dutch ships were often engaged in hostile action against each other. In fact, on the next leg of the journey, to Macao, de Rhodes's ship ran into four Dutch ships near the coast of Champa; these ships pursued it with all speed. Thanks to darkness, the Portuguese ship could escape by hiding in a small island near present-day Binh Thuan.[26] On May 29, 1623, the ship finally arrived in Macao, a seaport town of China, which the Portuguese had rented for two thousand *écus* a year. For de Rhodes, it was the end of a four-and-a-half-year journey after his departure from Europe. As he put it, "Think what a consolation it was to find myself in that great kingdom for which I had yearned so long!"[27]

As with any first-time traveler to China, de Rhodes was much awed by the size of the country, its population (which he estimated to be 250 million), its wealth, and its curiosities such as men wearing long hair and women with grotesquely small feet. In his memoir he extolled with enthusiasm the virtues of rice and especially of tea, which he believed prevents and cures headaches, relieves the stomach and aids digestion, and purges the kidneys against gout and gravel.[28]

---

25. *Divers voyages*, 42–43.

26. De Rhodes's attitude towards the Dutch grew worse on his return trip from China to Rome when he was arrested by some Dutch judges in Djakarta for saying Mass. He was put in jail for over three months and sentenced to leave the country and pay a fine of four hundred gold crowns. In addition, and for de Rhodes, a most horrendous sacrilege, the judges decreed that the holy images would be burned in the public square beneath a gallows on which a criminal would be hanged at the same time. See *Divers voyages*, pt. III, 13–27. He also blamed the "bloody persecution that has reduced the church in Japan, one of the most flourishing in the world, to near nothing" on the malice of two Dutchmen who aroused the fear of the king of Japan of an invasion by the Portuguese. And de Rhodes concluded with sarcasm: "It will be a great honor for the Dutch, who call themselves Christians, to have annihilated that church to satisfy their passion against other Christians!" (*Divers voyages*, 146.)

27. *Divers voyages*, 44.

28. See *Divers voyages*, 45–53. De Rhodes personally testified to the marvelous curative virtue of tea: "Speaking for myself, whenever I had migraine I would feel much relieved on taking tea. It seemed as if some hand completely removed my headache from me, because the greatest effect of tea is overcoming the foul vapors that rise to the head and make us sick" (51–52). However, tea may prevent sleep. Indeed,

As a missionary, of course, de Rhodes was most interested in learning about Chinese religions. For him, however, the three Chinese religions were nothing more than "superstitions," "idolatries," and "sorceries." In his view, the Chinese were "brilliant"; but insofar as their religions were concerned, "until now they have lived in darkness and profound ignorance of the most important thing in life, namely, knowledge of the true God and the proper way to serve him."[29]

The diocese of Macao, founded in 1576, was then part of the metropolis of Goa and extended over the whole of China and Japan. The Jesuits operated a college there named Madre de Deus. De Rhodes reported that all academic subjects were taught at the college as in any great European university. Later it was elevated to the status of a university which occasionally granted the degree of doctor in theology.

De Rhodes stayed at the college for a year to prepare himself for his mission in Japan by devoting himself to the learning of the language. Very probably he also learned some Chinese which, according to him, had some eight thousand characters. A mastery of Chinese, he thought, would require four years of full-time study.[30]

A NEW MISSION FIELD:
FIRST SOJOURN IN COCHINCHINA (1624–26)

De Rhodes's dream to be a missionary in Japan was not to be realized. Shogun Iemitsu, who succeeded his father Hidetada in 1623, was even more hostile to Christianity. Upon coming to power, he ordered a great number of Christians to be burnt in Yedo, present-day Tokyo. De Rhodes's superiors thought it wise not to send him to Japan. Instead, they dispatched him to Cochinchina where, as we saw in the last chapter, the order had started a mission in 1615.

In December 1624, de Rhodes and six other Jesuits left Macao for central Vietnam and arrived at Cua Han (present-day Da Nang) after nineteen days of voyage.[31] There were then three Jesuit residences, and de Rhodes was assigned

de Rhodes reported that in Vietnam when he had to stay up all night to hear confessions he would take tea and never fell asleep, and yet the following day felt as fresh as if he had slept. However, once when he tried to stay awake six nights in a row with tea he wound up "utterly exhausted." After all, there is some limit to what tea can do!

29. *Divers voyages*, 53.

30. However, de Rhodes certainly did not know written Chinese well. He himself confessed that "although I understood the Chinese language very well, I still did not know it well enough to make a long speech in it, so that I was forced to preach through an interpreter." This was one of the two reasons he gave why he failed to make many conversions during his ten-year stay in Macao from 1630 to 1640, the other reason being the "pride of the Chinese." See *Divers voyages*, 114.

31. Four were Portuguese: Gabriel de Martos, Gaspar Luís, António de Fontes, and Manoel Gonzales; one Italian: Gerolamo Maiorica; and one Japanese: Michael Maki, who knew Chinese well. See de Rhodes's letter to Nuno Mascarenhas, Assistant for Portugal, written in Cochinchina on June 16, 1625, *ARSI, JS* 68, f. 13rv, and Manoel Fernandes's letter to the general, written in Hoi An on July 2, 1625, *ARSI, JS* 68, f. 15rv.

to that of Thanh Chiem, commonly called Dinh Cham, where the seat of government of the Quang Nam province was located. At the residence, founded in 1623, were three other Jesuits: António de Fontes, António Dias, and more importantly, Francisco de Pina, who was fluent in Vietnamese. Under the latter's guidance, de Rhodes began studying the language in earnest, because, as he had seen in Salsette, only with a mastery of the local tongue could a missionary be effective.

Though discouraged at first by the difficulty of Vietnamese, which he compared to the twittering of birds because of its tones, de Rhodes applied himself with intensity to the study of the language. His learning experience has as much to say about his linguistic abilities as about his missionary method: "Every day I was given lessons, which I studied with the same application as I once studied theology in Rome. God willed that within four months I knew enough to be able to hear confessions and within six months to preach in the language of Cochinchina, as I have continued to do for many years since. I would advise all those wishing to come to our province to convert souls to take this trouble at the outset. I assure them that the fruits produced by presenting our mysteries in their own language are incomparably greater than those achieved through an interpreter, who tells them only what he pleases and cannot speak with the efficacy of words coming from the mouth of a preacher animated by the Holy Spirit."[32]

Besides having de Pina as teacher, de Rhodes was also taught by an extremely bright boy who, though not knowing de Rhodes's language, in three weeks taught him how to pronounce all the tones and himself learned "to read our letters, to write, and to serve Mass."[33]

As far as de Rhodes's apostolic activities during his first one-and-a-half-year sojourn in Cochinchina are concerned, they were rather meager, his main occupation being the study of the language. In the annual reports of 1625 and 1626, he was merely mentioned by name. He did go to the Hoi An residence but never to the one farther south at Nuoc Man (Qui Nhon).

From his 1625 letter to Nuno Mascarenhas and his later books, we learn of his collaboration with Francisco de Pina, especially in the conversion of Minh

---

32. *Divers voyages*, 72–73. There is no doubt that de Rhodes was a gifted linguist. He could write and speak fluently Latin, French, Italian, Portuguese, and Vietnamese; he could understand Konkani, Japanese, Chinese, and Persian. But he could not understand Dutch (for whom, as we have seen, he did not have much sympathy), as is clear from his account of his imprisonment by the Dutch authorities in Djakarta. As he told us, when he was brought to the court, a clerk "advanced to the center of the room and read the entire sentence for a solid hour, all in the Dutch language. I replied that inasmuch as that language was unknown to me I had not understood a thing of what had been said" (*Divers voyages*, pt. III, 25).

33. *Divers voyages*, 73–74. By "our letters" de Rhodes must have meant Latin, since the boy knew how to serve Mass, which required answering in Latin. The boy was later baptized, adopting de Rhodes's name with Raphael as the Christian name. Raphael de Rhodes became a second-level catechist (*ke giang*) and accompanied Giovanni M. de Leria (1597–1665), an Italian, in his mission to Laos. Raphael became quite wealthy and gave generously to the missionaries. On him and the Laotian mission, see *Histoire du Royaume*, 287; Marini, 492–540; Tissanier, 347; and Chappoulie I, 215–37.

Duc Vuong Thai Phi,[34] the last concubine of Lord Nguyen Hoang (1502–1613), the founder of the Nguyen dynasty. After hearing de Pina preach several times, Minh Duc asked for baptism which, however, had to be administered during the night for fear that her son, Prince Nguyen Phuoc Khe, who was hostile to the Christian faith, would prevent it.[35] Her Christian name was Mary Magdalene and she was often referred to by de Rhodes as Madam Mary. She had a small chapel built in the palace itself in Hue, and thanks to her position became a great source of support for the fledgling Christian community. During his second sojourn in Cochinchina (1640–45) de Rhodes visited her several times.[36]

De Rhodes's first stay in central Vietnam was marked by two tragedies: one was the death by drowning of Francisco de Pina in 1625, the other the opposition of the court. The first was a tremendous loss to the Christian community since de Pina was then the only one fluent in Vietnamese. The second would be, from the missionary point of view, a precious lesson for de Rhodes. Lord Nguyen Phuoc Nguyen was displeased with the missionaries because the expected Portuguese ships with merchandise and arms failed to show up. Opponents of Christianity took advantage of this fallout to proscribe Christian mission by accusing Christians of abandoning the cult of ancestors. They alleged that Christians had "no interest in succoring or paying respect to the souls of the departed relatives" and that "ours was a barbarous religion that obliterated all sentiments of gratitude toward parents from the heart."[37]

In de Rhodes's account, Christians themselves had a share of responsibility for this misunderstanding: "What provided the excuse for this ugly talk was the indiscreet zeal of a certain person who with scant prudence had wanted to abolish all ceremonies performed in that country for the relief of the departed. I have described them at length in my history of Tonkin, and really, although there are a few customs which Christians cannot practice without sin, most are quite innocent; and we decided they might be retained without prejudice to religious purity."[38]

We will analyze this text in detail later; suffice it here to note that de Rhodes has touched the central nerve of both Vietnamese religion and missionary methodology. At any rate, as a result of the accusation, the lord issued an edict

---

34. Her name is Minh Duc. Vuong Thai Phi is her title which means "most honored concubine of the Lord King."

35. See Gaspar Luís, "Missio Cocincinae. Anno 1625," *ARSI*, JS 71, f. 61v.

36. Of her de Rhodes wrote: "She became the mainstay of this whole new Church. Her example and influence were wonderfully instrumental in converting unbelievers and sustaining the faith of those who had already received baptism.... She has a most beautiful chapel in her palace that she continued to maintain through the most severe persecutions, where she is daily at her devotions, and to which she admits all Christians in the province.... She is today still the refuge of all our Fathers, and there is no Christian she would not help in any way she could" (*Divers voyages*, 75–76). Later, her son had her chapel removed.

37. *Divers voyages*, 76–77. If this is the charge, then the earliest Vietnamese opponents of Christianity were very shrewd indeed: they portrayed Christianity as destructive of the very heart of Vietnamese religion. Again and again, throughout the worst persecutions of Christians in Vietnam, the same charge was brought up. Any preaching of the Christian faith in Vietnam *must* deal with this issue.

38. *Divers voyages*, 77.

ordering the missionaries to leave all the churches and withdraw to Hoi An. Fortunately, the missionaries succeeded in making the lord change his mind.

Connected with this attempt to banish Christianity was the Vietnamese Christians' practice of wearing images, crosses, and rosaries around their necks as a witness to their faith. Lord Nguyen Phuoc Nguyen wanted to proscribe this practice. At first, the Vietnamese Christians resisted and were ready to die for their faith; but following the missionaries' advice about the difference between "brave" and "foolhardy," they took the sacred objects off. Here we are reminded of what de Rhodes said about the Indian Christians who after conversion behaved like the Portuguese. Though hairdo and clothes are by no means the same as sacred objects, just the same, by wearing these sacred objects ostentatiously, Vietnamese Christians set themselves apart from the general population, and this is not what is required by the Christian faith.

MISSION TO TONKIN (1627-30)

The closing of the doors to the Japanese mission opened up new fields for evangelization. As we saw in the last chapter, in 1626 Giuliano Baldinotti and Julius Piani were sent to Tonkin to explore possibilities to set up a Jesuit mission. And despite Baldinotti's political faux pas in contacting the Jesuits in Cochinchina directly to obtain personnel, the mission in Tonkin was not scuttled. Upon his return to Macao, Baldinotti submitted a report to Andrea Palmiero, the visitor, and requested that missionaries with a knowledge of Vietnamese be sent to Tonkin.

The obvious choice would be de Rhodes, because thanks to his fluency in the language, he would be able to "battle all the idolatry in Tonkin" and because, as he modestly put it, "I was not indispensable in Cochinchina."[39] Since it would be politically unwise to go straight from Cochinchina to Tonkin, de Rhodes, together with Pêro Marques,[40] whom Palmiero appointed as superior of the new mission in Tonkin, had to go back first to Macao in July 1626, and from there depart for Tonkin.

FIRST ENCOUNTER WITH TONKIN

The two missionaries had to wait for nine months before they could embark on a Portuguese merchant ship in March 1627 for Tonkin. They arrived at Cua Bang (present-day Ba Lang) on March 19, the feast of Saint Joseph. As de

---

39. *Divers voyages*, 80.

40. Pêro Marques (1577–1670), born in Nagasaki of a Portuguese father and a Japanese mother, went to Tonkin once (1627–30) and five times to Cochinchina (1618–26; 1637–39; February–July 1652; 1653–55; 1658–65). Since Marques did not speak Vietnamese, his work in Tonkin was taking care of the Japanese. He authored several annual reports on Cochinchina (1662–64): *ARSI JS* 71, ff. 379, 404, and *JS* 75, ff. 124–169v. On him, see Tissanier, 82; Marini, 378–89. His brother, Francesco, also a Jesuit, died a martyr in Japan.

Rhodes had been awed by China when he first saw it, and took care to inform his readers of the situation of the country, so also was he deeply impressed by Tonkin and took great pains to present an extensive description of it.[41]

It is not necessary to rehearse here all that de Rhodes has said about Tonkin.[42] He discusses the name of the country ("Tonkin," meaning "eastern capital"), its origin and its relation with China, its political system with a puppet king and a despotic lord (*chua*), its military might with about six hundred ships and a huge army, its educational structure with its three examinations, its judicial system, its fauna and flora, its commerce, its monetary system, and its tonal language.[43]

However, de Rhodes's most important reflections, for our purpose, are those that deal with the three religions of Tonkin, i.e., Confucianism, Buddhism, and Taoism, and with practices related to family life, sickness, funerals, and the cult of ancestors. Needless to say, these customs, both cultural and religious, have direct implications for de Rhodes's evangelization and catechesis, and we will take them up in our discussion of de Rhodes's inculturation and catechetical method in the next two chapters.

To resume our narrative, as soon as the Portuguese ship reached shore, a crowd rushed out to see who the newcomers were, where they came from, and what merchandise they were bringing in. De Rhodes took advantage of the people's curiosity to clarify in fluent Vietnamese (to their surprise!) the purpose of his mission. He explained that while most of the people who had just arrived were Portuguese merchants seeking to trade goods and arms, he had a precious pearl to sell so cheap that even the poorest among them could buy. When the people wanted to see the pearl, he told them that it could not be seen by bodily but only by spiritual eyes. The pearl, he said, was the true *way* (*dao*) that leads to the happy and everlasting life.

In a passage that throws a great light on his catechetical approach, de Rhodes wrote:

> Having heard of the Law which they call *dao* in scholarly language and *dang* in popular tongue, which means *way*, they became all the more cu-

---

41. See the first part of *Histoire du Royaume*, 116 pages long, entitled "De L'Estat temporel du Royaume de Tonkin." He also gives a very brief description of Tonkin in *Divers voyages*, 81–90.

42. Most of the information has been given in the first chapter under the section "Annam: Tonkin and Cochinchina."

43. Needless to say, this sort of travelog is what captivates the curiosity of Europeans. Most of the information de Rhodes gave on Tonkin is amazingly accurate and can be independently corroborated. One exception is the information on the educational structure with its three literary examinations: he wrongly said that the *thi den* or *thi dinh* was open to bachelors; in fact, only doctors were eligible to sit for such an examination (see the previous chapter for a description of the three literary examinations). Some other pieces of information, particularly regarding the number of ships (which he put at five hundred or six hundred), seems to have raised disbelief among his readers. In his later book, he took notice of this incredulity and reaffirmed what he had said: "Everyone is free to believe what he pleases, but I will nevertheless say that by God's grace I do not like exaggeration and that I hate lying to the point of horror. Still, I am not sorry for having told what I saw, and on one occasion, I very carefully counted 400 galleys in the king of Tonkin's forces, all exceedingly well outfitted..." (*Divers voyages*, 85). For other sources of information on Tonkin, see the works of Borri, Marini, and Tissanier.

rious to know from me the true law, the true way that I wanted to show them. Thereupon I talked to them about the sovereign Principle of all created beings. I decided to announce it to them under the name of the Lord of heaven and earth, finding no proper word in their language to refer to God. Indeed, what they commonly call *Phat* or *But* designates nothing but an idol. And knowing that the cult of idols was held in high esteem by the leaders and doctors of the kingdom, I do not think it proper to designate God with these words. Rather I decided to employ the name used by the apostle Saint Paul when he preached to the Athenians who had set up an altar to an unknown God. This God, he said, whom they adored without knowing him, is the Lord of heaven and earth. It was therefore under this name, full of majesty even in the hearts of the pagans, that I first announced to them that the true way consisted first and foremost in fulfilling our legitimate duties to the Lord of heaven and earth by the means he has revealed to us.[44]

As a result of de Rhodes's preaching, two persons and their families were baptized. During their two-week stay at Cua Bang, the two missionaries baptized thirty-two Vietnamese among whom there was an old schoolteacher and an influential magician. With the former, de Rhodes left a copy of prayers (probably in Chinese or *chu nom*) so he could teach them to his pupils, and to the latter he gave the charge of directing the first community of Christians. It was already typical of de Rhodes to involve lay people in teaching and governing the local church.

On Good Friday, with a tall tree he had had cut and made into a cross, de Rhodes organized a procession for the Portuguese and the Vietnamese. With the cross on their shoulders, the group climbed up to the highest and most visible hill, and planted the cross there. A short time later, as Lord Trinh Trang was sailing south to wage war against Cochinchina, he saw the cross from afar, and was pleased when told that it was the sign of the Portuguese and that it would attract Portuguese merchants to his kingdom.

Lord Trinh Trang, who was on his first expedition against Cochinchina, had known that the Portuguese merchants and the two Jesuits were in the country. Still fearful that they might be spies for Cochinchina, he despatched a eunuch to check them out. The latter brought the missionaries and the Portuguese to meet the lord. It was then that de Rhodes saw for the first time the powerful army of Tonkin and gave a detailed description of it in his memoirs.[45] Because of pressure of time, the lord could give them only a very short audience during which de Rhodes offered him as gifts a mechanical clock and an hourglass. Lord Trinh Trang told the missionaries to remain at An Vuc and wait for his return from the war.

---

44. *Histoire du Royaume*, 129–30. I will analyze this passage in detail later.
45. See *Histoire du Royaume*, 134–37; *Divers voyages*, 92.

At An Vuc the missionaries were given large lodgings. At the entrance of the house, they erected a cross on which de Rhodes had the words "The Cross of the Lord of Heaven and Earth" written in Chinese characters. During their stay at An Vuc, there was one important conversion. A Buddhist monk, aged eighty-five, who was revered as the head of all the monks in the Thanh Hoa province, joined the church, and was given the name Joachim. His conversion brought many others to the faith. He helped de Rhodes with the translation of Christian prayers and doctrines into Vietnamese. He also gave a piece of land to build a church which was blessed on May 3, 1627. It was the first church in Tonkin.[46]

Also in An Vuc, de Rhodes had the opportunity to meet one of Lord Trinh Trang's widowed sisters. This lady was greatly impressed by the solemn rituals with which one of the Christians had been buried. She wanted to know if de Rhodes could do anything to help her deceased husband receive eternal salvation. When he replied that he could do nothing to help one who has died in "faithlessness," the woman was deeply distressed. Though she did not become a Christian, she had her mother-in-law baptized.[47]

In Van No (present-day city of Thanh Hoa), the missionaries added social activities to evangelization. One of the converts, whose Christian name was Lina, opened a residence for the poor. There was also near the church in Van No, a leprosarium which the missionaries frequently visited. Many lepers became Christian. One of them, whose Christian name was Simon, was learned in Chinese letters. De Rhodes dictated to him "prayers and the commandments of the decalogue" so he could teach them to others.

Amidst these successes, there began opposition to the missionaries, especially on the part of Buddhist monks. They challenged de Rhodes to a debate. They wanted to open the debate with a list of accusations against the new religion. De Rhodes wanted an advance copy of the accusations, which the monks refused to give. As negotiations on procedural matters were going on, de Rhodes took the Bible and read aloud the first chapter of Genesis in Latin. The strange language caught the attention of the audience and they demanded an explanation. De Rhodes went on to explain the doctrine of God as "first Principle and creator of all things." Realizing that they had been outsmarted, the monks grew agitated and threatened violence. Fortunately, it was averted by a eunuch official who happened to come by.

Meanwhile, Lord Trinh Trang's expedition against Cochinchina turned into a defeat, and he had to withdraw. He stopped at An Vuc, where the missionaries went to see him a second time. They expected that the lord would be angry with them because he knew that the Portuguese had assisted Cochinchina. However, the lord gave them a warm welcome. De Rhodes gave him a book on astronomy

---

46. See *Histoire du Royaume*, 138–40.

47. See *Histoire du Royaume*, 141–42. We have pointed out above how de Rhodes firmly believed that without baptism one cannot be saved. Recall his practice of "hunting" orphaned children in Goa to baptize them.

written in Chinese.[48] He also demonstrated how the mechanical clock and the hourglass worked, which delighted the lord greatly.

In addition, de Rhodes took advantage of the meeting with the lord to discourse to him on the existence of God. He began with a lesson on astronomy and proceeded to argue for the existence of "the Great Artisan" of the universe. The conversation lasted for two hours, and de Rhodes notes that despite the fatigue of the journey, the attention of the lord and the royal officials did not slacken.[49] The lord allowed both missionaries to continue their stay in Tonkin and to preach.[50]

SOJOURN IN THE CAPITAL

The two missionaries followed the lord to Thang Long in a Portuguese ship. They arrived at the capital on July 2, 1627, and were lodged at the house of a certain Man Tai, a pagan, who was baptized later on his deathbed. But the most important conversion for the life of the new church was that of one of the sisters of Lord Trinh Trang and her daughter. Of the lady and her daughter, both named Catherine, de Rhodes wrote in a passage that provides rare information on the first catechism in Tonkin:

> The most illustrious and the first to receive faith and baptism was one of the lord's sisters. She was learned in Chinese letters and well versed in poetry; we called her Catherine.... Formerly, she had been so devoted to the cult of idols that the Buddhist monks called her *Thay*, that is, teacher, because of her abilities to instruct others. But having changed religion she also changed the object of her zeal, which she now applied to teaching a great number of young ladies whom she formed in the morals and piety of the Christian religion. Her daughter, also named Catherine, was also devoted to studying and meditating on the mysteries of our religion. Because she was a poet, she composed in beautiful verses for the use of catechism poems on the entire sacred history, beginning from the creation of the world to the coming, life, passion, resurrection, and ascension of our Lord. Furthermore, at the end of her poems, she added the history of our arrival in the kingdom of Tonkin and the beginnings of the preaching of the Gospel. The book did so much good in that not only the new Christians sang those verses at home, in town, and in the countryside, but also

---

48. It was a book written by Matteo Ricci, published in Peking in 1607, entitled *Hen kai t'ong hien t'u chu* (Development of the Heavenly Sphere).

49. See *Histoire du Royaume*, 152–53.

50. See *Histoire du Royaume*, 150–57. It is interesting to note how Confucius was influential in Vietnam in the following incident. When one of the "principal doctors of the kingdom, highly respected by the king" saw the clock, the hourglass, and the book on astronomy, he said to the king: "Sire, as to the mechanism of this clock, it is admirable and deserves a king's curiosity. But for the book, our Confucius suffices for us, and we do not need any other book in the kingdom" (155).

the pagans sang them, because they took pleasure in the sweetness of the songs, and thus were instructed in the mysteries and truths of the faith.[51]

During his sojourn in the capital de Rhodes, while by no means neglecting the Mass, sought to convert people who were educated and influential who could help him with spreading the faith and defending it against the attacks of pagan scholars. Unlike Matteo Ricci, de Rhodes was not learned in the Chinese classics nor was he, as we will see, well versed in the three religions of Vietnam. Hence, he was not equipped to institute *by himself* a dialogue with learned pagans on points of doctrine.

Once, during his second sojourn in Cochinchina, he attempted a discussion with a group of learned Buddhist monks on religious doctrines. But he could not carry it through, and had to rely on the help of Catechist Ignatius "who was present, to refute them, because he was very well versed in all their books and possessed special grace for disproving all the errors of these idolaters."[52]

To supplement his lacunas, de Rhodes sought to convert learned people and then made use of their talents. Thus, besides the two Catherines, he also converted Dr. Joachim, a seventy-year-old judge of the court (who was popularly called "Ong Nghe," i.e., Mr. Doctor), *licencié* John, and Dr. Peter.

In addition, de Rhodes attempted to convert Buddhist monks, because, as he shrewdly observed, "of all the pagans we tried to cultivate and convert to the knowledge of the true faith in Tonkin, we have found that none was more receptive to our religion and more constant in retaining it than those who had formerly been deeply attached to the cult of idols."[53] Thus, he brought to the faith a famous monk whom he christened Anthony and a group of twelve monks near Cau Giay, a suburb of the capital. Of course, the scholars and monks were not converted alone; they brought with them to the faith their families and others whom they influenced. In turn, they became zealous missionaries propagating their new faith.[54] One of the monks, baptized as Francis-Xavier, later became the first catechist and in 1643 became a Jesuit brother.[55]

Another event of great significance for our study of de Rhodes's catechetical work is his discovery of, as I will argue later, the catechism by Matteo Ricci. It happened quite by chance. One Buddhist monk and supervisor of the temple of the lord's mother, who had often come to listen to de Rhodes's preaching but was prevented by his wife from becoming a Christian for fear of losing his income, showed up one Sunday before Mass with a book written in Chinese. De Rhodes immediately recognized that it was the book written by one

---

51. *Histoire du Royaume*, 164–65. See also de Rhodes's letter to Nuno Mascarenhas, sent from Macao on January 16, 1631, *ARSI, JS* 80, f. 15rv. The success of this book was due in part to the well-known love of the Vietnamese for poetry. Unfortunately, we no longer have record of this book or of the poems it contained.

52. *Divers voyages*, 184.

53. *Histoire du Royaume*, 165.

54. See *Histoire du Royaume*, 165–71.

55. See *Histoire du Royaume*, 189–91; *Divers voyages*, 96; and *Relazione*, 184–86.

of the Jesuit missionaries in China and wondered how the monk came to own it.[56] The latter explained to the congregation that his father once accompanied the Vietnamese ambassadors to China and there met the "doctors of the Great West."[57] These gave his father a book, saying that those who believe and observe what was written in it would have a happy eternal life. His father in turn gave it to him, and he had been keeping it for thirty years. He said that he had compared the teaching of de Rhodes with that of the book, and found that the two coincided.

De Rhodes assured the congregation that the contents of the book were "nothing other than their catechism, without any difference neither in the order of the presentation of doctrines nor in the method of instruction."[58] This identity of the two teachings, said de Rhodes, confirmed the faith of the Christians.[59]

Meanwhile, Lord Trinh Trang continued to display great sympathy towards the missionaries. Four months after their arrival in the capital, he had a house and a church built for them. However, the lord's favorable attitude gradually changed into suspicion. It was aroused against the missionaries by several groups: the concubines who had to be dismissed by those men who became Christian; the eunuchs who were afraid of losing their jobs if the lord converted; the magicians whose alleged supernatural powers were overshadowed by the miracles that the Christians performed; and the Buddhist monks whose pagodas were deserted. De Rhodes was accused of being a magician who killed people with his breath (that was why the lord no longer allowed him to come near him); of bringing death to sick people (because he baptized people on the point of death); and of fomenting the destruction of statues in the pagodas.[60]

Fortunately, de Rhodes was able to disprove these allegations and to dispel Lord Trinh Trang's suspicions. Things turned for the worse, however, when the missionaries were accused of secretly collaborating with Lord Trinh Trang's enemies. A former Buddhist monk, having lost his income because of the conversion of his followers to Christianity, had joined the Mac dynasty to wage war against the Trinh. Upon being caught he hoped to save his life by promising to reveal a secret plot allegedly organized by the missionaries and the Christians together with Cao Bang and Cochinchina to overthrow the lord. As a result, on May 28, 1628, Lord Trinh Trang issued a decree forbidding his subjects, under

---

56. Matteo Ricci's "catechism," entitled *T'ien-chu Shi-i* (The True Meaning of the Lord of Heaven), was published in Peking in 1601. We will discuss this book at length later.

57. Even after independence from China, for diplomatic reasons Vietnamese kings since the Dinh dynasty (968–80) still kept the custom of making a triennial tribute to China. Ambassadors were chosen among the highest-ranking doctors.

58. *Histoire du Royaume*, 181. It is not clear whether the word "catechism" refers to a book or to the teaching of the faith. De Rhodes used the word to refer to both. If it refers to a book (which is unlikely), is it possible that we have here a first draft of the *Cathechismus* ?

59. We will discuss this book and its relationship with de Rhodes's *Cathechismus* in chap. 4.

60. See *Histoire du Royaume*, 191–99.

pain of death, to come to see the missionaries and to embrace the religion they preached.[61]

The missionaries were put under virtual house arrest and could communicate with their Christians only by letters.[62] Despite this edict, Christians managed to come and see them under various disguises. More important, deprived of Masses and the sacraments, they themselves organized prayer meetings during which the missionaries' letters were read.

EXILE FROM TONKIN AND RETURN TO THE CAPITAL

After ten months of clandestine activities, the missionaries were finally ordered to leave the country. Since his edict of May 1628, Lord Trinh Trang had tolerated their presence in the hope of attracting trade with Portuguese merchants. But when the Portuguese ships had not come during the sailing season, he realized that the missionaries no longer served a useful purpose. In March 1629 he gave de Rhodes and Pêro Marques twenty gold *écus* and pieces of precious cloth and ordered them to embark for Cochinchina and from there to go back to Macao.

The trip took place toward the end of March in a small boat which the lord provided, manned by thirty-six sailors and a captain.[63] Two Christians were allowed to accompany the missionaries, Catechist Ignatius Nhuan and Anthony Dinh, an ex-soldier.[64] Two catechists (Andrew and Francis) were left behind and given authority to confer baptism on those who were prepared for it.

During the voyage, the two priests did not fail to preach to the soldiers, while Catechist Ignatius entertained them with songs which he had composed on Christian doctrines. About a hundred miles south of the capital, the governor of Che Bo, who was a Christian, invited the missionaries to come to his house to baptize a number of catechumens he had instructed.

Arriving in An Vuc, where they had stayed when they first arrived in Tonkin in 1627, they found the old hospice built by one of the converts flourishing. However, the church they built, the first one in Tonkin, had been burnt down.[65]

---

61. See *Histoire du Royaume*, 210–11. The edict reads: "We, King of Tonkin, even though we are well informed that the European priests who are at our court, have so far taught our people no evil and pernicious doctrine. Nevertheless, we do not know what they will do in the future or what they are plotting in the present. Therefore, henceforward we forbid under pain of death all our subjects to go to them or to embrace the law they preach" (211). The edict was engraved on a post and planted at the entrance of the missionaries' residence. See de Rhodes's January 16, 1631, letter to Nuno Mascarenhas, Assistant for Portugal, written from Macao, *ARSI, JS* 80, f. 15v.

62. See *Histoire du Royaume*, 217. These letters must have been written in Chinese characters or *chu nom*. However, since de Rhodes did not know either writing system well, the letters must have been written with the help of other Christians. Needless to say, these letters are no longer extant.

63. See *Histoire du Royaume*, 225, and Cardim, 83.

64. See Gaspar do Amaral, "Annua de reino de Annam do anno de 1632," *ARSI, JS* 85, f. 160; idem, "Relaçaõ dos catequistas da Christamdade de Tumquim e seu modo de proçeder pera o Pe Manoel Diaz, Visitador de Jappaõ e China," *Real Academia de la Historia* (Madrid), *Jesuitas*, leg. 21 bis, Fasc. 16, 31–37r.

65. De Rhodes reported that a Christian woman, by the name of Ann, had found among the ashes

From there they proceeded to Nghe An, and then to Bo Chinh, the border town between the two countries.

In Nghe An the captain sent eighteen of his soldiers back to the north, since the journey had to be continued in a bigger ship. Before returning home, the soldiers asked de Rhodes for baptism. The reply he gave them is extremely significant since it sheds light on what he considered as the minimum requirements for baptism: "To their request we replied that if they believe with all their hearts in the true Lord and Creator of heaven and earth, and in his Son Jesus Christ our Savior, who has redeemed us with his blood, according to what we have announced to them, and if they are ready to reject their vain superstitions and renounce the cult of idols, which are nothing but false gods, we will baptize them."[66]

Before departing for Bo Chinh, the captain wanted to offer a sacrifice for a safe trip. De Rhodes dissuaded him from practicing what he considered "superstitious ceremonies" and urged him to place his trust in "the Lord God who rules the earth and the seas." During the voyage, a fierce tempest arose. As a result, the captain grew extremely angry at the missionaries and at Catechist Ignatius, whom he threatened to throw into the sea, for having deterred him from offering the sacrifice to the gods before the voyage. Thereupon, the missionaries invoked Saint Lawrence and recited the Our Father and the Hail Mary, and immediately the wind died down.

Arriving in Bo Chinh, the captain asked for baptism and was given the name Augustine; with him six other soldiers were also baptized. They then returned to the north, leaving their charges to the governor of Bo Chinh. Fearing that their coming to Cochinchina might provoke its lord to expel their Jesuit confreres, the two missionaries requested the captain to persuade the governor not to initiate their journey to Cochinchina himself but to free them to make their own arrangements for the trip, to which the governor agreed.

Meanwhile the missionaries made twenty-five converts, among whom there was a *licencié* well versed in Chinese letters to whom they gave a book of prayers so he could teach them to others. Afraid that the governor might change his mind, they decided to return to Nghe An. They were warmly welcomed by the provincial governor, who allowed them to preach freely. Their preaching met with great success, so that in less than eight months since they left the capital they baptized some six hundred people, without counting emergency baptisms.

Unfortunately, during this time they were in desperate financial straits, so that they had to send Anthony the ex-soldier back to Thang Long to ask for help. Anthony came back with thirty gold *écus* and with a letter from Gaspar do Amaral, who had arrived with Paul Saito in a Portuguese ship in Nghe An.

---

a crucifix which had been miraculously preserved. On it were written the words, in Latin on the one side and in Chinese on the other, "the sacred sign of the Lord of heaven and earth." See *Histoire du Royaume*, 128.

66. *Histoire du Royaume*, 231.

De Rhodes and Pêro Marques set out to see them at once. A eunuch came with Lord Trinh Trang's permission for the ship to come to the capital. He, however, strenuously objected to the presence of de Rhodes and Marques on the ship because the edict for their expulsion was still in force. However, the captain refused to go unless de Rhodes and Marques came along.

They reached Thang Long in November 1629. The missionaries immediately set out to minister to their communities, preaching and administering the sacraments, especially baptism, eucharist, and penance. At first, Lord Trinh Trang tolerated the presence of de Rhodes and Marques, but after six months, when the Portuguese ship returned to Macao, he ordered them to embark and leave the country.

Before his departure, de Rhodes had the brilliant idea of forming some of his closest collaborators, the catechists, into a quasi-religious community. They would make the three vows of not marrying until the return of the missionaries, of putting all their possessions in common, and of obeying the one among them who would be appointed their superior. During de Rhodes's last Mass, after communion, Francis-Xavier Duc, Andrew Tre, and Ignatius Nhuan pronounced their vows on their knees, their hands placed on the Gospel, in front of the whole congregation. Anthony Dinh the ex-soldier also took the three vows, but because of his lack of education he was not commissioned to preach and baptize but to take care of temporal matters in the new religious community.[67]

In May, de Rhodes and the other three Jesuits left Tonkin for Macao, de Rhodes for good, never to return.[68] He had worked in Tonkin for more than three years. By numerical standards alone, his mission had been a huge success: when he left, there were 5,602 Christians.[69] During the ten-month absence of the missionaries, from May 1630 to March 1631, the catechists he had trained baptized 3,340 people and built 20 new churches.[70]

After his departure, the church in Tonkin grew by leaps and bounds. According to de Rhodes, in 1639 there were 82,500 Christians and more than 100 churches.[71] In 1640, there were nearly 100,000 Christians,[72] and in the following year the church in Tonkin counted 108,000 Christians and 235 churches.[73]

---

67. See *Histoire du Royaume*, 255-56, and de Rhodes's letter to Nuno Mascarenhas, *ARSI, JS* 80, f. 16v. We will discuss this institution of catechists in detail as one of de Rhodes's catechetical strategies.

68. On his return to Macao de Rhodes brought with him two letters of Tonkinese Christians, one addressed to Pope Urban VIII and the other to the general Mutio Vitelleschi, both written in Chinese and translated into Latin by de Rhodes. See *Histoire du Royaume*, 259–61, and *Relazione*, 252–53. The original letter to the Pope is preserved at the Archives of the Propaganda Fide, *Miscellanee diverse*, vol. 16, ff. 208r–210v. The letter to Vitelleschi is preserved in *ARSI, JS* 80, ff. 12r–14r.

69. See Cardim, 85.

70. See *Histoire du Royaume*, 263–64.

71. See *Histoire du Royaume*, 292; *Tunchensis historiae*, II, 167.

72. See *Histoire du Royaume*, 303; *Relazione*, 296; *Tunchensis historiae*, II, 179.

73. See Cardim, 76. In *Histoire du Royaume*, 262-326, de Rhodes continued the history of the church in Tonkin after his departure, but this part does not interest us here since our focus is de Rhodes's activities themselves. Nevertheless, it is to be noted that after de Rhodes had left Tonkin, several Jesuits were sent to continue his work, notably Gaspar do Amaral, António Francisco Cardim, António de

FROM MACAO TO COCHINCHINA THE SECOND TIME (1640–45)

Banished from Tonkin, de Rhodes returned to Macao and stayed there for ten years, during which he taught theology at the Madre de Deus College and took care of Chinese Christians. In fact, it is the latter work that took the lion's share of de Rhodes's time and energy: "This [taking care of Chinese Christians] kept me so busy all day that if I wanted to do some studying to prepare sermons or theology courses, which I taught in our college, it had to be done at night. It was barely daylight before I was busy with my Chinese Christians or with those we were preparing for baptism."[74]

WHY DID DE RHODES STAY IN MACAO FOR A DECADE?

It is curious that a person of de Rhodes's talents was kept in Macao for a decade teaching theology (though trained in theology, de Rhodes was by no means temperamentally cut out to be a professor) and working with the Chinese (with whose language he was not familiar), rather than sent to Cochinchina, where his linguistic skills and missionary expertise would do the most good. Though we cannot derive certain answers to this question from written documents, it is possible to surmise some of the reasons for de Rhodes's marooning in Macao.

De Rhodes's missionary approaches and strategies in Tonkin, though extremely successful, were novel and aroused opposition among his confreres. Briefly, there were five issues at stake: (1) his establishment of the religious community of catechists with the three vows; (2) his making use of them as ordinary ministers of baptism; (3) his adaptation of local customs; (4) his adoption of religious terminologies, especially his baptismal formula; and (5) his advocacy for a native clergy.[75] No doubt the bitter *querelle des rites,* which was becoming a hot issue in the 1630s with the coming of the Dominicans and Franciscans to the Chinese mainland and the establishment of their missions in Fukien, placed de Rhodes's innovations under close scrutiny.

To obtain some light on these matters, the visitor Andrea Palmiero undertook a short fact-finding trip to Tonkin in 1631.[76] It appears that Palmiero approved

---

Fontes, António Barbosa, and Felice Morelli. In particular, do Amaral and Cardim have written many important reports on the Jesuit mission in Tonkin, and Morelli was so beloved by Lord Trinh Tac (1605–82), who had succeeded his father, Trinh Trang (1575–1657), that he was officially adopted by him as son. See *Histoire du Royaume,* 321–23.

74. *Divers voyages,* 115. Even though de Rhodes baptized a thousand persons during his stay in Macao, he considered his mission among the Chinese less than a success, both because of his lack of fluency in Chinese, which forced him to use interpreters, and because of the "pride of the Chinese who considered themselves the greatest people on earth." See *Divers voyages,* 114.

75. We will discuss these issues at length later.

76. Andrea Palmiero (1569–1635) was born in Lisbon. After having taught humanities for six years, philosophy for four, and theology for twelve years at the University of Coimbre, he went to India in 1617. He was successively visitor of the provinces of Malabar, Japan, and China. In 1627 he presided

what he saw there since the catechists continued to live in their community, to teach and baptize, and to lead the Christian communities. Furthermore, de Rhodes's adaptation of local customs was continued by his successors. Nevertheless, to avoid further conflicts between de Rhodes and his confreres, very probably Palmiero thought it wise to keep him in Macao.[77]

However, in 1639, events in Cochinchina once again made de Rhodes's missionary experience highly desirable. Recall that the Jesuits had arrived in this country in 1615, and that de Rhodes himself had spent almost two years (1624–26) at Thanh Chiem studying the language before being sent to Tonkin. By 1639, after twenty-five years of evangelization, the church in central Vietnam had 15,000 Christians and 20 churches.[78]

In 1629, Lord Nguyen Phuoc Nguyen (1613–35) decreed the expulsion of all missionaries out of Cochinchina. The Jesuits in Macao asked the Portuguese government to send a delegation to Lord Nguyen Phuoc Nguyen with the request that he withdraw the edict. The lord allowed the three Jesuits who had been in hiding to stay until the return of the Portuguese ship back to Macao. When Nguyen Phuoc Lan succeeded his father in 1635, he was even harsher towards the missionaries. The reason was that some Japanese in Hoi An had assisted his brother Nguyen Phuoc Anh in a revolt against him. As a result, the lord doubted the loyalty of the Japanese Christians and of the missionaries, and in 1639 he ordered the seven Jesuits to leave the country.[79]

Eager to continue the mission in Cochinchina, the new visitor Antonio Rubino looked around for someone to send there.[80] De Rhodes volunteered and was accepted. Thus began de Rhodes's second mission to central Vietnam.

---

in Kiangsi, China, over a meeting of eleven Jesuits and three Chinese doctors to determine the question of rites and the use of the word *T'ien* (heaven) and *Shang Ti* (the august emperor) to refer to God. He approved again the use of the dress of Chinese scholars as well as several Chinese rituals accepted by Matteo Ricci some thirty years earlier. See Louis Pfister, *Notices biographiques et bibliographiques sur les Jésuites de l'ancienne Mission de Chine (1552–1773)*, vol. I (Shanghai, 1932), 30, 195–96; Daniele Bartoli, *Dell'Historia della Compagnia di Giesu, La Cina, Terza Parte, Dell'Asia, descritta dal P. Daniello Bartoli della medesima Compagnia* (Rome, 1663), 119–21.

77. See Do Quang Chinh, 174–75.

78. This number was given by B. Roboredo in his report "Relação das perseguições da Missam de Cochinchina desde Dezembro de 1640 ate Abril de 1641" *ARSI, JS* 70, f. 1r. According to de Rhodes, the number is 12,000 (*Divers voyages*, 117). Cardim reported that already in 1629 there were 15,000 Christians in Cochinchina (Cardim, 96). Marini said the number of Christians in 1639 was 50,000. See Giovanni Filippo de Marini, *Delle Missioni de' Padri della Compagnia di Giesu nella Provincia del Giappone* (Rome, 1663), 360. At any rate, compare this number of 15,000 Christians and 20 churches in Cochinchina after twenty-five years of evangelization by 1639 with the number of 108,000 Christians and 235 churches in Tonkin after only fourteen years of evangelization! However, it must be noted that between 1627 and 1639, Macao sent only two Jesuits to Cochinchina whereas it sent fifteen to Tonkin. See Fortuné de Montezon and Édouard Estéve, *Voyages et Travaux des Missionnaires de la Compagnie de Jésus. Mission de la Cochinchine et du Tonkin* (Paris, 1858), 386–91.

79. The seven Jesuits were: Francesco Buzomi, António Dias, Joseph, Francesco Barreto, Roman Niti, António de Fontes, and Gaspar Luís. See Do Quang Chinh, 183.

80. Rubino (1578–1643), an Italian, studied philosophy in Rome and theology in Goa. After thirty-six years in India, Rubino came to Macao in 1638 and was named visitor of Japan and China the following year. He died a martyr in Nagasaki. De Rhodes gave a biography of Rubino in his *Histoire de la vie*, 6–87.

It was divided into four trips and lasted a total of fifty months, from 1640 to 1645.

First Sojourn: February–September 1640

In February 1640 De Rhodes left Macao on a Portuguese ship, and after four days arrived at Da Nang. Careful not to arouse the opposition of the Vietnamese mandarin, often referred to as Ong Nghe Bo,[81] who was fiercely hostile to Christians, he hid among the Japanese Christians. By means of gifts he succeeded in gaining the support of the Japanese captain who agreed to introduce him to Lord Nguyen Phuoc Lan. De Rhodes was warmly received by the lord, to whom he had brought expensive gifts, and was allowed to stay in the country, at least until the departure of the Portuguese ship.

At the court he met Minh Duc Vuong Thai Phi, whom de Pina had baptized some fifteen years earlier under the name of Mary Magdalene. He stayed at her house and celebrated Mass in her church. There he baptized ninety-four people, including three female relatives of the lord and a "famous priest of idolatry," that is, a Buddhist monk.[82]

De Rhodes was very pleased with his work in the capital, as he wrote in his July 16 letter to the general.[83] However, in Cochinchina, since the foundation of the mission twenty-five years earlier, no Christian had received the sacrament of confirmation, because of the lack of a bishop. On July 15, 1640, some Cochinchinese Christians wrote to Pope Urban VIII asking him to authorize the Jesuits to administer this sacrament. No doubt this lack of the sacrament of confirmation was one of the reasons why de Rhodes later strongly lobbied for the establishment of the hierarchy in Vietnam.[84]

After thirty-five days in the capital he returned to Hoi An where he met another Jesuit, Pedro Alberto, who had come to minister to the Japanese. The missionaries waited quietly until the Portuguese ship had left and then began working publicly again. The governor of Quang Nam, irritated by their obstinacy, ordered them to leave the country by whatever means, even "by walking on the water." De Rhodes and Alberto bought a small boat and piloted them-

---

81. We do not know the Vietnamese name of this man. Ong Nghe Bo (literally, Mr. Doctor Director of Provincial Department) is the title of the mandarin in charge of the finance and taxation department of a province. Cochinchina was then divided in four *dinh* (provinces), from north to south: Quang Binh, Chinh, Quang Nam, and Tran Bien. Each province is headed by a governor in charge of three departments, each with a director: justice, finance and taxation, worship and food. In taking hostile actions against the Christians this Ong Nghe Bo, responsible for finance and taxation, had overstepped his authority and jurisdiction.

82. See *Divers voyages*, 120–22.

83. See *ARSI, JS* 80, ff. 79–80r.

84. The letter was written in Chinese and was translated into Latin by de Rhodes and sent to Rome from Macao. The original Latin text is found in *ARSI, JS* 68, f. 47rv; a copy is found in the Archives of the Propaganda Fide, *Miscellanee diverse*, vol. 16, f. 78rv.

selves back to Macao with three Christians and arrived safe and sound on September 20, 1640.[85]

SECOND SOJOURN: DECEMBER 1640–JULY 1641

Three months later, on December 17, de Rhodes came back to central Vietnam with Benedetto de Mattos.[86] Arriving in Da Nang on Christmas Eve, they discreetly received the Christians to avoid arousing the anger of Ong Nghe Bo. At the beginning of 1641, leaving his confrere in Da Nang, de Rhodes went south to Quang Nam to visit the Christian communities.

At Ha Lam, de Rhodes was surprised and pleased to hear a question from the audience after he had lectured on the origin of the soul and original sin. A man asked him how he could logically reconcile his statement that the soul is created directly by God, without the contribution of the parents, and his teaching that original sin is transmitted through generations: "I was delighted to hear this doubt from the mouth of a Cochinchinese that had once troubled St. Augustine, the greatest doctor. I took care not to answer him with scholastic subtleties that might have encumbered his mind. I decided to give him a little comparison that satisfied him."[87]

De Rhodes used the analogy of the soul as a precious pearl, coming pure and beautiful from God's hand, but fallen into mud and sullied by it. The mud is the human body, derived from Adam. De Rhodes's explanation, despite its dualistic overtones, seemed to satisfy his questioner.

Upon his return to Da Nang, de Rhodes, thinking that Ong Nghe Bo would tolerate his and his companion's presence, at least until the departure of the Portuguese ship, decided to expand his activities. De Rhodes would visit the two southern provinces (Quang Nam and Tran Bien), and de Mattos the two northern ones (Quang Binh and Chinh). Everywhere he went, de Rhodes found vibrant Christian communities, directed and ministered by lay people. For example, at Cho Moi, there was an old man named Paul. Of him de Rhodes wrote: "He was the heart and soul of that whole church. Every Sunday and holy day he gathered together the Christians in a chapel he had in the enclosure of his house. There he instructed them, preached, and took care to help them in every way necessary to keep them in the faith they had received. His zeal extended to the pagans, and he disposed many for baptism."[88]

---

85. See *Divers voyages*, 124. De Rhodes recorded here a remedy against seasickness that the Vietnamese Christians had taught him. Take one of those fish that have been devoured by and found in the bellies of other fish, cook it well, adding a little pepper, and eat it on board ship. This, said de Rhodes, "imparts such vigor to the stomach that it can sail the sea without getting upset" (124).

86. Benedetto de Mattos (1600–1651), a Portuguese, came to China in 1630. He stayed in Fukien for five years (1630–35) and in Hainan for five years (1635–40). In 1640 he came back to Macao, and in December of the same year he went to Cochinchina with de Rhodes, which he left four months later. De Mattos came back to Hainan and died there. See Pfister, *Notices biographiques*, 1:208–11.

87. *Divers voyages*, 131.

88. *Divers voyages*, 134–35.

At Bau Goc and Vom, which he next visited, de Rhodes received much assistance from the catechists who instructed the catechumens while he was preaching or listening to confessions. Before leaving, de Rhodes had twenty books, which the Jesuits of Tonkin had printed, copied for religious instruction.[89] He then went to Ben Da where again he found the community administered by a sixty-year-old man named Philip.

On March 29, 1641, he left for the province of Tran Bien (Phu Yen), the southernmost territory of Cochinchina.[90] While he was there, a tragic incident happened to the Christians at Thanh Chiem in Quang Nam. It was reported by Antonio Rubino in his April 10, 1641, letter to de Rhodes: Ong Nghe Bo had unleashed a persecution against the Christians and had the sacred images burnt in public.[91] The news distressed de Rhodes considerably but he decided to stay on in Tran Bien. In two months he baptized 1,355 people. Meanwhile, his companion de Mattos, who visited the two northern provinces, administered 572 baptisms, though he did not baptize one of the lord's brothers for fear of being discovered by him.[92]

Upon his return to Thanh Chiem, de Rhodes found that de Mattos had left for Macao. De Rhodes's presence was discovered by Ong Nghe Bo who ordered him to leave the country immediately. On July 2, 1641, de Rhodes embarked on a ship for Manila, and from there he came back to Macao on September 21, 1641.

THIRD SOJOURN: JANUARY 1642–JULY 1643

At the end of January 1642, de Rhodes, accompanied by an unnamed Vietnamese catechist, left Macao for Da Nang. His first attempt was to appease Ong Nghe Bo with gifts, and he was left in peace for a while. In the company of the Portuguese, he went to the capital to meet Lord Nguyen Phuoc Lan, to whom he gave several clocks. These gifts earned a stay in the capital after the Portuguese had left. But, shortly afterwards, the lord ordered him to go to Da Nang and to return to Macao with the Portuguese.

De Rhodes returned to Da Nang but refused to embark for Macao. Instead, he secretly stayed behind, and for nineteen months, as the only priest in Cochinchina, traveled up and down the country, visiting the Christian communities.

---

89. *Divers voyages*, 137. See also de Rhodes's letter to the superior general in *ARSI, JS* 80, ff. 79–80r and Cardim, 106. These books were most probably the "catechism" of Matteo Ricci and the works of Gerolamo Maiorica in *chu nom*.

90. De Rhodes names this province *Ranran*, which derives from the name of the river Da Rang, which the Vietnamese call *Song Ba*. The province of Tran Bien was formerly a territory of the kingdom of Cham, definitively annexed by the Vietnamese in 1629.

91. See his letter in de Rhodes, *Histoire de la vie*, 22–24. In November 1640 the visitor Antonio Rubino, Br. Roboredo, and Francisco Marques left Macao for Japan by way of Manila. A storm forced them to land in Da Nang. They stayed there for four and a half months. It was during their stay that they witnessed the persecution by Ong Nghe Bo.

92. See Cardim, 112–13.

During these trips he was accompanied by ten new catechists, among them Andrew of Phu Yen, Ignatius of Quang Tri, and Vincent of Quang Nghia. Ignatius was a former mandarin and had a perfect command of the Chinese letters. During this time, de Rhodes baptized about one thousand people, slightly fewer than during his second sojourn.

In order not to irritate the Vietnamese authorities further, he followed the advice of the Portuguese and the catechists to absent himself for a while from the country. Before leaving, however, he decided to form a vowed community of catechists, as he had done in Tonkin in 1630. On July 31, 1643, on the feast of Saint Ignatius, in the course of the Mass, ten catechists professed the vows of chastity and obedience. Ignatius, being the most educated, the wisest, and at the age of thirty-four, the oldest, was appointed superior.[93]

De Rhodes divided them into two groups, five, with Damasus as leader, to work in the two southern provinces, and the rest, with Ignatius as leader, to work in the two northern provinces. On the same day, de Rhodes embarked on a Portuguese ship for Macao where he remained for seven months before returning to central Vietnam for the last time.

FOURTH SOJOURN: MARCH 1644–JULY 1645

In March 1644, de Rhodes returned to Da Nang where he was given a joyous welcome by the ten catechists and the Christians. During his absence the catechists had made excellent progress: the first group in the south, under Damasus, had baptized 293 people; and the second group in the north, under Ignatius, 303.[94] To booster their prestige, de Rhodes gave Ignatius and Damasus the title of *Thay*, i.e., master, and allowed them to wear a surplice while teaching.

Accompanied by his catechists de Rhodes went to Hue to meet Lord Nguyen Phuoc Lan and to present him with gifts. During his stay in the capital, de Rhodes tried to keep his contact with the Christians as secret as possible, for fear of arousing opposition by the authorities. However, he was able to see Minh Duc Vuong Thai Phi and to celebrate Palm Sunday Mass in her church. During the Holy Week he was back in Da Nang, celebrating two Masses on Easter Sunday, one for the Portuguese in Hoi An, and the other for the Vietnamese. Upon the request of Minh Duc Vuong Thai Phi, he returned to the capital and there converted a favorite goldsmith of the lord.

Continuing north he reached the border with Tonkin. There he was invited by a nearby community of Christians in Tonkin to visit them. Fearing that his visit to Tonkin would create problems for the Christians, he sent Catechist Ignatius instead. The delegation who came to see him with the invitation de-

---

93. See *Divers voyages*, 160–61.
94. See de Rhodes's annual report written on August 1, 1644, in Cochinchina in *ARSI, JS* 71, ff. 240–51.

scribed to him how "there were at least a thousand Christians who were living very holy lives although they had never seen a priest."[95]

Returning south, de Rhodes stopped at the capital where he baptized thirty people. While there, he was invited by a court magistrate to a debate with "idol-atrous priests," i.e., Buddhist monks. From a catechetical point of view, it is interesting to note how de Rhodes proceeded: "I began my talk by describing the justice of God, who is the supreme King of the world. I showed how rig-orous God is towards those who refuse to obey him, to the point of punishing them with eternal fire, and on the other hand, how God is gentle and gracious towards those who live rightly, and the care God has for them, both in this life and the next — which I explained by means of the story of the three children God saved in the furnace in Babylon."[96]

When some of the monks challenged de Rhodes with citations from their religious books, he was lost and had to rely on the expertise of Ignatius who, thanks to his knowledge of the Chinese classics, succeeded in confounding them with their own books.

Up to this point, the church in Cochinchina, despite occasional harassment from the authorities, had experienced peace and relative toleration. Things changed dramatically in July 1644. Ong Nghe Bo of Quang Nam province had just come back from the capital with the order to put Catechist Ignatius to death. Ignatius had routed the Buddhist monks when he came to the aid of de Rhodes in the latter's debate with them. After their defeat, the monks went to enlist the help of Tong Thi Toai who nurtured an intense hatred of Ignatius.[97] When the soldiers of Ong Nghe Bo came to the house of the cate-chists in Hoi An to arrest Ignatius, they did not find him but arrested instead Catechist Andrew who was then nineteen years old. They delivered Andrew to Ong Nghe Bo who put him to death on July 26, 1644. He was the first martyr of Cochinchina.[98]

After the death of Andrew, persecutions grew more intense. Many Christians, men and women, were subjected to brutal torture. Ong Nghe Bo ordered de Rhodes to leave for Macao. Ostentatiously boarding the Portuguese ship, de Rhodes rejoined his nine catechists on their boat some three miles off the coast. For more than a month, they had to hide by day and work by night.

On September 15, 1644, de Rhodes sent Ignatius to the northern provinces, whereas he and the other catechists went south. One day, while they were in

---

95. *Divers voyages*, 181.

96. *Divers voyages*, 183.

97. Tong Thi Toai had been the wife of Lord Nguyen Phuoc Lan's older brother Nguyen Phuoc Ky, the heir apparent, who died in 1631. After her husband's death, she was involved with her brother-in-law who upon coming to power took her as his concubine, and over the opposition of many mandarins, gave her the title of "queen." Catechist Ignatius had been a mandarin and most probably had opposed Tong Thi Toai. It was natural then that Tong Thi Toai wanted him killed. Tong Thi Toai aided her father in his collaboration with Lord Trinh Trang during his war on Cochinchina in 1648. Ten years later, the government discovered Tong Thi Toai's complicity and condemned her to death.

98. De Rhodes has written a book on Andrew's martyrdom. See his *La glorieuse mort d'André Catechiste de la Cochinchine* (1653). See a shorter report in *Divers voyages*, 194–200.

Qui Nhon, their boat was discovered by the soldiers. They were arrested and delivered to the district judge who, however, let them go free. During this time, de Rhodes was able to add three more young men to his group of catechists, now numbering twelve.

De Rhodes continued his missionary work amidst much difficulty. After Christmas 1644, he was arrested with Ignatius and was brought before six magistrates who questioned him on the doctrines he was preaching. To everyone's surprise, they were set free by the lord's order. The provincial governor, however, commanded him to leave his province.

On February 15, 1645, he returned to Hoi An where two Portuguese ships had recently arrived from Macao. He was informed that there was also a Spanish ship on which there were two Spanish Franciscans and four Clares.[99] The lord and his wife, much intrigued by the nuns hidden behind veils and with shorn heads, entertained them and the two Franciscans lavishly for ten days, with sumptuous banquets and mock military battles of all kinds.

On June 1, 1645, de Rhodes and eight of his catechists took a boat and left for Quang Binh, the northernmost province. On the way, mistaken for spies for Tonkin, they were arrested and brought back to the capital for incarceration. De Rhodes was condemned by the lord to death by decapitation, but the sentence was commuted to perpetual exile, after the lord's former teacher persuaded him that de Rhodes had committed no crime in preaching the new religion. After twenty-two days of imprisonment in Hoi An, de Rhodes left Vietnam forever on July 3, 1645, bringing with him the head of the martyr Andrew.

During the fifty months de Rhodes spent in Cochinchina between 1640 and 1645, he baptized some 3,400 people, without counting the baptisms administered by the catechists: 94 during the first sojourn, 1,877 during the second, "more than a thousand" during the third, and 432 during the fourth.

Compared with his mission in Tonkin which produced 5,602 conversions, his second mission in Cochinchina produced significantly fewer, though it was much longer and much more strenuous (fifty versus thirty-eight months). There are several reasons for this state of affairs. The population of Cochinchina was much less dense than that of Tonkin; de Rhodes operated alone most of the time, without the assistance of other missionaries; and there was much more extensive persecution by the authorities, especially by Ong Nghe Bo.

But the smaller number of conversions in Cochinchina is amply made up by the number of martyrs, the "seed of Christians." Whereas Tonkin can boast of one martyr in 1630,[100] Cochinchina had three. We have already mentioned the

---

99. In 1640 Portugal broke loose of Spanish domination. The Portuguese in Macao joined in the uprising. The Spaniards in the Philippines sent a ship to Macao to reinforce those who wished to be loyal to the Spanish crown. The Spaniards were badly beaten by the Portuguese who took them prisoners and sent them back to the Philippines. They also sent away the four Clares who had come to Macao to establish a convent, accompanied by two Franciscans. The ship left Macao in February 1645, but a storm forced it to take refuge in the harbor of Cham in Cochinchina. That was where de Rhodes met the six religious. See *Divers voyages*, 238–49.

100. In 1630, a brother of Trinh Trang's ordered the decapitation of a young neophyte named Francis.

martyrdom of Andrew of Phu Yen. The other two were Catechists Ignatius and Vincent. Ignatius, a former mandarin well versed in the Chinese classics and one of the most effective co-workers of de Rhodes (whom Tong Thi Toai had wanted killed), was probably arrested together with de Rhodes, seven other catechists (among whom was nineteen-year-old Vincent), and a thirteen-year-old boy also named Ignatius. They were brought to the capital in June 1645.[101] After a month and a half in prison, they appeared before Lord Nguyen Phuoc Lan for interrogation. The lord promised them freedom if they renounced the "way of the Portuguese." Ignatius and Vincent explained that they did not follow the "way of the Portuguese" but the "way of the Lord of heaven and earth." Given their adamant refusal to renounce their faith, the lord pronounced the death sentence on Ignatius and Vincent, and ordered the other catechists and the young boy flogged, their heads shorn, and one finger cut. The sentences were carried out on July 26, 1645, three days after de Rhodes left for Macao.[102]

THE RETURN FROM MACAO TO ROME

De Rhodes's superiors in Macao decided that a man of his experience could render a vast service to the missions by going back to Europe to fetch spiritual and temporal help. De Rhodes was charged with three tasks: to impress the Pope of the extreme need to send bishops to Tonkin and Cochinchina; to seek material help from Christian princes for the missions; and to ask the superior general to send more missionaries to the countries of Asia.[103]

In December 1645, de Rhodes began his return journey to Rome which he had left some twenty-seven years earlier. It was a three-and-a-half-year journey, full of mishaps and adventures, including imprisonment by the Dutch, which took de Rhodes to Malacca, Java, Djakarta, Macassar, Persia, Upper Armenia, Anatolia, Smyrna, and finally, Rome.

Upon his arrival in Rome on June 27, 1649, de Rhodes immediately set out to realize his plan of having a hierarchy established in Vietnam.[104] In his first report to the Propaganda Fide on August 2, 1650, he pointed out to the cardinals of the congregation that there were 300,000 Christians in Vietnam, with an average annual increase of 15,000. Pastoral care of that number of Christians would require at least 300 missionary priests from Europe. Such a large number

---

Converted in 1628, this young man was a carrier of the litter of this prince. Francis was wont to devoting himself to the burial of poor people. The prince was extremely displeased that his carrier performed what he considered to be a dirty work and strictly forbade him to continue. Francis refused to obey the prince since he regarded this work of mercy as part of his Christian duties. The prince ordered him to renounce his Christian faith, and when Francis would not, he was put to death. See de Rhodes, *Relazione*, 258–59; *Histoire du Royaume*, 265–66; *Tunchensis historiae*, II, 146–47.

101. De Rhodes, *Relation des progrez*, 124.

102. See Saccano, 41–42; de Rhodes, *Histoire du Royaume*, 271–73.

103. See *Divers voyages*, pt. III, 2.

104. For a detailed narrative of de Rhodes's activities in Rome to secure the establishment of a hierarchy in Vietnam, see Chappoulie I, 102–13.

of foreign missionaries would not only be hard to obtain but would also meet with opposition from the governments of both Tonkin and Cochinchina.

The best solution would be to create a native hierarchy, beginning with the ordination to the priesthood of catechists who met requisite conditions. De Rhodes anticipated objections to his proposal by the Portuguese government in virtue of the *padroado* system. He suggested that the Holy See appoint bishops as "apostolic vicars" *in partibus infidelium,* under the jurisdiction of the Propaganda Fide, without the knowledge of the Portuguese crown.

On August 1, 1651, the Propaganda Fide proposed to Pope Innocent X to send to Vietnam one patriarch, two or three archbishops, and twelve bishops as apostolic vicars. The Pope did not make any immediate decision. In May 1652, since no decision had been made, de Rhodes addressed a letter to Pope Innocent X in which he repeated the substance of the report he had presented to the Propaganda Fide, emphasizing that the Vietnamese church had suffered martyrdom and that there were well-prepared candidates for the priesthood among the catechists he had trained. The Congregation, in its meeting with the Pope on July 30, 1652, judged that it might be necessary to send a secular priest to Vietnam for a fact-finding mission before making any episcopal appointment.

The Pope thought there was no better candidate for the episcopacy in Vietnam than de Rhodes himself, but the latter declined the appointment, not only because being a Jesuit he was barred from seeking the episcopacy but also because having been expelled from the country, he would not be able to return to it officially. Instead, on August 19, 1652, he was made prefect of the mission and was charged with recruiting candidates for the episcopacy.

On September 11, 1652, de Rhodes left for Paris where he met the Reverend Bagot, a Jesuit, director of a group of twelve students who formed the Société des Bons Amis. De Rhodes's missionary plan received an enthusiastic response from the group. Three priests of the group were judged worthy candidates for the episcopacy: François Pallu, François de Montigny-Laval, and Bernard Piques. De Rhodes also obtained financial help from the duchess of Aiguillon for the support of the eventual hierarchy.

On learning that Rome was about to send French bishops to Vietnam, Portugal voiced fierce opposition. The Portuguese ambassador made it known to the Pope that no French missionaries could be sent to Vietnam; that Portugal would be responsible for the nomination and maintenance of any Vietnamese clergy; and that should French missionaries be sent, there would be war against them.[105] In the face of this attack by Lisbon, the Holy See did not see it wise to proceed with de Rhodes's project.

Meanwhile the Jesuit general, believing that de Rhodes's presence in the project of establishing a hierarchy in Vietnam would prevent it from being realized, decided to make him superior of the Jesuit mission in Persia. On No-

---

105. See Adrien Launay, *Nos missionnaires, précédés d'une étude historique sur la Société des Missions-Étrangères* (Paris, 1886), 17.

vember 16, 1654, de Rhodes left Marseilles for his new mission. He settled in Isfahan where he had stayed for three months in 1648 during his journey back to Rome.

But de Rhodes's dream for Vietnam did not die. On September 9, 1659, the Propaganda Fide published a decree, confirmed by Pope Alexander VII, establishing two apostolic vicariates with two bishops: François Pallu (1626–84), bishop of Heliopolis, apostolic vicar for Tonkin, and also responsible for the Chinese provinces of Yunnan, Kuchu, Hukuang, Kiangsi, and Szechwan, as well as Laos; and Pierre Lambert de la Motte (1624–79), bishop of Beryte, apostolic vicar of Cochinchina, and also responsible for the Chinese provinces of Tchekiang, Fukien, Kwantung, Kiangsi, the island of Hainan, and other nearby islands. A few months later, the Propaganda Fide named Ignatius Cotolendi (1630–62) bishop of Metellopolis, apostolic vicar of Nankin, and also gave him responsibility for the Chinese provinces of Chansi, Chensi, Chantung, and Pekin, as well as for Korea and Tartar.[106]

One can only surmise the joy with which the news of the establishment of a hierarchy in Vietnam filled the heart of de Rhodes in Isfahan. But the old missionary did not rest on his laurels; with alacrity he began learning Persian and soon knew it enough to preach. In a letter to a Jesuit in Lyon he wrote: "Since the time I came to this country, God has given me the grace to learn the Persian language. I know it enough now to preach. Ordinarily I would go to the villages, looking for sick children and baptize them when they are on the point of death.... We need time and patience, as in China."[107] De Rhodes died in Isfahan on November 5, 1660.

---

106. See Chappoulie I, 114–28.
107. Quoted in Chappoulie I, 113.

3

The Missionary Strategies of Alexandre de Rhodes

Cultural, Religious, Liturgical, and Ecclesial Adaptations

Like his fellow Jesuit missionaries Matteo Ricci in China and Roberto de No-bili in India, de Rhodes was profoundly sensitive to the cultural and religious traditions of the people he was evangelizing. He was convinced that successful missionary work required not only mastery of the native language but also familiarity with the people's customs and culture. That de Rhodes took enormous pains to learn about the countries and peoples he evangelized is supported by his many memoirs in which he provided us with a detailed and for the most part surprisingly accurate account of the sociopolitical histories, cultural practices, and religious traditions of both Tonkin and Cochinchina.[1] In addition, he

---

1. It is appropriate here to review de Rhodes's memoirs of his missionary work. De Rhodes's earliest writing on his missionary work is his June 16, 1625, letter, written in Portuguese and addressed to Nuno Mascarenhas, Assistant for Portugal, in which he related his first travel from Macao to Cochinchina, his study of the language, and his imminent undertaking of the mission in Tonkin. This handwritten, almost two-page letter (15.5 x 23 cm.) is now located in *ARSI, JS* 68, f. 13rv.

After he was expelled from Tonkin in May 1630, de Rhodes returned to Macao and there on January 16, 1631, he wrote a three-and-one-half-page letter (20 x 30 cm.) in Portuguese to Nuno Mascarenhas in which he reported the missionary work of both himself and Pêro Marques in Tonkin. The letter is now located in *ARSI, JS* 80, f. 15r–16v.

The third and major document is de Rhodes's lengthy history of Tonkin. We possess a manuscript of this two-volume history written in Latin in *ARSI, JS* 83 and 84, f. 1–62v. Thanks to the date recorded on the margin, we gather that it was composed in 1636 when de Rhodes was in Macao, teaching theology at the Madre de Deus College. It was published first in Italian in Rome in 1650 (*Relazione de' felici successi della Santa Fede...*) in 326 pages, in 12.5 x 18 cm. format. The French translation by Henri Albi was published in Lyon in 1651 (*Histoire du Royaume de Tunquin...*) in 326 pages, in 12.5 x 18 cm. format. The Latin original was published last in Lyon in 1652 (*Tunchinensis Historiae libri duo...*). Vol. I has 89 pages, and vol. II 200 pages, both in 12.5 x 18 cm. format. The last part of this most important work (chaps. 37–51) details the situation of the church in Tonkin until 1646, which means that it was not written in Macao in 1636 but later, possibly after the author had come back to Rome (June 27, 1649).

In 1644 de Rhodes wrote a report in Portuguese on the martyrdom of Andrew of Phu Yen: *Relaçao do glorioso Martirio de Andre Cathequista Protomartir de Cochinchina alanceado, e degolado em Cachao nos 26 de Julho de 1644 tendo de Idade dezanove annos.* The report is sixteen pages long, in 11 x 21 cm. format. It is found at *Real Academia de la Historia de Madrid, Jesuitas,* Legajo 21 bis, fasc. 17, f. 228–

also described the ways in which he attempted to inculturate the Christian faith and practices into the local situation.

In this chapter we will examine some of the most significant challenges seventeenth-century Vietnam posed to de Rhodes's missionary work and the strategies he used to meet them. One convenient way to understand these challenges is to examine briefly the reasons why de Rhodes was banished from both Tonkin and Cochinchina. Some of these reasons originated from the cultural and religious heritage of Vietnam. We will then study the ways in which de Rhodes attempted to meet these challenges in the areas of cultural practices, religious traditions, liturgical celebrations, church organization, and catechetical ministry.

REASONS FOR DE RHODES'S EXPULSIONS

De Rhodes was expelled from Tonkin in May 1630 and from Cochinchina in July 1645. The reasons for such expulsions were, of course, many and diverse, some of which, mainly economic and political, played a predominant role at the time but are now no longer of great interest for our study. Others, both cultural and religious, continue to be of abiding relevance for contemporary Christian mission and catechesis in Vietnam.

Economic and Political Reasons

As has been pointed out in the first chapter, the relationships between the missionaries on the one hand and the Portuguese merchants and military on the other in the seventeenth century were at best ambiguous. Under the *padroado* system, the missionaries were maintained and protected by the Portuguese government. Arriving in Tonkin and Cochinchina on Portuguese ships, and presented to the lords of the two countries with great reverence by the Portuguese merchants and military officers, de Rhodes and his fellow missionaries would have had a difficult time distinguishing themselves from their compatriots, at least in the eyes of the local authorities. It was no accident that the religion they preached was then known in Vietnamese as *dao Hoa Lang*, literally, way

---

234v. In 1653, de Rhodes wrote a longer account of the martyrdom of Andrew entitled *La glorieuse mort d'André Catéchiste de la Cochinchine...* in 109 pages.

The last and major work is *Divers voyages et missions...*, first published in Paris in 1653 and republished in 1666, 1681, 1683, 1854, and 1884. The book is composed of three parts. The first two parts are paginated continuously and have 276 pages. The third part begins with new pagination. The book has been translated into German by Michael Pachtler (Freiburg: Herder, 1858) and into English by Solange Hertz (Westminster, Md.: The Newman Press, 1966). We have a Latin manuscript, written in Macassar in June 4, 1647, entitled *Alexandri Rhodes è Societate Jesu terra marique decem annorum itinerarium*. It is located in *ARSI, JS* 69, f. 95r–140v. It contains sixty-one chapters, with chaps. 50–58 and the last part of chap. 61 missing. This Latin manuscript forms the second part of *Voyages et missions*, though the French printed text differs considerably from the Latin manuscript.

or religion of the Portuguese.[2] De Rhodes himself was called "the Father of the Portuguese," that is, "the Father of the Christians."[3]

Engaged in an internecine war, the lords of both Tonkin and Cochinchina sought to place their respective countries at an advantage by means of commercial trade with the Portuguese and above all by obtaining Western firearms. They regarded missionaries as useful pawns in their bid for power, allowing them to stay and preach in their lands as long as they could attract foreign trade, and expelling them when their usefulness vanished.

There is, however, no evidence whatsoever of de Rhodes's ever attempting to persuade the Portuguese to trade with or sell arms to either Tonkin or Cochinchina. At most he tried to gain the goodwill of the lords with harmless presents such as clocks and rare books in order to be allowed to stay and preach in their territories.[4]

Well aware of the political and military rivalries between Cochinchina and Tonkin, de Rhodes was extremely careful to avoid any direct contact with his confreres and the Christians in one part of the country while he was working in another. In 1630, when banished from Tonkin by Lord Trinh Trang and ordered to go directly to Cochinchina and to leave from there for Macao on Portuguese ships, he sought to avoid that route for fear of arousing the anger of the lord of Cochinchina against his Jesuit confreres and the Christians. In 1645, when at the border between Tonkin and Cochinchina he was invited by a nearby community of Christians to cross into Tonkin to visit them, he denied himself the pleasure of seeing the Christians of the north again, for fear that his visit would create difficulties for the Christians of both sides.

Ironically, despite all his painstaking caution, the *immediate* cause of de Rhodes's expulsion from both Tonkin and Cochinchina was political and economic. In 1630, it was triggered by the accusation of a former Buddhist monk that de Rhodes and the Christians were involved in a plot with Cao Bang and Cochinchina to overthrow Lord Trinh Trang. In 1645, the apparent cause for banishment was the charge of espionage for Tonkin. At the time, there was a rumor that Lord Trinh Trang had just died and that his successor, Lord Trinh Tac, was preparing an invasion of Cochinchina. The political situation was ex-

---

2. In the seventeenth and eighteenth centuries, Vietnamese authorities, both in Tonkin and Cochinchina, called Christianity *dao Hoa Lang* (way of the Portuguese) and Christians *dao Hoa Lang nhan* (people of the Portuguese law). Whether these terms were purely descriptive or were used by opponents to disparage the new religion, it is hard to say. Most probably, initially, they were descriptive, and subsequently, became abusive. At any rate, the term *dao Hoa Lang* was subjected to a vigorous discussion by the Jesuit priest Isidoro Luci, missionary to Tonkin between 1694 and 1716. See *ARSI, JS* 89, f. 545–48v.

3. See Saccano, 2–3.

4. It is true that these gifts could be very expensive and cost all the money de Rhodes had to live on for a year. De Rhodes wrote about the gifts he had to give to Lord Nguyen Phuoc Lan on his return to Cochinchina in 1640: "I went to the king with the most beautiful presents I could find. It's true that to buy them I had used just about all the money I had brought from Macao to keep me all year, but God provided, for a good Christian named Andrew and his wife sent me all the money needed to reimburse me, saying they wanted the satisfaction of providing the presents destined to win the king's heart" (*Divers voyages*, 121).

tremely tense. De Rhodes and his eight catechists were arrested as they were sailing to the northernmost province of Quang Binh. Brought to the capital for trial, de Rhodes was condemned to decapitation by Lord Nguyen Phuoc Lan, but his death sentence was commuted to permanent exile on the intervention of the lord's former teacher.

Besides these political reasons, there was also an economic one. In 1630, after tolerating the presence of de Rhodes and Pêro Marques for ten months despite his earlier edict of expulsion, Lord Trinh Trang finally ordered them to leave the country, since the Portuguese ships, which he had hoped to attract with the presence of the missionaries, did not come during the season of favorable weather.

Cultural Reasons

In his account of the various customs of the Vietnamese in Tonkin, de Rhodes mentioned polygamy, noting that this practice was common among the well-to-do.[5] As a Christian, he could not but regard it as immoral,[6] and as a missionary, he made the dismissal of "concubines"[7] the condition for baptism.[8]

---

5. See *Histoire du Royaume*, 99.

6. De Rhodes argued for monogamy on the basis of Genesis's account of the creation of Adam and Eve: "Furthermore, God did not give the man two or three wives but only one, because they became one and not many flesh, as Adam prophetically affirmed." But, in an attempt at inculturation, he also appealed to a Vietnamese proverb: "The Vietnamese themselves say: 'The husband and the wife give one another their bones and flesh.' Just as the man has a right to the body of the woman, so that as long as he lives, she may not attach herself to another man, so the woman has a right to the body of the man, so that as long as she lives, he may not take another woman" (*Cathechismus*, 77–78).

7. The term "concubine," which in Western languages has an illicit ring about it, is hardly appropriate for the position of the secondary wife or wives in a Vietnamese polygamous marriage. Though polygamy can be practiced for a variety of reasons, the duty of producing a male heir to continue the cult of ancestors may often be one of them. Not rarely did the first wife herself have a say in allowing her husband to take a second wife. Of polygamy in Vietnam Léopold Cadière, a missionary priest of the Missions étrangères de Paris who has worked in Vietnam for over fifty years, and a careful observer of the Vietnamese way of life, has this to say: "Je ne sais pas ce qui se passerait, si tous les Annamites avaient deux ou trois femmes.... Mais j'avouerai que la polygamie, telle qu'elle existe en Annam, adoptée pour des motifs qui ne manquent pas d'une certaine noblesse, ne produit pas les effets néfastes qu'on reproche d'ordinaire à cette institution" (Cadière I, 67).

8. In his instructions to catechists preparing catechumens for baptism, de Rhodes said that there were four kinds of people they must not admit to the sacrament, one of them being people engaged in polygamy: "Husbands must have only one wife, the legitimate one, and married women must be the legitimate wives; otherwise, they must ask for a certificate of repudiation before baptism." And he added a wise observation, more for the benefit of future missionaries: "Experience has taught me that in these pagan countries, catechumens promise a lot to obtain baptism, but they tend not to keep their promises after reception of baptism, especially in matters regarding concubines" (*Cathechismus*, 319).
De Rhodes must have remembered the case of a wealthy man in Qui Nhon whom he called "a bad Christian" and of whom he spoke at length as a warning for other Christians. This man had a concubine and, in spite of de Rhodes's repeated entreaties, could not bring himself to dismiss her. Once when he was seriously ill, he asked for confession but de Rhodes refused him the sacrament as long as he still retained his concubine. De Rhodes related that as long as the man thought death inevitable, the man promised him he would do what he was required, but he kept delaying until, regaining his health, he made mock of God whom he thought he no longer needed. But de Rhodes added: "But God certainly made mock of him. A heavy storm arose over the whole sea and land of Cochinchina.... By God's grace

There was no doubt that de Rhodes's opposition to polygamy aroused Lord Trinh Trang's anger and was one of the reasons for his banishment from Tonkin. Embittered by what they considered a cruel treatment by their husbands who dismissed them in order to become Christians, the concubines brought their plight to the lord's attention. In response to their complaints, Lord Trinh Trang sent de Rhodes the following message: "What is this way that you have been preaching in my kingdom? You have ordered that my subjects must have only one wife, while I want them to have several so that they may have as many children as possible who are faithful to me. Cease and desist, therefore, from preaching this way. If you do not obey, know that I can have you decapitated and thus prevent you from doing what I have forbidden."[9]

After this incident, Lord Trinh Trang only rarely invited the missionaries to the court. As a result, little by little, the missionaries lost the lord's good will.

RELIGIOUS REASONS

Finally, there were religious reasons for de Rhodes's expulsion. These can be summarized under two headings: the worship of what de Rhodes regarded as idols and the cult of ancestors. By idols de Rhodes meant the statues of various religious personages such as the Buddha, Confucius, deities and spirits, national heroes, and immortals that were found in all Buddhist pagodas, Taoist temples, and Confucian shrines. Christians were denounced to Lord Trinh Trang, especially by Buddhist monks, with claims that they had destroyed these statues. As a result, the lord issued an edict forbidding all his subjects under most grievous pains to embrace the Christian religion. The edict was affixed on the door of the missionaries' house, in the presence of the missionaries and a large number of Christians.

Fortunately, de Rhodes was able to see Lord Trinh Trang in person and defend himself and the Christians against this false accusation. Surprisingly, the lord was persuaded by de Rhodes's defense and allowed the missionaries to continue to preach "provided that we break no idols." De Rhodes assured the lord that "we have never taught the Christians to break the idols; on the con-

---

not one of our Christians was involved in this misfortune with the exception of that wretch who was still convalescing. Still he thought he had escaped, because he had himself carried into one of his houses where he thought himself safe. But God knew where to find him all right. That house, which the storm had loosened in its joints, was completely demolished a few days later by a heavy rain. All others in it were saved. It was only that wretch, whom God's hand pursued after his mercy had long proved futile, who was buried in the ruins whereas his guilty soul was buried in hell—at any rate, he died without the sacraments and in a state of disobedience to God and the church" (*Divers voyages,* 175–76). This story is interesting insofar as it reveals de Rhodes's belief not only about concubinage but also about divine justice.

9. *Histoire du Royaume,* 192. Given the angry tone of the message, de Rhodes suspected that it was not authored by Lord Trinh Trang, who had shown the missionaries great kindness and generosity, but by the messenger who had a large number of wives. Despite the threat of capital punishment, the missionaries resolved "to continue as usual to combat and condemn the practice of having many wives" (193). See also *Divers voyages,* 104–5.

trary, we have expressly forbidden them to cause the statues any injury and have strongly urged them to live in peace with everyone."[10]

Much more serious is the charge that Christian missionaries required the Vietnamese Christians to abandon the cult of ancestors. Later we will see de Rhodes's description of the Vietnamese funeral customs and veneration of ancestors. Here suffice it to note that this charge is an oft-repeated one, especially during the persecution of Vietnamese Christians in the nineteenth century. The charge of destroying the cult of ancestors was already leveled against Christians during de Rhodes's first sojourn in Cochinchina (1624–26). Taking advantage of Lord Nguyen Phuoc Nguyen's displeasure with the missionaries because the expected Portuguese ships with merchandise and arms had failed to arrive, opponents of Christianity accused Christians of many crimes among which "the major one was their having no interest in succoring or paying respect to the souls of their departed relatives, saying that ours was a barbarous religion that obliterated all sentiments of gratitude toward parents from the heart, which nature impressed in every one."[11]

As a result of this accusation, Lord Nguyen Phuoc Nguyen issued an edict ordering all Jesuit missionaries to leave the churches they had built. Fortunately, the Jesuits succeeded in courting the favor of the lord's eldest son, who obtained his father's permission for them to stay in their houses a hundred days longer. The pretext for this extended stay was the need to organize the funeral for de Pina who had drowned sometime earlier. Meanwhile, the Jesuits persuaded the lord to change his mind and to revoke the edict.

The same charge was brought by the notorious Ong Nghe Bo against de Rhodes during his second sojourn in Cochinchina, when on July 25, 1644, the latter came to him to request the release of Catechist Andrew. Ong Nghe Bo told de Rhodes that Lord Nguyen Phuoc Lan was angry at him because he "had the audacity to make the rounds of his kingdom and to corrupt the souls by means of a new way which destroyed all the sentiments of the religion which their ancestors had professed."[12] By "the sentiments of the religion which their ancestors professed" Ong Nghe Bo no doubt meant the cult of ancestors.

That this was what he meant is confirmed by the question Lord Nguyen Phuoc Lan asked Catechist Ignatius a year later, on July 26, 1645, trying to

---

10. *Histoire du Royaume*, 199. That this was the missionaries' policy is borne out by two facts. First, when a number of new Christians wanted to remove the statues in a temple they had built before their conversion and to turn the temple into a church, de Rhodes refused the offer and advised them to let it naturally fall into ruins "for fear that in breaking the idols against the will of those who adore them, we would attract their hatred and persecution; which is the reason why canon law has very wisely forbidden to do so" (197). Second, when a certain wealthy man became a Christian, he wanted to convert the house he had built for the worship of idols into a church and asked de Rhodes to bless it. De Rhodes consented to the request only after assuring himself that no "idols" had been installed in it and therefore there was no need to remove them beforehand (197). Of course, this policy does not mean that there might not have been some indiscreet and excessively zealous converts who actually destroyed statues they considered as idols.

11. *Divers voyages*, 76–77.

12. *La glorieuse mort*, 17.

make him renounce his Christian faith: "How can you not abandon this law that teaches you to despise and hate your father and mother? Don't you know that every year thousands of people are killed in Japan, simply because they follow the way of the Portuguese?"[13]

If the charge that Christian missionaries required the repudiation of the cult of ancestors were true, Christianity not only would have shaken the very foundations of Vietnamese religions but also would have torn apart the fabric of Vietnamese cultural and societal structures. As we have seen in the first chapter, the cult of ancestors, central to the Vietnamese indigenous cult of spirits, was reinforced by Confucianism when the latter penetrated into Vietnam. It provided continuity across generations and bound all the Vietnamese together, from the king as the august Son of Heaven to the humblest citizen in the country. There is no doubt that this cult of ancestors, if viewed as contrary to the Christian faith, would constitute one of the most serious challenges to Christian mission. It would be natural then for rulers of the country to take every possible measure not only to banish de Rhodes but also to proscribe Christianity, if both de Rhodes and Christianity posed a threat to this cult of ancestors.

Having seen some of the key reasons for de Rhodes's expulsions from Vietnam,[14] we will now examine the strategies with which he attempted to meet the various challenges to his missionary work.

DE RHODES AND CULTURAL PRACTICES

De Rhodes's profound knowledge of the Vietnamese language no doubt contributed to the astounding achievements of his mission. His experiences in Salsette near Goa where he noticed how his countryman Etienne Crucius's perfect mastery of the local dialects facilitated large-scale conversions, his own language studies in Central Vietnam during the years 1624–26, and his relative lack of success among the Chinese in Macao during the decade 1630–40 because of his inability to preach in their tongue convinced de Rhodes that mastery of the languages of the peoples to be evangelized was the first and fundamental condition for the effective preaching of the Gospel.[15] It may be said that learning local languages well is the sine qua non first stage of "inculturation" that missionaries must undergo. This first stage is all the more urgent if language is not merely a means of communication but a "house of Being," a way of *experiencing* reality of which religion is an *expression*. Language,

---

13. Saccano, 8.

14. To these political, cultural, and religious reasons, others could be added such as the implacable hatred of some powerful personages at the court (e.g., Madame Tong Thi Toai and the mandarins), the example of persecutions in Japan of which the lords were well aware, and misunderstandings of Christian rituals, e.g., baptism, as sorceries. See Do Quang Chinh, 138–45; 238–47.

15. See *Divers voyages*, 72–73.

in the words of Sri Lankan theologian Aloysius Pieris, is indeed a *theologia inchoativa*.[16]

That de Rhodes believed that language is incipient theology is implied by his view that the Hebrew language was the only valid medium to transmit God's revealed teachings, and that nations that lost the Hebrew language after the confusion of languages at Babel, e.g., China, fell into heresies such as Taoism, Confucianism, and Buddhism.[17]

Besides knowledge of the language, de Rhodes also vehemently insisted on the need for missionaries to adapt to, and for indigenous neophytes to preserve, local cultural practices, unless these were contrary to Christian morality. He was scandalized by the fact that Indian Christians in Goa were required to abandon their native costumes and to dress in the Portuguese fashion. He also vigorously protested against the obligation imposed upon Chinese male Christians to wear their hair short.

De Rhodes's two criteria for judging the preservability of a particular cultural practice were whether it was required by Jesus himself and whether it was opposed to the Gospel. These norms are implied in both his question about the Indian Christians — "I don't know why they are asked to do things that the Lord would not have asked of them"[18] — and his statement to Chinese male Christians who were compelled to cut off their long hair — "I used to tell them that the Gospel obliged them to lop off their spiritual errors but not their long hair."[19]

CULTURAL ADAPTATIONS IN PERSONAL LIFE

It was along these principles that de Rhodes evaluated Vietnamese cultural customs and behaved accordingly, first in his personal life and then in his ministry. Fortunately, de Rhodes had much latitude to adapt to local customs in his personal life. In China the Jesuits had already adopted the gown of the literati, and the visitor Andrea Palmiero had approved this practice in 1627.

When the Jesuits first came to Vietnam, they wore Vietnamese robes and sandals.[20] Though de Rhodes has not left any information on his personal wardrobe, from the many portraits of de Rhodes and from an engraving included in Giovanni Filippo de Marini's 1663 work, which shows a missionary preaching in the Far East, we gather that de Rhodes often wore a Vietnamese hat and a Vietnamese robe with large sleeves, an open and folded-over neck, and the front buttoned down under the right arm. He did not wear any over-

---

16. *An Asian Theology of Liberation* (Maryknoll, N.Y.: Orbis Books, 1988), 70–71.

17. See *Cathechismus*, 103–4. De Rhodes seems to have derived this understanding of the Hebrew language from Augustine. See *City of God*, bk. XVI, chap. 11.

18. *Divers voyages*, 21.

19. *Divers voyages*, 21.

20. Borri, who was in Cochinchina between 1618 and 1621, reported that the Jesuits "wear a very loose cotton cassock, which they call *Ehingon*, ordinarily of blue color, and they appear in public thus attired, without any other robe or coat" ("Relation," 55).

coat like European priests. As to footwear, de Rhodes did not make use of embroidered shoes (*van hai*) or boots (*giay ong*), reserved for mandarins and wealthy people, but heelless slippers (*giay da lang*) common among middle-class Vietnamese.[21] But de Rhodes went further than his colleagues in wearing long hair, like Vietnamese men, letting it fall freely in long braids on his shoulders.[22]

Perhaps these seventeenth-century sartorial and hairstyle adaptations do not appear to us to be of great significance today. However, these innovations were not considered trivial at the time. Indeed, in the following century, they were deemed important enough for the protonotary and apostolic visitor to Central Vietnam, Pierre-François Favre, to order all missionaries to wear their hair according to the fashion prescribed by the Council of Trent for ecclesiastics and no longer the long hair of Vietnamese custom. The same visitor also required all missionaries to Central Vietnam, especially the Jesuits, to wear the black silk cassock with black buttons and a black silk overcoat.[23]

Like any good missionary, de Rhodes also adapted himself to and took pleasure in Vietnamese foods and cuisine. With genuine delight he described the taste of various indigenous fruits[24] and native delicacies such as fish sauce (*nuoc mam*) and bird's-nest soup.[25] He enthusiastically endorsed tea as a remedy against headaches, stomach troubles, and kidney complaints.[26] He even made use of folk medicine against seasickness and vouchsafed its effectiveness.[27]

---

21. See de Marini, *Delle Missioni de' Padri della Compagnia di Giesu nella Provincia di Giappone* (Rome, 1663). For a discussion of the many portraits of de Rhodes, see L. Cadière, "Iconographie du P. De Rhodes," *BAVH* XXV (1938): 27–61. De Rhodes noted that most Vietnamese walked barefooted, especially in the countryside, because the ground was muddy almost everywhere. See *Histoire du Royaume*, 5.

22. De Rhodes noted that as a sign of independence from China, the Vietnamese kings who overthrew the Chinese domination ordered their men not to bind their hair into a bun wrapped with a net like the Chinese but to let it fall freely on their shoulders in long braids. See *Histoire du Royaume*, 5.

23. See Pierre François Favre, *Lettres édifiantes et curieuses sur la visite apostolique de M. de La-Baume, évêque d'Halicarnasse à la Cochinchine en l'année 1740* (Venice, 1746), 187.

24. He frankly confessed that once he ate ten to twelve quinces at a time. See *Histoire du Royaume*, 50.

25. See *Histoire du Royaume*, 48, and *Divers voyages*, 65–66. Fish sauce is made from several layers of raw fish and salt placed in a large pot. As the fish decompose, they yield a golden, quite pungent liquid. It is diluted in a small quantity of water and used as a condiment in all Vietnamese cooking. The birds' nests are those of sea swallows who make their nests with their saliva on cliffs near the sea. These nests "are so white and taste so good, not when eaten alone, but when cooked with fish and meat." They are "a delicacy for the greatest lords" (*Divers voyages*, 66).

26. See *Divers voyages*, 45–53.

27. Seeing that de Rhodes was afflicted with seasickness, his Christians told him that "they had with them a remedy that so strengthened the stomach that it was in no way inconvenienced by this complaint, which is caused by the motion of the ship or by sea vapors. One must take one of those fish that have been devoured by, and which are found in the bellies of other fish, then cook it well, adding a little pepper, and take it before boarding the ship; this imparts such vigor to the stomach that it can sail the sea without getting upset." De Rhodes assured us that he never suffered any more seasickness after the use of this "medicine": "I wish with all my heart that it may prove of use to my reader, and especially to those wishing to come work with us beyond the Great Sea, which they will be able to cross without nausea!" (*Divers voyages*, 124). For de Rhodes's observations on Vietnamese traditional medicine, see *Divers voyages*, 189–91.

As admirable as these adaptations to local costumes and foods may be, and however strongly recommended they are by mission methodology, they still are limited to what Louis Luzbetak terms "the surface level of culture ... the *who, what, where, when, how,* and *what kind...,* the symbols *minus* their meanings."[28] The question is whether de Rhodes has gone beyond these basic cultural building blocks and sought to transform their social functions, meanings, and values within the total context of the Vietnamese culture in the light of the Gospel.

CULTURAL ADAPTATIONS IN MINISTRY

In his description of the "temporal state" of Tonkin de Rhodes recounted several cultural customs some of which he regarded as religiously neutral, others as morally objectionable.[29] Among the latter, we have already mentioned polygamy. As we have seen, de Rhodes's opposition to this practice was one of the reasons for his expulsion from Tonkin. De Rhodes considered it immoral and made the dismissal of "concubines" a condition for the reception of baptism. No doubt, for him, polygamy was both contrary to the Gospel and forbidden by Jesus, the two criteria he used to adjudicate the acceptability of a cultural practice.

On biblical grounds, he condemns polygamy by appealing to the Genesis account of the creation of one man and one woman.[30] In his exposition of the sixth commandment, he explicitly invokes both God's law and Christ's teaching against polygamy: "A legitimate marriage is one of one man and one woman so that as long as one partner is alive, no other partner may be taken. Consequently, polygamy as well as divorce is contrary to the divine law. Indeed, at the beginning, it was not so, as the Lord Jesus himself has taught with his own divine mouth. In fact, at the beginning, God gave Adam only one woman, Eve, and he remained with her until his death, for nine hundred thirty years."[31]

In addition to these Christian grounds, de Rhodes also sought to buttress his opposition to polygamy by appealing to a Vietnamese proverb: "Hai vo chong gui xuong gui thit nhau," literally, the husband and the wife give one another their bones and flesh. In itself the proverb is no argument against polygamy; it simply affirms the mutual commitment between the husband and the wife and in principle can be applied to the husband and his "concubine(s)" since the latter is/are truly and legally his wife/wives. Nevertheless, it serves as an instruc-

---

28. Louis J. Luzbetak, *The Church and Cultures: New Perspectives in Missiological Anthropology* (Maryknoll, N.Y.: Orbis Books, 1988), 225.

29. See *Histoire du Royaume,* 93–109; 112–16. I leave aside the *religious* practices which de Rhodes described under the heading of the three "superstitious sects" and the cult of ancestors. I will discuss them in the next section.

30. See *Cathechismus,* 77–78.

31. *Cathechismus,* 299–300.

tive example of how de Rhodes attempted to inculturate a Christian doctrine and practice, especially when it repudiates a local custom.

Besides outright rejection, de Rhodes also attempted either to impose a Christian meaning to theologically neutral cultural practices or to transform them in such a way that their potentially objectionable elements were purified. As an example of the first strategy, de Rhodes took advantage of a rather curious practice in Tonkin as an entry point for evangelization:

> I noted one custom among them that might suggest that our holy faith had been preached at one time in that kingdom, where nevertheless all memory of it has been obliterated by now. As soon as children were born, I often saw the parents put a crossmark on their foreheads with charcoal or ink. I asked them what good this would do to the child and why they daubed this mark on its forehead. "That," they used to tell me, "is to chase away the devil and keep him from harming the child." I immediately rejoined, "But how could that frighten devils, who are spirits?" They admitted to me they knew nothing more about it, but I did not neglect to disclose its secret to them by explaining the power of the holy cross. This often served me as a means of converting them.[32]

With regard to other cultural practices, de Rhodes neutralized their potentially superstitious elements by christianizing them. An example of this second strategy is the oath of allegiance that soldiers had to swear to the lord of Tonkin. Once a year, toward the end of the sixth month of the lunar calendar (roughly July), in the presence of a literary doctor representing the lord, every soldier had to pronounce aloud the oath of fidelity to the lord in front of a richly decorated altar "dedicated to the gods or rather to the devils."[33] After the swearing ceremony, each soldier received from the doctor a certificate marked with *minh* (clearly), or *bat minh* (not clearly), or *thuan* (average), indicating the degree of his loyalty to the lord. According to these grades, the soldier would be rewarded with a cloak of various length and quality.

The danger of swearing loyalty to the lord consisted for Christians in its association with gods and devils and its superstitious formula. A Christian soldier, with de Rhodes's approval, substituted the official formula with one inspired by the Christian faith: "I swear to the true God of heaven and earth, Father, Son, and Holy Spirit, the company of the blessed spirits, and the whole court of heaven that I shall render faithful service to my king (Trinh Trang) until death. If I lie, if I swear falsely, and against my conscience, I shall be glad to be killed at

---

32. *Divers voyages,* 86–87. See also *Histoire du Royaume,* 103–4. This custom, not reported by any other missionary, is probably part of the practices to protect the child from the harms of the evil spirits. Other practices include not naming the child with the name of an older child who has died, that is, taken away by the evil spirits, and naming the child with obscene names. In both cases, the intent is to deceive the evil spirits into thinking that the child is so ugly that it is not worth taking him or her away. See *Histoire du Royaume,* 112–13.

33. *Histoire du Royaume,* 35.

this moment by the true God, the Lord of heaven and earth, and be consumed by God's lightnings."[34]

Another example has to do with the celebration of Tet, the Vietnamese New Year, arguably the most solemn cultural feast in Vietnam. The Vietnamese had the custom of erecting, on the evening of the last day of the year, a bamboo pole (*cay neu*) in front of their house to invite their deceased parents (*ruoc ong ba*) to come and share in the family's celebration of the New Year. This pole is about fifteen to eighteen feet tall, higher than the roof of the house. Near the top of the pole is attached a small wicker basket or a bag containing a few mouthfuls of areca nut and betel (*mieng trau*) and several pieces of gilded paper money (*tien ma*).

The purpose of this custom is to welcome and assist the deceased parents. Areca and betel are the host's typical welcoming offerings to guests, and money is given to dead parents so that they may pay their debts before the beginning of the New Year. The Vietnamese believe that it is a bad omen not to pay before the New Year debts incurred during the previous year. Obviously, the dead ancestors are believed to have the same needs as the living, so that they are provided with the same things that the living require in their daily life. The bamboo pole serves as a sign to direct the ancestors to the houses of their descendants where they are invited.[35]

De Rhodes regarded the custom of erecting the bamboo pole, especially the offering of paper money to ancestors with which they may pay their debts, as nothing but "foolish imagination" and "superstition."[36] However, the New Year was such a culturally central celebration and afforded such a pastorally enriching opportunity that he was determined to keep the custom, and at the same time to transform the elements he deemed objectionable. He advised the Christians to attach to the *cay neu* a crucifix rather than the wicker basket or the bag with offerings: "One could see almost on all the streets of the city this venerable sign of our salvation raised above the housetops, causing terror to demons and joy to angels. The lord himself saw it as he was carried around the principal streets on New Year's Day.... Seeing these crosses raised high, he said: That is the sign of the Christians."[37]

De Rhodes also invested the New Year celebrations with Christian meanings. The Vietnamese celebrate the New Year in three days: the first day (*mong mot*) is reserved for the cult of ancestors; the second (*mong hai*) for near relatives; and the third (*mong ba*) for the dead. De Rhodes, on the other hand, asked the Christians to dedicate the three days to the Trinity: "The first day in memory of

---

34. *Histoire du Royaume*, 37.

35. See *Histoire du Royaume*, 105. In certain parts of Vietnam, people paint the alleys leading to the house with white chalk with the same intention.

36. *Histoire du Royaume*, 105. As to the practice of paying all one's debts before the New Year, de Rhodes found it quite laudable. But he considered it vitiated by the superstitious motives which inspired it, namely, to avoid bad luck in the coming year or to avoid bringing shame to one's ancestors.

37. *Histoire du Royaume*, 201.

the benefits of creation and conservation, which is dedicated to God the Father; the second in thanksgiving for the inestimable benefit of redemption, which is dedicated to God the Son; and the third in humble gratitude to the Holy Spirit for the grace of being called to be a Christian."[38]

Finally, not only was de Rhodes interested in christianizing Vietnamese cultural customs but he was also careful not to introduce practices that would set Christians apart as a culturally separate group. During his first stay in Cochinchina, the Christian community ran into a potentially fatal difficulty. Lord Nguyen Phuoc Nguyen had issued an edict forbidding Christians to wear images, crosses, and rosaries around their necks. As de Rhodes noted, many Christians considered it cowardice unworthy of the Christian name to conceal the insignia of their faith, and were ready to shed their blood in defiance of the lord's edict.

De Rhodes himself had nothing but the greatest reverence for religious objects and a profound admiration for those who wore them.[39] However, in this case, the outward display of religious objects, besides exposing the Christians to unnecessary death, would set them culturally apart from the other Vietnamese, just as Portuguese fashion set Indian Christians, and short hair set Chinese male Christians, apart from their compatriots. For all these reasons, de Rhodes and his fellow Jesuits persuaded, not without difficulty, the Christians to forgo wearing these sacred objects. In this way, the Vietnamese Christians "gave unbelievers no excuse for showing disrespect for the piety of our Christians."[40]

In sum, de Rhodes's attitude toward Vietnamese cultural practices was subtle and complex. (1) Generally, those practices he considered morally unacceptable, he would firmly reject, appealing to the law of the Gospel and the teaching of Christ, his twin criteria for acceptability, and when possible, invoking Vietnamese wisdom embodied in proverbs and sayings to support his position. (2) Practices that were apparently good, he preserved and gave them a Christian meaning. (3) Practices that were in his judgment liable to superstition but possessed a strong potential for pastoral and spiritual enrichment, he purified them by omitting their objectionable elements or by transforming them with a Christian interpretation. (4) Finally, he was in principle opposed to introducing into the Vietnamese culture Christian practices which, though laudable in themselves, would set the Vietnamese Christians culturally apart from their compatriots.

---

38. *Histoire du Royaume*, 201. Giovanni Filippo de Marini also refers to this custom of dedicating the first three days of the year to the Trinity. See "Relation," 260–61.

39. See his admiration for the piety of Tonkinese Christians: "They each wear two crosses, one on the breast and the other up their sleeve; and they say the former serves as their shield, the latter as their sword. They never travel abroad without taking with them their little oratories, which they open up as soon as their reach their lodgings" (*Divers voyages*, 101–2).

40. *Divers voyages*, 78.

DE RHODES AND VIETNAMESE RELIGIOUS TRADITIONS

Though de Rhodes's interest in Vietnamese cultural practices and customs was genuine, his was not that of a pure ethnologist. His efforts at understanding the Vietnamese culture were directed primarily toward a more effective preaching of the Gospel. Obviously, among the many cultural challenges to his missionary work, the Vietnamese religious traditions stood out as the most powerful and persistent. Consequently, he gave them the lion's share of his attention. Following a long-standing tradition, he spoke of the "Three Religions" (*tam giao*), both in China[41] and in Vietnam.[42] In addition to these three religions, de Rhodes also spoke at length of the cult of Heaven and the spirits (including the ancestors) which we have identified as the heart of the Vietnamese indigenous religion.

As mentioned above, de Rhodes believed that the loss of the Hebrew language at the Tower of Babel, and with it of the tradition of divine revelation, was responsible for the emergence of false religious doctrines, especially in China:

> After the confusion of the languages came the kingdom of the Chinese from whom the Vietnamese received their religions. Because the Chinese, after the confusion of the languages, lost the language in which the true way was found, and because they had no books in which the true way was contained, they were divided into different false ways, just like those who have lost their true way are dispersed in many ways that are false. The Chinese were divided into three main false ways, without counting many less important but equally false ones. The first is that of the literati called *Nho* religion; the second is that of those who worship demons and perform sorcery called *Dao* religion; and the third is that of idolaters, called *But* religion.[43]

As can be surmised from the above quotation, de Rhodes cannot be expected to offer a historically accurate and objective account of the history, doctrines, and practices of the Three Religions of China and Vietnam. It would be insufferable

---

41. For de Rhodes's exposition of the "Three Religions" in China, see *Divers voyages*, 53–55. He called them three "kinds of superstition." The first was "that of the king and the nobility, who adore the material heavens, including the stars" (53). The second kind are "idolaters, who adore certain deities who were once their kings.... One of their false gods is a certain Confucius who ... gave them their laws and invented their letters" (54). "The third sect is that of the sorcerers, who are many and very wicked. These are the ones who have waged the cruelest war against us in all these kingdoms" (54). Needless to say, these characterizations of Taoism, Confucianism, and Buddhism, respectively, are nothing but caricatures. They say more about de Rhodes's attitude and that of Christians of his times toward these religions than about these religions themselves. At any rate, de Rhodes believed that thanks to the imminent conversion of King Ming Yong-Lee, inspired by his Christian general Achilles, "all China will soon be worshiping Jesus Christ and will expel all the devils it has honored till now" (56).

42. De Rhodes discussed the Vietnamese religions mainly in *Histoire du Royaume*, 61–92; *Divers voyages*, 86–89; and *Cathechismus*, 104–24.

43. *Cathechismus*, 104–5.

pedantry to point out the numerous inaccuracies in his presentation of these religions. Not that de Rhodes intentionally distorted or falsified them. To be sure, he did intend to offer his Christian readers an accurate account of these religions, but he did not have at his disposal all the tools of modern scholarship to verify the historical accuracy of his information. More often than not, most of his information was second- or thirdhand. Furthermore, his interest was less historical and phenomenological than apologetic. That is, he was less engaged in presenting a balanced account of these religions and more concerned with highlighting their errors, or superstitions as he called them, so as to rebut them and to help catechumens reject them in favor of Christianity.

In what follows we will examine not so much the accuracy of de Rhodes's account of the Three Religions as his understanding of and attitude toward Buddhism, Taoism, Confucianism, and the cult of ancestors, and how he met the challenges these religious traditions posed to his missionary work.[44]

DE RHODES AND VIETNAMESE BUDDHISM

When de Rhodes came to Tonkin in 1627, he wished that when Vietnam threw off the yoke of the Chinese domination it had also rejected the religions and "superstitions" imported from China. Unfortunately, these religions continued to flourish, in particular Buddhism, which enjoyed, de Rhodes noted, a greater prestige in Vietnam than in China. He remarked that "there are today in the kingdom of Tonkin innumerable pagodas and idols. There is not a small village that does not have a pagoda with idols where people come to practice their superstitious devotion. However, these pagodas are filthy and badly kept; the bonzes who serve there are greedy, appropriating all the offerings for their own use and for their wives and children, and not taking care of the decorations of the pagoda and the statues of their gods."[45]

While he had little esteem for the Buddhist monks, de Rhodes greatly admired the devotion of the Buddhist faithful. Twice a month, he notes, they would come to the pagodas to make their prayers and offerings: "They perform these practices with great piety; there is hardly anyone among them, however financially deprived, who would not bring offerings on those occasions and place them reverently at the feet of these dusty statues."[46]

For Buddhist teachings, however, de Rhodes had nothing but condemnation. For him, Buddhism teaches two pernicious errors. The first, which de Rhodes

---

44. De Rhodes varied the order of his exposition of these religious traditions in his various works. In *Histoire du Royaume*, he followed the order Confucianism, Buddhism, Taoism, and the cult of the dead. In *Divers voyages*, he simply said: "The Tonkinese have among them the same three types of religion as the Chinese, but the piety they display toward the souls of the relatives surpasses anything we could imagine in Europe. They go to incredible lengths to find suitable places for their tombs. They believe the happiness of the whole family depends on the respect they show the dead" (87). In *Cathechismus*, de Rhodes followed the order Buddhism, Taoism, Confucianism, and the cult of ancestors.

45. *Histoire du Royaume*, 69.

46. *Histoire du Royaume*, 70.

calls the "external way," promotes the worship of idols, and the second, which is worse and which he calls the "internal way," teaches atheism, that is, the teaching that "nothingness is the origin of all things, and that at death all things return to nothingness as to their ultimate end."[47]

To rebut the errors of Buddhism, de Rhodes adopted three strategies: first, attacking its founder (*argumentum ad hominem*); second, showing how Buddhism was mistaken for the true religion by the Chinese (historical argument); and third, arguing for theism and monotheism (theological argument).

De Rhodes presents the Buddha as "one who had a violent and evil temper; from his tender age he gave himself up to magic and had two demons as friends from whom he learnt both his conduct and his teaching."[48] The Buddha was also, says de Rhodes, a deceiver. To the common people he taught the worship of idols (the "external way"), since they could not be dissuaded from the innate belief that God exists and that there would be recompense for the good and punishment for the wicked. But to his clever disciples he taught atheism (the "internal way"), saying privately that his teaching on idols was merely designed to amuse the simple-minded folk.[49]

But, de Rhodes asks, how could the Chinese, who were so advanced culturally, accept such a nonsensical doctrine and religion, and do so from the Indians who were their cultural inferiors? De Rhodes answered this objection by recounting how the Chinese envoy sent by Emperor Ming of the Han dynasty to search for the writings of the true religion of the West (i.e., Christianity) stopped prematurely in India because of fatigue, and was given the writings of the Buddha. He brought the Buddhist scriptures back to China and these were mistakenly circulated throughout China as containing the true religion of the Great West.[50]

But de Rhodes's most important strategy against Buddhism was his doctrinal arguments for theism over against atheism and for monotheism over against idolatry. We will examine these arguments when in chapter 5 we study the ways in which de Rhodes presents the doctrine of God to the Vietnamese. Suffice it here to note that it is the third strategy alone that retains its validity today, since both the *argumentum ad hominem* and the historical argument suffer from fatal flaws.

While postponing consideration of de Rhodes's arguments for theism and monotheism, let us examine the ways he refutes what he takes to be two main

---

47. *Cathechismus*, 107. De Rhodes takes *nirvana* and *sunyata* to mean nothingness.

48. *Histoire du Royaume*, 66.

49. See *Histoire du Royaume*, 66–67, and *Cathechismus*, 106–7.

50. See *Histoire du Royaume*, 68, and *Cathechismus*, 108–10. De Rhodes very probably derived this story from Matteo Ricci. See Matteo Ricci, *The True Meaning of the Lord of Heaven*, translated, with introduction and notes, by Douglas Lancashire and Peter Hu Kuo-chen (St. Louis: Institute of Jesuit Sources, 1985), 455. According to one tradition, Emperor Ming (58–75 C.E.) of the Han dynasty saw in a dream a large golden figure. One of his ministers assured him that the figure was that of the Buddha. The emperor sent ambassadors to search for him. In this way Buddhism was introduced into China between 64 and 75 C.E.

teachings of Buddhism. The first, which the Buddha preached to the masses (his "external way"), concerns the transmigration of souls. De Rhodes finds this teaching "ridiculous" on three counts. First, the existence of previous lives is impossible because we have no memory of it. Second, it contradicts another teaching of the Buddha that the human soul is mortal. If the human soul dies, how can it transmigrate? Third, it clashes with common sense which is contained in a Vietnamese and Chinese proverb: "Life is a journey, death a return." How can the soul return home if it continues to transmigrate?[51]

The Buddha's second teaching, which he taught to his select disciples only (his "internal way"), affirms that the human soul is mortal. De Rhodes advances five arguments against it. First, as has been shown above, it contradicts the Buddha's teaching on the transmigration of souls. Second, it opens the door to immorality, since if the soul perishes, there would be neither reason nor incentive for observing the moral laws. Third, it goes against the common desire of everyone to leave something behind to be remembered by, such as a famous deed or a beautiful tomb. Fourth, it flies in the face of the fact that there are certain spiritual operations that are independent of the body, such as understanding and willing. Fifth, it oppugns the widespread and sacred practice among the Vietnamese to honor and take care of their parents after their death.[52]

While he was adamantly opposed to what he took to be Buddhist doctrines, pastorally, as we have seen in chapter 2, de Rhodes took great pains to convert Buddhists because, given their deep religious devotion, once converted to Christianity they would be the most ardent believers and zealous missionaries. In particular, he sought to engage in public disputations with Buddhist monks (though not always successfully), because when any one of them became a Christian he usually brought with him many of their followers. Indeed, among de Rhodes's converts, both in Tonkin and Cochinchina, many had been Buddhist monks and became his most effective collaborators.

DE RHODES AND VIETNAMESE TAOISM

Of the Three Religions in Tonkin, de Rhodes considered Taoism the crassest and the most pernicious because "it is the most widespread and the most devoted to the service of the devil."[53] This assessment was based not so much on Taoist philosophy (Taoism as *tao chia*), of which he gave a brief exposition in *Cathechismus*, but on Taoist religious practices (Taoism as *tao chiao*) he observed in Tonkin.

De Rhodes summarizes Taoist doctrines in a saying of Lao Tzu which to him

---

51. See *Cathechismus*, 116–17. De Rhodes gives the proverb in both the Sino-Vietnamese form, "Sinh qui da, tu qui da," and the Vietnamese form, "Song thi gui, chet thi ve."

52. See *Cathechismus*, 118–20. Note the ways in which de Rhodes skillfully exploits Vietnamese culture to reject the Buddhist doctrines of the transmigration and the mortality of the human soul.

53. *Histoire du Royaume*, 72.

was nothing but a meaningless conundrum: "Tao, that is, the law or the way, has made one; one has made two; two has made three; three, lastly, has made everything."[54] He takes Taoism as well as Buddhism to hold that "nothingness" is the origin of all things and therefore to deny the doctrine of creation: "They [i.e., Taoists] make emptiness and nothingness the first principle of all things. Now, is it not absurd that emptiness or nothingness creates something?"[55]

De Rhodes charges that this implicit atheism or at least ignorance of the true God and creator leads Taoism to the worship of demons and the practice of sorcery. In his history of Tonkin, de Rhodes gives a detailed description of how even the lord and court officials gave credence to Taoist sorcerers, especially in the healing of diseases. Sicknesses were believed to be caused by angry ancestors, so that the first thing to do in the case of illness is to ask Taoist sorcerers to identify the disgruntled forebear.

Taoist sorcerers, de Rhodes tells us, were plentiful, and most were blind and poor people trying to make a living with this profession. The sorcerer would kill a chicken, throw its two legs into a pot of boiling water, and inspect its nails to determine the cause and progress of the disease.[56] A sacrificial banquet would be offered to appease the dissatisfied ancestor. Later, the sorcerer would, de Rhodes observes with sarcasm, bring the foods home for his wife and children to enjoy. Throughout the night, chanting and ringing of bells would be carried out continuously to keep the malevolent ancestor at bay. Meanwhile, de Rhodes does not fail to note with a chuckle, the sick person's health deteriorates because he or she is deprived of necessary sleep and rest by this superstitious pandemonium.

De Rhodes also mentions the sorcerer's method of healing the sick by bringing a paper boat and a few soldiers to a river. There the boat, representing the angry ancestor, is submerged into the water, while the soldiers fire some shots to scare the illness-causing ancestor away. Sometimes, the sorcerer would remove the sick person from the bed and substitute him or her with another individual

---

54. *Cathechismus*, 112. De Rhodes cites the terse Sino-Vietnamese text: "Dao sinh nhat, nhat sinh nhi, nhi sinh tam, tam sinh van vat" (112). This quotation is taken from the Tao Te Ching, chap. 42, which reads in full: "Tao produced the One. The One produced the two. The two produced the three. And the three produced the ten thousand things. The ten thousand things carry the *yin* and embrace the *yang,* and through the blending of the material force (*ch'i*) they achieve harmony." See *A Source Book in Chinese Philosophy,* translated and compiled by Wing-Tsit Chan (Princeton: Princeton University Press, 1963), 160.

In this cryptic statement, Tao Te Ching seems to be saying that though there are many beings, there is only one Being and that Being (the One) comes from Non-Being (Tao). The One (Being) is the original material force or the Great Ultimate, the two are the *yin* and the *yang*, the three is their blending with the original material force, and the ten thousand things are things carrying *yin* and embracing *yang.* For de Rhodes, who followed Greek metaphysics, to say, as Tao Te Ching does, that Being comes from Non-Being is pure nonsense.

55. *Cathechismus*, 112.

56. De Rhodes also remarks that the Tonkinese were so superstitious that they would not undertake anything important such as travel by sea or by land, war, and wedding without consulting the chicken legs to discern the possible outcome. See *Histoire du Royaume,* 75–76.

in the hope of confusing the ancestor. This was done, to no avail, in the case of the lord of Tonkin's eldest son who died despite the sorcerer's trick.

There was another custom, abominable in de Rhodes's eyes, of harnessing a horse as the sick person lies dying. The sorcerer would have the horse readied to transport the soul away, while the relatives would weep profusely, imploring it to remain with them. As de Rhodes says, the soul is indeed carried away, not by the horse but by "the devils straight to hell."[57]

Finally, what shocked de Rhodes the most is that after the sick person passed away, the family would still make use of the services of the Taoist sorcerer who had failed to cure their loved one. Together with him, the family would go to a medium who invoked the devil under the name of the deceased.[58] The devil would enter the medium whose face would take on terrifying colors. De Rhodes believed that God allowed this demonic possession to punish the superstitiousness of these people. Then, the deceased person would allegedly converse with various members of the family. De Rhodes notes with sarcasm that the soul does not fail to ask that the family offer him or her meats and drinks, which, of course, will go to the sorcerer and the medium. At other times, the sorcerer would deceive the family by making the dead speak through a mirror and say what he wants.[59]

From de Rhodes's vivid descriptions of these practices, it is highly likely that he was an eyewitness to many of them during his three-year mission in Tonkin. No doubt he considered religious Taoism, with its use of witchcraft and magic, a serious threat to the Christian faith. As mentioned above, he regarded it as the most pernicious of the Three Religions imported from China to Vietnam because of its widespread popularity, even with the ruling class, and its worship of demons. For people who lacked medical knowledge and whose main weapons against diseases and death were magic and witchcraft, religious Taoism must have been exceedingly attractive.

De Rhodes's strategy against religious Taoism was a mixture of the natural and the supernatural. On the one hand, he would simply show by his actions that such practices as divining chicken feet and consulting the horoscope were totally useless and could sometimes hinder the prosecution of a worthy project. For example, once, when twenty merchant ships were preparing to sail and the chicken feet were interpreted to be a bad omen, their captains decided to postpone the trip, whereas de Rhodes persuaded the captain of his boat to set sail. His boat had a peaceful voyage and arrived on time, while the others had to

---

57. See *Histoire du Royaume*, 75.

58. De Rhodes related that at least twice he had to perform exorcism on female mediums who later became Christian. One of them was a certain Monica who was very pious but who "before being baptized had practiced superstitious magic and even the diabolical art of medium" (*Histoire du Royaume*, 250). The other was a medium "whose stock in trade is making the devil speak through their mouths, especially at funerals, where magicians pretend to call up the souls of the deceased to console the children" (*Divers voyages*, 142–43).

59. See *Histoire du Royaume*, 77–78.

wait for fifteen or twenty days, and even then sailed in foul weather.[60] He also invoked the action of the lord of Cochinchina who refused to heed his advisors who, on the basis of the horoscope, told him that it would be inauspicious to undertake an assault against his northern rival who had invaded his territory. Despite the presumed bad omen, the lord of Cochinchina succeeded in repelling his attacker.[61] With these actions de Rhodes hoped to convince pagans of "the futility of their religion and of their foolish superstitions."[62]

On the other hand, de Rhodes sought to demonstrate that Christian sacred objects and rituals were much more powerful and effective than those of Taoism, even for the healing of diseases and the resuscitation of the dead: "By means of the holy cross and holy water, those good Christians drove away devils as a matter of course and cured all sorts of diseases. By giving them four or five drops of this sacred water to drink, they cured some blind people and even brought two dead people back to life."[63]

Once, a pagan chief with a Christian wife asked de Rhodes to send some Christians to his town to cure many of his subjects who had fallen sick. De Rhodes dispatched six catechists whose miraculous healing would put any Taoist sorcerer to shame:

> They started out, weapons in hands to make war on the devil, who was held to be the cause of these ailments. These were the cross, holy water, blessed palms, holy candles, and pictures of the Virgin that I had given them at baptism. They went, planted crosses at the entrance, the middle, and the end of the town, and visited the sick, saying a prayer, and giving them a few drops of holy water to drink. In less than a week's time they cured 272 sick people. News of it spread throughout the kingdom. The chief of the town came to thank me with many tears. This heartened the Christians greatly, and many pagans were thereby convinced of their errors.[64]

At other times, de Rhodes would commend some Christians for their efforts directly to frustrate the magical powers of Taoist sorcerers with Christian means. He recounts with obvious pleasure the work of two Christians who, through their prayers and by the power of the crucifixes they carried in their sleeves, successfully thwarted the attempt of a medium to invoke the devil. Again, he reports with pride the work of a young Christian by the name of Martin who, by the power of Jesus Christ, dispatched into hell the demon whose power was

---

60. See *Histoire du Royaume*, 76.

61. See *Histoire du Royaume*, 96–97. Here de Rhodes also mentions the superstitious custom that Tonkinese men had of returning home, if upon setting out on a journey, they met a woman or sneezed or heard someone sneeze. All these things were deemed to bring bad luck.

62. *Histoire du Royaume*, 98.

63. *Divers voyages*, 97.

64. *Divers voyages*, 97–98. See also *Histoire du Royaume*, 185–86. In the latter account, de Rhodes says that 270 (rather than 272) people were cured and that the sick would throw up a "filthy and putrid liquid, symptom of a diabolical possession and sign of healing" (p. 186).

invoked by a sorcerer to make a human statue made of sticks walk and a heavy stone jump.[65]

In sum, then, with regard to Vietnamese Taoism, while not exhibiting much understanding of the subtle doctrines of philosophical Taoism, de Rhodes possessed a remarkable firsthand knowledge of religious Taoism and its practices of magic, witchcraft, and sorcery. He was rightly concerned by the large appeal it had with the masses. Pastorally, he sought to counter it by showing that Taoist practices are useless and that Christian practices are far superior to the Taoist ones. No doubt de Rhodes believed that Christian sacred objects such as holy water had a curative virtue and recommended their use together with prayers and faith in Jesus.[66]

There was, of course, a danger that replacing Taoist witchcraft and magical arts with Christian sacred objects would produce a similar superstitious attitude toward the latter. To prevent this, de Rhodes sternly warned Christians not to look for material gains from healing with sacred objects. Indeed, he reported, as a cautionary tale for others, that one of the Christian leaders was punished by God with death because he had accepted a reward from the chief of the town in which he had performed some healings.[67] Furthermore, he inculcated in his neophytes faith in the power of God rather than in the objects themselves and insisted on the necessity of the virtue of humility.[68]

DE RHODES AND VIETNAMESE CONFUCIANISM

Of the Three Religions de Rhodes held Confucianism, of which he gives the Vietnamese name, *dao nho,* in highest esteem. In evaluating Confucianism he carefully distinguishes between the teaching of Confucius and the cult rendered to him. With regard to Confucius's teaching, de Rhodes recognizes that "Confucius, in the books we have received from him, gives proper instructions to form good morals."[69] He alludes with approval to Confucius's emphasis on the necessity of cultivating one's character prior to regulating the family and governing the state.[70] He concedes that in Confucius's teachings on law, politics, and the administration of justice, "there is nothing contrary to the principles

---

65. See *Histoire du Royaume,* 78–80.

66. De Rhodes notes the Tonkinese Christians' reverence for holy water: "They have such reverence for holy water that they come to fetch it from five or six days' journey away. They carry some in porcelain receptacles attached to their arms on beautiful bracelets. They give it to all the sick to drink, with marvelous results. Every Sunday I was obliged to bless at least 500 large jars of this sacred water to satisfy their pious desires." See *Divers voyages,* 102.

67. See *Histoire du Royaume,* 186–87; *Divers voyages,* 98.

68. See *Histoire du Royaume,* 86, where a young Christian named Matthew, who had succeeded in preventing a Taoist sorcerer from performing his tricks, was advised to "humble himself and to keep secret the grace that God has given him and not to divulge what he had done lest the pagans would react by ill-treating the Christians."

69. *Histoire du Royaume,* 62.

70. See *Histoire du Royaume,* 62–63. The allusion is to *The Great Learning* text. See Chan, *A Source Book in Chinese Philosophy,* 86–87.

of the Christian religion that should be rejected or condemned by those who follow them."[71]

De Rhodes's most serious objection to Confucius is the latter's silence on the existence of "the supreme creator and Lord of all things, source and origin of all holiness and goodness."[72] He argues that either Confucius knew or did not know that this divine creator exists. If he did not, then he could not be good and holy. If he did but did not teach this truth to others, he would not be worthy to be called good and holy either.[73]

Furthermore, even when Confucius spoke of "the first principle of all things," he made it out to be "bodily, insensible, lacking in knowledge, deprived of reason and soul, and incapable and unworthy of worship and adoration."[74] Granted that Confucius prescribed the cult of heaven, still it was a duty Confucius reserved for the king and did not make incumbent upon everybody. Finally, de Rhodes reproaches Confucius for never mentioning eternal life and the immortality of the soul, thus opening the door for atheism and immorality of all sorts.[75] For all these reasons, he does not deserve, in de Rhodes's judgment, to be called and treated as a "saint."

Confucius's disqualification for the title of "saint" brings us to the issue of the cult rendered him. De Rhodes describes in detail how the Tonkinese "worshiped" Confucius:

> The Tonkinese, young and old, hold Confucius in such high regard that they revere him like a god, and inculcate this respect in their children from the tenderest age. On the first day when the children begin school to learn the Chinese characters, the teacher, before accepting them as his students, would kneel with them and teach them the first lesson of how to invoke

---

71. *Histoire du Royaume,* 63. De Rhodes limits himself to making general observations on Confucius's teachings; he does not discuss at any length such basic Confucian concepts as the rectification of names (*cheng-ming*), humaneness (*jen*), the gentleman (*chün-tzu*), the mean (*chung*), and reciprocity (*shu*).

72. *Cathechismus,* 113.

73. De Rhodes reports that he once used this line of argument in a sermon in a church in Tonkin where there were, besides Christians, a group of Confucianists. The Christians "listened to him with great satisfaction, whereas the Confucianists . . . were very saddened and confused, though they remained obstinate in their old error" (*Histoire du Royaume,* 62). Of course, they could reply that though Confucius never spoke of *Ti* (the Lord) or *Shang-ti* (the Lord on High), he often spoke of *T'ien* (Heaven) as purposive and as the Master of all things. He repeatedly referred to the *Tien-ming,* that is, the mandate or will or order of Heaven. See, for instance, *The Analects,* 2, 4: "At fifteen my mind was set on learning. At thirty my character had been formed. At forty I had no more perplexities. At fifty I knew the Mandate of Heaven. At sixty I was at ease with whatever I heard. At seventy I could follow my heart's desire without transgressing moral principles." See Chan, *A Source Book in Chinese Philosophy,* 22.

74. *Histoire du Royaume,* 63.

75. See *Histoire du Royaume,* 63–64. It is true that Confucius was reluctant to speak of spiritual beings and life after death, as is testified by this statement from *The Analects,* 11, 11: "Chi-lu (Tzu-lu) asked about the spiritual beings. Confucius said: 'If we are not yet able to serve human beings, how can we serve spiritual beings?' 'I venture to ask about death.' Confucius said: 'We do not yet know about life, how can we know about death?" (Chan, *A Source Book in Chinese Philosophy,* 36). Clearly, Confucius's ultimate attitude is not denial of and skepticism about the afterlife, but his humanistic concern about the present welfare of human beings.

Confucius and implore his assistance. The purpose is to obtain a quick mind and facility in learning what will be taught, what the locals call *sang da,* literally, bright stomach. . . . Even the doctors and men of letters have fallen to this folly. Before presenting themselves for the examinations to obtain a degree, they would make vows and offer prayers to Confucius in the hope of enjoying success, and when they have received their degrees, they would prostrate themselves before a small altar dedicated to Confucius to render him thanks. This is a foolish superstition much in vogue among the pagans.[76]

Against this cult of Confucius, de Rhodes adopted several distinct strategies. First, he corrected the false rumors that the Jesuits condoned it: "We have trouble persuading converted Christians not to genuflect before his statues, which almost all have in their houses; and those who started the rumor that the Jesuits permit their neophytes this idolatry are very badly informed."[77]

Second, de Rhodes recognizes the legitimacy of rendering Confucius the kind of reverence and honor due to other teachers (such as kowtowing to the ground) which does not exceed "a purely political cult."[78]

Third, de Rhodes demands that if there are pagans present at the cult to Confucius, in order to avoid misleading them and giving scandal, Christians must explain beforehand that such reverence "is not done to Confucius as to a god but only as a teacher from whom one has received writings and political guidance."[79]

Fourth, since very few Christians would have the courage to make such a public protestation, de Rhodes urges most vigorously that "such reverence to Confucius be omitted, lest it becomes a trap to someone."[80]

In sum, de Rhodes's attitude to Confucianism was ambivalent. On the one hand, he acknowledged its profound and beneficial influence on the Vietnamese society, especially in its moral, social, and political teachings. On the other hand, he found its doctrines on fundamental matters such as the existence of

---

76. *Histoire du Royaume,* 64–65.

77. *Divers voyages,* 54. De Rhodes does not name those who spread this rumor against the Jesuits, but it is likely that these were other missionaries who were opposed to the Jesuits' method of inculturation such as the Dominicans and Franciscans. Of course, Matteo Ricci and the Jesuits who agreed with him did allow Christians to participate in the Confucian rites such as the ceremonies of awarding degrees, because they believed that these had social and civil and not religious significance. On the other hand, they did not give a blanket permission to take part in all the rites performed in the Confucian temples, especially where animal sacrifices were involved, because they smacked of superstition. Opponents of the Jesuits forbade participation in any and every Confucian rite, because they saw all Confucian rites as having a religious significance and therefore superstitious.

78. *Cathechismus,* 114. The Latin text uses the well-known phrase of *cultum publicum,* whereas the Vietnamese text simply says that the cult of Confucius should not go beyond the norms of politeness. The Latin phrase echoes the interpretation that Matteo Ricci gave to the Chinese cult of Confucius. For a succinct presentation of Ricci's position regarding the cult of Confucius, see George Minamiki, *The Chinese Rites Controversy from Its Beginning to Modern Times* (Chicago: Loyola University Press, 1985), 15–24.

79. *Cathechismus,* 115–16.

80. *Cathechismus,* 116.

a creator God, the immortality of the soul, and the afterlife seriously defective. The same ambivalence is shown with the regard to the cult of Confucius. As a civil and political act, it is a legitimate practice. On the other hand, given its potential for superstition, de Rhodes was more a rigorist than a probabilist in proscribing it altogether.

In establishing this policy, de Rhodes differed from his confreres in China who took a pastorally more lenient position. The reason is that his confreres in China were scholars who believed they could prove, on the basis of the Chinese classics and with the help of rationalist neo-Confucian philosophers, that such a cult had, strictly speaking, no religious meaning. By contrast, de Rhodes was no scholar of Confucianism; his knowledge of the Confucian classics was minimal. But he was deeply in touch with the common people for whom many of the gestures and objects in the Confucian rites, whatever their original symbolism, were susceptible to superstitious interpretation. Therefore, he thought it wise, pastorally, to forbid them altogether. Such a strategy seems unduly narrow and might have offended some Vietnamese Confucian scholars and deterred them from accepting Christianity.[81] For the majority of Vietnamese Christians, however, it offered at the time useful guidelines in dealing with such a confusing situation.

DE RHODES AND VIETNAMESE INDIGENOUS RELIGION

As has been said in chapter 1, the Vietnamese indigenous religion is characterized by a belief in a multitude of spirits (among whom *Ong Troi,* that is, the transcendent and personal deity and creator, occupies the supreme place) and above all by the cult of ancestors. This is the primary religious matrix into which the Three Religions were amalgamated.

With regard to the cult rendered to Heaven (*Te Nam Giao*), it would seem that in 1628 de Rhodes had the opportunity to see King Le Than Tong go to the temple to offer, in his capacity of the Son of Heaven (*thien tu*), the *Nam Giao* sacrifice. On the last day of the year, Lord Trinh Trang, escorted by his army, went to bathe in a river, a gesture symbolizing relinquishment of the old life and reception of the new life.[82] At midnight (*giao thua*), a cannon discharge marked the end of the old year and the beginning of the new year. On the morning of New Year's Day, the lord, followed by all the mandarins, forty thousand soldiers, three thousand horses, and three hundred elephants betook himself to the palace of King Le Than Tong. At the lord's arrival, the king came out of his palace and was carried to the temple where, as the representative of the people before Heaven, he offered the *Nam Giao* sacrifice. At the end of the ceremony,

---

81. This seems to be the case of at least two influential mandarins. The first was the teacher of Lord Nguyen Phuoc Lan and the second a magistrate at the court. Both of them showed great sympathy for de Rhodes and Christianity, but both refused to become Christians. See *Divers voyages,* 182–85.

82. See Tissanier, 266.

three cannon shots were fired to alert the people of the conclusion of the sacrifice. Then the king was escorted back to the palace where the lord and the mandarins presented him with their New Year best wishes.[83] De Rhodes has nothing but the greatest respect for the *Te Nam Giao,* which he interprets as a "sacrifice offered to the heavenly King"[84] and uses it to illustrate the fatherhood of God.[85]

With regard to the cult of ancestors among the Vietnamese, de Rhodes gives a detailed and surprisingly accurate description of it: "There is perhaps no other nation on this inhabited earth that honors and venerates the souls and bodies of the dead more than the people of Tonkin."[86]

This respect for the dead is manifested, says de Rhodes, in three ways. First, no money is spared to procure the most magnificent coffin for the deceased. Second, a most solemn funeral is organized with the attendance of as many notables as possible. Third, no expenses are dispensed with to look for, with the help of a geomancer, an appropriate burial site so that the dead person may enjoy a peaceful rest and his or her descendants may live in prosperity.[87]

While admiring these marks of respect for the deceased,[88] de Rhodes takes great offense at the Vietnamese celebrations of the death anniversary which he correctly calls *le gio.* The central event of these celebrations is the sumptuous funeral banquet. De Rhodes describes it in details available only to an eyewit-

---

83. For a detailed description of this ceremony, see *Histoire du Royaume,* 11–13.

84. *Cathechismus,* 21.

85. See *Cathechismus,* 22–23.

86. *Histoire du Royaume,* 86.

87. See *Histoire du Royaume,* 80–82. De Rhodes mentions that this belief in the necessity of selecting an auspicious burial site and the use of geomancers to find such a site were also widespread in Cochinchina, especially among the lords: "They [i.e., the princes] firmly believe that the good fortune of their whole family depends on the place they choose to bury their parents, especially their mothers, convinced that if they can find a really suitable place to bury them, all their progeny will continue in the royal line; that if the burial place is unsuitable, their fortune will soon leave them and they will certainly lose their crowns" (*Divers voyages,* 170).

De Rhodes also describes in detail the mourning for the dead: "It is an inviolable custom of all the people of this country for the children to mourn their father and the wife for her husband for three years" (*Histoire du Royaume,* 83). During the mourning period, different costumes are worn, depending on the degree of relationship to the dead. For three years, men let their hair grow over their eyes, whereas women cut theirs short. Widows are forbidden to remarry during this period. After the mourning, the body is exhumed, the bones washed with perfumed water and then placed in a small urn. If the person dies outside of his or her birthplace, he or she will be brought back there.

88. De Rhodes was not reluctant to put on the most solemn funerals possible to impress upon non-Christians that Christians were no less respectful of the dead. At least twice the strategy worked. When a Christian soldier died in 1627, "we put on the most magnificent and solemn funeral possible in which all our Portuguese people and the new Christians took part in good order. The rituals were celebrated in public, in full view of a great number of pagans who not only were deeply edified by the charity of the Christians but also were impressed with favorable feelings toward our religion" (*Histoire du Royaume,* 141). News of the funeral reached one of Lord Trinh Trang's sisters, who sent for de Rhodes to receive information about Christianity.

The second time happened in 1630 when one of the soldiers was burned to death by cannon powder. Lord Trinh Trang asked the Christians to hold the funeral for him: "We took charge and assembled for this purpose more than one thousand Christians who accompanied the body to the burial site" (*Histoire du Royaume,* 218). This earned a respite in the lord's opposition to de Rhodes.

ness.[89] At the beginning of the banquet, the eldest son addresses his deceased father, expressing the gratitude of the children.[90] Then he and the entire family prostrate themselves to the ground and invite the deceased to come and share in the meal. At the end of the banquet, the eldest son, in the name of his siblings and all the people in the family, asks the deceased father or mother to protect them and grant them health, wealth, and longevity. Once again they prostrate themselves to the ground as if to receive the blessings from their ancestors.

De Rhodes discerns three "gross errors" in this practice. First, it presupposes that the deceased parents can freely come and go as they please or when invited, ignoring the barriers separating them from us. Second, it foolishly believes that the dead need food and drink like the living. Third, it wrongly supposes that the deceased have the power to grant our requests for protection and good things.[91]

Besides the anniversary banquet, de Rhodes also mentions two other practices connected with the cult of the dead. First, there was the custom of making houses and furniture in bamboo and paper and burning them, in the belief that the dead will make use of them. Rich people, de Rhodes notes, would spend a fortune on these things. Second, during the sixth month of the lunar calendar, there was the practice of making paper clothes and burning them for the use of the souls that have no one to take care of them (the Vietnamese call them *co hon,* literally, orphaned souls). Twice a month, school children would raise money to buy rice and cook it, then put part of the cooked rice on the roofs of houses for the *co hon.*[92]

To combat all these superstitious customs, de Rhodes uses a two-pronged approach, first by opposing them with the doctrine of the spirituality of the soul, and secondly by substituting alternative Christian practices. The human soul, de Rhodes argues, is spiritual and therefore does not need food, clothes, houses, or other material things, much less if these things are burned. With unvarnished sarcasm he writes:

> How would the Vietnamese dare to offer to their deceased parents these imaginary things for their use? You may say: By being burned, these things

---

89. See *Histoire du Royaume,* 84–89. De Rhodes narrates in vivid details the grandiose celebrations organized by Lord Trinh Trang of Tonkin for his deceased father at which de Rhodes must have been present (86–88). He also mentions the festivities put on by Lord Nguyen Phuoc Lan of Cochinchina for his departed ancestors to which the four Spanish Poor Clares and two Franciscan priests were invited. See *Divers voyages,* 248.

90. At the beginning of the banquet, the eldest son would make the following address to his deceased father, which de Rhodes reports and deserves to be quoted in full for the touching sentiments of filial piety expressed therein: "My deeply honored Father, welcome to your house from which you have been long absent. You have been away from your beloved children who owe so much to you. You have fed, raised, and educated us with so much care, for whom you have procured many good things with so much pain. All our consolation and all our desire is to know that you dwell among us and to perform for you all the obligations we owe you for your kindnesses. Please accept with pleasure this humble offering which we have prepared in gratitude for the good things you have given us and in this way allay in some measure the sorrows we feel because of your absence" (*Histoire du Royaume,* 85).

91. See *Histoire du Royaume,* 84–85.

92. See *Histoire du Royaume,* 89–92.

become something else. You hit the nail on the head: by being burned, they become partly flames and partly ashes. But then, which part do you send to your parents? If it is ashes that you send, how can they live well amidst ashes? How can they be dressed properly and cleanly with ashes? If it is flames that you send, then indeed you are sending them flames, because these works of error and sin, which you perform and which you learned from your parents, are like flames to increase the sufferings of your deceased parents. Just as the joy of the saints in heaven increases when the good teachings they have taught are put into practice by their disciples after their death, so also those who have taught and practiced perverse teachings suffer more pains and torments in the other life, even if they are dead, on account of the new sins of those they have taught.[93]

De Rhodes was deeply aware that filial piety, especially as it is demonstrated toward the deceased parents, belongs to the very core of the Vietnamese culture. Hence, rather than simply ridiculing these superstitious customs, he was solicitous to replace them with practices acceptable to the Christian faith, lest the Christians be accused of failing in this most sacred duty of filial piety. As he carefully notes, "there are two months in the year, the seventh and the last, that are devoted by all people to celebrating the memory of their deceased parents, which no one would miss. This should be a shame to the Christians, who are less observant in these duties of piety and charity to the souls of the departed."[94]

The alternative practices are offering prayers for the souls in purgatory and works of charity. Votive masses and prayers were no doubt offered for the dead in seventeenth-century Vietnam.[95] With regard to works of charity, he explicitly

---

93. *Cathechismus*, 122–23. See also *Histoire du Royaume*, 90. It is to be noted that whereas de Rhodes took a rigorous position toward anniversary banquets, in 1658 his successors in Tonkin, Onuphre Borges and Joseph Tissanier, allowed Tonkinese Christians to do prostrations in front of the ancestral altar and to prepare banquets for the deceased provided they did not invite them to eat. The reason for this, says Tissanier, is to allow Vietnamese Christians to keep some of their native customs and not to make the Christian religion too odious by abolishing some indifferent practices. See Tissanier, 169–70. In the middle of the eighteenth century, Jesuit missionaries António de Vasconcellos and Stefano Lopes allowed Vietnamese Christians to prepare, on the death anniversary, a banquet at the tomb of the deceased. There was a plate of meat, sweet things, and areca and betel. On the one end of the tomb there was placed a cushion, and on the other a pipe and tobacco. All around the tomb there were flowers, gilded paper, incense sticks, and lighted candles. The family members would prostrate themselves to the ground to greet the deceased and invite him or her to come and take part in the banquet. Then a second round of prostrations was made to thank the deceased for having accepted the offerings which they then ate. All these rituals were performed to express gratitude to the deceased. See Favre, *Lettres édifiantes*, 31-32, and Do Quang Chinh, 319–20.

94. *Histoire du Royaume*, 88–89. Actually, besides the New Year (*Tet*), the two most important Vietnamese festivals for the dead are *Thanh Minh* and *Trung Nguyen*. *Thanh Minh* (Pure Light) is celebrated on the third day of the third month of the lunar calendar. On this day, the Vietnamese visit the tombs of their family members to clean them (*tao mo*). *Trung Nguyen*, also known as *Vu Lan*, is celebrated on the fifteenth day of the seventh month. It is dedicated to prayers and sacrifices for the wandering souls.

95. De Rhodes relates that one Christian named Secunda had died and subsequently appeared to one of her relatives who saw "on a nearby mountain a huge ball of fire in the midst of which Secunda stood moaning and accusing all her relatives of extreme cruelty because they did not bother in the least to help her in her misfortune" (*Divers voyages*, 215). Upon hearing this, de Rhodes immediately said Mass for the deceased woman who was never seen again in such a deplorable state.

suggested that instead of burning paper clothes for the dead, Christians should use the money to buy real clothes for the living poor. He noted that his suggestion was well received by both Christians and pagans so that one poor person received some twenty-eight robes in one year as the result![96]

For a Christian missionary, local religions inevitably pose the most difficult challenges to the work of evangelization. As Vatican II acknowledges, these non-Christian religions do contain elements of goodness and truth which must be regarded as "a preparation for the Gospel" and that "whatever good is found in the minds and hearts of men and women or in the rites and customs of peoples, these elements not only are preserved from destruction, but are purified, raised up, and perfected for the glory of God, the confusion of the devil and the happiness of humanity."[97] It is clear that de Rhodes's missionary strategy of *Aufhebung* vis-à-vis the Vietnamese religions is not completely at odds with Vatican II's recommendations.

However, though he did acknowledge the presence of some good elements in non-Christian religions, he did not view them in as positive a light as the council. In this he was very much the child of his age. For him non-Christian religions were so vitiated by superstition and idolatry that little, if anything, in them (except some teachings of Confucius and the respect for the dead and filial piety in the Vietnamese indigenous religion) could be accepted without a radical purification by the Christian faith.

ADAPTATIONS OF CHRISTIAN LITURGY

So far we have seen how de Rhodes modified or substituted certain Vietnamese cultural and religious usages such as the swearing of the loyalty oath, the erection of a bamboo pole *(cay neu)* on New Year's Eve, the three-day celebration of the New Year, Taoist magical arts, Confucian rites, and ancestor worship with Christian practices or at least with practices acceptable to the Christian faith. Next, we will investigate de Rhodes's reverse attempts to help the Vietnamese make sense of the Christian liturgical celebrations.

1. De Rhodes reported that the Vietnamese Christians celebrated Christmas with great solemnity. Most interesting is his practice of administering baptism *in public* and *during the Mass* so that the connection between the physical birth of Jesus and the spiritual birth of catechumens would be made transparent. The congregation sang, besides religious songs, *Christmas carols,* which means they had been translated into Vietnamese. Furthermore, de Rhodes respected the cul-

---

96. See *Histoire du Royaume,* 90–91.
97. *Lumen Gentium,* no. 17. See also Vatican II's *Nostra Aetate* (Declaration on the Relation of the Church to Non-Christian Religions), no. 2: "The Catholic Church rejects nothing of what is true and holy in these religions.... Let Christians, while witnessing to their own faith and way of life, acknowledge, preserve and encourage the spiritual and moral truths found among non-Christians as well as their social life and culture."

tural custom of not allowing women to go out at night, so that he told them to come to the Christmas Day Mass only. After the Mass, he exposed the statue of the Infant Jesus for the faithful's adoration.[98]

2. On the feast of the Purification of the Virgin, de Rhodes organized the solemn blessing of the candles. The catechumens carried them during the procession into the church and afterward were allowed to bring them home. De Rhodes noted that they had these candles lighted when they were on their deathbed to prepare for a holy death. Moreover, these candles also helped Christians break the taboo common among the Vietnamese of not using the word "death" but rather a circumlocution, especially in front of a person of rank.[99]

3. With regard to fasting, de Rhodes noted that Vietnamese non-Christians observed an extremely rigorous fast in honor of their "idols." They abstained not only from meat and eggs but also from milk products and fish of all kinds, not merely for a few months but for the whole life. Given this custom, de Rhodes encouraged Christians to practice fasting beyond the minimum church requirements, not only during Lent but also during Advent.[100]

4. On Palm Sunday, there was the blessing of the palms in which not only Christians but also pagans participated. Since there were no olive trees in Vietnam, de Rhodes substituted olive branches with those of local coconut trees. Christians kept these blessed branches at home to chase away demons and evil spirits. On Holy Friday the cross was exposed for veneration by the faithful.[101]

5. One of de Rhodes's most interesting paraliturgical innovations, and one that is still in use, is what is known as *ngam dung,* that is, standing meditation. To enable the Christians to participate in the liturgy of the Holy Week, in particular the Tenebrae, and to obviate their ignorance of Latin, de Rhodes composed in Vietnamese the mysteries of the Passion in fifteen *ngam* (meditations). Each of the meditations is declaimed, with the accompaniment of drum and gong, by a faithful who stands (*dung*) on a platform in the middle of the church. Behind the platform there is a crucifix and a fifteen-branch candelabrum. At the end of each meditation, a candle is extinguished, followed by the common recital of one Our Father, seven Hail Marys, and one Glory Be. This well-attended liturgy, which resembles the classical Vietnamese theater (*cheo, tuong*), with its dialogues between the assembly and the declaimer, and the use of drum and gong, is still celebrated in many parts of Vietnam on every Friday of Lent and each evening of the Holy Week.[102]

6. De Rhodes has not provided us with detailed information on how he celebrated the sacraments and how he adapted them to the needs of the Vietnamese. Concerning the celebration of the eucharist, given that the mission in China had

---

98. See *Histoire du Royaume,* 200.
99. See *Histoire du Royaume,* 201–2.
100. See *Histoire du Royaume,* 202–3.
101. See *Histoire du Royaume,* 203.
102. See *Histoire du Royaume,* 203–4.

failed to make use of Pope Paul V's authorization to celebrate the Mass, recite the breviary, and administer the sacraments in Chinese, it is highly likely that de Rhodes celebrated the Mass in Latin and not in Vietnamese.[103] Furthermore, we learn that de Rhodes celebrated the Mass with the head uncovered. In China as well as in Vietnam, no one was permitted to appear before the king with the head uncovered, except criminals as a sign of shame. De Rhodes justified his practice of celebrating the Mass with the head uncovered with the argument that while the priest appears before God as the representative of Christ, he is also the representative of sinners imploring God for the remission of their sins. Hence, he can appear before God with the head uncovered.[104]

For those who could not attend Sunday Mass because of distance or because of the absence of the priest, de Rhodes encouraged them to meet together for prayer and devotions.[105] Moreover, a calendar was composed and distributed to Christians to facilitate remembrance of Sundays, holy days of obligation, and fast days.[106]

It is known that in his administration of baptism de Rhodes used the baptismal formula in Vietnamese. His Vietnamese baptismal formula is: "Tao rua may, nhan nhat danh Cha, va Con, va Spirito Santo. Amen."[107] For reasons

---

103. On June 27, 1615, the Holy Office issued the instruction *Romanae Sedis Antistes* allowing the Chinese mission three things: to wear a head cover during the divine offices; to translate the Bible into literary Chinese; and for future Chinese priests to celebrate the Mass, recite the breviary, and administer the sacraments in literary Chinese. Whereas the first authorization was immediately enacted, the last two were postponed *sine die*. On September 9, 1659, Pope Alexander VII issued the bull *Super Cathedram* permitting the ordination to the priesthood of Chinese men who could read Latin, even though they could not understand it. For the question of Chinese liturgies, see François Bontinck, *La Lutte autour de la liturgie chinoise aux XVIIè et XVIIIè siècles* (Paris: Béatrice-Nauwelaerts, 1962).

104. See Tissanier, 270.

105. This practice was extremely important for the faith life of the Christian community, especially because most of the time during 1640–45 de Rhodes was practically the only priest in all of Vietnam. We are told that near the border between Tonkin and Cochinchina, "there were at least a thousand Christians who were living very holy lives although they had never seen a priest" (*Divers voyages*, 181).

106. See *Histoire du Royaume*, 249.

107. Literally, the formula means: "I wash you, in the one name of the Father, the Son, and the Holy Spirit." De Rhodes's translation of the baptismal formula was subjected to discussion by the Jesuits both in Macao and Vietnam between 1640 and 1645. In 1645, a meeting was held in Macao to discuss it, presided over by João Cabral and Alvare de Semedo, vice-provincials of Japan and China respectively. At the meeting, the baptismal formula in Vietnamese proposed for approval read: *Tao rua may nhan danh Cha, va Con, va Spirito santo*, literally, "I wash you in the name of the Father, and the Son, and the Holy Spirit." Note the absence of the word *nhat*, i.e., "one," after the word *nhan*. At the end of the meeting, thirty-one of thirty-five fathers, half of whom were professors of theology and several of whom knew Vietnamese, approved this formula and rejected the formula proposed by de Rhodes. Among those who were unfavorable to de Rhodes's formula were the two vice-provincials and several missionaries who had been or would be in Vietnam, such as António Barbosa, Gaspar do Amaral, Giovanni Filippo de Marini, B. Cittadelli, A. Ferreira, F. Rangel, P. Alberto, and F. Montefusculi. See *Manoscritto em que se prova, que a forma do Bauptismo pronunciada em ligoa Annamica he verdadeira*, in ARSI, JS 80, ff. 35–38v; *Circa formam Baptismi Annamico Idiomate*, in ARSI, JS 80, ff. 76–80v (written in Macao in 1648); Marini's letter, written probably in 1652 to J. L. Confalonieri, Assistant for Italy, about the baptismal formula adopted by de Rhodes for the Vietnamese, in ARSI, JS 80, f. 96; Marini's letter written from Tonkin in 1655 to F. de Tavora, Assistant for Portugal, on the same subject in ARSI, JS 80, ff. 88–89v. On this theme, see Do Quang Chinh, 303, and idem, *Lich Su Chu Quoc Ngu 1620–1659* (Saigon: Ra Khoi, 1972), 68–76.

unexplained, de Rhodes left the words *Spirito Santo* untranslated, even though he could easily have found the Vietnamese equivalents for them.[108] The reason de Rhodes used the Vietnamese formula for baptism is probably so that it could be used in the administration of the sacrament by catechists and other lay Vietnamese Christians who did not know Latin.

With regard to the baptismal rites themselves, de Rhodes took pains to explain gestures and things that may suggest magic. He reported that once as he was about to baptize eighty catechumens and was using the blessed salt in a plate as part of the ceremony, a man rushed into the church and shouted to the catechumens: "Wretched people! Be careful! He is performing sorcery with the thing in the plate!" De Rhodes had to explain to the people that the plate contained nothing but ordinary salt that had been blessed.[109]

Lastly, in the administration of the sacrament of penance, de Rhodes found that the practice of auricular confession for women, even in public, with a board separating the confessor from the penitent, was offensive to the Vietnamese, especially to pagans. Once, de Rhodes relates, soldiers came into the church to listen to what the women were telling him. He resolved the problem by using two adjoining houses, the women staying in the one house and making their confessions through the wall to the priest who stayed in the other.[110]

7. De Rhodes repeatedly referred to books of prayers that he dictated to those who were leaders of the community so they could teach them to others.[111] Unfortunately, no such books survived to help us form an idea of how de Rhodes translated what he calls "Catholic prayers." Of course, these were not liturgical texts, as de Rhodes still used Latin for sacramental celebrations. There is no doubt that such prayers include the Our Father, the Hail Mary, the Glory Be, the acts of faith, hope, and charity, the act of contrition, the Apostles' Creed, morning and evening prayers, and various litanies.[112]

DE RHODES AND CHURCH ORGANIZATION

Besides the multiple challenges of culture, religion, and worship, one of the most practical and urgent problems facing de Rhodes as he carried out the task of *plantatio ecclesiae* was the day-to-day organization of church life. In his work

---

108. The Vietnamese words for Holy Spirit are *Thanh Than*. The current baptismal formula is: "Cha rua con, nhan danh Cha va Con va Thanh Than."

109. See *Histoire du Royaume*, 194–95.

110. See *Histoire du Royaume*, 247. Of course, auricular confession, possibly in a confessional box, was the only form of celebrating the sacrament of penance available in the seventeenth century. It is the close proximity between the foreign priest and the female penitent and the *sotto voce* confession that caused the scandal.

111. See, for example, *Histoire du Royaume*, 139, 145–46, 236. On Day Four of *Cathechismus*, de Rhodes says that at this stage catechumens should be given the Our Father, the Hail Mary, and the Apostles' Creed to learn by heart (133).

112. Of course, de Rhodes may not be the first to translate these prayers into Vietnamese. It is likely that other Jesuits, in particular Francisco de Pina, might have already translated them.

of evangelization de Rhodes most often had to shoulder the burden alone. In 1615 there were only three Jesuits — Francesco Buzomi, Diego Carvalho, and António Dias — in Cochinchina. The first group to arrive in Tonkin in 1626 was made up of only two: Giuliano Baldinotti and Julius Piani.

It was only in 1625 that the number of Jesuits in Cochinchina reached fifteen, of whom there were eleven priests and four brothers.[113] During his mission in Tonkin from 1627 to 1630, he was practically working alone, since his companion Pêro Marques did not know the language. During his second mission to Cochinchina from 1640 to 1645, he was alone, traveling back and forth from Macao. At one time, he writes, "never did I feel God's help so near. I was the only priest in a large kingdom, and I can truthfully say that my parish stretched over at least 120 leagues. Nevertheless, I ministered to it and visited it all within two years; as far as I know, I did not neglect to stay anywhere for as long as necessary to secure the good of souls."[114]

Not only were priests extremely scarce and the number of converts rapidly increasing, but the missionaries were also often opposed by the Vietnamese religious and political leaders. Twice de Rhodes was banished from Tonkin. In Cochinchina, after several exiles, he was condemned to death, his life spared at the last minute by the intervention of the lord's teacher. Not rarely did he have to work clandestinely, hiding from place to place or under house arrest, and the Christians were forbidden to have contact with him.

Under these severe constraints, how could de Rhodes carry out his task of evangelization and *plantatio ecclesiae*? He found the solution to this challenge in the laity. Everywhere he went, de Rhodes immediately formed a nucleus of lay leaders, made up of former Buddhist monks, mandarins, doctors, *licenciés*, persons of noble birth, and commoners, not only men but also women. We will shortly speak of the corps of elite leaders, namely, the catechists. Here suffice to recall the names of the two Catherines, mother and daughter, who composed books on the Bible and Christian doctrine; Madame Minh Duc Vuong Thai Phi, who built a chapel in the lord's palace where she gathered the Christians for worship; Lina, who built a hospice for the poor; Simon, who taught Christian doctrine to his fellow lepers; Dr. Joachim, Dr. Peter, and *licencié* John, who dedicated themselves to catechesis. These lay leaders not only "pastored" the Christian communities, gathering them in prayer and worship, preaching and teaching, confirming and strengthening the faith of their brothers and sisters, but also became missionaries themselves, evangelizing the non-Christians and baptizing them when the priests were absent.

---

113. For a list of these Jesuits, see Do Quang Chinh, 279. See also the letter of Manoel Fernandes written to father general from Hoi An on July 2, 1625, in *ARSI, JS* 68, f. 15r; the letter of Gabriele de Martos written to father general from Cochinchina on July 5, 1625, in *ARSI, JS* 68, f. 17; and the annual report made by Gaspar Luís on January 1, 1626, in *ARSI, JS* 57, 61r., 64v.

114. *Divers voyages,* 154–55. At one time, he was so glad to meet two Spanish Franciscans unexpectedly because "the first thing I wanted to do was make my confession, not having for a whole year received the sacrament I had administered to thousands" (*Divers voyages,* 239).

De Rhodes's empowerment of the laity, even if necessitated by circumstances, is particularly significant in view both of the Vietnamese culture and the attitude of other missionaries elsewhere. In a patriarchal society such as Vietnam, it is remarkable that so many Christian women assumed important positions in the church. Similarly, in a traditionally hierarchical culture such as the Vietnamese, it is surprising that leadership in the church came from below as it were.

Furthermore, whereas the missionaries in China and Macao were distrustful of the natives and were reluctant to have them ordained, de Rhodes went out of his way to promote the local laity, allowing them to be "ordinary ministers" of baptism and encouraging them to lead the assemblies in prayers and devotions. It is because of his trust in these leaders that he thought the Vietnamese Christian Church had reached sufficient maturity to have their own priests and even bishops. Consequently, he marshaled all the means at his disposal to have a hierarchy established in Vietnam.

The Vietnamese lay Christian leaders did not disappoint de Rhodes's trust in them. They discharged their responsibilities with enthusiasm and remarkable success. Again and again de Rhodes marveled at the depth of their faith, their courage and patience under persecutions, the uprightness of their moral lives, and even their power to perform miracles.

Just to take two examples, one from Tonkin, the other from Cochinchina. Anthony, a "sacristan" at Vu Xa, brought two hundred people to baptism a few months after becoming a Christian. He, de Rhodes writes, began "to labor as a catechist and an apostle, to preach, to announce our mysteries, to shake the consciences, to vanquish the spirits, and to defeat the demon."[115] The old man Paul in Cho Moi, writes de Rhodes, "was the heart and soul of that whole church. Every Sunday and holy day, he gathered together Christians in a chapel he had in the enclosure of his house. There he instructed them, preached, and took care to help them in every way necessary to keep them in the faith they had received. His zeal extended to the pagans, and he disposed many for baptism."[116]

Without lay leaders like these, de Rhodes could not have accomplished what he did. Together with him, they deserved to be called the cofounders of Vietnamese Christianity.

DE RHODES AND THE INSTITUTION OF CATECHISTS

Of the lay leaders, the catechists played an indisputably preponderant role. De Rhodes's closest collaborators, they were the pillars with which de Rhodes built the church in Vietnam. In chapter 2, we have seen how de Rhodes founded quasi-religious communities of catechists, in both Tonkin and Cochinchina.

---

115. *Histoire du Royaume*, 168.
116. *Divers voyages*, 134–35.

The history of the institution of catechists in Vietnam is a complex one. Immediate collaborators of priests and intermediaries between the laity and the clergy, they performed all ministries not requiring holy orders. During the first years of the Vietnamese Church, they replaced the missionaries during their absence. Later, the institution evolved into a stable, quasi-religious organization called *Nha Duc Chua Troi* (House of the Lord of Heaven), whose members lived in the presbytery with the parish priests.[117] Our immediate interest here is to see how the organization of catechists was a strategy with which de Rhodes met the pastoral challenges of his mission.

Of these catechists de Rhodes writes: "What helped me wonderfully in the cultivation of this fine vineyard and propagating our holy faith was the assistance of the catechists who, to tell the truth, accomplished everything under God in the great strides made by this Church. Given the fact that I was the only priest who could preach, because the priest who was working with me did not know the language, I decided to keep some Christians with me who were not married and who were filled with zeal and piety, to help me in the conversion of souls. Many offered me their services, but I chose those I thought most capable and started a seminary, which was so successful that we might say it was what kept us going."[118]

To help him carry out his mission effectively, de Rhodes looked for people with the following qualifications. First, they had to be relatively young to be able to endure the physical hardships of apostolic life which often required continuous travel and long hours of teaching. The oldest catechist was Ignatius at the age of thirty-four, and the youngest ones were Andrew, aged seventeen, and Vincent, aged sixteen, when they were made catechists in 1642. The average age of the first catechists was twenty-five.

Second, the catechists had to be of at least average intelligence since their primary function was to teach the Christian doctrine. To judge from the doctrinal sophistication of *Cathechismus,* which is a manual written for them, their intelligence must have been above average, if not superior. Furthermore, a knowledge of the Chinese characters and possibly of the Confucian classics was required, since at the time no one would be respected as a teacher without a knowledge of these things, and since in their apostolic activities the catechists might be called upon to converse with educated pagans. Tonkinese Catechist Francis Xavier had been a Buddhist monk for seventeen years and was well versed in Chinese letters. Another Tonkinese catechist, Ignatius Nhuan, was "knowledgeable in the Tonkinese religions" and "composed in Vietnamese a song in elegant verse and with perfectly agreeable music in which he rebutted all the errors and superstitions by making them sound absurd and ridiculous."[119]

---

117. A comprehensive history of the institution of catechists in Vietnam remains to be written. For a treatment of this theme, see Do Quang Chinh, 329–78.

118. *Divers voyages*, 102–3.

119. *Histoire du Royaume*, 238.

Cochinchinese Catechist Ignatius was by far the most learned in Chinese letters and philosophy. He had been a mandarin in the service of Lord Nguyen Phuoc Khe. De Rhodes had to enlist his help in his disputations with the Buddhist monks.

Those who lacked the knowledge of the Chinese characters were required to spend a year in study before being admitted to the rank of catechists.[120] Thus, the sixteen-year-old Vincent was required to study with other student catechists,[121] and Andrew, the future martyr, was assigned to Catechist Ignatius to improve his knowledge of the Chinese letters.[122] Indeed, de Rhodes adamantly refused to make a catechist out of anyone who lacked an average education. Thus, the ex-soldier Anthony, despite his fervor and zeal, was made a "coadjutor" rather than a catechist and was put in charge of material affairs rather than catechetical teaching.

Third, the catechists had to be able to devote themselves full-time to the ministry. Hence the requirement of celibacy, at least during their ministry.[123] Married men, who had to take care of their families, were not admitted to the rank of catechists in spite of their learning and social rank. Thus, in 1643, Dr. Philip, and in 1645, Bartholomew, were refused when they asked to leave their wives and families in order to become catechists.

Fourth, to achieve maximum success in their ministry, the catechists had to be able to work in harmony with one another and in the discipline of the community. Hence the vows of poverty and obedience. In Tonkin, they made the vow of "not keeping any money or possession as one's own but to place in common all the alms which the Christians would give them."[124] They also vowed "to obey the one who will be nominated their superior,"[125] whereas the catechists

---

120. Besides the study of the Chinese letters and Christian doctrine, it is likely that the Tonkinese catechists were also taught the *chu nom* and the Roman script, at least from 1632 to 1639. It is well to remember that Gaspar do Amaral was in Tonkin from 1629 to 1638, and António Barbosa from 1636 to 1642. The former composed his *Diccionario anamita-português-latim,* the latter his *Diccionario português-anamita,* both now lost. In the case of the catechists of Cochinchina, it is almost certain that they were introduced to the Roman script. During his ten-year stay in Macao (1630–40), de Rhodes worked on the first draft of his *Cathechismus* and his *Dictionarium.* From 1640 to 1645, he must have received help from the Cochinchinese catechists, especially the learned Ignatius, to perfect his Romanization of the Vietnamese language. At any rate, the letters of Catechists Igesico Van-Tin and Bento Thien, both written to Giovanni Filippo de Marini in the new script on September 12, 1659, and on October 25, 1659, respectively, show that they had mastered the new writing system. See *ARSI, JS* 81, ff. 246–246v, and *ARSI, JS* 81, ff. 247–247v.

121. See Saccano, 49–50.

122. See *La glorieuse mort,* 77.

123. In 1630 the first Tonkinese catechists made *temporary* vows of celibacy, i.e., they promised not to get married until the return of the Jesuits. When Andrea Palmiero came to Tonkin in 1631 with three other Jesuits, he granted the catechists the permission to make perpetual vows of celibacy. In 1643 the catechists of Cochinchina made *perpetual* vows of celibacy. See *Histoire du Royaume,* 256, and *Divers voyages,* 161.

124. *Histoire du Royaume,* 256. However, the Cochinchinese catechists did not make the vow of poverty. Nevertheless, they did live a community life, first with de Rhodes, and later with Metello Saccano, de Rhodes's successor.

125. *Histoire du Royaume,* 256.

of Cochinchina vowed "to obey the Fathers of the Society of Jesus who will come to preach in their country or those who will be deputized by them."[126]

Fifth, and most important, the catechists had to be men of profound faith and exemplary life and, in addition, animated by an ardent desire to serve the church. De Rhodes describes the ten young men of Cochinchina whom he accepted as catechists as "having the same desire to belong to God entirely and to be totally devoted to the church."[127]

Once de Rhodes had chosen his catechists, he trained them by having them live, travel, and work with him. This is particularly the case with the catechists in Cochinchina. It was "on-the-job training" as it were. No doubt, he also gave them special instructions on Christian doctrines of which *Cathechismus* represents a summary.

Because the catechists lived in community, there was a need for some rules and guidelines. When de Rhodes left the Tonkinese catechists in 1630, he "left behind rules and guidelines for their conduct, which they have faithfully observed."[128] Unfortunately, we do not know exactly what these rules and guidelines were. However, we possess a manuscript written in 1647 which provides us with some good ideas about them.[129] It contains twenty-seven general rules; articles 1–7 deal with spiritual life; articles 8–13 prescribe the conduct to be observed during apostolic activities; and articles 14–27 describe these activities themselves.

As implied by their names,[130] the catechists' principal task was to teach Christian doctrines. Article 17 of the above-mentioned Rule recommends that they teach catechism, especially to the educated. Of course, they also taught the catechumens, preparing them for baptism. Some of them even went to evangelize abroad: in 1638, Catechists Andrew, Thomas Thang, and Jerome of

---

126. *Divers voyages*, 161. Moreover, the Cochinchinese catechists swore "to serve the church for all their lives." It is clear that the catechists of Tonkin made a *temporary* vow of obedience, whereas those of Cochinchina a *perpetual* one. At any rate, in 1631, the Tonkinese catechists obtained from Andrea Palmiero, visitor of Japan and China, the permission to make the three vows in the perpetual way. See *Histoire du Royaume*, 264, and *Relazione*, 201.

127. *Divers voyages*, 156.

128. *Histoire du Royaume*, 257. See also *Relazione*, 250: "We gave the catechists a certain rule and a guide of life which they must always observe."

129. See *Instrucção para os cathequistas deste Reino de Anam, ou Tumkin* in ARSI, JS 80, ff. 45–48v.

130. There are different Vietnamese words for catechists which indicate their ranks. As we have seen, de Rhodes established two ranks of catechists: those who teach and those who take care of temporal affairs of the community. We know that Anthony the ex-soldier was allowed to profess vows but was made a "coadjutor" rather than a catechist because of his lack of education. He was the only coadjutor among de Rhodes's catechists, both in Tonkin and Cochinchina.

Among the catechists of Cochinchina, two, that is, Ignatius and Damasus, were given by de Rhodes the title of *Thay,* literally, master, and were allowed to wear a surplice while teaching. According to Saccano and Tissanier, this title was given by de Rhodes only to very capable and experienced catechists and means "doctor" (see Saccano, 35, and Tissanier, 200–201). These were called in Vietnamese *Thay giang dao* (master who preaches religion), or *Thay giang* (preaching master), or simply *Thay* (master). Those who were not yet advanced were called *ke giang dao* (the one who preaches) or *ke giang* (the one who preaches). Later, the title of *Thay giang* was used for those who had made perpetual vows, whereas *ke giang* was for those with temporary vows. See Do Quang Chinh, 357–66.

Tonkin accompanied Giovanni Battista Bonelli in his mission in Laos.[131] Again, in 1642, other catechists accompanied Giovanni M. de Leria in his mission also to Laos.[132]

One of the most important liturgical ministries of the catechists was conferring baptism. Because of the scarcity of priests, de Rhodes allowed them to baptize, not only in case of emergency but also as a general rule.[133] When he and Pêro Marques were exiled from Tonkin for the first time, they gave Catechists Francis Xavier Duc and Andrew Tri "the order to baptize whoever was ready for it."[134] During the ten months when the Jesuits were absent from Tonkin (from May 1630 to March 1631), the catechists baptized 3,340 people.[135] In 1643, when there was no priest in Cochinchina, the catechists baptized 596 people.[136] After de Rhodes's definitive departure from Cochinchina in July 1645, during seven months his catechists baptized 200 more according to Saccano,[137] and 2,226 according to de Rhodes.[138]

That the founding of the institution of catechists was a stroke of pastoral genius on de Rhodes's part is beyond a shadow of doubt. Without their collaboration, the mission of de Rhodes and other Jesuits would have been severely curtailed. Furthermore, during the missionaries' prolonged absence, without the catechists' teaching, baptizing, and pastoring the communities, the Vietnamese Church would have survived only with much difficulty, if at all.

Moreover, the institution of catechists has provided the Vietnamese Church with two magnificent fruits: vocations to the priesthood and martyrdom. All the Vietnamese priests in the seventeenth century, with the exception of the Jesuit Cristoforo Cordeiro, had been catechists for many years. The first two Vietnamese priests, John Van-Hue and Benedict Hien, who were ordained in 1668, had been catechists for over thirty years. In 1670, Apostolic Vicar Pierre Lambert de la Motte ordained seven catechists.[139]

Among de Rhodes's catechists, the Vietnamese Church boasts of its first martyrs: Andrew of Phu Yen, Ignatius of Quang Tri, and Vincent of Quang Nghia.[140] If the blood of martyrs is the seed of Christians, then the institution of catechists was the cradle in which the martyrs were born, nurtured, and came to full maturity.

---

131. See *Histoire du Royaume*, 284–87.

132. See *Histoire du Royaume*, 287–88.

133. This permission to catechists to be "ordinary ministers" of baptism provoked heated discussion among the Jesuits in Macao in 1630. As a result, the visitor Andrea Palmiero decided to make a fact-finding trip to Tonkin. Apparently the visitor approved de Rhodes's policies regarding the catechists' taking vows and administering baptism.

134. *Histoire du Royaume*, 226.

135. See *Histoire du Royaume*, 263–64.

136. See *Divers voyages*, 162–63.

137. See Saccano, 69.

138. See *Relation des progrez*, 42.

139. See Nguyen Huu Trong, *Les origines du clergé vietnamien* (Saigon, 1959).

140. See *La Glorieuse mort*; Saccano, 12–20; and E. Ferreyra, *Noticias summarias das perseguições da Missam de Cochincina, principiada, et continuada pelos Padres de Companhias de Jesu* (Lisbon, 1700), 50–93.

The challenges to de Rhodes's mission in Vietnam were multiple and diverse. They came from the Vietnamese cultural practices and religious traditions, from Christian liturgical celebrations, from the organization of the Vietnamese infant church, and from the very tasks of evangelization and catechesis. To meet all these challenges de Rhodes availed himself of all the means at his disposal: polemics against errors, adaptation of cultural customs, translation of Christian texts, inculturation of Christian practices, empowerment of lay leaders, and foundation of a quasi-religious institution of catechists. But there is another powerful weapon in his arsenal: the catechism. To this we will turn in the remaining chapters.

4

Cathechismus

History, Structure, and Method

Honored as the first theological work ever written in Vietnamese, de Rhodes's *Cathechismus* is also a prime example of how Christian faith and praxis were inculturated into an alien culture. Of course, it is neither the first nor only catechism written for Asian peoples, nor did de Rhodes compose his catechism on an intellectual island, cut off from the influence and assistance of others. Consequently, in this chapter we will first attempt to understand *Cathechismus* by tracing its history in the context of seventeenth-century catechisms. We will then examine its structure and method.

THE *CATHECHISMUS* AND SEVENTEENTH-CENTURY COUNTER-REFORMATION CATECHISMS

The development of catechism as a genre was intertwined with the Protestant Reformation, the Tridentine Counter-Reformation, and the Christian missions in the New World and Asia.[1] Rooted in the ancient practice of linking catechesis with the profession of faith in baptism and with the sacrament of penance, modern catechisms took their origins in the Reformers' efforts to remedy the state of alarming religious ignorance among the laity. Both Catholic and Protestant catechisms, despite their profound theological differences, share a common pastoral concern, namely, to dispel the ignorance of the true Christian faith and to transmit the Christian doctrines in their integrity and wholeness.

---

1. For a detailed history of catechisms from 1450 to 1870 with extensive bibliography, see Pietro Braido, *Lineamenti di storia della catechesi e dei catechismi: Dal "tempo delle riforme" all' età degli imperialismi (1450–1870)* (Turin: Editrice Elle Di Ci, 1991). For a comprehensive and readable history of catechisms with special focus on the catechisms in the English language, see Berard Marthaler, *The Catechism Yesterday and Today: The Evolution of a Genre* (Collegeville, Minn.: The Liturgical Press, 1995).

REFORMATION AND COUNTER-REFORMATION CATECHISMS

Luther's *Deutsch Catechismus* (the Large Catechism) and *Enchiridion: Der kleine Catechismus für die gemeine Pfarherr und Prediger* (the Small Catechism), both published in 1529; Calvin's *Christianae religionis institutio* (1536, 1539, 1559), *Instruction et confession de Foy* (1537), and *Le Catéchisme de l'Eglise de Genève: c'est à dire Le formulaire d'instruire les enfants en la Chrestienté: faict en manière de dialogue, où le ministre interroge et l'enfant répond* (1542); and the Heidelberg Catechism (1563), all these writings, to mention only the best-known works, established the catechism as a potent remedy for religious ignorance, as a test of orthodoxy, as a theological genre with its distinctive structure, and as a form of instruction characterized by the question-and-answer format and by memorization.[2]

Before the Council of Trent (1545–63) responded to the Protestant Reformation by mandating the composition of a catechism, Peter Canisius (1521–97) and Edmund Auger (1530–91), both Jesuits, had already sought to counteract the Protestant Reformation with their catechisms. The former produced *Summa doctrinae christianae per questiones tradita et in usum christianae pueritiae nunc primum edita* (1554, revised in 1566 to take into account the teachings of Trent and to be more explicitly anti-Protestant), *Catechismus minimus* (1556), and *Parvus Catechismus Catholicorum* (1559). Auger wrote his *Catéchisme et sommaire de la religion Chrestienne* (1563) and *Petit catéchisme et sommaire de la religion chrestienne* (1568) specifically as a rebuttal of Calvin's *Le catéchisme de l'Eglise de Genève.*[3]

The Council of Trent's mandate to produce a catechism bore fruit three years after its closure when, in 1566, the *Catechismus ex decreto Concilii Tridentini ad Parochos Pii Quinti Pont. Max. iussu editus* was published. The work of a four-member committee, the catechism, popularly known as the *Roman Catechism,* is addressed to those charged with teaching the faith (the *parochos*) and is structured in four parts: (1) faith and the Apostles' Creed, (2) sacraments, (3) commandments and divine law, and (4) the nature and necessity of prayer.

The intent of the *Roman Catechism* is profoundly pastoral. Its preface insists that the aim of catechesis is to promote a loving knowledge and imitation of the crucified Christ. It recommends that religious instruction be adapted to the age, intelligence, and spiritual condition of the addressee.[4]

During the immediate post-Tridentine period, the most important catechisms are indisputably those of Jesuit Cardinal Robert Bellarmine (1542–1621). In 1597 he published *Dottrina cristiana breve perché si possa imparare a mente,*

---

2. See Braido, *Lineamenti di storia della catechesi e dei catechismi,* 39-56, and Marthaler, *The Catechism Yesterday and Today,* 21–32.

3. See Braido, *Lineamenti di storia della catechesi e dei catechismi,* 57–65, 75–77, and Marthaler, *The Catechism Yesterday and Today,* 42–50.

4. See Braido, *Lineamenti di storia della catechesi e dei catechismi,* 66-74, and Marthaler, *The Catechism Yesterday and Today,* 33–41.

and in the following year *Dichiarazione più copiosa della Dottrina cristiana.*
Both works, written in the question-and-answer format (the first with 96, the
second with 273 questions), were guided by two principles: only basic truths
should be communicated, and the learner's capacity to assimilate them must
be taken into account. In 1598, Pope Clement VIII approved both catechisms,
mandated their use in all papal territories, and urged their diffusion throughout the world. Thanks to papal endorsement, Bellarmine's works knew an
extraordinary success: they have at least fifty-six translations (including Asian
languages) and more than five hundred editions.[5]

DE RHODES AND COUNTER-REFORMATION CATECHISMS

Did de Rhodes know these Counter-Reformation catechisms? Though he
never mentioned any of them by name, there is little doubt that he knew them
all. First of all, with regard to Auger, his works were written in French, de
Rhodes's mother tongue, and were widely used in France, particularly at Avignon (de Rhodes's hometown) and Lyon.[6] Jean-Claude Dhôtel reports a total
of twenty-two editions of these two catechisms in France from 1563 and 1582,
with translation into Spanish, Italian, and Dutch and a large diffusion in Jesuit
high schools.[7]

As for Peter Canisius's catechisms, even if de Rhodes had not known them
as a young boy, he must certainly have known them as a student in the upper
grades at the Jesuit high school in Avignon. By order of the Jesuit superiors,
Auger's works were used in the lower grades of high school, whereas Canisius's in the Latin version were used in the upper grades, so that from 1566
onward, thanks to Jesuit educational institutions, Canisius's catechisms were
diffused throughout France.[8]

With regard to the *Roman Catechism* and Bellarmine's catechisms, it is extremely likely that de Rhodes knew them during his six-year sojourn in Rome,
first as a novice and then as a student of theology at the Roman College
(1612–18). De Rhodes has not given us much information on his theological
studies in Rome, but from his remarks on how it would take as much time

---

5. See Braido, *Lineamenti di storia della catechesi e dei catechismi,* 82–86, and Marthaler, *The
Catechism Yesterday and Today,* 50–52.

6. Friedrich J. Brand cites some of Auger's letters in which the author reports the phenomenal sale
of his catechisms. For example, in his letter of April 25, 1564, Auger writes: "The catechism is printed in
Paris with the approval of the doctors and it will be published in Toulouse and Avignon, and here, of the
4,600 copies there is none left." See Brand, *Die Katechismen des Edmundus Augerius S.J. in historischer,
dogmatisch-moralischer und katechetischer Bearbeitung* (Freiburg I. B.: Herder, 1917), 51.

7. See Jean-Claude Dhôtel, *Les origines du catéchisme moderne d'après les premiers manuels im-
primés en France* (Paris: Aubier, 1967). Recall that de Rhodes attended the Jesuit high school in
Avignon.

8. See Dhôtel, *Les origines du catéchisme moderne,* 81, and G. Bedouelle, "L'influence des
catéchismes de Canisius en France," in Pierre Colin et al., *Aux origines du catéchisme en France*
(Tournai: Desclée, 1989), 67–86.

to learn Chinese as to study theology[9] and how he studied Vietnamese as intensely as he had studied theology in Rome,[10] it can be safely assumed that de Rhodes's theological studies were arduous and were undertaken with utmost seriousness.

The theological curriculum at the Roman College at the beginning of the seventeenth century was deeply inspired by the Counter-Reformation. Cardinal Bellarmine, the symbol of the Counter-Reformation, had been a professor of theology at the Roman College from 1576 to 1588. Furthermore, his catechisms, which were influenced by the Council of Trent and the *Roman Catechism,* were made obligatory by Clement VIII for all pontifical territories, including. Avignon, de Rhodes's home town.

Granted that de Rhodes knew the Counter-Reformation catechisms, and perhaps even used them as texts for his theology courses at the Madre de Deus College in Macao during the decade of 1630–40, was he influenced by them in composing his own catechism? No doubt he had easy access to these catechisms which must have been readily available at the Jesuit university in Macao. Of course, a full answer to this question is possible only after a thorough examination of the method and contents of *Cathechismus.* Suffice it to note here that as a whole, de Rhodes's catechism differs significantly, in both its method and contents, from those of the Counter-Reformation. It does not follow the question-and-answer format favored by Canisius, Auger, and Bellarmine. Like the *Roman Catechism,* it was written as a manual for catechists, but it does not adopt the four-pillar structure of the *Roman Catechism,* i.e., creed, sacraments, commandments, and prayer, which became standard with most post-Tridentine catechisms.

Furthermore, the anti-Protestant polemic, a hallmark of post-Tridentine catechisms, is entirely absent from *Cathechismus.* Not that de Rhodes was irenic towards the Protestant; on the contrary, he relished doctrinal disputations with them, even at the risk of his life, as is clear from one of his encounters with the Calvinists:

> But both going and coming from my native town, I found myself in danger of ending my travels in the Rhone River. Coming down from Lyon, I got into a boat with some highly insolent Calvinists, who began at once to read aloud from a heretical book that contains a thousand blasphemies against the sacred mysteries of the Catholic faith, causing these errors to be heard and this venom tasted by several who were present. I spoke up immediately and began refuting the false teachings they were uttering. This

---

9. *Divers voyages,* 56: "Because they [i.e., the Chinese] have 80,000 characters, that is to say, as many as there are words, no one knows them all. To learn an adequate number of them, our Fathers devote four years of study, with the same application as necessary for learning the whole theology curriculum."

10. *Divers voyages,* 72–73: "Everyday I was given lessons, which I studied with the same application as I once studied theology in Rome."

made them so angry they wanted to toss me overboard, and they would
have done so if the Catholics had not resisted them. As for me, I did not
offer them any resistance beyond telling them that I would be very much
obliged to them if they were to give me on the spot what I was going to
the ends of the earth to search for. As for the heresies they wanted to read,
I said I would oppose them while I had breath.[11]

In contrast to the catechisms of Canisius and Auger, for instance, *Cathechismus*
does not dwell at all on the differences between Catholics and Protestants. Perhaps a hint of anti-Protestantism might lie behind de Rhodes's affirmation of
the Pope as "the sovereign ruler, the holy *papa* in the nation of Rome, vicar of
the Lord Jesus Christ, successor of Saint Peter."[12] But that is about it.

These profound differences between Counter-Reformation catechisms and
Cathechismus will be accounted for in due course in terms of the latter's social and cultural situation, its ecclesial context, its method, and its intended
audience.

EARLY CATECHISMS IN ASIA

Missionaries to the New World and Asia were confronted with a host of
difficulties in their effort to evangelize the native peoples: vast expanse of territories, scarcity of means of communication, multiplicity of languages, diversity
of cultures, scandalous behaviors of colonizers, resistance of local political and
religious leaders, rivalries among the religious orders, lack of a central ecclesiastical government, and abuses of the *padroado* system, just to mention a few.
In spite of all these obstacles and challenges and their own human frailties,
missionaries to these two continents from the sixteenth century onward have
worked tirelessly and courageously to bring the Good News to these newly
discovered lands.

One of the necessary tools for evangelization was no doubt the catechism.
Missionaries to Latin America were not slow to compose a slew of them, even

---

11. *Divers voyages*, 8. De Rhodes was no less polemical against other Protestants, especially the
Dutch, as we have seen in chap. 2. He was kinder to the Anglicans who treated him well during his
trip back to Rome. Sir Aaron Becket, the English governor for the Indies, treated him so generously that
de Rhodes thought he was a Catholic. But from the conversation, de Rhodes found out that he "was
enmeshed in the common misfortune of that poor country which, once the delight of true piety, shortly
lost the thing that had caused her to be held in reverence by all other nations for so many centuries"
(*Divers voyages*, pt. III, 29–30). On another occasion, de Rhodes defended the Real Presence, abstinence
from meat, clerical celibacy, and communion under one species from the attack of an Anglican minister
(see *Divers voyages*, pt. III, 4–43).

De Rhodes also attempted to persuade the patriarch of Armenia to renounce "the errors of Euty-
ches and Dioscorus" (*Divers voyages*, pt. III, 69) and to accept the authority of the Pope. Obviously
ecumenical dialogue was nonexistent in those days!

12. *Cathechismus*, 312.

before Canisius, Bellarmine, Jerome de Ripalda,[13] and Gaspar Astete,[14] and of course, especially after the Council of Trent.[15]

DE RHODES AND THE FIRST CATECHISMS IN ASIA

In Asia, with a lot fewer missionaries and with vastly more linguistic obstacles than in Latin America, the production of catechisms was understandably less abundant. For our purpose of understanding *Cathechismus,* we can leave out of consideration the earlier catechisms by Roberto de Nobili (1577–1656), important though they were for India.[16]

While de Rhodes had not explicitly mentioned de Nobili, he had repeatedly invoked the authority and example of Francis Xavier (1505–52) whom he called "the second apostle of the Indies" after the Apostle Thomas and the "founder of that great church [i.e., Japan] that has given heaven so many martyrs."[17] As he began his mission in Goa in 1542, Francis Xavier produced *Catechismo breve,* a small catechism almost identical to the one published by John de Barros in Lisbon in 1539. In 1545 he published a set of guidelines for catechists (*Instruzione per i catechisti*) and in the following year a short catechism in the form of a commentary on the Creed (*Dichiarazione sopra gli articoli della fede cattolica*).[18]

In a letter to his companions in Europe written in Cochin on January 29, 1552, Francis Xavier outlined a catechetical method that is strikingly similar to the one followed later by de Rhodes in his *Cathechismus.*[19] In general outline, Francis Xavier's catechetical approach is made of three successive steps: (1) A

---

13. Jeronimo de Ripalda (1536–1618), a Jesuit, produced an influential catechism entitled *Doctrina Christiana* in 1591.

14. Gaspar Astete (1537–1601), a Jesuit, wrote *Doctrina Christiana y documentos de crianza* in 1592 which by 1900 had gone through six hundred editions.

15. See Braido, *Lineamenti di storia della catechesi e dei catechismi,* 99-122, and Marthaler, *The Catechism Yesterday and Today,* 54–62.

16. Of de Nobili's voluminous writings the most important from the catechetical perspective is his *Kandam* or *Gnanopadesam* which is divided into five parts: the first deals with rational truths about God; the second revealed truths; the third the mysteries of Christianity: the Trinity, incarnation, redemption, sacraments, Mary, judgment; the fourth some prayers: the sign of the Cross, Our Father, Hail Mary, the Creed, the decalogue; and the fifth lists thirteen notes of the true religion. Then follow twenty-six catechetical sermons which summarize the first three parts. Finally comes a "refutation of calumnies" which responds to five series of objections: against Christianity in general, against the incarnation, against the veneration of images, against the social status of the Christian, and against the preachers of the Christian faith. See Braido, *Lineamenti di storia della catechesi e dei catechismi,* 124–27. It is highly likely that de Rhodes knew of the missionary work of de Nobili, especially during his lengthy stay in Goa.

17. *Divers voyages,* 35. It was in Goa in 1621 that de Rhodes heard of the beatification of Francis Xavier. See *Divers voyages,* 28.

18. The text of the two catechisms is found in *Epistolae S. Francisci Xaverii aliaque eius scripta,* ed. G. Schurhammer and J. Wicki (Rome: Inst. Hist. S.I., 1914–15), vol. I, 339–67.

19. See *Cartas y escritos de San Francisco Javier,* annotated by P. F. Zubillaga (Madrid: BAC, 1953), 405. In this letter Francis Xavier informed us that he had translated his catechism *Dichiarazione del simbolo* into Japanese but "written in our letters." Is it not likely that when he was studying Japanese de Rhodes used this text? Also, is it not likely that Xavier's Romanization of Japanese might have inspired de Rhodes to do the same for Vietnamese?

kind of natural theology which argues that there is a creator of the universe; that the world is not *ab aeterno* but has a beginning; that the sun, the moon, and the heaven are not gods or living creatures; that the human soul survives the death of the body; that the rational soul is different from the sensitive; and that the pagan "religious sects" are erroneous on the above-mentioned points. (2) An exposition of the Christian mysteries which include the Trinity; the creation of the world; the fall of Lucifer; the sin of Adam; the promise and the coming of the Son of God; Jesus' passion, death, resurrection, and ascension; and the last things. (3) The law of God, the commandments, and baptism.[20]

The convergences between Francis Xavier's catechetical approach and de Rhodes's are so extensive and substantial that one must wonder whether the latter has not intentionally adopted the former. Though it is not possible to document a textual influence of Francis Xavier on de Rhodes's *Cathechismus,* nonetheless there are persuasive reasons for an affirmative answer to the question of whether de Rhodes was influenced by his fellow Jesuit. One of the reasons is de Rhodes's profound admiration for both the contents and method of Francis Xavier's teaching, as evidenced by the following report of an incident that happened during de Rhodes's ten-year sojourn in Macao:

> I had the great consolation of meeting a 150-year-old man who had been baptized in the old days by the hand of the great Apostle of the Indies, St. Francis Xavier, when he was in Japan. I was privileged to hear his confession and to have a long talk with him. I was delighted to learn from what he said, and even more from the solid virtues displayed in his manner of living, of the *wonderful instruction St. Francis used to give those he converted to the faith and the method he employed in confirming them in their initial resolve.*[21]

It is clear from this account that de Rhodes was familiar with and had high regard for both Xavier's teachings and catechetical method.

Another catechism with which de Rhodes might have been acquainted is *Catechismus christianae fidei in quo Veritas nostrae religionis ostenditur et sectae Japonenses confutantur,* published by Alessandro Valignano, S.J. (1538–1606), in Lisbon in 1586. Valignano had been appointed visitor of the missions to East Asia in 1573. When he came to Japan in 1579, he noted the pronounced westernizing tendencies of his confreres' missionary methods, advocated especially by such Jesuits as Francisco Cabral, João Rodrigues, and Camillo

---

20. See Braido, *Lineamenti di storia della catechesi e dei catechismi,* 131.

21. *Divers voyages,* 115. Emphasis added. De Rhodes's admiration for Francis Xavier is also apparent in the following statement: "It was there [i.e., Goa] that the great Apostle of the Indies, St. Francis Xavier, began his conquests, filling all those countries with Christians and all heaven with saints. He is credited with having baptized at least 3,000 to 4,000 persons with his own hand. We learn from one of his letters that in one year alone he baptized 100,000. Within ten years he had journeyed and preached Jesus Christ in over 300 kingdoms. The glorious deeds of his lifetime surpass anything that has ever been heard of, and the miracles he performed before and after his death are so numerous they can scarcely be counted" (*Divers voyages,* 19). There is also another similarity between Francis Xavier and de Rhodes: both took care to train catechists and lay leaders to teach and guide the Christian communities.

Costanzo. Such westernization was manifested both in the missionaries' attitude toward the Japanese culture and rituals and in the use of religious language. Over against these trends Valignano recommended instead a gradual inculturation into the Japanese culture and way of life.[22]

In addition, with the help of the Japanese versed in local religions Valignano composed the *Catechismus christianae fidei* as a handbook for the catechists to refute Japanese religious errors and to teach the Christian faith. It is divided into two books. The first, made up of nine "discourses" directed to those who prepare themselves for baptism, deals with natural religious truths, and in chapters 8 and 9 with revealed truths (the Trinity, creation, salvation, the incarnation, death and resurrection of Jesus). The second book, composed of seven chapters, treats the laws of God, the sacraments, and the last things.[23]

There are several convergences between Valignano's catechism and that of de Rhodes. Both were written as manuals for catechists; both were animated by a concern for inculturation; both had the preparation for baptism as their main focus; both were engaged in refuting errors of local religions; and both proceeded with a presentation first of natural and then of revealed truths. Because of the lack of historical sources, it is not possible to trace a direct influence of the former on the latter. However, it seems more than likely that de Rhodes knew Valignano's works. After all, de Rhodes wanted to be a missionary in Japan and spent his first year in Macao learning Japanese (May 1623–December 1624). As part of his preparation for ministry in Japan, he would certainly have had to familiarize himself with Valignano's manuals of catechesis which had gained popularity by the 1620s.[24]

Another catechism to be mentioned, not so much to establish its literary connection with de Rhodes's *Cathechismus* as for the purpose of comparison, is *Vera et brevis divinarum rerum expositio,* attributed to Jesuit Michele Ruggieri (1543–1607).[25] Ruggieri left Rome for Goa in 1578 and went to Macao in 1579. He came to Canton several times between 1580 and 1581, and in 1583 he and Matteo Ricci succeeded in establishing the first mission in Chaoching. He worked in China until 1588, when he returned to Italy and there spent the last years of his life.

---

22. See his *Risolutioni che il Visitatore dette intorno alle dimande della Consulta che si fece in Giappone nell'anno 1581 in diverse parti* of January 1582.

23. For the common people Valignano composed a catechism in Japanese, *Dochirina Kirishitan* (1591?), which presents the classical loci of modern catechesis: the sign of the cross and the Our Father, Hail Mary, *Salve Regina;* the creed; the Ten Commandments and the precepts of the church; the seven capital sins; the sacraments; and elements of Christian life (the works of mercy, theological and moral virtues, the gifts of the Holy Spirit, the beatitudes, etc.). See Braido, *Lineamenti di storia della catechesi e dei catechismi,* 132–33.

24. It is interesting to note that it was Valignano who, following his arrival in Macao in 1578, decided that the only way for missionaries to have any success in their work is by way of mastering the local languages. It was he who assigned to Michele Ruggieri and Matteo Ricci the task of studying the Chinese language. No doubt it is in line with this policy that de Rhodes was sent to Cochinchina to learn Vietnamese in the years 1624–26.

25. The text is available in *Opere storiche del P. Matteo Ricci,* ed. Tacchi Venturi (Macerata: Giorgetti, 1913), 498–540.

Vera et brevis divinarum rerum expositio, published in 1582, is a lengthy dialogue between an "ethnicus philosophus" and a "sacerdos christianus" divided into thirteen chapters. The chapters deal with the following themes: (1) the existence of the one God; (2) God's nature and attributes; (3) errors regarding the knowledge of God; (4) God the creator of all things; (5) angels and the first parents; (6) the immortality of the human soul; (7) God as the lawgiver and the threefold law of nature, Moses, and the Gospel; (8) the incarnation; (9) the articles of faith; (10) the Ten Commandments; (11) religious life according to the counsels; (12) the sacraments and in particular baptism; and (13) God as remunerator and the last things.

In Fukien, Ruggieri dictated through a Chinese secretary a translation into Chinese of this Latin text — which has little resemblance, however, with the original — entitled *T'ien-chu Chen-lu,* that is, *True Record of the Lord of Heaven.* The text was revised by Matteo Ricci and a Confucian scholar over a period of five months and was published in 1584.[26] It has sixteen chapters dealing with the following themes: (1) existence of a true God; (2) God's nature and attributes; (3) human knowledge of God; (4) creation of everything by God; (5) angels and the first parents; (6) the immortality of the human soul; (7) life after death; (8) promulgation of God's law in three phases: natural law, the Mosaic law, and the law of the Gospel; (9) the incarnation of the Son of God; (10) the nature of the law of the Gospel; (11) mysteries of faith; (12) the Ten Commandments in general; (13) the first three commandments; (14) the last seven commandments; (15) religious life; and (16) baptism.

As a whole, *T'ien-chu Chen-lu* preserves the general structure of the Latin original but omits its more abstract contents. There is no mention of the Trinity; of the sacraments, only baptism is mentioned; there is no discussion of the hierarchical church and the Holy See; and an exposition of the Buddhist and Chinese understanding of the soul takes precedence over that of the immortality of the soul.

There is some likelihood that de Rhodes might have known Ruggieri's catechism, either in the Latin or the Chinese versions or both, especially during his decade-long professorship in Macao. There are parallels between the structures of Ruggieri's and de Rhodes's catechisms which, significantly, do not follow the four-pillar organization of post-Tridentine catechisms. Furthermore, there are convergences in their treatment of the knowledge of God as creator and remunerator, of God's attributes, of the angels and the first parents, of the three-

---

26. The original title of this work is *True Record of the Lord of Heaven: A New Compilation from India.* After Ricci completed the first draft of his own catechism, *The True Meaning of the Lord of Heaven,* in 1596, Ruggieri's work was destroyed. But after 1637 it was revised, with additions and deletions, by John Monteiro and two others, and published under the new title *True Record of the Sacred Teachings Concerning the Lord of Heaven.* The text of the earlier version is available in *ARSI, JS* I, 189. For a study of this Chinese catechism in comparison with the Latin text, see L. Wieger, "Notes sur la première catéchèse écrite en chinois 1582–1584," *Archivum Historicum S.I.,* I (1932): 72–84. See also Pasquale d'Elia, ed., *Fonti Ricciane: Storia dell'introduzione del Cristianesimo in Cina scritta da Matteo Ricci, S.I.* (Rome: La Libreria dello Stato, 1942–49), vol. I, 197, n. 2.

fold law, of the commandments, and of baptism. These convergences could be accounted for by the common theological heritage both had received at the Roman College and, more probably, through the work of Matteo Ricci, as we will see below. At any rate, the similarity in the structures of the two authors' works, which departs from the standard post-Tridentine structure, could scarcely be accidental.[27]

MATTEO RICCI'S *THE TRUE MEANING OF THE LORD OF HEAVEN* AND DE RHODES'S *CATHECHISMUS*

So far we have considered de Rhodes's *Cathechismus* in relation to catechisms which circumstantial evidence suggests might have influenced its composition. There is, however, one catechism for which both external evidence and internal analysis of *Cathechismus* confirm a direct link, and that is Matteo Ricci's *The True Meaning of the Lord of Heaven*.[28]

In chapter 2 we mentioned how de Rhodes discovered by chance that one of the Buddhist monks owned a copy of Ricci's "catechism." Here is de Rhodes's account of this discovery:

This man whose spirit was still seized by the teachings of Christian doctrine which he had heard came one Sunday morning to our church when the Christians were prepared to hear Mass. He showed them a book in Chinese letters. On its first page there was printed the holy name of Jesus written in big characters. I took a look at it and immediately recognized that the book had been brought in from China and was a work authored by one of our Fathers. I was completely flabbergasted by how this work could have fallen into the hands of a Buddhist monk.

He explained to me how his father had accompanied the ambassador who was sent, once every three years, as was the custom, to do homage and pay tribute to the king of China. His father brought this book back from the court of Peking, considered it a treasure, and upon his death left it to his son as an heirloom. His father told him that he had received it as a gift from the Doctors of the Great West while accompanying the ambassador to Peking. These doctors assured him that whoever believed and observed what was written in this book would lead a holy life and would go to heaven after leaving this world. After his father's death, which made him an orphan at the age of only ten, he kept this book with devotion in

---

27. For a comparison between Ruggieri and de Rhodes, see Nguyen Chi Thiet, 331–37.

28. For an English text, see *The True Meaning of the Lord of Heaven (T'ien-chu Shih-i),* translated, with introduction and notes, by Douglas Lancashire and Peter Hu Kuo-chen, S.J. (St. Louis: Institute of Jesuit Sources, 1985). References to Ricci's work will cite the pages of this edition. Léopold Cadière opines that de Rhodes knew Ricci's work and would carry it around with him during his mission so that he could give it to learned Vietnamese to read. See his "Le titre divin en annamite. Etude de terminologie chrétienne," *Revue d'Histoire des Missions* (December 1931), supplement to the December issue, 1–21 (with separate pagination).

a box for some thirty years. From time to time he would open the book, read it, but did not understand anything of it. Recently, after hearing our sermons, he began to have some understanding of it.

I asked him whether he understood the meaning of those big letters on the first page of the book and he honestly replied that he did not. Then I showed him the same letters in another one of our books which explained the holy name of Jesus. This gave our new Christians a great joy; indeed, it strongly confirmed their belief in the truths they had been taught when they recognized, as I made them see, that the contents of the book that the Buddhist monk had brought was nothing other than their catechism, without any difference, neither in the order of the themes treated nor in the method of instruction.[29]

Even though de Rhodes did not name the author of the book ("one of our Fathers") nor its title, there is no doubt that it was Ricci's *T'ien-chu Shih-i*.[30] The Buddhist monk, we are told, had kept the book for some thirty years before he showed it to de Rhodes sometime in 1629/1630, which would date his father's reception of the book in the first decade of the seventeenth century. Ricci's book, which was first published in Peking in 1603, would have been a worthy gift to a member of the Vietnamese ambassadorial delegation.[31]

It is not clear what de Rhodes meant by "another one of our books." It is unlikely that it referred to de Rhodes's own *Cathechismus* which was not yet printed. If it was not de Rhodes's *Cathechismus* (the "our" here does not imply authorship but possession), what book was it? It could have been any of the books then available in Chinese or *chu nom*.[32]

---

29. *Histoire du Royaume*, 180–81.

30. According to Nguyen Hong, this catechism was that of Michele Ruggieri. See Nguyen Chi Thiet, 59. I myself argue that it was that of Matteo Ricci.

31. One difficulty in identifying the Buddhist monk's book with Ricci's work is the reference to "the holy name of Jesus written in big characters" on "the first page" (not the cover) of the book. The title of Ricci's book is *T'ien-chu Shih-i* and does not contain the word Jesus. De Rhodes did not say that the word Jesus was *printed* on the first page but "marqué" and "peint en gros caractères" on it. Could it be that whoever presented the monk's father with Ricci's book "marked" or "painted" the word Jesus on the first page of the book as part of the dedication? At any rate, I am not aware of any Chinese catechism published before 1600 with the word "Jesus" as part of its title.

Pietro Braido notes that since Ricci's *T'ien-chu Shih-i* is not a catechism proper, the catechism used in China is the translation of *Doutrina* by João da Rocha, S.J., but does not give any information on its full title in Chinese which may contain the word "Jesus" (see *Lineamenti di storia della catechesi e dei catechismi*, 129). Actually, da Rocha was a missionary in Nanking in 1600, and he translated into Chinese the catechism of Marco Jorge, S.J., which was published in 1619. In this case, the book appeared some twenty years after the Vietnamese ambassadorial delegation came to Peking.

On the other hand, it is extremely unlikely that the book was Ruggieri's *T'ien-chu Chen-lu*, for two reasons. First, as was mentioned above, after Ricci completed the first draft of his book in 1596, Ruggieri's work was destroyed. Second, because Ruggieri's book was produced shortly after his arrival in China, it made frequent use of Buddhist terminology (note its subtitle: *A New Compilation from India*) and paid little attention to indigenous Chinese religious traditions such as Taoism and Confucianism. It does not seem appropriate that the "Doctors of the Great West" would present such a book as gift to a member of the Vietnamese embassy.

32. De Rhodes would carry these books around with him during his missionary travels and give them to his potential learned converts to read. Once, as he was in exile from Tonkin, de Rhodes gave

"Their catechism" (i.e., that of the Vietnamese Christians) can mean either the Christian doctrines or the book of catechism. The former meaning is more likely here, that is, the Christian doctrines de Rhodes taught the first Christians in Tonkin. What de Rhodes was claiming is that both the *order* in which he presented the Christian doctrines and the *method* he used to teach them are similar to Ricci's *T'ien-chu Shih-i.*[33] To see whether his claim is justified, it is necessary to examine briefly the contents and the method of Ricci's work.

The True Meaning of the Lord of Heaven is often described not as a "catechism" in a strict sense but as a "pre-evangelical dialogue,"[34] and rightly so. Its express purpose is not to expound the *mysteries* of the Christian faith which are beyond the grasp of reason. Rather it intends to show that self-cultivation, which, according to Confucianism, is the main task of human beings, cannot be successfully achieved without faith in and service to the true God. To support his thesis Ricci does not appeal to the Christian Scripture but to the Confucian classics. In his exposition Ricci studiously avoids anything that exceeds the range of pure reason.[35] Indeed, of the eight dialogues that make up the book, only the tiny last part of the last dialogue (seven pages out of four hundred!) mentions the Christian mysteries of creation, the fall, the incarnation, the ascension, and baptism.

Methodologically, Ricci's book is guided by the principle of "Ch'in ju p'ai fo," that is, "Draw close to Confucianism and repudiate Buddhism." Hence, it is organized as a series of eight dialogues between a Western Christian scholar and a Chinese Confucian scholar.

The contents of *The True Meaning of the Lord of Heaven* can be briefly summarized as follows.[36] (1) Exposition of the existence of the one God ("the Lord of Heaven"), creator of heaven and earth, God as governor and sustainer;

"books written in Chinese" to the governor of Bo Chinh with the hope of converting him (see *Histoire du Royaume*, 235). To Lord Nguyen Phuoc Nguyen's teacher, who later saved his life by persuading the lord to commute the death sentence he had imposed on de Rhodes to exile, de Rhodes "presented with some books written in Chinese characters that our Fathers had put together, in which they explain the Christian truths" (*Divers voyages*, 182–83). Similarly, says de Rhodes, "another great lord who was a captain and commanded part of the king's troops," whom a Vietnamese Christian named John attempted to convert, "was reading our books and giving them to others to read" (*Divers voyages*, 186).

33. It may be asked why de Rhodes did not mention either Ricci or the title of his work. I can only hazard a guess. Perhaps it would have been imprudent for de Rhodes to tie his teaching and catechetical method too closely with Ricci since by 1650 (when the Italian version of *Histoire du Royaume* was published) severe attacks had been mounted against him and his missionary method. In 1643, the Dominican Juan Baptista Morales had denounced the Jesuit practices to the bishop of Manila and submitted to the Propaganda Fide a series of seventeen propositions describing what he regarded as questionable practices of the Jesuits. These propositions were forwarded to the Holy Office. The theologians of the Holy Office examined these practices as described by Morales and found them unacceptable. Their decisions were communicated to the Propagande Fide, which issued a decree condemning the Chinese rites and the Jesuit practices on September 12, 1645, with the approval of Pope Innocent X.

34. *True Meaning*, 15.

35. Explaining the essential content and method of his book, Ricci says: "Now you, Sir, desire to learn the principles of the teachings of the Lord of Heaven. I shall therefore state them plainly for you, and my explanations will be based solely on reason" (*True Meaning*, 71).

36. For an overview of Ricci's book, see *True Meaning*, 25-31, and Ricci's own summary in Latin on pp. 460–72.

(2) refutation of the false opinions regarding the Lord of Heaven found in Chinese religious and moral traditions; (3) affirmation of the immortality of the human soul and its radical difference from birds and other animals; (4) affirmation of the human soul as a pure spirit which does not form an organic unity with the world; (5) refutation of various erroneous doctrines regarding reincarnation; (6) affirmation that our moral life must be intentional and governed by motives; affirmation of heaven and hell in which our good and evil deeds will be remunerated; (7) discussion of the Confucian teaching that human nature is naturally good and affirmation of the Christian teaching that this natural goodness must become "virtuous goodness"; (8) presentation of some Western customs, especially of the practice of celibacy, and brief explanation of why the Lord of Heaven appeared in Jesus.

An extended comparison between Ricci's *T'ien-chu Shih-i* and de Rhodes's *Cathechismus* will reveal both substantial similarities and significant differences.[37] A list of similarities would include the following:

1. Use of natural reason: Both insist that the true religion must be in accord with natural reason, and therefore reason is an indispensable tool to discover the true religion.[38]

2. Use of Chinese canonical writings: Both appeal (Ricci much more than de Rhodes) to the Confucian classics to prove some of their ideas.[39]

3. Existence of God: Both make use of some scholastic arguments (e.g., efficient causality[40]) and similar images (image of the kingdom and the king[41]) to prove the existence of the supreme Lord of all things; both invoke the same argument (the order of the universe[42]) and the same images (the universe as a palace[43] and image of birth from parents[44]) to prove the necessity of the creator.

4. The name of God: Both argue that the term *T'ien* (heaven) as applied to God does not signify the material firmament[45] and that God can be named as Lord of heaven[46] (*Shang-ti* in Chinese and *Duc Chua Troi* in Vietnamese).

5. The cult of heaven: Both argue that cult should be rendered not to the material heaven but to the Lord of Heaven, and both reject the cult to the earth.[47]

6. Etymology of the Chinese word for God: Both argue that the Chinese word for heaven is composed of two characters: one and great.[48]

---

37. See Tan Phat, 61-108, and Nguyen Khac Xuyen, pt. 2, chap. 3.
38. See *True Meaning*, 71; *Cathechismus*, 11.
39. This is the leitmotif of *The True Meaning*; see *Cathechismus*, 12, 21.
40. See *True Meaning*, 77; *Cathechismus*, 28–29.
41. See *True Meaning*, 57; *Cathechismus*, 9.
42. See *True Meaning*, 78–79; *Cathechismus*, 12–13.
43. See *True Meaning*, 77–78; *Cathechismus*, 39–40.
44. See *True Meaning*, 81–82; *Cathechismus*, 12.
45. See *True Meaning*, 125–26; *Cathechismus*, 12–13.
46. See *True Meaning*, 121–23; *Cathechismus*, 9.
47. See *True Meaning*, 127–28; *Cathechismus*, 16.
48. See *True Meaning*, 127; *Cathechismus*, 13–14. The Chinese word for "heaven" was traditionally

7. Incomprehensibility of God's nature: Both relate the story of a minister who repeatedly asked his king to give him more time to find the answer to the king's question about the nature of God.[49] Both also relate the story of Augustine meditating on the mystery of God on the beach at Ostia and his encounter with a child who told him that human intelligence can never fathom the divine mystery.[50]

8. Universality of the Christian religion: Both argue that the religion of the Lord of Heaven is neither a new religion nor a religion peculiar to a particular country but an ancient and universal religion.[51]

9. Degrees of fatherhood: Both refer to three degrees of fatherhood — our physical father, the king, and God — to speak of different kinds of honor and veneration due to each of them.[52]

10. Attitude toward Chinese religions: Both entertain great respect for Confucianism and little esteem for Buddhism and Taoism.[53]

11. Origin of Buddhism in China: Both narrate the story of how Buddhism was mistaken by the Chinese as the true religion of the West.[54]

12. Interpretation of certain philosophical concepts: Both misunderstand the Taoist *Wu*, the Buddhist *K'ung,* and the Neo-Confucianist *T'ai-chi, Li,* and *Ch'i.*[55]

13. Reincarnation: Both use the same arguments to refute the doctrine of reincarnation (e.g., no memory of former lives, immateriality of the human soul).[56]

14. The human soul: Both use the doctrine of three kinds of souls: vegetative, sensitive, and intellectual.[57]

15. The immortality of the human soul: Both use the same arguments to prove that the human soul is immortal: the veneration of ancestors and our natural fear of the deceased person and not of dead animals.[58]

This is by no means a complete list of the similarities between Ricci and de

---

held to be composed of the characters "one" and "great." In recent times it has been shown that this etymological explanation is erroneous.

49. See *True Meaning,* 91; *Cathechismus,* 33–34.

50. See *True Meaning,* 91; *Cathechismus,* 141–42. There is a slight difference between Ricci and de Rhodes here. Ricci places the Augustine story in the context of the knowledge of God's nature in general, whereas de Rhodes places it in the context of understanding the mystery of the Trinity. The latter's use of the story is more faithful to Augustine.

51. See *True Meaning,* 67; *Cathechismus,* 25.

52. See *True Meaning,* 433; *Cathechismus,* 17–21.

53. The whole purpose of *The True Meaning* is captured in the slogan: "Draw close to Confucianism, repudiate Buddhism." See *Cathechismus,* 104–18.

54. See *True Meaning,* 453–54; *Cathechismus,* 109–11. De Rhodes added that the Chinese emperor, whose name is Minh of the Han dynasty, was advised during a dream to seek the "way of the great West" at the time of Jesus' birth, "true legislator and only master" (see *Cathechismus,* 165–66).

55. See *True Meaning,* 99–121; 187–89; *Cathechismus,* 31–33; 105–12.

56. See *True Meaning,* 239–57; *Cathechismus,* 116–17.

57. See *True Meaning,* 145–57; *Cathechismus,* 45–46.

58. See *True Meaning,* 161–65; *Cathechismus,* 129–32.

Rhodes. Clearly, these resemblances, at times verbatim, cannot be accounted for simply by a common culture and a similar theological formation. Rather they are incontrovertible evidences of de Rhodes's familiarity with and use of Ricci's work in composing his *Cathechismus*. To this extent de Rhodes's claim that his catechism is similar to the Chinese catechism (which we have argued to be Ricci's) in the order in which Christian doctrines are treated and in the method of instruction is largely justified.

On the other hand, the dissimilarities between the two works are so numerous and substantial that it would be wrong to say that *Cathechismus* is a clone or even a pale imitation of *T'ien-chu Shih-i*.[59] A close analysis of both the contents and method of *Cathechismus* given below will support such a conclusion. Suffice it here to note that the similarities we have pointed out above are confined basically to the first two "days" of *Cathechismus* and that, besides differences in format (Ricci's is dialogue whereas de Rhodes's is continuous exposition), de Rhodes's intended audience and especially his reliance on divine revelation, instead of only on pure reason (as is Ricci's procedure), to develop his themes and arguments make *Cathechismus* an entirely different work. It belongs to the catechism genre proper rather than being a "pre-evangelical dialogue" like *T'ien-chu Shih-i*. As a consequence, whereas Ricci's discussion of Christian doctrines is given in seven meager pages, de Rhodes's explication of them forms the heart of his book.[60]

HISTORY AND STRUCTURE OF *CATHECHISMUS*

De Rhodes's *Cathechismus*, together with his *Dictionarium*, was published in Rome in 1651 with the assistance of the Propaganda Fide. They were the first Vietnamese *printed* works in the new script.[61] The significance of *Cathechismus* lies in two areas, namely, cultural-linguistic and catechetico-theological. In the first respect, it represents a landmark in the process of Romanizing the Vietnamese language and is an immense contribution of Christianity to the Vietnamese culture. An investigation of this aspect lies outside the scope of our present work.[62] In what follows we will continue our examination of the catechetical contribution of *Cathechismus*, reserving the study of its theology to the next chapter.

---

59. Hence, de Rhodes's statement is a gross exaggeration. Such an overstatement, however, is understandable since, for de Rhodes's audience, any similarity between de Rhodes's catechesis and an ancient Chinese text would constitute a proof of the authenticity and correctness of his teaching.

60. For a comparison between Ricci and de Rhodes, see Nguyen Chi Thiet, 338–51.

61. We emphasize "printed" because we do know that there were *handwritten* texts in the new script before the publication of de Rhodes's works, such as the now lost dictionaries of Gaspar do Amaral and António Barbosa.

62. A brief discussion of this aspect as well as de Rhodes's *Dictionarium* has been given in chap. 1.

HISTORY

As we have argued above, de Rhodes was familiar with the major Counter-Reformation catechisms and with some of the first catechisms prepared for Asia, especially those by Francis Xavier, Alessandro Valignano, Michele Ruggieri, and Matteo Ricci. In preaching and teaching, first in Tonkin and later in Cochinchina, de Rhodes of course drew upon his own theological knowledge which he had acquired at the Roman College. But he knew that he had to adapt both the method and contents of his catechesis to the Vietnamese people who, despite their many similarities with the Chinese, had their own language, culture, and religions.

Because of cultural and religious similarities between the Chinese and the Vietnamese, de Rhodes thought he could borrow from the earlier works of his confreres in China, especially those of Alessandro Valignano and Michele Ruggieri (probably) and of Matteo Ricci (certainly), and he did so extensively. But his experiences in Tonkin and Cochinchina convinced him that the catechisms of his predecessors, illustrious as they were, and their catechetical methods, however effective in their contexts, could not be replicated, like a recipe, for his new mission field. To be an effective missionary and to meet the needs of his Vietnamese audience, he had to devise a catechetical method of his own and to write his own text.

This effort eventually gave birth to *Cathechismus*. It was probably not a project conceived on the spur of a moment and produced in a short period of time. Though de Rhodes has not left us an account of how he arrived at the idea of writing a catechism and how he went about composing it,[63] it is more than likely that *Cathechismus* was a child of necessity. De Rhodes simply *had* to write down something on the basis of which to preach and teach because he had to find, *for the first time,* Vietnamese words that would be appropriate equivalents of Christian concepts and Latin terminologies, especially as he began his ministry in Tonkin in 1627.

He had learned the Vietnamese language two years earlier, in Cochinchina, with the help of Francisco de Pina. His lessons must have included some theological terms, since he was able to hear confessions within four months and to preach within six.[64] However, there is little doubt that the theological vocabularies in *Cathechismus* are far more numerous and sophisticated than those he had been taught. In developing his glossary of Vietnamese theological terms and in his efforts at Romanizing them, de Rhodes was assisted by the dictionaries of Gaspar do Amaral and António Barbosa. In addition, he must have been helped by his catechists who themselves had to determine whether the Vietnamese words that de Rhodes used were adequate to the theological concepts they were intended to express.

---

63. *Cathechismus* does not have the usual preface or introduction in which the genesis of the work is normally explained.

64. See *Divers voyages,* 73.

Cathechismus[65] was in all likelihood composed during the years 1636–45, that is, during the later years of de Rhodes's professorship in Macao and his second mission to Cochinchina, when he had gained a mastery of the Vietnamese language and the Romanizing system.[66] At any rate, it must have been completed after *Histoire du Royaume de Tunquin* (1636), since in this memoir de Rhodes made no mention of his *Cathechismus* (or his *Dictionarium*), and before *Divers voyages et missions* (1647), since in this work de Rhodes referred twice to his *Cathechismus*.[67]

Cathechismus received permission for publication by the vicar general of the Society of Jesus Gosswin Nickel on July 8, 1651. On October 2, 1651, in a meeting of the Propaganda Fide, the cardinals ordered all current printing jobs of its press to be temporarily suspended in order to complete the publication of de Rhodes's catechism as soon as possible. Probably, therefore, copies of it were available at the beginning of 1652.

It goes without saying that the printing of both *Cathechismus* and *Dictionarium* was a laborious and costly enterprise. Technically, it required making new types for the Romanized Vietnamese with its own diacritical marks. Fortunately for de Rhodes, the printing costs were underwritten by the Propaganda Fide.[68] To assist the printers who were unfamiliar with the new writing system, de Rhodes must have supervised the entire printing process to make as few errors as possible.[69]

Cathechismus was printed in two languages, each page having two columns, the right featuring the Vietnamese text, the left its Latin translation. To facilitate cross-checking the two texts, each text is divided into small sections having the same meaning, each section marked with the same alphabet, from *a* to *z*. The book is printed in quarto, with 319 pages.

---

65. Note de Rhodes's spelling with an *h* after *t*. There were three spellings current in the seventeenth century: *catechismus* (the more common), *cathechismus*, and *catecismus*.

66. Do Quang Chinh persuasively argues that 1636 is the *terminus a quo* and 1645 the *terminus ad quem* of the composition of both *Cathechismus* and *Dictionarium*. After 1636, because both works demonstrate that de Rhodes achieved a much surer command of the Romanization technique, especially in the use of diacritical marks, perhaps thanks to the works of Gaspar do Amaral and António Barbosa, than that he had shown in his earlier letters. Before 1645, because after this date de Rhodes was undertaking a long and arduous journey to Rome which would have afforded him little time to work on such demanding projects (de Rhodes left Macao on December 20, 1645, and arrived in Rome on June 27, 1649). Furthermore, between 1640 and 1645, de Rhodes was working off and on in Cochinchina with periods of absence (totaling about sixteen months) in Macao. It is highly likely that during his second mission to Cochinchina de Rhodes received much help from his catechists, especially the ex-mandarin Ignatius, in composing his two works. See Do Quang Chinh, *Lich Su Chu Quoc Ngu 1620–1659* (History of the National Script 1620–59) (Saigon: Ra Khoi, 1972), 83–84.

67. See *Divers voyages*, 74 and 96.

68. It is interesting to note that both works have the following description of the author: "*Ab Alexandro de Rhodes è Societate Iesu, ejusdemque Sacrae Congregationis Missionario Apostolico.*" The title "apostolic missionary of the same Sacred Congregation" (i.e., of the Propaganda Fide) is a subtle indication that de Rhodes was not a missionary by authorization of the Portuguese crown by virtue of the *padroado* system, but under the jurisdiction of the Congregation of Propaganda Fide.

69. In spite of the painstaking proofreading, there are two full pages of typographical errors in *Cathechismus*! See pp. 3–4.

STRUCTURE

As has been pointed out, to compound its strangeness, the book does not have the usual preface or introduction in which to explain its nature and purpose. Perhaps it was felt that the title is self-explanatory: the book is billed as a "catechism for those who wish to receive baptism in order to enter the holy way [religion] of the Lord of heaven."[70] The fact that it was published by the Propaganda Fide may suggest that the catechism was intended for the use of mission countries. No detailed information on the author is given nor is the book dedicated with the usual flourish to a high-born person, as were de Rhodes's two memoirs.

One would know that the strange-looking script on the right column of the page is Vietnamese (*Tunchinensis*) only by reading the vicar general Gosswin Nickel's *nihil obstat*.

Cathechismus is also distinctive in that it adopts neither the time-honored question-and-answer format of Counter-Reformation catechisms nor the dialogue structure popularized by Ruggieri's and Ricci's works. Rather it uses the expository method, perhaps because this was felt to be more appropriate for a manual of catechesis.

Furthermore, the book is not divided into chapters but "days," and there are no titled subdivisions within each day. Each day is of roughly the same length, apparently so that each day's material can be treated in one day,[71] and the material of the whole book should/could be covered in eight days.[72]

That de Rhodes intended his *Cathechismus* to be covered in eight days is implied by the following account of the first months of his mission in Tonkin:

> Toward September [i.e., of 1627], that is, four months after our arrival in the capital, we moved into a new house, part of which we turned into a church. From the time we first moved in, so many people came to see us that we had to preach six times a day, three in the morning and three in the afternoon, to satisfy the demands of those who kept coming to listen to us, one group after another. The fruits we gathered from our labor and from the seeds of God's Word which we sowed were so great that we had to take two days out of the week to administer baptism to those who wished to receive it. Ordinarily, each group had 20 and sometimes 40 persons, among whom there were people of distinction, even from the lord's family.
>
> At the beginning we had to engage in dispute with certain curious and contentious people who came to listen to us with the intention to contra-

---

70. The full Vietnamese title reads: "Phep giang tam ngay cho ke muan chiu phep rua toi, ma beao dao thanh duc Chua Troi."

71. This is implied by the opening lines of the second day — "Praise be to God! *Yesterday* we said that..." (*Cathechismus*, 27) — and those of the third day — "*Yesterday* we have explained briefly that..." (*Cathechismus*, 58). Emphasis added.

72. See *Divers voyages*, 96: "I have explained it [i.e., catechetical method] at length in my *Catechism*, which I divide over the course of eight days, wherein I try to propound all the main truths in which idolaters require instruction."

dict the doctrines we were teaching. This not only disturbed the order of our sermons, taking away the precious time which was allotted to them, forcing us to answer their questions and resolving their doubts, but also sowed confusion in the minds of others and prevented the Gospel from producing its fruits.

 We therefore decided not to allow anyone to ask questions unless he or she had assiduously listened for *eight days* to the doctrines we were teaching. As a result, either these contentious people withdrew, too impatient to wait until the end, or they listened attentively to us during this time, and had their doubts eventually cleared up and had nothing more to object to us. In this way we did not lose time and there was less danger of troubling the well-intentioned people with frivolous questions.[73]

De Rhodes's baptismal catechesis, with its eight-day cycle, was not as lengthy as patristic catechumenate but not as cursory as Francis Xavier's which, because of the great number of people who came to him, was often limited to the rudiments of the Christian faith — the *Credo, Pater,* and *Ave Maria*. Indeed, if each day's material is divided into six lectures, as de Rhodes reported, each lasting, let's say, about an hour, it could without difficulty be treated adequately.

 Although the book is called a catechism, it is also a manual of catechesis, as is clear from the occasional instructions de Rhodes gives to catechists on when and how to present certain doctrines.[74] However, *Cathechismus* is not a how-to book, explicit methodological instructions being minimal. It is essentially an exposition of the Christian faith, and the catechetical method is found, not in the few asides about *how* to illustrate a particular teaching, but in the very *selection, structuring,* and *explication* of the doctrines to be taught.

DE RHODES'S CATECHETICAL METHOD

 As mentioned above, in *Cathechismus* de Rhodes has not provided us with a preface and/or introduction in which his catechetical method would be explained. However, elsewhere he did expound at some length on how Christian doctrines should be taught. To understand both de Rhodes's catechetical enterprise and *Cathechismus,* we will have to analyze these texts carefully as well as to examine the actual ordering of doctrines in *Cathechismus* itself.

FOUNDATIONAL TEXTS ON CATECHETICAL METHOD

 Given the extreme importance of the passages in which de Rhodes explains how Christian doctrines should be taught in Vietnam, it is necessary to quote them here in full, despite their length, and in chronological order.

---

73. *Histoire du Royaume,* 173–75. Emphasis added.
74. See *Cathechismus,* 133; 166–69; 261; 316–19.

The first text occurs in the context of de Rhodes's arrival in Tonkin in March 1627. After telling the curious crowd who had gathered around the newly arrived Portuguese merchants that he had a precious pearl to sell so cheap that everybody could afford to buy, that is, the true *way*, de Rhodes added:

Text A

Having heard of the law which they call *dao* in scholarly language and *dang* in popular language, which means the *way*, they became all the more curious to know from me the true law, the true way that I wanted to show them. Thereupon I talked to them about the sovereign Principle of all created beings. I decided to announce it to them under the name of the Lord of heaven and earth, finding no proper word in their language to refer to God. Indeed, what they commonly call *Phat* or *But* designates nothing but an idol. And knowing that the cult of idols was held in high esteem by the leaders and doctors of the kingdom, I do not deem it proper to designate God with these words. Rather, I decided to employ the name used by the apostle Saint Paul when he preached to the Athenians who had set up an altar to an unknown God. This God, he said, whom they adored without knowing him, is the Lord of heaven and earth (*duc Chua troi dat*). It was therefore under this name full of majesty even in the hearts of the pagans that I first announced to them that the true way consisted first and foremost in fulfilling our legitimate duties to the Lord of heaven and earth by the means God has revealed to us.[75]

The second, and most important text, constitutes de Rhodes's *magna carta* of the catechetical method which he developed explicitly for the Vietnamese people:

Text B

Among those who announce the doctrine of the Gospel to other kingdoms of pagans there are many who are of the opinion that it is necessary first to destroy the errors of paganism and disabuse the minds of pagans of these erroneous views before establishing and teaching the doctrines and principles of the Christian religion. This method, they claim, follows the order God has given to a prophet, saying: I have commanded you to destroy and pull up, to build and plant.

Others, as far as the most august mystery of the Holy Trinity is concerned, maintain that it should be expounded to catechumens only after they have been disposed to receive baptism in order to avoid troubling their minds with doubts which this most sublime and ineffable mystery might induce.

From my own experience, however, I believe that between these two options there is another method of teaching more appropriate for the people

---

75. *Histoire du Royaume*, 129–30. This text has already been quoted in chap. 2.

of this kingdom. This method requires that one not attack the errors of the Tonkinese sects before establishing the truths knowable by the light of natural reason, such as the creation of the world, the end for which the sovereign Principle of created things has made and ordered the rational creatures, the obligations incumbent upon them to know and serve God. The goal is to build in the hearers' minds a sort of firm foundation on which the rest of their faith can be supported and not to turn them off, which often happens, by our rebutting and ridiculing their devotions, false though they are, and their superstitious observances.

I have often been more successful, as far as I can tell, in impressing upon them feelings of piety and natural love toward the Creator and the First Principle of their being. Then, by means of a narrative of the history of the universal flood and of the confusion of languages, I inspire in them a sense of fear of God whom they must fear and adore. Then follows a refutation of the idolatry which, incidentally, the devil himself has not introduced into the world until after the flood.

In this I am in perfect agreement with others that we must not expound to the pagans whom we wish to convert the mysteries of the Holy Trinity, the incarnation and the passion of the Son of God, and sow the holy seed of these great truths in their hearts before we have uprooted the errors and superstition of idolatry.

Nevertheless, I do not believe that we should wait until the time of baptism to propose to the catechumens the faith in the Trinity of the divine persons. On the contrary, we must begin with an exposition of this mystery, and then it will be easier to go from there to the incarnation of the Son of God, who is the Second Person, and to what he has suffered to save the world lost by sin, and to his resurrection and other mysteries of our religion. After all, this is the order and method followed by the apostles in the symbol of the faith which they have left us.

For myself, during the many years I have been engaged in teaching the pagans, I have not found anyone who objected to our faith with regard to the exposition of the incomprehensible mystery of the Trinity. On the contrary, I have always found that they had more difficulty in believing the Incarnation. The reason for this is that they do not find it strange that God, whose nature they recognize by the light of natural reason to be incomprehensible and exceeding the scope of our knowledge, is also less amenable to explanation by our discourses with regard to his properties and persons whom we propose to their belief.

On the other hand, we have the greatest trouble in convincing them that the one who is pure spirit, eternal, and immortal, and who reigns in heaven crowned with glory, was clothed in the flesh, born in time, subject to death, and exposed to all sorts of shame and misery.

That is why, when it is time to propose to the catechumens the mysteries of Passion, we must do it with skill and a little differently from when we present them to Christians by observing three things. First, we must throw in much sharper relief the miraculous events that occurred in the death of Jesus Christ, such as nature recoiling from the crime committed against his person, the sun withdrawing its rays and refusing to shine upon the earth guilty of such an execrable sacrilege, the tombs opening up, the rocks bursting asunder, the earth shaking, and all the creatures experiencing pains at the death of their creator. From all this the conclusion is drawn that if he died, it is because he chose to do so of his own free will and that he granted his murderers the power which he had to kill him, in order to redeem and save the human race.

Secondly, after explaining the great love and the wonderful virtues which Jesus Christ has shown in his suffering and death, it is appropriate to expose to them for the first time the image of the cross for their adoration, with lighted candles and other similar ceremonies of devotion.

Thirdly, we must never explain the passion and death of the Redeemer without adding immediately the narrative of his glorious resurrection, of how he rose by his own power on the third day, and how he went out in triumph from the tomb where he had been placed. In this way it is made clear that if he could give himself life by overcoming death, he was the Lord of life and death, and that in principle he could have prevented his own death and could have been delivered from the hands of the Jews, had he so wanted.

These things should be repeated often and impressed upon their minds so that they may conceive more love and respect for the Savior. Experience has taught me that the deeper love and devotion they have for the Savior's passion, the firmer they become in their Christian faith, and the more constant in their practice of virtues.[76]

The third text contains de Rhodes's reflections on the ease with which he succeeded in converting the "idolatrous priests [i.e., Buddhists monks], who are usually the most obstinate." This success de Rhodes attributed to the particular method he used in catechizing Vietnamese pagans:

Text C

I found them marvelously open to reason. I baptized 200 of them who will be of unbelievable help to us in converting others. One of them brought me 500 of those he had disabused of error by teaching them the truths of faith, and they have since become our most fervent catechists. They were all delighted when I pointed out to them how our religion conforms to right reason, and they admired above all God's Ten Commandments, finding that nothing more reasonable could be uttered

---

76. *Histoire du Royaume*, 175–78.

or more worthy of being laid down by the Supreme Ruler of the world. My favorite method was to propose to them the immortality of the soul and the afterlife. From thence I went on to prove God's existence and providence. Advancing thus from one degree to the next, we gradually came to the more difficult mysteries. Experience has shown us that this way of instructing the pagans is very useful. I have explained it at length in my catechism, which I divide over the course of eight days, wherein I try to propound all the main truths on which the idolaters should be taught.[77]

De Rhodes's Catechetical Method: Seven Principles

These three fundamental texts give us in a nutshell the method de Rhodes adopted in his catechesis in Vietnam. Before examining whether and if so, how *Cathechismus* embodies these methodological principles, it would be helpful to lay them out in systematic form:

1. No catechetical method is universally applicable. A method that is apt for "other kingdoms of pagans" (Text B) may not be effective in Vietnam. One has to discover through "experience" (this word is used repeatedly in Texts B and C) which method is most appropriate and effective for the people one is catechizing.

2. Experience has taught de Rhodes that two approaches were counterproductive in Vietnam. The first *begins* with an attack of the Vietnamese religious beliefs and practices. A critique of these religious traditions is, de Rhodes concedes, *necessary* since they do contain doctrinal errors and superstitious practices, but it should not be undertaken as the *preliminary* step before one teaches the truths of Christianity.

The Vietnamese people are deeply religious; preliminary "rebutting and ridiculing" (Text B) of their religions would, as is often the case, offend their religious sensibility and close their ears and hearts to the Gospel. This "refutation of idolatry" will be done only *after* one has spoken of the existence of God, creation, the fall, the flood, the Tower of Babel (Text B). De Rhodes notes that this order is not only logically and psychologically sound but also *historically* correct, because, according to him, it was only *after* the flood that the devil brought idolatry into the world (Text B).

3. The second approach to be rejected for the Vietnamese people concerns the *ordering* of Christian doctrines. Some missionaries maintain that the doctrine of the Trinity should not be presented to catechumens at the beginning of catechesis but should be postponed toward its end, right before baptism. The reason for this order is to "avoid troubling their minds with doubts" (Text B). De Rhodes rejects this proposal for three reasons. Theologically, the doctrine of

---

77. *Divers voyages*, 96.

the Trinity is presupposed by the doctrine of "the incarnation of the Son of God, who is the Second Person" (Text B). Experientially, in the many years of teaching pagans, de Rhodes has not found anyone objecting to the doctrine of the Trinity. Traditionally, the proposed order is not the one followed by the creed. Hence, de Rhodes recommends that the exposition of the trinitarian mystery be done at the *beginning* of catechesis (Text B).

4. This does not mean that one *starts* with the doctrine of the Trinity. Rather one must commence with truths "knowable by the light of natural reason," such as the creation of the world, the aim of human life, and the obligations of knowing and serving God (Text B). Other "natural" truths with which one should begin catechesis for the Vietnamese include "the immortality of the soul and the afterlife" (Text C). The goal is to establish in the hearers' minds "a sort of firm foundation on which the rest of their faith can be supported" (Text B) so that Christianity is shown "to conform to right reason" (Text C). This is one of the reasons why Vietnamese Buddhist monks admired and accepted the Christian doctrines and ethics (Text C).

5. The most difficult Christian doctrine to teach the Vietnamese, in de Rhodes's experience, is that of the incarnation, passion, and death of the Son of God. To the Vietnamese mind it seems to contradict God's spirituality, eternity, immortality, and omnipotence. Interestingly, de Rhodes notes that presenting christological doctrines to pagans requires a *different* method from the one used to explain them to believers (Text B). To make them credible, de Rhodes suggests a triple strategy: highlighting the cosmic wonders associated with Christ's death, fostering devotion to the suffering Christ, and connecting Christ's passion with his resurrection. The point is to affirm as strongly as possible the freedom with which Jesus accepted his passion and hence his lordship over all his enemies and all things, including humankind's most powerful adversary, death (Text B).

6. As one attempts to tailor one's catechetical method to the local situation, its religious language must be pressed into service. In so doing two guidelines should be observed. First, words that at first sight seem equivalent to Christian concepts may not be appropriate; attention must be paid to their different philosophical and religious contexts (e.g., *but* or *phat* are not appropriate equivalents of God, given the polytheistic context in which they were used). Second, biblical usage provides a useful guide in coining new theological terms (e.g., *Duc Chua troi dat* for God, on the basis of Acts 17:23–25). This second rule makes it clear that de Rhodes's method is governed by divine revelation and not by natural reason, that is, "by the means God has revealed to us" (Text A).

7. Finally, in catechesis it is necessary to link doctrine with praxis, instruction with worship. Christian truths are shown to have practical implications both for worship, e.g., devotion to the Passion of Christ (Text B) and ethics, e.g., "our legitimate duties to the Lord of heaven and earth" (Text A) and "the practice of virtues" (Text B).

METHOD IN THE *CATHECHISMUS*

To what extent has *Cathechismus* exemplified these methodological principles? A close analysis of de Rhodes's catechism will confirm that it has observed his method point-by-point.[78]

THE ORDERING OF DOCTRINES

As has been mentioned above, *Cathechismus* is divided into eight days. Furthermore, it is clear that as far as *content* is concerned, de Rhodes has also divided it into two parts: the first is composed of Day One to Day Four, and the second of Day Five to Day Eight. Each part is then symmetrically made up of four days, with Day Five marking a decisive turning point in both the method and content of catechesis: "What follows should not be expounded to all but only to those who, having heard what has been said above, have already despised idols and false religions and are prepared to receive baptism by fasting and other works of piety. At this stage, they may be given Our Lord's Prayer, the Hail Mary, and the Apostles' Creed to learn by heart."[79]

1. The double goal of the first four days is then (*a*) to lead the catechumens to "despise idols and false religions" and (*b*) to make a personal decision to accept baptism and to corroborate this choice with works of piety. In other words, the aim of all catechesis is Christian conversion. How is this objective achieved? Day One opens with reflections on the precariousness of life and our natural desire for longevity or better still, eternal life. These thoughts naturally lead to the time-honored doctrine of the two ways, the one leading to heaven, the other to hell.[80] The way to heaven is constituted by the cult of "heaven," and the way to hell by the cult of "idols." This double way, says de Rhodes, happens to be the philosophy "commonly found among the Vietnamese."[81]

To determine which way is true requires the use of right reason, since "the true way must necessarily conform to reason."[82] This use of reason as the means to build a common ground between Christianity and the Vietnamese pagans helps de Rhodes to carry out his plan to establish a basis upon which their eventual faith can rest (principle 4). It is important to note here that despite de Rhodes's metaphor of natural reason as the "foundation" of faith, he is no

---

78. For an exposition of de Rhodes's catechetical method, see Nguyen Chi Thiet, 293–310.

79. *Cathechismus*, 133. In a way de Rhodes is following the patristic *disciplina arcani* by concealing certain theological doctrines and religious practices from catechumens and pagans.

80. This corresponds with de Rhodes's statement that "my favorite method was to propose to them the immortality of the soul and the afterlife" (Text C). Note the difference between this eschatological orientation of de Rhodes and Matteo Ricci's starting point in reflections on the duty of self-cultivation (see *True Meaning*, 65). Ricci's approach is dictated by his audience, which is the Confucian scholar whose central focus is the perfection of the individual, de Rhodes's by the religious tradition of his Vietnamese pagans.

81. *Cathechismus*, 11.

82. *Cathechismus*, 11.

crypto-Enlightenment, rationalist theologian attempting to justify Christian beliefs at the bar of reason or to demonstrate the reasonableness of the Christian mysteries by means of philosophical arguments. Rather his appeal to reason only serves the purpose of finding an entry point into the culture and religions of the people whom he was catechizing and of instituting a dialogue between Christian faith and the Vietnamese cultural and religious traditions. In other words, the search for a common ground is purely methodological. Substantively, however, de Rhodes's theology is shaped by divine revelation and not by what reason can discover (principle 6).

2. This primacy of faith over reason is made abundantly clear in Day Two. After arguing, on the basis of reason and Vietnamese religious practices (e.g., the *Nam Giao* sacrifice), that the way to heaven is by means of the cult of "the supreme Father and Lord of all things, who creates and preserves heaven and the earth and all things,"[83] de Rhodes relates the story of a pagan philosopher who was asked by his king to find the answer to the problem of the nature of God. The philosopher asked for one day, then two, then four more days to reflect on his answer and at the end confessed his inability to produce one. Then adds de Rhodes: "This non-Christian philosopher is like someone who, contemplating the immensity of the ocean, sees it better the more he moves away from the beach. We, however, *assisted by the Lord of Heaven*, will dare to say something about who the true artisan of heaven and the earth and all things, the supreme Lord is."[84]

This "assistance by the Lord of Heaven" is nothing other than divine revelation. Indeed, to arrive at an adequate understanding of God and divine nature, we have to have recourse to both reason and revelation: "These attributes of the sovereign creator of all things, Lord of heaven, the earth, and all things are made known to us not only by God's revelation in his book but also by natural reason impressed in our hearts by God."[85]

3. This appeal to revelation allows de Rhodes to speak on Day Three of the creation of angels (in particular, of Lucifer and Michael), of the material world, of Adam and Eve, of the earthly paradise; of the temptation and fall of Eve and Adam; of the consequences of original sin; of the necessity of the baptism of children. On Day Four he continues the sacred history with the narrative of the first patriarchs, in particular Cain and Abel, Seth, Enoch, and Methuselah, and Noah and the flood.

4. It is only *after* having taught these truths that de Rhodes, according to

---

83. *Cathechismus*, 19–20. See also p. 34: "We affirm that there is as it were a light in the human heart which manifests the existence of God, since without God as creator and lord who is the first cause and original source, nothing of this entire world would exist."

84. *Cathechismus*, 34, emphasis added. Recall that Ricci relates the same story and mentions explicitly the story of Augustine meditating on the mystery of God and his encounter with a child on the beach of Ostia. See *True Meaning*, 91–92. De Rhodes's use of the image of the ocean implicitly refers to Augustine. De Rhodes will relate the story of Augustine in his exposition of the Trinity. See *Cathechismus*, 141–42.

85. *Cathechismus*, 50.

his method (principle 2), undertakes his critique of the errors and superstitious practices of the Three Religions and of the Vietnamese indigenous religion. By this time, de Rhodes hopes, the catechumens will have been convinced of the truths of Christianity and would be psychologically disposed to perceive the errors of their religions. Only at this stage, then, is an attack against the Vietnamese religions pastorally opportune and effective. As we have seen in chapter 3, de Rhodes's knowledge of the *doctrines* of these religions leaves a lot to be desired, though he displays a remarkable familiarity with their *practices*. The point here is not whether de Rhodes's knowledge of the Vietnamese religions is accurate but that, contrary to many other missionaries, he does not begin his exposition of the Christian truths with an attack against the Vietnamese religions with the risk of alienating his audience. Rather he makes the rejection of the Vietnamese religions a *natural* consequence of accepting the truth of Christianity.

5. The predominance of faith over reason, which de Rhodes has already affirmed in Day Two, becomes even more explicit in Day Five. As has been mentioned above, Day Five marks a radical turning point in the spiritual development of the catechumens. Enlightened by divine revelation and fortified by grace, they have been enabled to recognize the errors of their religious traditions and have decided to embrace the Christian truths. It is appropriate then at this stage to introduce the two most sublime Christian mysteries, the Trinity and the Incarnation: "We have established at the beginning that there exists a first principle of all created things, knowable by the light of natural reason.... His incomprehensible essence and his attributes are such that no created intellect can grasp them unless it is elevated by God with a supernatural light. This light is twofold. The first is the light of faith by which God reveals himself and divine matters to us in this life through his words.... The second light is called the light of *gloria;* the created intellect, elevated and enlightened by it, sees the divine essence clearly, as it is."[86]

Faithful to his method, de Rhodes proceeds to expound the mystery of the Trinity at the beginning of the second phase of catechesis, in Day Five, *before* the mystery of the Incarnation, rather than at the end, immediately prior to baptism, as his colleagues used to do (principle 3).

6. In his exposition of the christological doctrines, de Rhodes introduces a method rarely practiced by Counter-Reformation catechisms. Differently from his explanation of the Trinity, which is couched in abstract scholastic terms, de Rhodes's exposition of the christological mysteries is concrete and scripture-based. In fact, it is narrative theology at it best. De Rhodes devotes part of Day Five and the entire Day Six to telling the stories of Jesus' infancy and public ministry, with particular emphasis on Jesus' miracles. Instead of explaining christological and mariological doctrines in the abstract, de Rhodes anchors

---

86. *Cathechismus,* 133–34. With this explicit appeal to the light of faith and with the exposition of the mysteries of the Trinity and Incarnation, de Rhodes goes beyond the "pre-evangelical dialogue" of Matteo Ricci and undertakes catechesis proper.

them in the appropriate *stories* of Mary's and Jesus' lives: Mary's immaculate conception is placed in the context of her birth, her perpetual virginity in the birth of Jesus, the hypostatic union of the one divine person of the Logos in his two natures in the annunciation, Jesus' divinity and the authenticity of his teaching in the miracles he performed. In this way, these doctrines appear to catechumens not as abstract propositions but as life-giving teachings intimately connected with the words and deeds of Jesus.

7. In his exposition of Jesus' passion and death in Day Seven, de Rhodes carries out his threefold strategy to the letter: highlighting the miraculous elements of Jesus' death, fostering devotion to the suffering Christ, and linking Jesus' death with his resurrection (principle 5). With regard to the first strategy, de Rhodes made good use of his astronomical knowledge to explain how the solar eclipse at Jesus' death could not be a natural occurrence but had to be a miracle.[87] Indeed, de Rhodes adds that Dionysius, "a pagan gentleman and a famous mathematician," saw this solar eclipse at Hieropolis in Egypt, and later, when he heard St. Paul mention it in Athens, he recognized that it had happened on the day and at the hour of the eclipse he observed at Hieropolis. Thereupon, de Rhodes says, he embraced the Christian faith.[88]

To foster devotion to the suffering Christ de Rhodes reminds the catechists that after speaking of Jesus' death, they should "display some beautiful representation of the Lord Jesus Christ on the cross, if possible with candles and incense, and address those present with the following words or words to this effect."[89] There follows a long prayer[90] composed by de Rhodes himself in which the catechumens are urged to express their repentance for their past sins and their gratitude and love for Christ: "Would that I had never offended you, O my most beloved Lord, but because the past is no longer in my power, I am firmly resolved to serve you in the future with all my heart and obey your commandments with all my strength until I depart from this world. I also renounce all the vain idols and all the diabolical religions I have foolishly adhered to till now; and you, my true God, who suffered and died on the cross, I adore you and bless you for ever and ever. Amen."[91]

To link Jesus' passion with his resurrection, de Rhodes follows his account of

---

87. Basically, de Rhodes's argument is as follows: Normally, a solar eclipse happens only with the new moon, that is on the first or thirtieth day of the month, when the moon stands between the sun and the earth. Now Jesus' death occurred during the Passover which always took place at *full* moon. Hence, the solar eclipse at that time was a divine miracle. This is how de Rhodes describes it: "At this moment, the moon found itself opposite to the meridian line of the sun and was hidden by the earth; it suddenly turned, moved up to the meridian line of the sun and immediately came to a standstill under the sun, and eclipsed it, not only for certain regions as was normal, but for the entire world" (*Cathechismus*, 228–29). No doubt, de Rhodes's "scientific" explanation of the solar eclipse at Jesus' death made a deep impression on the Vietnamese who were terrified by phenomena of solar and lunar eclipses. See *Histoire du Royaume*, 195–96; 237–38.

88. See *Cathechismus*, 229–30.

89. *Cathechismus*, 232–33.

90. The prayer runs from pp. 233–38 of *Cathechismus*. It goes without saying that this prayer is an eloquent testimony to de Rhodes's own spirituality.

91. *Cathechismus*, 237–38.

Jesus' death immediately with a narrative of Jesus' descent into hell, resurrection, apparitions, and ascension. The point of the narrative is to demonstrate that death did not affect Jesus' divinity and that Jesus' power and glory shone forth in his resurrection: "On the third day, after the holy death of the Lord Jesus Christ (the day on which the Lord had often foretold that he would rise from the dead), when dawn had just begun, his most holy soul, surrounded by the souls of the just who had been released from the prison of the *limbo* and by a great number of angels, approached the tomb and reunited with his most holy body, raising it immediately, glorious and impassible."[92]

ADAPTATION OF THEOLOGICAL TERMS

One of the principles governing de Rhodes's catechetical method is the adaptation of theological terminology from local religious traditions (principle 6). As mentioned above, de Rhodes had to find for himself Vietnamese words that would be equivalent to Christian theological concepts and Latin terms, especially during the composition of *Cathechismus*. We will examine here some of the most important Vietnamese terms that de Rhodes adopted in his catechism.[93]

1. Terms for God

No doubt most prominent among theological terms is the word for God. We know that when Christian missionaries arrived in China, they were faced with the problem of deciding which of the three available terms, *t'ien* (heaven), *shang-ti* (sovereign on high), and *t'ien-chu* or *t'ien-ti* (lord of heaven) would be the appropriate equivalent for *Deus*. Ricci argued that it would be inappropriate to designate God with words such as "Supreme Ultimate" (*T'ai-chi*) and "Principle" (*li*), as the Neo-Confucianist philosophers appeared to him to have done. Rather he was in favor of using the three words mentioned above interchangeably to designate God.[94]

As is well known, Ricci's proposal was not officially approved. On March 26, 1693, Charles Maigrot, vicar apostolic of Fukien, issued a *mandatum* in which he declared not only that the "Chinese rites" were forbidden to Christians but also that of three terms, only *t'ien-chu,* and not *t'ien* and *shang-ti,* would be inappropriate for God.[95]

---

92. *Cathechismus*, 243.
93. On this subject, see Do Quang Chinh, 297–304.
94. See the second dialogue of *True Meaning*.
95. The use of *T'ien-chu* for God is ratified by Clement XI's decree *Ex illa die* (1715) and Benedict XIV's decree *Ex quo singulari* (1742). Benedict's decision is expressed in the following statement: "Cum Deus Optimus Maximus congrue apud Sinas vocabulis europaeis exprimi nequeant, ad eumdem verum Deum significandum, vocabulum *Tien Chu,* hoc est, Caeli Dominus, quod a sinensibus missionariis, et fidelium longo ac probato usu receptum esse disgnoscitur, admittendum esse: nomina vero *Tien* (caelum) et *Xang Ti* (supremus imperator) penitus rejicienda." See *Collectanea Sacrae Congregationis de Propaganda Fide,* 1622–1886, vol. I, (Rome, 1907), 133.

Fortunately, when de Rhodes reached Tonkin in March 1627, he did not have to contend with the "Chinese Rites" controversy. The dispute really started only later, in 1643 when Juan Baptista Morales submitted his seventeen *dubii* to the Propaganda Fide regarding the Jesuit practices in China. But de Rhodes was faced, as we have seen in Text A above, with the issue of whether he should use the two Vietnamese words *but* and *phat* to designate God. Since they were used for the Buddha whom de Rhodes regarded as an idol, he rejected them outright. Inspired by Saint Paul's example, he opted for the expression "the Lord of heaven and earth" (see Acts 17:24 and Luke 10:21) which he translated into Vietnamese as *Chua Troi Dat*.

One of the greatest contributions of de Rhodes to the Vietnamese theological vocabulary is his use of the expression *Duc Chua Troi Dat* to refer to God. The earliest missionaries transliterated the Latin *Deus* into Vietnamese and used the expression *Chua Deu* (Lord Deus). The disadvantage of this transliteration is that it fails to convey the meaning of who God is. More importantly, it does not attempt to inculturate the Christian notion of God into the Vietnamese culture.

Of course, de Rhodes knew the three Chinese words which were also used in Vietnam in literary language, though pronounced somewhat differently (*Thien*, *Thuong De*, and *Thien Chua*). Indeed, in his *Dictionarium*, de Rhodes lists all three terms.[96] However, he preferred the expression *Chua Troi Dat* because it evokes the creative power of God. In fact, it is composed of three words, one Sino-Vietnamese (*Chua*) and the other two pure Vietnamese (*Troi* or *Bloi* and *Dat*). The word *Chua*, from the Chinese *Chu*, means "lord" and was used as the title of the two heads of the states of Tonkin (*Chua* Trinh) and of Cochinchina (*Chua* Nguyen).[97] *Troi*[98] and *Dat*[99] are pure Vietnamese terms of everyday use for heaven and earth respectively. By using these two common words rather than the learned terms of *thien* and *dia*, de Rhodes succeeded in conveying the nearness of God to the common Vietnamese people.

In *Catechismus*, de Rhodes often adds a prefix *Duc* to this expression: *Duc Chua Troi Dat*.[100] The word *Duc* (noble) is a title and indicates the highest honor.[101] Sometimes, the expression is shortened to *Chua Troi*[102] and *Duc Chua Troi*.[103] Given the number of times this last expression is used in *Catechismus*, it seems to be de Rhodes's favorite term for God, and indeed, this

---

96. For *Thien* and *Thien Chua*, see *Dictionarium*, col. 762–63, translated as "coelum" and "coeli Dominus" respectively. For *Thuong De*, see *Dictionarium*, col. 788, translated as "rex supremus."

97. De Rhodes lists *Chua* in *Dictionarium*, col. 117, and gives the following translation and notation: "Dominus." *Duc Chua bloi dat*: Lord of heaven and earth, name used by the Vietnamese people to designate God. *Chua*: Ruler of the whole kingdom which we call king.

98. *Dictionarium*, col. 45. The old spelling is *bloi*, translated as "coelum."

99. *Dictionarium*, col. 208, translated as "terra." De Rhodes also gives the Sino-Vietnamese equivalent *dia*.

100. See *Catechismus*, 117, 24, etc.

101. See *Dictionarium*, col. 240–41. De Rhodes says that this prefix *Duc* indicates "titulus summi honoris" and is added to words such as God, Jesus, Mary, angel, king, lord, queen.

102. See *Catechismus*, 12, 15, etc.

103. See *Catechismus*, 12, 15, and on practically every page.

term, together with the term *Thien Chua,* is the most commonly used word today among Vietnamese Christians for God.

Cathechismus also uses other expressions for God: *Duc Chua Ca* (the noble supreme Lord),[104] *Chua Ca tren het moi su* (supreme Lord above all things),[105] *Duc Tho ca* (the supreme Artisan),[106] and *Thuong De* (sovereign on high or august emperor).[107]

Thanks to de Rhodes's early adaptation of *Duc Chua Troi Dat* as well as other terms, among which also is *Thuong De,* for God, Vietnamese Christianity was spared the painful controversies that wrought havoc with the Chinese Church and severely impeded the preaching of the Gospel in that land.

In connection with terms referring to God, let us also examine de Rhodes's translation of "religion," which is the way to worship God. From Text A, it is clear that he was familiar with the Vietnamese terms *dao* (Sino-Vietnamese) and *dang* (pure Vietnamese), both meaning "way" and used by the Vietnamese to refer to their religions. It is interesting that de Rhodes does not translate *dao* or *dang* with the Latin *religio* but *lex* (law).[108] This word may wrongly suggest that for de Rhodes Christianity is a series of do's and don'ts. Nothing is farther from the truth. Rather, *lex* indicates that Christianity is a way of life, and is the correct equivalent of the Vietnamese words.

2. Combining Old Words into New Ones

To find equivalents for Christian terms for which there are no ready translations, de Rhodes resorted to combining existing words into new ones to convey the special meaning of the Christian terms. Here are a few examples.

To translate "angel," de Rhodes combines *thien* (heaven) with *than* (guardian spirit) into *thien than.*[109] For "human soul," *linh* (spirit) and *hon* (vital principle) are combined into *linh hon.*[110] For "paradise," *thien* (heaven) and *dang* (house) are combined into *thien dang.*[111] For "virgin," *dong* (child) and *than* (body) are combined into *dong than.*[112]

Whenever there are composite words that seem to be equivalent to the Latin

---

104. *Cathechismus,* 71, 79, 80, 84, etc.

105. *Cathechismus,* 16, 19, 21, 24, etc.

106. *Cathechismus,* 34, 39, 40, 60, etc.

107. *Cathechismus,* 21, 22, etc.

108. See *Dictionarium,* col. 204–5.

109. *Cathechismus,* 62, 63, 64, 65, etc.; *Dictionarium,* col. 741, 763, 792. In col. 240, de Rhodes also gives *Duc thanh thien than* (holy angels) and *Duc thanh Anjo giu minh* (holy guardian angels).

110. *Cathechismus,* 116, 117, 118, 119, etc.; *Dictionarium,* col. 336–37. Here de Rhodes also gives two expressions which express Vietnamese anthropology: the man is said to have *ba hon bay via* (three souls and seven spirits) and the woman *ba hon chin via* (three souls and nine spirits).

111. *Cathechismus,* 62, 274, etc.; *Dictionarium,* col. 200, 703. In the last column, de Rhodes also gives, together with the Sino-Vietnamese expression *thien dang,* the pure Vietnamese expression *nha bloi,* literally, house of heaven or heavenly house. However, this term is not used today.

112. *Cathechismus,* 145, 146, 149, 175; *Dictionarium,* col. 236. Here de Rhodes also gives *dong trinh,* which is now commonly used rather than *dong than.*

terms, de Rhodes takes them over, such as *ma qui* (devil),[113] and *dia nguc* (hell).[114]

3. Paraphrasing Technical Terms

When combination of words is not possible and when there are no ready equivalents, de Rhodes turns to paraphrasing. "Baptism" he translates as *phep rua toi*, literally, powerful rite of washing sins away.[115] For "supernatural mysteries" he uses the circumlocution of *su be tren khoi tinh the giai nay*, literally, things above the nature of this world."[116] "Original sin" is *toi to ne truyen cho*, literally, sin that the progenitors transmit.[117] "Purgatory" is *noi giai toi*, place where sin is absolved.[118] "Trinity" is *mot duc Chua troi ba ngoi*, literally, one Lord of Heaven with three thrones.[119] "Incarnation" is *duc Chua troi ra doi cuu the*, the Lord of heaven coming into the world to save it.[120] "Hypostatic union" is *duc Chua troi buoc lai va xac va linh hon ay cung ngoi thu hai*, literally, the Lord of Heaven binding his body and soul to the Second Person.[121] "Apostle" is rendered as *day to ca*, the supreme servant.[122]

This list, by no means exhaustive, shows how imaginative and resourceful de Rhodes was in finding Vietnamese words to convey the meaning of highly abstract and technical concepts and terms, especially in trinitarian and christological theologies, that have become part of the Western theological tradition. Many of his paraphrases given above are no longer in use.[123] Contemporary Vietnamese theological vocabulary has replaced them with more exact terms. Nevertheless, Vietnamese Christianity owes an immense debt to de Rhodes for introducing these technical terms into its theological glossary.

4. Retention of Foreign Words

Curiously enough, despite his extensive translation work, de Rhodes has kept quite a few foreign words, both Latin and Portuguese, in *Cathechismus*. Many of these he could easily have translated into Vietnamese. Indeed, some of them, such as *Sanctissima Trinitas*, *apostolus*, and *gloria*, have been paraphrased in *Cathechismus*; others, such as *angelus* and *gratia*, are found in *Dictionarium*.

---

113. *Cathechismus*, 84, 85, 86, 143, 182, etc.; *Dictionarium*, col. 441, 627. Strictly, *ma* means the soul of the dead and corpse, and *qui* means the malevolent soul of the dead.

114. *Cathechismus*, 57, 67, 171, 274, 275; *Dictionarium*, col. 219, 535. Literally, the Sino-Vietnamese words *dia nguc* mean earth and prison respectively.

115. *Cathechismus*, 133, 319.

116. *Cathechismus*, 61.

117. *Cathechismus*, 93.

118. *Cathechismus*, 239; *Dictionarium*, col. 823.

119. *Cathechismus*, 167, 170.

120. *Cathechismus*, 143.

121. *Cathechismus*, 152.

122. *Cathechismus*, 247.

123. Except *thien than* (angel), *linh hon* (soul), *thien dang* (heaven), *dia nguc* (hell), *phep rua toi* (baptism), and *toi to tong* (original sin). These terms are still used in contemporary theological Vietnamese.

At any rate, there are about 150 common and proper foreign nouns in *Cathe-chismus*. Here are the most important ones: *gratia, gloria, angeli, firmamentum, deus, Sanctissima Trinitas (Trindade, Santissima Trindade), ecclesia, ecclesia catholica apostolica, evangelio, crux, coena, latria, duleia, hyperduleia, Spiritu Sancto, Christus Domini, Christo, myrrha, apostolo, lymbo, sacramento, bonum est diffusivum sui.*

Of great interest is the fact that, as we have seen above, de Rhodes left *Spiritus Sanctus* untranslated in the baptismal formula. The reason he did not translate *Spiritus Sanctus* is probably that the word *spiritus (than)* is associated in Vietnamese with either angel or devil,[124] and the word *sanctus (thanh or thanh hien)* is given in Vietnamese to Confucius.[125] Both connotations are of course erroneous for the Holy Spirit, and that is probably why de Rhodes avoided them.[126]

5. Use of Vietnamese Proverbs and Sayings

Though proverbs and sayings, strictly speaking, do not fall under the rubric of theological terms, nevertheless de Rhodes's skillful use of them to make a theological point makes it appropriate to examine here their role in *Cathechismus*.

Unlike the Chinese, the Vietnamese do not possess philosophical texts comparable to the Confucian classics which would serve as the standard texts for general education.[127] Rather, their philosophical wisdom and ethical teaching are embodied primarily in thousands of sayings and proverbs. Furthermore, the Vietnamese have a predilection for poetry and song. Hence, their proverbs and sayings are always couched in rhythmic verses rather than in prose (in the popular six-eight meter called *luc bat*) and even put into songs *(ca dao)*.[128] De Rhodes's use of Vietnamese proverbs and sayings in catechesis bespeaks his sensitivity to and appreciation for the Vietnamese popular culture.

As repositories of popular wisdom, proverbs and sayings are most often used to clinch an argument in matters in which universal agreement is to be expected. It is natural then that de Rhodes uses them mainly in his discussion of matters

---

124. See *Dictionarium*, col. 740–41 and 763.

125. See *Dictionarium*, col. 747–48. De Rhodes refuses this title to Confucius.

126. It is interesting to note that the contemporary Vietnamese word for the Holy Spirit is a combination of precisely these two words — *Thanh Than* — so that the current baptismal formula is: *Cha rua con, nhan danh Cha, va Con, va Thanh Than.*

127. There are of course many ancient writings in Chinese and in *Nom* characters by Vietnamese literati, but none of them achieved the normative status accorded to "Confucian" classics. For a list of these writings, see Vu Dinh Trac, *Viet Nam trong Quy Dao The Gioi* (Orange County, Calif.: Vietnam Catholic Association in the United States of America, 1985), 51–60.

128. That is why the younger Catherine wrote her catechism and the entire sacred history in "beautiful verses" and not only the new Christians "sang these songs in their homes, in the city and in the countryside," but the "pagans sang them as well" (see *Histoire du Royaume*, 164–65). Likewise, the learned catechist Ignatius "composed in the native language a song with elegant verses and with a lovely tune in which he shows the absurdity of and ridicules all the errors and superstitions" (*Histoire du Royaume*, 238).

accessible to human reason. The purpose is to show that Christian teachings in these matters conform to reason and popular wisdom.

Below is a list of Vietnamese proverbs and sayings found in *Cathechismus* with English translation and the contexts in which they are used:

1. *Khi sinh ra chang co dem mot dong ma lai; khi chet cung chang co cam mot dong ma di.*[129] "At birth, one cannot bring a cent into the world; at death, one cannot take a cent away." The proverb confirms the precariousness of human life and the superiority of the soul over the body.

2. *Song thi gui, chet thi ve.* Also in literary form: *Sinh la ki da, tu la qui da.*[130] "Life is a journey, death a return." This proverb teaches that there is an afterlife.

3. *Kien thang kha ke nguu giac, ly ngu nang phuc nhan tam.*[131] "The horns of buffaloes are tied with solid ropes, the hearts of humans are drawn by solid reasons." This proverb affirms the duty of living according to reason.

4. *Thien phu dia tai.*[132] "Heaven covers, the earth supports." This saying affirms the existence of a creator and divine providence.

5. *Tu tao thien lap dia.*[133] "Since the creation of heaven and the establishment of the earth." This saying affirms that the world has a beginning and therefore is created.

6. *Sung ban pha thanh.*[134] "Cannons destroy the city." Though the proverb says that cannons destroy the city, we must understand that it is not the cannons but the shooter that destroys the city. Hence, when we say that "heaven" does this or that, we must understand that it is the Lord of Heaven that does this or that.

7. *Hai vo chong gui xuong gui thit nhau.*[135] "The husband and the wife give one another their bones and their flesh." This proverb affirms the indissolubility of marriage.

LINKING DOCTRINE WITH PRAXIS, INSTRUCTION WITH DEVOTION AND WORSHIP

De Rhodes's last catechetical principle requires that the practical implications of doctrines be unveiled to catechumens and that instruction be accompanied by worship and devotions (principle 7). Accordingly, throughout *Cathechismus* de Rhodes urges that catechumens be led, through their understanding of the Christian doctrines, to perform a radical conversion to God and to accept baptism. That is why the book culminates with an immediate preparation for this sacrament.

---

129. *Cathechismus*, 7.
130. *Cathechismus*, 9, 49, 117.
131. *Cathechismus*, 11. This proverb is in Sino-Vietnamese form. Interestingly, this proverb is also quoted by Ricci, but is said to be a Western saying! See *True Meaning*, 101.
132. *Cathechismus*, 12. This proverb is said to be of Chinese origin.
133. *Cathechismus*, 12. This proverb is said to be of Chinese origin.
134. *Cathechismus*, 13.
135. *Cathechismus*, 78.

Before arriving at that final act of self-surrender to God, however, the cat-echumens are gradually initiated into a process of intellectual and spiritual development punctuated by a series of devotional acts with, as has been noted, Day Five as a major turning point. In carrying out this initiation de Rhodes is constantly pointing out how for the catechumens, accepting the truths of Chris-tianity means taking decisions that change the direction of their lives and affect their daily behavior.

This is evident in the opening lines of *Cathechismus* which describe the two ways, of heaven and hell, eternal life and eternal death: "You must know that there are two dwellings in the afterlife: one is good, the other bad, one is above, the other below, paradise and hell."[136] At once then the catechumens are presented with a radical and life-transforming choice.

At the end of Day One, once again the catechumens are urgently encouraged to make a decision for God and to adore and pray to God: "Now that this holy law of God has enlightened Vietnam, let no one among you close the spiritual eyes of your heart and soul. Rather, with all your heart and strength embrace the way that is in conformity with reason. Detest and renounce the darkness of your errors and the blindness of your sins you have committed so far. Receive this law with your whole heart, rendering thanks to the Creator and Lord for the light of the new law, though it is more ancient than heaven. And so that the Lord God may enlighten you in the future, prostrate yourselves before God to adore and pray to him."[137]

Day Two also concludes with an exhortation to respond with an act of love to God's infinite love in creating us: "Because true love is not shown by clever words but by great deeds, and as the infinitely good God has deigned to instruct us, true love is shown by keeping God's commandments perfectly. Therefore, to respond with at least a measure of gratitude for such goodness, let us resolve to keep God's commandments fully, with God's help, without which we can do nothing."[138]

In concluding his instruction on original sin on Day Three, de Rhodes draws out its practical implications for the catechumens after they have become Chris-tian: "Therefore, utmost care must be taken to baptize the babies, even those of pagans, who are on the point of death before the use of reason, and in-deed with prudence we should baptize them, even without the knowledge and against the will of their parents, when they are on the point of death, before they breathe their last."[139]

On Day Four, after his attack on the doctrinal errors and superstitious practices of the Vietnamese cult of ancestors, de Rhodes comes to a practical conclusion: "Consequently, these erroneous acts and false honors should be re-

---

136. *Cathechismus*, 8.
137. *Cathechismus*, 26.
138. *Cathechismus*, 56.
139. *Cathechismus*, 93. Of course, a different theology of original sin and grace available today will reject de Rhodes's pastoral approach to infant baptism.

sisted, for they are nothing but offences and mockeries against the parents and increase their pains."[140]

On Day Five, now that the catechumens have resolved to renounce their false religions and embrace the Christian faith, de Rhodes immediately introduces them to the basic Christian prayers, i.e., the Our Father, the Hail Mary, and the Creed. To overcome an arid and abstract presentation of the trinitarian and christological doctrines which follow, de Rhodes, at the end of the day, recommends the performance of the typical Vietnamese gestures of *vai* and *lay* (bowing and prostration). Note the careful and detailed rubric he lays out to express the various elements of the Christian doctrines:

> At this point, we should show a beautiful picture of the Blessed Virgin Mary carrying her infant son Jesus, our Lord, so that people may adore him humbly by bowing their heads to the ground. First, a triple adoration should be made to the three divine persons in the one divine essence, thus confessing the mystery of the divine Trinity by this external adoration. The knees should be bent only once, to confess the one divine essence. The head should be bowed to the ground three times, demonstrating our adoration to the three divine persons, imploring each of them to forgive our sins. The head should be bowed to the ground once more to render reverence and adoration to the Lord Jesus Christ, man and mediator, humbly asking him to make us worthy to receive the fruits of his abundant redemption and to forgive all our sins.
>
> Lastly, reverence should be shown to the Blessed Virgin by bowing the head to the ground once, though we know that the Blessed Virgin is not God, but because she is the mother of God, all-powerful over her son, we hope to obtain pardon for our sins through her holy intercession.[141]

Day Six, which deals with Jesus' public ministry, ends with another exhortation: "Let us detest the hard-heartedness of the Jews, let us adore the Lord, and let us embrace ardently in our minds his divine teaching in order to be enlightened now and to obtain eternal life later."[142] De Rhodes's exposition of Jesus' passion, death, and resurrection on Day Seven is, as we have seen above, accompanied by the ritual of adoration of the cross and a long prayer to the suffering Christ. Moreover, at the end of the day, another ritual concludes the catechetical session: "Let us adore the Lord Jesus seated on the high throne of heaven. Let us ask him pardon for our lives spent in iniquities and at the same time implore the grace to serve him with all our hearts in the future, rejecting all superstitions and other sins of our past lives. Here we should present a beautiful

---

140. *Cathechismus*, 123.

141. *Cathechismus*, 166–68. De Rhodes carefully explains to the catechumens, who were used to worshiping idols, that "when we kneel, adore, or pray before the images of the Lord Jesus Christ or of the saints, our mind must be directed to the one who is represented by the images and adore or venerate the saint who is there represented" (168).

142. *Cathechismus*, 206–7. De Rhodes's "anti-Jewish" rhetoric, which is pronounced throughout his catechism, is part of the theological heritage he received.

picture of the Lord Christ holding the globe in his hands, so that all may adore the Lord Jesus as the true Lord and the sovereign king of heaven and earth."[143]

Finally, on Day Eight, we arrive at the climax of the weeklong catechesis. The day opens with reflections on eschatology (general judgment, the end of the world, the final resurrection, the coming of Christ, heaven and hell). Then, for the first time in his book, de Rhodes makes reference to himself as a missionary coming from afar to preach the Good News of salvation to the Vietnamese people. This self-referential invocation adds poignancy and urgency to the challenge he makes to the catechumens to choose the way of life:

> On the order of our Lord Jesus Christ, the King of kings, I have come here to bring you the good news and to invite you all to receive these supreme joys of the blessed. I will show the way, and if you are willing to follow it, you will escape the unimaginable torments of eternal misery which the damned together with the devil suffer eternally and will possess the undescribable happiness in eternity. Either of these two ends will necessarily happen to each of us, as is attested by the supreme and infallible divine truth. While the goodness of the supreme God permits you the time, *choose the good and straight path,* that is, during the present life of which we cannot promise ourselves the tomorrow. If you are wise, *grasp at once the divine ladder which I will show you.* By climbing it, you will certainly reach the eternal joys of heaven; God himself promises it. And you will escape the eternal pains of hell. Who among you can live with eternal fires?[144]

After this emotional appeal, de Rhodes proceeds to show the "good and straight path" by expounding the Ten Commandments. Finally comes the supreme moment of decision. To perform the acts of choice for God, the candidates are urged to pray on their knees for God's grace by reciting the Our Father and the Hail Mary. They are then guided through five series of questions to which they are to respond "with the mouth and the heart" and to signify their consent "by crossing their arms on their breasts."[145] These five series of questions, which neatly summarize the contents of de Rhodes's eight-day catechesis, are designed to elicit the basic acts of faith, fear, hope, love, and contrition. Once again, de Rhodes urges catechists to "show the picture of our Savior Jesus Christ on the cross, so that all may conceive sorrow in their hearts, open up their interior senses, and express externally whatever their spirits and feelings suggest."[146]

The catechumens are then dismissed so that "each can weep in private over his or her sins, at least for one night."[147] On the next day, only candidates are admitted to baptism who fulfill the following four conditions: rejection of idols

---

143. *Cathechismus*, 261.
144. *Cathechismus*, 277–78. Emphasis added.
145. *Cathechismus*, 307.
146. *Cathechismus*, 316–17.
147. *Cathechismus*, 317.

from one's hearts and houses; forgiving one's enemies and repairing all damages; monogamous marriage for both man and woman (securing a certificate of repudiation, if necessary); and paying off all debts.[148]

It is clear therefore that throughout his catechesis, de Rhodes was at pains to unfold the practical implications of the Christian doctrines for everyday life. Furthermore, catechesis was for him much more than instruction in Christian beliefs by means of concepts. With frequent use of sacred images (e.g., of Mary, the crucified Christ, and the risen Christ), bodily gestures (e.g., bowing, genuflection, prostration, crossing of arms over the breast, weeping), devotional prayers (e.g., the Our Father, the Hail Mary, the Creed, the acts of faith, hope, love, fear, contrition), and personal exhortations, de Rhodes aimed at moving not only the intellect but also and above all the imagination and heart of his catechumens toward the ultimate goal of catechesis, that is, total and radical conversion to God signified in the reception of sacrament. This last point brings us to considering another aspect of de Rhodes's catechetical method, namely, the use of St. Ignatius's method as deployed in *The Spiritual Exercises*.

THE *CATHECHISMUS* AND *THE SPIRITUAL EXERCISES*

Even though the audience and structure of *Cathechismus* and *The Spiritual Exercises* differ profoundly from each other — the former directed to non-Christians, the latter to Christians; the former promoting the catechumen's conversion and reception of baptism, the latter the Christian's choice of a state of life according to God's purpose — significant similarities between the two works warrant a close, albeit brief, comparison.

Of course, being a Jesuit, de Rhodes was familiar with both the text of *The Spiritual Exercises*[149] and the practice of the four-week retreat in the Ignatian tradition.[150] That this familiarity showed itself in de Rhodes's catechism is more than likely, and a comparison of the structure and basic themes of *Cathechismus* with those of *The Spiritual Exercises* will confirm de Rhodes's indebtedness to *The Spiritual Exercises*.[151]

---

148. See *Cathechismus,* 318. De Rhodes wisely adds: "Experience has taught me that in these pagan countries, catechumens promise a lot to obtain baptism, but they tend not to keep their promises after reception of baptism, especially in matters regarding concubines" (319).

149. For a modern English translation of *The Spiritual Exercises,* see *The Spiritual Exercises of Saint Ignatius of Loyola,* a translation and commentary by George E. Ganss (Chicago: Loyola University Press, 1992). For an introduction to Ignatian spirituality, see David Lonsdale, *Eyes to See, Ears to Hear* (Chicago: Loyola University Press, 1990).

150. From Ignatius's day until now, all Jesuit novices must make the spiritual exercises for the full thirty days. Since 1616 all Jesuit priests make the exercises for thirty days during their final year of spiritual training called "tertianship." As a Jesuit, then, de Rhodes was quite familiar with the spiritual exercises. It is interesting to note that when on his way back to Rome he was put in jail by the Dutch in Djakarta, he took advantage of his time of confinement to perform his spiritual exercises: "I remained ten days in this retreat, where in truth I was never so consoled" (*Divers voyages,* pt. III, 17).

151. For a sustained comparison between *The Spiritual Exercises* and *Cathechismus,* see Tan Phat, 109–47.

THE STRUCTURE OF *THE SPIRITUAL EXERCISES*

Before comparing de Rhodes's *Cathechismus* with Ignatius of Loyola's *Spiritual Exercises,* it is useful to say a brief word on the latter. *The Spiritual Exercises* is no doubt a synthesis of Ignatius's spiritual experience and theological vision. Written in 1521 at Manresa, at least in substance,[152] published in 1548, and slightly revised by Ignatius until his death in 1556, the book is essentially a manual to guide exercises which are to be carried out by a retreatant, ordinarily with counsel from a director. The retreatant's goals during the exercises are to (1) remove disordered attachments; (2) discern how one can best serve God; and (3) come to the decision to order one's life toward God not from some disordered attachment more pleasing to self than to God. To do so, the person "retreats" from ordinary occupations for about thirty days and makes four or five contemplations a day, alone with God, in complete solitude.[153]

The Spiritual Exercises opens with twenty annotations on the meaning of the spiritual exercises, on how the retreatant should make them, and on how the director should direct them. Like Garcia de Cisneros's *Ejercitario,*[154] *The Spiritual Exercises* is divided into four weeks.

The aim of the First Week is the spiritual purification of the soul, enabling it to advance toward God. To bring about this purgative act, Ignatius reminds the exercitant of the "principle and foundation" of not only the spiritual exercises but also the entire Christian life. This "principle and foundation" consists of four elements: (1) the goal: glorification of and service to God and one's eternal salvation; (2) the means to the goal: proper use of the creatures; (3) a vital preliminary attitude: keeping oneself "indifferent" or undecided until the sound reasons for choice become clear; and (4) the norm for the choice among the options one faces: that which is likely to result in the greater glory of God. With this "principle and foundation" in mind, and in order to feel sorrow for his or her sins, the exercitant makes five meditations every day on three themes: (1) the fall of the angels, of the first parents, and of the one cast in hell through one single mortal sin; (2) the retreatant's personal sins; and (3) hell. These meditations are accompanied by daily particular and general examinations of conscience, culminating in confession and communion.

The Second Week, pursuing the illuminative way, opens with a contemplation of Christ the King's call to extend his kingdom throughout the world. Its fundamental goal is to help the exercitant make a choice or election of the state of life in which he or she can best serve and glorify God. This choice requires

---

152. Very probably, the earliest version contains the meditations on the Kingdom and Two Standards, the division into four weeks and their meditations, some instructions for making an election, and some of the rules for discernment for the First Week.

153. Retreats for groups, however, were already practiced during Ignatius's lifetime. Preaching the topics of *The Spiritual Exercises* became more frequent after the founding of retreat houses in about 1660.

154. Ignatius knew this work through the Benedictine Dom Juan Chanones, the abbot of Montserrat, who was Ignatius's director and first spiritual father and to whom he made a general confession in 1522.

a deep and interior knowledge of Christ, and to achieve this, the exercitant is asked to make a series of meditations on the mysteries of Christ's childhood and public life.

Furthermore, to assist the exercitant in the election of the state of life, he or she is led to meditate on three themes. The first meditation is on "two standards" (*de dos banderas*): the one of Satan, the mortal enemy of human nature; and the other of Christ, our supreme commander and lord. To rally under Christ's banner, one must choose poverty as opposed to riches, shame and contempt as opposed to worldly honor, and humility as opposed to pride. The second meditation, designed to test the exercitant's readiness to follow Christ, is on the three classes of persons (*tres binarios de hombres*) with their respective attitudes toward God: postponers, half-hearted, and wholeheartedly decisive. The third meditation is on the three ways of being humble (*tres maneras de humildad*): the first consists in obedience to God's law and is a habitual and serious purpose never to commit a mortal sin, or even to deliberate about committing it; the second is "indifference" to creatures and a habitual determination never to enter into deliberation about committing even a venial sin; and the third, which is the most perfect, is the desire to be conformed to Christ in all things by choosing, out of pure love for Christ, actual poverty, contempt, and being regarded as a useless fool.

All these exercises were geared toward helping the exercitant make the most important act of the Second Week, namely, the choice or decision (*elección*) either of a state of life or any other matter concerning his or her conduct to live more perfectly in that state of life already chosen. Ignatius points out that there are three times at which such a decision may be made, the first two being higher and more excellent, and the third safer and more reliable. In the first, the person is so moved and attracted by God that he or she carries out what is proposed without any doubt. In the second, the person makes the decision as the result of the spiritual consolations or desolations he or she receives, and by applying the rules of discernment of spirits. If the person has not made a choice at these two times, there is the third at which the person is not being moved one way or another by various spirits and uses his or her natural faculties in freedom and peace in considering both the advantages and disadvantages of the decision taken.

After the election or reformation of life has been achieved, the exercitant is confirmed in his or her decision during the last two Weeks by contemplating Christ's sufferings in the Third Week and his triumph in the resurrection and apparitions in the Fourth. By means of these contemplations the person partic-ipates in the whole of the paschal mystery and grows in intimacy with Christ. The whole course of the exercises culminates in the contemplation to obtain love for God and ends with Ignatius's justly famous prayer of self-offering: *Sume et suscipe*. Thus, the purgative and illuminative ways of the First and Second Weeks are brought to completion in the unitive way of the Third and especially Fourth Weeks.

THE *CATHECHISMUS* IN LIGHT OF *THE SPIRITUAL EXERCISES*

At first sight, it would seem that the two works have little in common since, as has been pointed out above, they are intended for different audiences and aim at achieving different effects. It must be remembered, however, that Ignatius's *Spiritual Exercises,* though directed primarily to Christians searching for a state of life in which they can best serve God, can be and have been adapted to a variety of circumstances and audiences, including non-Christians in search of a religion in which they can most truthfully and effectively serve God and arrive at their own salvation.[155]

An exhaustive comparison between de Rhodes's catechism and Ignatius's spiritual masterpiece is of course out of the question here. We will rather focus on aspects in which it is apparent that de Rhodes followed Ignatius's *Spiritual Exercises* in composing his *Cathechismus.* Essentially, what links the two works together is their pervasive effort at assisting people in making a radical conversion to Christ the King and a total commitment to his service. It is this common concern that allows de Rhodes to adopt the basic structure, conversion strategies, and key ideas of *The Spiritual Exercises* in his catechesis.

1. Structure

By structure is meant not only the practical ordering of the various themes treated in the two books into weeks or days but also their theological architectonic principle that throws light on and imparts unity to their entire theology.

(*a*) Like *The Spiritual Exercises, Cathechismus* regards glorification of and service to God and eternal salvation as the final end of the human person, as the "principle and foundation" of human existence. Of course, speaking to the Vietnamese, de Rhodes couches this "principle and foundation" in terms of longevity and presents the fulfillment of this end as the duty of the "gentleman": "Let us humbly ask the excellent Lord of heaven to help us understand well the law of the Lord. To do so we must consider that no one in this world lives a long life; there are indeed not too many who would live to seventy or eighty years of age. Let us therefore look for the way to live a long life, that is, to live eternally. This task is incumbent upon a gentleman."[156]

---

155. The question may be asked whether *The Spiritual Exercises* can be adapted for the use of non-Christians. The answer depends on whether the "principle and foundation" of which Ignatius speaks is knowable to reason alone. George Ganss rightly notes that "[i]f the words alone of the Foundation are considered without any context, all the truths in it are such that they could be learned from reason alone, for example, by Plato or Aristotle. This fact is occasionally useful with non-Christian retreatants or in missionary countries" (*The Spiritual Exercises of Saint Ignatius,* 208). It seems that de Rhodes makes use of this principle and foundation in the first four days of *Cathechismus* in this way. Ganss, however, notes, again correctly, that Ignatius developed his principle and foundation in the Christian context and that for him God the Creator is the triune God. It is in this Christian sense that de Rhodes explicates this principle and foundation in the last four days of his catechesis.

156. *Cathechismus,* 1.

However, de Rhodes immediately makes it clear that by a long life he means supernatural happiness or eternal salvation and that it is the reward for the right cult of the true God.[157] He insists that, to use the words of Ignatius, "human beings are created to praise, reverence, and serve God our Lord, and by means of doing this to save their souls."[158] On the very first day of his catechesis, de Rhodes broaches the theme of God the *Creator* and urges the catechumens to search for the Creator of all things and to render him worship and adoration worthy of God's supreme status so as to obtain perfect and eternal happiness.[159] Like Ignatius, de Rhodes makes faith in God the Creator and worship of him the "principle and foundation" of human existence, and like Ignatius who makes this faith and worship the cornerstone of the spiritual retreat, de Rhodes makes belief in and worship of God the Creator the structure and goal of catechesis.

Given the extreme importance of the truth of God's creation and the final end of human existence, de Rhodes devotes the entire second day to this theme, proving that "the Lord of heaven is the first efficient cause of all the creatures"[160] and rebutting the errors of regarding *Muc moi, nguc hoang, ban co,* and *thai cuc* (beings mentioned in various Chinese philosophical writings) as the creator.[161]

(*b*) Ignatius follows reflections on creation and the ultimate end of human existence with a meditation on the sins of the angels, the first parents, the damned, and the retreatant. Similarly, de Rhodes follows his reflections on faith in God the Creator with an instruction on the sins of the angels, the first parents, the patriarchs (on the third day), and the errors and sins of non-Christian religions (on the fourth day).

(*c*) For the exercitant, the Second Week is the most dramatic and transforming spiritual exercise. Through a series of meditations on Christ's kingdom, his infancy and public ministry, the two standards, the three classes of persons, and the three ways of humility, the exercitant is trained to make an election for a state of life (or reformation of life) which will be confirmed and deepened in the remaining Weeks Three and Four. This election is the heart and soul of the spiritual exercises, so much so that those who are unable or unwilling or halfheartedly disposed to make it are advised to discontinue the exercises.[162]

---

157. De Rhodes immediately warns the catechumens that "there are two dwellings in the afterlife: the one is good, the other is bad; the one is above, the other below; the one is paradise, the other hell" (*Cathechismus*, 8).

158. *The Spiritual Exercises of Saint Ignatius*, 32. The English translation will be taken from the Ganss volume. See n. 149 above.

159. See *Cathechismus*, 9: "In this country, whoever wishes to become a mandarin, must serve and wait upon the king....How much more should all in this world find out who is the true lord and the creator of heaven and the earth and all things in order to adore him. It is incumbent upon us to discover who is the creator of all things in order to adore him. Only in this way can we go to paradise and obtain infinite happiness."

160. *Cathechismus*, 28.

161. See *Cathechismus*, 29–33.

162. See *The Directory*, XVIII, 4. For an English translation of the *Directorium*, see W. H. Longridge,

Similarly, for de Rhodes, by the end of the fourth day, catechumens must have made a decision to despise "the idols and false religions and are prepared to receive baptism by fasting and other works of piety."[163] Only if they have made this election can they be introduced to the two central Christian mysteries of the Trinity and Incarnation. Structurally, then, the first four days of *Cathechismus* would correspond to the first two weeks of *The Spiritual Exercises*. They are designed to assist the catechumens to make a radical conversion from the errors of their religions to the worship of the true God and to follow the standard of Christ. Both the Second Week of *The Spiritual Exercises* and the Fourth Day of *Cathechismus* represent a transforming turning point in the life of the retreatant and the catechumen respectively.

Whereas the retreatant's election has as its object a state of life (or reformation of life) in the service of Christ the King on the basis of the "principle and foundation" of God's creative act and our ultimate end, the catechumen's choice is presented by de Rhodes as having a double focus: first, conversion to the true God, the supreme lord and creator of all things, known through reason; and conversion to the service of Jesus the King, known through revelation. What is presupposed as the principle and foundation in *The Spiritual Exercises* is made explicit and elaborated in *Cathechismus*, namely, faith in God the Creator and eternal beatitude.

(*d*) Lastly, just as the Third and Fourth Weeks of *The Spiritual Exercises* are intended to strengthen the exercitant's election by means of a series of contemplations on Jesus' passion and resurrection, so Days Five through Seven of *Cathechismus* are designed to deepen the catechumen's decision to abandon the idols and to follow Christ by means of a presentation of Jesus' infancy, public ministry, passion, and resurrection. Indeed, the subject matter of the Fifth and Sixth Days corresponds to that of the Second Week (the Incarnation, the infancy of Jesus, his public ministry, in particular his miracles); and the subject matter of Day Seven corresponds to that of the Third and Fourth Weeks (the passion and resurrection of Jesus). The goal of the catechesis during these days is to achieve, in the words of Ignatius, "an interior knowledge of Our Lord, who became human for me, that I may love him more intensely and follow him more closely."[164]

The Spiritual Exercises of Saint Ignatius of Loyola, Translated from the Spanish with a Commentary and a Translation of the Directorium in Exercitia (London: Robert Scott Roxburghe House, 1919), 311: "The disposition which S. Ignatius used to require in those who were going to make the Exercises of this Week is that they should give evidence of fervour and a desire of going on to deliberate about the choice of a state of life. So that if a man should be unwilling to do this, or only half-hearted about it, it would be better, even if he should wish to continue the meditations, to put him off for a month or two. For this is a matter which cannot be brought to a successful issue unless it be undertaken with fervour of spirit. It requires indeed all that greatness, courage, and constancy of soul which springs from an increase of devotion."

163. *Cathechismus*, 133.

164. *The Spiritual Exercises of Saint Ignatius,* 56. It would be interesting to compare Ignatius's and de Rhodes's presentations of the mysteries of Jesus' life from infancy to resurrection. In general, it may be said that de Rhodes tends to use the miracles to highlight Jesus' divinity and that in his presentation

2. Conversion Strategies

By "conversion strategies" are meant the techniques, mostly psychological and spiritual, employed to move the mind and heart of the exercitant or of the catechumen respectively to make the life-transforming election. Years of making the Ignatian exercises have familiarized de Rhodes with their conversion techniques, and he skillfully exploited them in his catechesis to bring the catechumens to the renunciation of idolatry and the worship of the true God.

(*a*) The first technique is the examen of conscience, both particular (concentrated on a single objective, such as correcting the predominant weakness or a sin) and general (aimed at a detailed knowledge of one's thoughts, words, and deeds). De Rhodes repeatedly urges his catechumens to acknowledge their sins, especially those of idolatry and superstition, and to accept the Christian message: "If in the past you have not known the true Lord of heaven and earth and have not worshiped God rightly, there is now a light shining upon you, as the way of the Lord is being announced."[165] Again, after presenting the passion and resurrection of Jesus, he adds: "Now let us adore the Lord Jesus seated on the high throne of heaven. Let us ask him pardon for our lives spent in iniquities and at the same time the grace to serve him with all our hearts in the future, rejecting all superstitions and other sins of our past lives."[166]

(*b*) *The Spiritual Exercises* prescribes an abundant use of the practices of meditation and contemplation. By "meditation" is meant discursive mental prayer, especially suited to beginners in the purgative phase, in which the three powers, namely, memory, intellect, and will, are employed to reason out principles and to form convictions in view of action. By "contemplation," the second basic method of mental prayer, Ignatius means attending to the persons, their words, and their actions, largely by means of the imagination. It consists in a mental gazing on the scene painted by the text which is being meditated upon, particularly by the Gospels.[167]

De Rhodes makes extensive use of both meditation and contemplation in his exposition of the Christian doctrines, especially in his narrative of Jesus' life, passion, and resurrection. In meditation, he has recourse to rational arguments to prove those Christian truths that are in principle accessible to human reason, e.g., the existence of God and the necessity of the First Cause. He does not however limit himself to appealing to the memory and intelligence of his audience; he also attempts to move their will to accept the Christian faith by concluding his presentations with passionate and insistent exhortations to surrender to Christ. Thus, after narrating the resurrection of Lazarus and the Jews' opposition to Jesus, de Rhodes makes this stirring exhortation: "Meanwhile let

---

of Jesus' passion and death he emphasizes Jesus' freedom and sovereignty to achieve the same goal. See Tan Phat, 120–27.

165. *Cathechismus*, 24–25.

166. *Cathechismus*, 261.

167. By "contemplation" then Ignatius does not mean what many writers on ascetical or mystical theology call "active or acquired contemplation" and "passive or infused contemplation."

us detest the hard-heartedness of the Jews, let us adore the Lord, and let us embrace ardently in our minds his divine teaching in order to be enlightened now and obtain eternal life later."[168]

Furthermore, de Rhodes not only paints in dramatic tone various events of Jesus' life to make them come alive to his catechumens but also, as we have seen above, recommends the display of holy pictures (e.g., that of the Virgin Mary holding the child Jesus at the end of de Rhodes's explanation of the Incarnation on Day Five, of Jesus on the cross, and of Jesus holding the globe after de Rhodes's presentation of Jesus' death and resurrection respectively on Day Seven). In this way, the catechumens can concretely and pictorially contemplate the incarnation of the Second Person of the Trinity, his passion and death, and his glorification as "the true Lord and the sovereign king of heaven and earth."[169]

(c) Besides meditation and contemplation, Ignatius also recommends a third method of mental prayer referred to as "the application of the senses." The *Directory* explains this method of praying as follows: "The application of the senses differs from meditation in that meditation is more intellectual and more concerned with reasoning, and is altogether more profound.... The application of the senses on the other hand is not discursive, but merely rests in the sensible qualities of things, as sights, sounds, and the like, and finds in them enjoyment, delight, and spiritual profit."[170] Ignatius calls for the activation of the five external senses in contemplating the mysteries of Jesus' life,[171] and he himself gives an example of how to use the senses to see, hear, smell, taste, and touch hell.[172]

De Rhodes's most powerful and dramatic application of the five senses occurs in his famous prayer to the crucified Jesus in front of a picture of Jesus on the cross surrounded by candles and incense. Here is a representative extract of de Rhodes's prayer:

> Look at the Lord of heaven, your redeemer, hung upon the *crux* for your sake, all his members torn. Consider his innocent hands, which had worked so many miracles, streaming with blood; see his holy feet, which were exhausted in search for your eternal salvation, pierced by horrible nails. Observe the divine side pierced by the cruel lance; look at this supremely elegant face covered with blood and spit, and gaze upon this forehead one time so serene and now bloodied by a crown of thorns.[173]

In addition, de Rhodes often exhorts the shedding of tears as a way of repenting for one's sins. Thus, immediately before baptism, he would send the catechu-

168. *Cathechismus*, 206–7.
169. *Cathechismus*, 261.
170. *Directory*, 314.
171. See *The Spiritual Exercises of Saint Ignatius*, 60–61.
172. See *The Spiritual Exercises of Saint Ignatius*, 46–47.
173. *Cathechismus*, 234–35.

mens away "so that each can weep in private over his or her sins, at least for one night."[174]

(*d*) Another technique recommended by Ignatius to focus the mind of the exercitant on the importance of making the election is the appropriate abstention from food and drink.[175] De Rhodes, too, recommends fasting to the catechumens during the eight days of catechesis and especially shortly before the reception of baptism "so that...they may approach, better prepared, the sacred bath of baptism."[176]

(*e*) Lastly, Ignatius suggests that every meditation or contemplation be accompanied by a "colloquy," that is, a prayer "in the way one friend speaks to another, or a servant to one in authority — now begging a favor, now accusing oneself of some misdeed, now telling one's concerns and asking counsel about them."[177] It is the heart's prayerful and spontaneous response in love to God occasioned by the divine truth being meditated upon.

Scattered throughout *Cathechismus* are de Rhodes's insistent recommendations to the catechumens to address God in prayer. The book opens with an exhortation to prayer: "Let us humbly ask the excellent Lord of heaven to help us understand well the law of the Lord."[178] The First Day ends with another call to prayer: "And so that the Lord God may enlighten you in the future, prostrate yourselves before God to adore and pray to him."[179] As a response to the doctrine of the Trinity, de Rhodes, as we have seen, suggests that the catechumens genuflect once in honor of the unity of God and bow their heads three times to the ground in honor of the Trinity.[180] A bowing of the head to the ground is also recommended to honor Mary, the mother of God.[181]

The most celebrated colloquy is of course the lengthy prayer in front of the picture of Jesus on the cross already alluded to.[182] Indeed, this prayer seems to have been composed as a direct response to Ignatius's suggestion at the end of the meditation on sin:

> Imagine Christ our Lord suspended on the cross before you, and converse with him in a colloquy: How is it that he, although he is the Creator, has come to make himself a human being? How is it that he has passed from eternal life to death here in time, and to die in this way for my sins? In a similar way, reflect on your self and ask: What have I done for Christ? What am I doing for Christ? What ought I to do for Christ? In this way,

---

174. *Cathechismus*, 317.
175. See his eight rules regarding the taking of food in *The Spiritual Exercises of Saint Ignatius*, 88–89.
176. *Cathechismus*, 318.
177. *The Spiritual Exercises of Saint Ignatius*, 42–43.
178. *Cathechismus*, 5.
179. *Cathechismus*, 26.
180. See *Cathechismus*, 167.
181. See *Cathechismus*, 168.
182. See *Cathechismus*, 233–38.

too, gazing on him in so pitiful a state as he hangs upon the cross, speak out whatever comes to your mind.[183]

Prayers are also addressed to the risen Christ as the true lord and supreme king of heaven and earth.[184] Finally, as the catechumens prepare themselves to perform the acts of faith, fear, hope, love, and repentance, de Rhodes warns them that "because these acts are supernatural, they must pray on their knees for God's grace by reciting the Our Father and the Hail Mary. They must ask for the intercession of the Blessed Virgin Mary, the Mother of God, so that these acts may be performed well...."[185]

3. Basic Theological Themes

Besides its structure and conversion strategies, *Cathechismus* is indebted to *The Spiritual Exercises* for some of its key theological themes. Because the theology of *Cathechismus* will be analyzed in detail in the next chapter, suffice it briefly to mention here, without elaboration, these principal themes which echo faithfully those of *The Spiritual Exercises*.

First and foremost is the "principle and foundation" which presents in a nutshell God's plan in creating human beings. Humans can and must use their freedom in their wise and rightful use of other creatures to achieve the purpose of their existence: to praise, reverence, and serve God, and in so doing to obtain salvation. The fundamental attitude that humans must develop is "indifference," that is, remaining undetermined and impartial to every and any option until the reasons for a wise choice are clearly perceived. This indifference never implies unconcern or lack of interest; rather, it indicates interior freedom from disordered inclinations.

Second, there is a balanced emphasis on the need of using both natural reason and divine revelation in order to discern the will of God for oneself at the present moment.[186]

Third, there is a strong emphasis on the necessity and urgency of making a choice or election, because there are fundamentally only two options available: salvation and perdition. Just as Ignatius speaks of the two standards, de Rhodes speaks of two eternal destinies for humans, namely, heaven and hell.

Fourth, both Ignatius's and de Rhodes's christology highlight the divinity and majesty and lordship of Christ. Their favorite appellation for Christ is the King. At the same time, both nurtured a tender devotion to Christ the Sufferer, the Poor, the Humble.

Fifth, both conceive Christian life fundamentally as an *imitatio Christi*, a sharing in the sentiments of Christ, and a generous and obedient response to

---

183. *The Spiritual Exercises of Saint Ignatius*, 42.
184. See *Cathechismus*, 261.
185. *Cathechismus*, 306–7.
186. For Ignatius's rules for discerning the spirits, see *The Spiritual Exercises of Saint Ignatius*, 121–28.

Christ's call to establish his kingdom throughout the world. Only in this way can one's life be lived *ad majorem Dei gloriam.*

In this chapter we have sought to understand *Cathechismus* by placing it in the context of seventeenth-century catechisms, especially those composed in Asia, and by examining its methodology, both in terms of what de Rhodes himself has said about how catechesis should be carried out and in terms of the Ignatian exercises. It still remains to study in detail the theology itself of *Cathechismus,* and to this task we will turn in the next chapter.

5

The Theological Message of the *Cathechismus*

Christian Doctrines in the Vietnamese Context

In catechesis what is of ultimate importance is not the *how*, that is, the method, but the *what*, that is, the message of God's self-communication transmitted in and through religious education. It is this message, and through it, the reality of God's self-gift, and not the catechetical methodology as such, that must be accepted so as to receive salvation. Of course, the message, though distinguishable from the method, cannot be separated from it. Method and message form an indivisible whole. Nevertheless, the method, however brilliant and original it may be, cannot bring about, with divine grace, conversion in the hearer unless it communicates the Christian message faithfully and integrally.

This message, according to Christians, is nothing other than the Good News of Jesus. Because the Good News was not only announced but made actual by Jesus in his life, death, and resurrection, the Good News proclaimed *by* Jesus of Nazareth became in due course the Good News *about* Jesus the Christ, the proclaimer transformed into the proclaimed, the messenger into the message.

Of course, this message did not come to us unadorned by cultural and sociopolitical trappings. By the seventeenth century, when it reached de Rhodes and his contemporaries, it had taken on Jewish, Greek, Roman, and Germanic theological formulations. More importantly, its medieval heritage had been challenged by the Reformation which was in turn countered by the Council of Trent and its aftermath, the so-called Catholic Counter-Reformation.

When de Rhodes was a theology student at the Collegium Romanum in Rome (1614–18)[1] and later when he was a theology professor at the Madre de Deus College in Macao (1630–40), it was the post-Tridentine theology that

---

1. According to the program of studies specified by the *Ratio Studiorum* promulgated by Claudius Aquaviva in 1599, de Rhodes's theological training would have included the study of Scripture, the Fathers, and the commentaries on Saint Thomas Aquinas. See Joseph Brucker, *La Compagnie de Jésus: Esquisse de son institut et de son histoire* (Paris: Beauchesne, 1919), 441.

he learned and taught. And it is this theology that de Rhodes employed to communicate the Christian message in his *Cathechismus*.

In the previous two chapters we have examined de Rhodes's missionary strategies and catechetical method. In this chapter we will study his theology. It is of course impossible and unnecessary to examine all the theological themes of *Cathechismus;* we will devote our attention only to those that are of greatest significance from the missionary and catechetical perspectives.

REASON AND REVELATION: TWO WAYS OF KNOWING GOD

For one engaged in mission and catechesis, several preliminary questions suggest themselves: What is the role of reason and faith in our knowledge of God? Can the "pagans," through the use of their reason, know anything about God apart from Christian revelation? Are there religious truths which are in principle knowable to reason and yet have been revealed to us because of the weakened state of our reason? Are there, on the contrary, divine truths that human reason is absolutely incapable of knowing independently from revelation, so that to know them at all, reason must receive them from God's revelation?

These questions are not abstract issues for ivory-tower theologians to speculate about; they have practical consequences for the missionary and the catechist. If indeed reason cannot know anything about God apart from Christian revelation, so that Christian faith and/or tradition are the only channels through which knowledge of God is made available, as fideism and traditionalism hold, then the missionary and the catechist cannot, methodologically speaking, presume to build a common ground between the native cultures and Christianity. The Good News that the missionaries announce to non-Christians would sound like a totally foreign tongue to decipher with their own cultures, languages, and histories offering no helpful clues.

If, on the contrary, there is nothing about God that cannot be known by pure reason, as rationalism maintains, then the Christian faith is rendered otiose, and mission and catechesis redundant. God would no longer be the Absolute Mystery to whom we surrender ourselves in trust and love.

Natural Knowledge of Religious Truths

Following the lead of Ignatius of Loyola, de Rhodes was concerned to impress upon the catechumens that their decision to reject idols and to accept Jesus Christ as their supreme king must be based upon a careful and objective examination of various rational grounds, free from the sway of disordered affections. Furthermore, following Ricci, de Rhodes wants to show that the Christian faith is harmonious with reason and the ancient wisdom of the Chinese and the Vietnamese peoples.

De Rhodes's stance in the matter of the relationship between reason, understood to include not only philosophy in the narrow sense but culture in general on the one hand, and Christian faith on the other can be described as dialogic-critical. To establish a dialogue with non-Christian peoples, as we have seen in the last chapter, he attempts to build in the catechumens' minds what he calls "a firm foundation"[2] on which faith can be supported and which consists of "the truths knowable by the light of natural reason, such as the creation of the world, the end for which the sovereign Principle of created things has made and ordered the rational creatures, the obligations incumbent upon them to know and serve God."[3]

Among truths knowable by natural reason de Rhodes includes matters in cosmology (creation of the world), anthropology (the purpose of human existence and the immortality of the human soul), and ethics (service to God).[4] These truths de Rhodes finds asserted by the desires of the human heart, by the Vietnamese popular wisdom as expressed in proverbs and customs, and by philosophers such as Confucius in their writings.

Among truths knowable by pure human reason de Rhodes lists first and foremost the existence of God as the Creator and Lord of all things: "First of all, we affirm that there is as it were *a light in the human heart* which manifests the existence of God, since without God as Creator and Lord who is the first cause and original source, nothing of this entire world would exist."[5] Elsewhere de Rhodes describes in detail what human reason knows about God and God's nature: "These attributes of the sovereign creator of all things, the Lord of heaven, the earth, and all things are made known to us not only by God's revelation in his book but also *by natural reason* impressed in our hearts by God: that God is infinite in essence, eternal in duration, immense in presence, most wise in counsel, omnipotent in action, all-good and generous in communication, most just and inscrutable in judgment."[6]

Next on the list is the spirituality and immortality of the soul: "The true law, however, which recognizes the sovereign Lord, creator of all things, first principle and last end, not only in virtue of divine revelation but also *under the light of natural reason,* teaches that the human soul is spiritual and immortal."[7]

---

2. *Histoire du Royaume,* 176: "quelque fondement assuré sur lequel le reste de leur créance se puisse aucunement appuyer."

3. *Histoire du Royaume,* 175–76: "quelques principes connaissables par la seule lumière de la nature, comme la création du monde, de la fin pour laquelle le souverain principe de l'être a fait et ordonné la créature raisonnable, et des obligations qu'elle a de le reconnaître et de le servir."

4. De Rhodes goes on to specify that the service to God includes "feelings of piety and natural love toward the Creator and the First Principle of their being" (*quelques sentiments de piété et d'amour naturel envers le Créateur et le premier principe de leur être*). It is clear that these three truths form the "principle and foundation" of which Ignatius's *Spiritual Exercises* speaks.

5. *Cathechismus,* 34, emphasis added. Note that the Latin text says: "Primo dari Deum supponimus tanquam lumine ipso naturae certum." Instead of *lumine naturae* the Vietnamese text says that there is "a light in the human heart."

6. *Cathechismus,* 50, emphasis added.

7. *Cathechismus,* 126, emphasis added.

The third truth knowable by unaided reason is our moral obligation to worship and serve the true God. Indeed, the worship of God must be in accord with reason, otherwise it should not be undertaken at all: "Therefore, the true law is the law of reason, the law of right order. If our actions are conformable to reason, we earn merit. If they are contrary to reason, we fall into sin."[8]

REVELATION OF TRUTHS ACCESSIBLE TO REASON

These three sets of truths are, according to de Rhodes, *in principle,* available to human reason. However, de Rhodes is well aware that the human intellect has been weakened by sins, and therefore these truths might not be known by all, quickly, and without admixture of errors.[9] As a result, even these naturally knowable truths have been revealed by God:

> Indeed, three times did the sovereign author of all things give humans the holy law. First, when God impressed in human hearts the natural law so that they may immediately distinguish right from wrong, good from evil. Natural reason and the light of God's face are etched in our hearts so that if we do not walk on the right path we will be inexcusable, as the Lord said to Cain in former times: "If you have done well, will you not receive good things? But if you have done evil, your sin will be immediately at your door."
>
> However, because the light of reason was *badly darkened by sins,* not only original but also personal, people could hardly distinguish false from true, wrong from right. Consequently, God gave to Moses, his friend, and through him, to the Jewish people, the written law which contains the Ten Commandments of the decalogue.... It was the second publication of the divine law.
>
> But because this carnal people, though they were not ignorant of the law of God, failed to keep it, the divine Master, Jesus Christ our Lord, came to promulgate himself the law of grace, establishing friendship with us. With this law the holy Teacher and Lord not only taught us the way to eternal life but also with grace and divine assistance which he merited, he gave us the necessary strength to keep it. That is why this law is called the law of grace.[10]

---

8. *Cathechismus,* 11.

9. Among the three consequences of original sin de Rhodes mentions "ignorance of the right path leading to eternal life" (see *Cathechismus,* 170).

10. *Cathechismus,* 177–79, emphasis added. There is a parallel passage on pp. 279–80: "Although this light of the face of God was sealed on us, it has been considerably darkened by sins. Therefore, the good Lord, more than two thousand years after the creation of the world, deigned to inscribe on two stone tablets his law which is contained in the Ten Commandments. This law God gave to God's servant Moses, so that Moses himself would teach it to the Jewish people who were then the people of God. But because this carnal people no longer observed the divine law properly, God sent God's Son Jesus Christ to teach the divine law and to give us by God's grace the strength to observe it. The Lord Jesus came not to abolish the law but to perfect it, in order to give us his divine example in fulfilling it."

Thus, in God's second and third giving of the law, revelation of truths intrinsically accessible to natural reason is made *morally* necessary because, as de Rhodes puts it, "the light of reason was darkened by sins, not only original but also personal." Consequently, revelation, according to de Rhodes, has, besides dialogue, an additional role, namely, critique. It will have to purify our natural knowledge of religious truths of defects and errors and bring it to the fullness of truth. In *Cathechismus* this critique is performed during the Fourth Day when the doctrinal errors and the superstitious practices of the "Three Religions" and the Vietnamese indigenous religion are exposed and rejected. But this corrective function should be performed, in de Rhodes's catechetical methodology, only *after* the truths knowable by the light of natural reason have been established.

REVELATION OF INACCESSIBLE MYSTERIES

Besides this morally necessary revelation, there is, according to de Rhodes, another which is *absolutely* necessary, that is, revelation of truths that are intrinsically beyond the ken of natural reason. These are truths that are dealt with in *Cathechismus* from the Fifth Day onwards. Among these truths de Rhodes includes the Trinity; the Incarnation; the life, passion, death, and resurrection of Jesus; the events surrounding the risen Christ; grace; the sacrament of baptism; the commandments; and Christian life in the church.

The following excerpt explains the essentials of de Rhodes's theology of revelation:

> We have established at the beginning that there exists a first principle of all created things, knowable by the light of natural reason. It is similarly known that there exists a single first principle, infinite, eternal, immense, all-powerful, omniscient, containing in itself all goodness and perfection, incomprehensible, such that nothing more perfect can be conceived.
>
> But God's incomprehensible essence and attributes are such that no created intellect can grasp them unless it is elevated by God with a supernatural light. This light is twofold. The first is the light of faith by which God reveals himself and divine matters to us in this life through God's words. Although knowledge through this light is still obscure and surpasses all natural reason, nevertheless it is very certain, founded as it is on the witness of the first principle or first truth. This first principle cannot be deceived by anyone because it knows all things, nor does it deceive anyone because it is at the same time supreme goodness which cannot lie.
>
> The second light is called the light of glory; the created intellect, elevated and enlightened by it, sees the divine essence clearly, as it is. This light is given only to the blessed in the eternal happiness. When the king of China resided quietly in his royal palace, no one outside the court could see him. Much less can one see the King of kings as he is, without coming first to his heavenly court in the beatitude of the age to come.

For us to obtain this light of glory, the merciful God gives us in this life the supernatural light of faith; through it we assent firmly and unchangeably to God's revelation to the saints in the Catholic Church, and through the church to us. Going forward thus in this world by the light of faith, we will finally arrive at the eternal happiness in order to see clearly by the light of glory that which we have firmly believed in this life.[11]

In this passage de Rhodes clearly distinguishes two levels of knowledge, the one dealing with things knowable by pure reason, such as God's existence and perfections (discussed in the first four days of *Cathechismus*), the other with things that cannot be grasped by it, such as God's "incomprehensible essence and attributes." For the knowledge of these mysteries the created intellect must be "elevated by God with a supernatural light." This light, given to us in this life and called the "light of faith," enables us to understand and adhere to things which God has revealed by means of words and deeds. Though superior to natural reason, it is still obscure. In eternal beatitude, it will be perfected. Called the "light of glory," it will empower the blessed to see God "as he is."

In sum, for de Rhodes, reason and revelation are not mutually contradictory. On the contrary, they complement one another. There are certain religious truths that are in principle accessible to pure human reason. However, because of sins, not all humans can grasp them easily, quickly, and without error. Revelation of these naturally knowable truths is in the present circumstances *morally* necessary. Furthermore, there are religious truths that are by their nature inaccessible to human reason. These are mysteries in the strict sense. To know them, revelation is *absolutely* necessary. In this life, revelation gives us the light of faith to understand and assent to them; in eternal life, we will receive the light of glory to see God as God is.[12]

INTERPRETATION OF SCRIPTURE

Whereas de Rhodes's theology of reason and revelation, which is the heritage of Saint Thomas, is agreeable to most contemporary Catholic theologians, there are two further aspects of it that may come under criticism. The first concerns his hermeneutics of Scripture. Born before the rise of the historical-critical method, de Rhodes took the Bible as a historical record reporting events accurately as they actually occurred. This literal reading of the Bible is operative

---

11. *Cathechismus*, 133–36.
12. Clearly, de Rhodes's theology of faith and reason is in complete accord with that of Saint Thomas Aquinas. See *Summa Theologiae*, I, q. 1, a. 1. The same theology is stated by Vatican I in its constitution *Dei Filius*. One may note the predominantly intellectualistic approach of de Rhodes's theology of revelation and faith common to post-Tridentine theology. However, from *Cathechismus* as a whole, it is clear that the personalistic and, to a lesser extent, communitarian dimensions are central to his theology of revelation and faith.

in his interpretation of creation,[13] the fall of the first parents,[14] and the patriarchs.[15] The same literal reading is practiced in de Rhodes's recounting of Jesus' infancy,[16] his miracles,[17] his parables,[18] the cosmic events surrounding his death and resurrection,[19] and the eschatological realities.[20]

It would be anachronistic to criticize de Rhodes's biblical hermeneutics from the perspective of the contemporary historico-critical method. His intention in narrating the biblical events is not to verify their historicity, but presuming the reliability of the biblical accounts, he attempts, in the manner suggested by *The Spiritual Exercises,* to re-create, through the imagination, the biblical scenes with their persons, words, and actions so as to move the hearer's memory, intellect, and will to make a decision for Christ. In this de Rhodes was enormously successful, as the number of his converts testifies, and it is by this criterion that his biblical exegesis should be judged.

Primitive Revelation and the Hebrew Language

It has been noted that de Rhodes understood the longevity of the patriarchs literally.[21] This he did, not simply because he took for granted the accuracy of the biblical reports, but because he wanted to argue that God's revelation of the true law and religion, which God first gave to Adam, was transmitted orally without interruption to the last patriarch, namely, Abraham, and through him

---

13. See *Cathechismus,* 58–82. De Rhodes speaks of the creation of the "empyreal heaven" as the dwelling place for the blessed and of the "spiritual light" on the first day. This spiritual light, "a purely spiritual and intellectual substance," is taken to mean the nine choirs of angels among whom Michael and Lucifer play an important role. Of the garden of paradise, which was created on the third day, de Rhodes writes: "On the same day God produced a paradise of delights, a magnificent garden, always cool with a perpetual spring season, never with the discomfort of excessive cold or heat, where the trees are covered with ripe fruits throughout the year." Such a garden must have sounded like a true heaven for de Rhodes's audience, most of whom were peasant farmers.

14. See *Cathechismus,* 82–92.

15. See *Cathechismus,* 94–104. Here de Rhodes takes the longevity of the patriarchs to be factual. The purpose is, as we will see below, to establish the continuity of divine revelation communicated by God from Adam to Abraham. Of Enoch, de Rhodes says that according to the Bible, he was taken up by God and has not died. Calculating the date of this event to his time, de Rhodes says that Enoch is still alive and is more than four thousand years old!

16. See *Cathechismus,* 159–65.

17. See *Cathechismus,* 179–206.

18. For example, de Rhodes takes the parable of the Rich Man and Lazarus (Luke 16:19–31) as factual and concludes that Lazarus "bearing during this brief life all the trials with patience and virtue, has been enjoying eternal happiness for more than sixteen hundred years and will possess the beatitude of glory eternally," whereas the Rich Man "has been consigned to unquenchable fires for more than sixteen hundred years and will be eternally tormented with no hope whatsoever of escape" (*Cathechismus,* 128; see also 47–48). Contemporary readers may chuckle at de Rhodes's careful calculation of the number of years of Lazarus's happiness and the Rich Man's misery, but the point de Rhodes wants to make, namely, that there is an afterlife and that God is infinitely just, is well taken.

19. See *Cathechismus,* 238–51.

20. See *Cathechismus,* 264–77.

21. Thus de Rhodes carefully lists the age of Adam, Methuselah, Noah, Shem, and Abraham so as to show that there was a direct transmission of God's revelation of the true religion among these patriarchs, from Adam to Abraham. See *Cathechismus,* 94–104. It is highly likely that de Rhodes follows Augustine's *City of God,* especially bk. XV, in his account of the patriarchs.

to David and the prophets until the coming of Jesus. This primitive revelation was preserved, de Rhodes holds, by means of the Hebrew language. It was at the Tower of Babel that the confusion of languages occurred, and as a result of the loss of the Hebrew language among non-Hebrew peoples, such as the Chinese, religious errors and various sects arose:

> Since Abraham was born about three hundred years after the flood and since Noah survived the flood by three hundred and fifty years, Abraham could receive the tradition of the divine law either from Shem or from Noah himself. He kept it for his family and transmitted it as well as the Hebrew language to the entire kingdom of Judea of which Abraham was the ancestor. The other kingdoms lost the Hebrew language in the confusion of languages as well as the tradition of the divine law, and as a result degenerated into false sects.
>
> After the confusion of languages came the kingdom of the Chinese from whom the Vietnamese received their religions. Because the Chinese, after the confusion of the languages, lost the language in which the true law was found, and because they had no books in which the true law was contained, they were divided into different laws, just like those who have lost the true way are dispersed in many ways that are all false.[22]

De Rhodes's account of how Chinese religions arose strikes us today as fanciful, and his theory of primitive revelation unnecessary and unfounded. But the point he attempts to make, namely, that the Jewish people were the carrier of divine revelation, is well taken, whether or not the Hebrew language was the indispensable means to preserve whole and entire God's revelation.[23] Further, even if one is inclined to dispute the necessity of the Hebrew language for the faithful preservation of divine revelation, still it is possible to emphasize the linguistic character of God's self-communication, as contemporary theologians have noted.

THE CHRISTIAN WAY

Divine revelation makes known to us not only a set of truths to believe but also and above all a manner of living to follow. To designate this way of life, de Rhodes uses the Sino-Vietnamese word *dao*, literally, way or path.[24] More specifically, he describes Christianity as the way of *return*. This is due to the fact that the Vietnamese view human life as a journey *back* to the source of all beings, as is implied in the proverb, "Life is a journey, death a return."[25]

---

22. *Cathechismus*, 103–4.

23. De Rhodes's view on the necessity of the Hebrew language for the preservation of divine revelation may have been derived from Augustine's *City of God*, bk. XVI.

24. The alternative Vietnamese word is *dang*. The Latin text uses the word *lex*, and not *via* or *religio*, to translate the Vietnamese expression.

25. The Vietnamese proverb reads in Sino-Vietnamese, "Sinh ki da, tu qui da," and in popular Vietnamese, "Song thi gui, chet thi ve."

Moreover, as path or way, *dao* also indicates a manner of living consonant with the return journey which will lead the travelers to their destination. In this sense, the Vietnamese *dao* retains the etymology of *religio* as *re-eligere*, that is, to choose again. On the way back to the source of all beings, one must *choose* a way of life that leads to the goal of one's journey. It is the choice of a way of life, in this case, conversion to the true God and being a disciple of Jesus, that is the ultimate purpose of de Rhodes's catechesis, just as the election of a state of life is the retreatant's goal in Ignatius's *Spiritual Exercises.*

By describing the Christian faith as a *dao*, de Rhodes realizes two fundamental principles of Vietnamese philosophy. The first insists on the unity between thought and action embodied in the expression *tri hanh hop nhat*, literally, knowing and doing in unity. De Rhodes shows that Christianity, as a body of revealed truths and a concrete way of life, responds to the need of the Vietnamese to unite thought and action in their lives.

The second principle affirms the unity of God and humanity encapsulated in the phrase *thien nhan hop nhat*, literally, heaven and humanity in unity. For the Vietnamese, true morality is that which enables the human person to realize his or her full potential. Authentic morality is *nhan dao*, literally, the human way. But the *nhan dao* must be in conformity with the *thien dao*, that is, the way of heaven or God. De Rhodes argues that Christianity is the way of heaven because it leads its adherents back to God.

At the same time, while he attempts to inculturate Christianity into the Vietnamese culture, de Rhodes also emphasizes its universality. In this sense, he insists that Christianity is not "the Portuguese way." In Vietnam, at the beginning of the Christian mission, Christianity was called *Hoa Lang dao*, literally, the way of the Portuguese.[26] To deny that Christianity is limited to any particular nation or people, and to affirm its catholicity, de Rhodes uses the analogy of the sun. Although it shows itself to one country after another, and not to all the countries at once, the sun belongs to all. Similarly, Christianity, though it has appeared first in the West, de Rhodes argues, is common to all peoples.[27]

GOD: THE CREATOR AND LORD OF HEAVEN AND EARTH

The challenge facing de Rhodes in Vietnam, at least among the common people, was not unbelief or atheism, which after all arose as a philosophical problem only in the West in the modern age, but what can be termed "overbelief" or the belief in a multitude of spirits (or "gods") exercising power over the course of human history and individual lives, whether these are the Buddha, Confucius, or the dead ancestors. The urgent need in mission and catechesis in Vietnam, as de Rhodes saw it, was therefore not to prove, by means of philo-

---

26. De Rhodes uses the expression *Dao Pha lang* in *Cathechismus*, 25.
27. See *Cathechismus*, 25–26.

sophical arguments, that there is a deity in the abstract (deism). Rather, it was to show that there is only one true God who is the Creator and Lord of heaven and earth (as de Rhodes's Vietnamese word for God — *Duc Chua Troi Dat* — implies) and who is the Father of Jesus. Hence, in *Cathechismus,* the belief in God is intimately connected with the belief in God's creative act, providence, and remuneration (monotheism) and with the belief in the Trinity (trinitarianism). The only true God, therefore, is the Father of our Lord Jesus Christ. The sole goal of catechesis is therefore to bring the catechumens to an act of faith in the God revealed by Jesus.

Consequently, it is of critical importance to remember that in the first four days of *Cathechismus,* though focusing on religious truths that are in principle accessible to natural reason, de Rhodes makes ample use of Scripture, and not only rational arguments, to argue for the existence of God as creator and remunerator.[28] This does not mean that de Rhodes belittles in any way the value of rational arguments; on the contrary, as we will see, he makes good use of them. The point here is that in the first four days of *Cathechismus,* as in the First Week of *The Spiritual Exercises* (especially with its "principle and foundation"), Jesus Christ is already, though discreetly, present.

THE NAME OF GOD: "THE NOBLE LORD OF HEAVEN AND EARTH"

As we have seen in chapter 2, when de Rhodes came to Tonkin in 1627, his first sermon to the Vietnamese who had gathered on the beach to meet the Portuguese merchants dealt with God: "Thereupon I talked to them about the sovereign Principle of all created beings. I decided to announce it to them under the name of the Lord of heaven and earth, finding no proper word in their language to refer to God."[29]

Indeed, there were two words, *But* and *Phat,* but de Rhodes found them objectionable, because in popular parlance they were used to designate the Buddha. De Rhodes had another option, taken by the first missionaries, that of simply transliterating the Latin *Deus,* pronounced in Vietnamese as *Chua Deu* (Lord *Deu*). Such a move, however, had the unfortunate effect of suggesting that the word *Deu* is the proper name of the Christian God, a divinity different from the God the Vietnamese already worship.

To avoid this misunderstanding, Francesco Buzomi proposed that the Chinese word *t'ien chu* (in Vietnamese: *thien chu*) be used. However, some of his fellow missionaries feared that the use of this new name might create theological confusion and pressured the visitor of the Vietnamese mission to mandate the use of *Chua Deu.* Buzomi vigorously protested against such an order,[30] and a gen-

---

28. Of course, this procedure is in full harmony with de Rhodes's view that religious truths which are intrinsically available to human reason have been revealed by God, given the presence of sins, so that all may know them, quickly, easily, and without admixture of errors.

29. *Histoire du Royaume,* 129.

30. See his letter to the superior general in *ARSI, JS* 68, f. 8v.

eral meeting of Jesuit missionaries in Cochinchina in 1626, in which de Rhodes participated, decided that the expression *Thien Chu* be adopted, pending the coining of a better term.

This better term de Rhodes produced in 1627 when he first came to Tonkin. It was clear that *Chua Deu*, a transliteration of the Latin word, is a bizarre term and, worse, has no connection with the native culture. *Thien Chu* is an improvement, but it is a Chinese word which remains strange to the masses. And, as we have seen, *But* and *Phat* have unacceptable polytheistic connotations. Inspired by St. Paul's speech to the Athenians (Acts 17:24), de Rhodes chose the expression *Duc Chua Troi Dat*. As has been explained in chapter 4, the expression literally means "the noble Lord of heaven and earth." By means of this expression and its variations, de Rhodes succeeds in achieving three important things. First, he inculturates the Christian concept into the Vietnamese culture. The word *Duc* is widely used as a honorific title for various important personages, such as the king (*Duc Vua*), the lord (*Duc Chua*), the queen (*Duc Chua Ba*), and even for Confucius (*Duc Khong Tu*) and the Buddha (*Duc Phat*). The word *Chua* means lord and was used as a title for the lords of Tonkin and Cochinchina. The word *troi* means heaven, and *dat* means earth; together *troi dat* means the entire creation. All the four words are pure Vietnamese, and therefore are known to the masses. Thus, the expression *Duc Chua Troi Dat* becomes the permanent property of the Vietnamese language.

Second, de Rhodes corrects a possible doctrinal error in some Vietnamese expressions about heaven such as *toi lay troi*, literally, "I adore heaven." The Vietnamese *troi* means both sky and heaven. In the second meaning, it can also stand for *Ong Troi*, literally, Mr. Heaven, a transcendent, personal, benevolent, omnipotent, and omniscient God. There was, however, the possibility of confusing the material sky with heaven as a shorthand for God and of worshiping the material sky. By affirming that God is the "noble Lord of heaven and earth" de Rhodes neutralizes the danger of divinizing the sky.[31]

Third, by using the expression *Duc Chua Troi Dat* for God, de Rhodes maintains both the transcendence and sovereignty of God (implied in *Duc Chua*) and the immanence and nearness of God (conveyed by *troi dat*). God is recognized as the Lord of the "heaven that covers and of the earth that sustains," as the Vietnamese proverb says.[32]

GOD: CREATOR AND LORD OF HEAVEN, EARTH, AND ALL THINGS

For de Rhodes, searching for God is the consequence of our natural desire for happiness: "To obtain this happiness, one must first of all ask who produces the heaven which covers us, who produces the earth which supports us, who

---

31. See *Cathechismus*, 16.

32. De Rhodes quotes this expression in *Cathechismus*, 12, in both the Sino-Vietnamese form (*Thien phu dia tai*) and in the Vietnamese form (*troi che dat cho*).

produces all the things that nourish us. Ask to find, find to worship, that is the way of merit."[33]

Now, among the Vietnamese, notes de Rhodes, this search has led to two forms of worship: "One is to worship heaven as the principle of all things; the other is to accord the idol the first place."[34] De Rhodes, then, devotes his attention first to rebutting the belief that the material heaven is the principle of all things and should be worshiped.[35] He easily disposes of this belief by arguing that heaven is like a house and therefore cannot build itself but must be built by its owner. Hence, it is reasonable not to adore heaven but its maker. That is why de Rhodes says that to the expression "I adore heaven" the words "the Lord of" must be added to read: "I adore the Lord of heaven." And if it is not reasonable to worship heaven which is above us, much less is it to worship the earth which we trample under foot.[36] Thus, God appears as the Lord of the house which is heaven-and-earth.

So far de Rhodes's argumentation for the worship of the one true God is anything but original. What is original is his appeal to the Vietnamese sacrifice of *Nam Giao* to show that belief in God the Creator and worship of God are deeply rooted in the Vietnamese culture. De Rhodes distinguishes three levels of veneration commensurate to three authorities: the parents, the king, and "the supreme Father and Lord of all things, who creates and preserves the heaven and the earth and all things."[37]

It is to this Lord of all things that the king offers the sacrifice of *Nam Giao* on the Vietnamese New Year's Day: "Thus, it is apparent that the Vietnamese, following their reason, venerate three different kinds of father, even though they have not recognized clearly that the Supreme Father is the Supreme Ruler, to whom, in the presence of the mandarins and the nobility, the king of Vietnam offers the sacrifice in the name of his subjects. These, in accompanying their king in his sacrifice, also worship in silence, together with their king, the Supreme Ruler who is the Great Father of all things, even though they do not know him."[38] This is de Rhodes's masterstroke in his attempt to inculturate the belief in God into the Vietnamese culture.

---

33. *Cathechismus*, 8.

34. *Cathechismus*, 11.

35. It would seem that de Rhodes has misunderstood the Vietnamese belief in "heaven." Heaven (in Vietnamese: *Ong Troi*, literally, Mr. Heaven) is not the material sky but a transcendent and personal being, benevolent and just, whom the Vietnamese invoke daily, especially in moments of joy and suffering. See Cadière III, 43–50. It seems certain that here de Rhodes is following Matteo Ricci's rejection of the sky as the principle of all things, especially in view of the fact that the former adopts the latter's tracing of the etymology of the Chinese character for heaven to two characters, *one* and *great*. See *Cathechismus*, 13–14, and *True Meaning*, 127.

36. See *Cathechismus*, 16. Here again de Rhodes follows Ricci. See *True Meaning*, 127.

37. *Cathechismus*, 19–20.

38. *Cathechismus*, 22. To these three degrees of reverence correspond three kinds of reward and punishment. With regard to the reward and punishment by God, de Rhodes writes: "As to the Supreme Father, Creator and Lord of all things, he is the Supreme Judge. To those who observe his law, God gives not only material rewards in this world but also eternal recompenses in the future life. Those who do

After arguing that neither heaven nor earth should be worshiped and that adoration and cult should be rendered only to the Lord of heaven and earth, de Rhodes goes on to show where this true Lord comes from and who he is. With regard to God's *origin,* de Rhodes affirms that "the true Lord of heaven and earth is not created by anyone, since the Lord of heaven is the first efficient cause of all creatures."[39] To illustrate his point, he makes use of the image of a tree. The tree with all its branches is derived from its root, which is not derived from any other root but is self-sufficient. Were one to seek another root, one would be forced to go on ad infinitum, which is absurd. Hence, one must "stop at this first root and cause of all things who is the true creator of the heaven and the earth and all things."[40]

But as has been said above, de Rhodes's primary concern is not to prove the existence of God in the abstract but to rebut the erroneous beliefs in the creator found among the Vietnamese. Thus he proceeds to argue that the four beings believed by popular religion and Chinese philosophy to be the creator, namely, *Muc moi,*[41] *Nguc hoang,*[42] *Ban co,*[43] and *Thai cuc* with its two elements *yin* and *yang*[44] cannot be so. It is clear that de Rhodes has little understanding of these philosophical concepts, especially the last one, and his caricatures make them easy targets for him to destroy.

It would be unfair to fault de Rhodes for his lack of philosophical sophistication; after all, he was refuting popular beliefs and not offering a scholarly critique of philosophical concepts. Indeed, *Cathechismus* is not a philosophical treatise like Ricci's *The True Meaning of the Lord of Heaven,* and even Ricci himself, despite his learning, did not understand correctly concepts such as *Wu*

---

not worship God the Father but the demon and other things, God will punish in this life by taking away their material possessions, their health, and even their lives. Furthermore, he will send them to hell to punish with eternal pains" (*Cathechismus,* 24).

39. *Cathechismus,* 28. De Rhodes's Vietnamese expression for God is *coi re dau moi su,* literally, the first trunk and root of all things. The Latin translation uses *prima causa efficiens,* which is too abstract and metaphysical.

40. *Cathechismus,* 29. Of course, de Rhodes's argument should not be taken to imply the temporal priority of God as if God were a being, albeit the first and the greatest, in the chain of beings. Rather, God as first cause of all things is transcendent to all things. In other words, God is not *a* being but *Being Itself.* Whether de Rhodes's hearers understood his reasoning correctly, and not as the popular chicken-and-egg argument, is doubtful.

41. See *Cathechismus,* 29–33. *Muc moi* is said by de Rhodes to be mentioned in "the books of a false sect." This sect is presumably Taoism. Since he is believed to be a human being, he cannot be the creator.

42. *Nguc hoang,* literally, the king of hell, is said by de Rhodes to be mentioned in the Taoist books as the nephew of Lao Tzu. Since he had a father and a mother, de Rhodes argues, he cannot be the creator.

43. *Ban co* is said by de Rhodes to be a human person and therefore is disqualified as the creator. In fact, in Taoism there is the myth that the world is created from the corpse of P'an-ku who emerged from the egglike lump.

44. *Thai cuc* is the Vietnamese word for T'ai-Chi. De Rhodes takes it to be a kind of corporeal substance without intelligence and without life from which two other substances proceed, *am* (*yin*) and *duam* (*yang*). But, de Rhodes asks, how can something without intelligence and without life be the creator of heaven and earth?

of Taoism, *T'ai-chi, Li,* and *Ch'i* of Neo-Confucianism, and *K'ung* of Chinese Mahayana Buddhism.[45]

With regard to the *nature* of God, it is important to note that contrary to the non-Christian philosopher who could not answer his king's question on who God is, a story de Rhodes inherits from Ricci, de Rhodes says that "assisted by the Lord of heaven, we will dare to say something about who the true artisan of the heaven and the earth and all things, the supreme Lord, is."[46] Clearly, de Rhodes is relying not only on reason but also on divine revelation, even when he discusses the existence of God, God's creative act, and God's nature.

On the basis of Scripture, then, de Rhodes demonstrates first of all God's infinite power. Contrasting God with a human architect, he shows how God differs from the architect in three ways. First, God creates the universe *ex nihilo,* whereas the architect must use preexisting materials and requires the help of many workers. Second, God creates by a mere act of the will, whereas the architect can complete his work only after a long time. Finally, the creatures continue to depend on God for their preservation, even after God's creative act, whereas the building once made begins to exist independently of the architect.

De Rhodes goes on to discourse on God's other perfections such as infinite wisdom, divinity, infinite essence, eternity, and goodness. But lest his discussion become abstract and removed from the daily life of his catechumens, de Rhodes hastens to show that to each of God's perfections corresponds an act of worship on our part. Thus, to God's infinite majesty and essence, we owe the highest worship and adoration, first in our souls and then in our bodies. To God's omnipresence, we must offer God worship everywhere. In God's eternity, we must place our hope for eternal life. In God's infinite wisdom, we must anchor our faith that God knows everything. Because of God's infinite power, we must practice on the one hand humility, recognizing our inability to do anything by ourselves, especially in matters related to the life of grace, and on the other hand trust in God for whom nothing is impossible. To God's love and goodness we must return gratitude and love, and because love is proved by deeds, we must observe God's commandments. Lastly, to God's justice, we must implore forgiveness for our past sins and resolve to mend our ways.[47]

De Rhodes's reflections on God the Creator offer no novelty and represent nothing more than standard post-Tridentine theology. However, he succeeds in putting a personal stamp on this traditional theology, first by relating it to the Vietnamese culture, especially the *Nam Giao* sacrifice, and in the process also correcting some of the erroneous Vietnamese views on the creator, and secondly by suffusing an otherwise arid body of truths with a living spirituality. It may be said that in investing the doctrine of God with a comprehensive spirituality, de Rhodes is simply elaborating the first statement of Ignatius's "principle and

---

45. See *True Meaning,* 47–48.
46. *Cathechismus,* 34.
47. See *Cathechismus,* 50–57.

foundation": "Human beings are created to praise, reverence, and serve God our Lord, and by means of doing this to save their souls."[48]

ANGELS AND DEMONS

Following tradition de Rhodes classifies the creatures in three categories: purely material beings, purely spiritual beings, and partly material and partly spiritual beings.[49] To the second category de Rhodes devotes a large exposition in his *Cathechismus*. He identifies these spirits with the "spiritual light" which God created on the first day.[50] Of them he says:

> The second kind consists of beings with a spiritual nature, without any material or corporeal admixture, which are sublime, intelligent, and absolutely incorruptible. Though having a beginning, they will never have an end but rather will endure forever. Such are the nine choirs of angels, innumerable heavenly citizens whom God has placed at the head of corporeal creatures to carry out the will of God in all things. They are endowed with the highest intelligence and free will so that, by subjecting themselves to the Lord God, they may obtain eternal happiness.[51]

Following the traditional angelology as developed by Pseudo-Dionysius in his *Celestial Hierarchies* and medieval theologians, de Rhodes goes on to describe in detail the nine choirs of angels arranged in three hierarchies containing three choirs each.[52] Then follows a dramatic account of the struggle between the two angelic chieftains, Lucifer and Michael. Its purpose is to explain the existence of evil and the reality of temptations which the catechumens experience: "Immediately, Lucifer, turned into the devil and called Satan, fell like a lightning with his companions from heaven down into the Tartar. Some of them, however, were allowed by God the sovereign Judge to remain in the air until the end of the world. These devils are the tempters who seduce humans to all sorts of impiety; from them originate all false sects, lies, perjuries, enmities, quarrels, impurities, killings, stealings, and finally all the sins which humans committed under their seduction."[53]

For contemporary readers, de Rhodes's angelology is little more than a dated piece of neoplatonic speculation. However, given the belief, extremely widespread among the Vietnamese, in the pervasive presence of spirits, both

---

48. *The Spiritual Exercises of Saint Ignatius*, 32.

49. See *Cathechismus*, 35–36. Note that de Rhodes translates "angels" into Vietnamese by coining a new word, *thien than*, literally, genies or spirits of heaven. At times, curiously, he left the word *angelus* untranslated in *Cathechismus*, perhaps to avoid the misunderstanding that the angels are like *ma* (souls of the dead) or *qui* (demons or malevolent souls of the dead).

50. See *Cathechismus*, 59–60.

51. *Cathechismus*, 35–36. See also a parallel text on p. 44.

52. De Rhodes may have been influenced in his angelology by his teacher at the Roman College, Del Bufalo de' Cancellieri, who wrote *De substantia, natura angelorum* (Rome, 1622).

53. *Cathechismus*, 67–68.

benevolent and malevolent, in their lives, de Rhodes's angelology performs an indispensable function in his catechesis for the Vietnamese.[54] Differently from Ruggieri and Ricci,[55] de Rhodes provides a lengthy exposition on the angels and demons to counteract the cult of spirits and demons promoted especially by Vietnamese Buddhism and Taoism. He argues that spirits and demons are creatures and therefore must not be worshiped, and that they have become evil by their own free will.

HUMAN BEINGS: SUPREME GLORY OF THE UNIVERSE

As mentioned above, the third kind of beings created by God consists of humans who are both material and spiritual. Following closely the Book of Genesis's double account of the creation of Adam and Eve, de Rhodes describes humans as made "according to God's image and likeness" and "as a summary of all God's work and as the highest glory of the universe . . . raised to grace, that is, friendship with God, endowed with numerous supernatural gifts in order to obtain with the blessed angels the supernatural end of eternal beatitude."[56]

Male and Female

After relating the creation of Eve from the side of Adam, de Rhodes makes two points that are of special importance for the Vietnamese. First, repeating "the holy doctors," he says:

> God did not make the woman from the bone of Adam's head, because the head of the woman is the man, and she must obey him. Though she may, should he err, admonish him gently, she may not inveigh against him, because she is subjected to him and is not his head. But God did not make the woman from the man's feet either, but from his rib, because the man should not treat his wife like a slave, but love her like a companion.[57]

Though by today's standards de Rhodes's view of the woman still suffers from the sexism of traditional Christian anthropology, it marked, in the seventeenth century, a significant departure from the customs of the Vietnamese society. The

---

54. The belief in spirits forms the core of the Vietnamese indigenous religion. See Cadière, I, 6–23; III, 53–66.

55. Ruggieri briefly mentions the creation of three kinds of beings, among whom there are the angels divided into nine choirs. He also mentions the fall of an eminent but proud angel and many followers of his: "Fuit igitur quidam, multis ille quidem donis decoratus, qui ausus est sibi felicitatem summam arrogare, nec divino auxilio indigere se professus est, et ad eandem elationem, tum exemplo tum consilio, multorum aliorum mentes commovit" (*Vera et Brevis Divinarum Rerum Expositio,* chap. 5). But Ruggieri's discussion of the angels and their fall pales in comparison with de Rhodes's. Ricci does not mention angels at all, though he does speak of spirits and distinguishes them from human souls. See *True Meaning,* 175–83.

56. *Cathechismus,* 72.

57. *Cathechismus,* 77.

men of de Rhodes's audience might readily nod appreciative approval at his affirmation that they are the head of the women and that the women must obey them. But they might very well have been irked by his statement that the women can admonish them (though gently) and that they should not treat women as their slaves but must love them as their companions.

Second, basing himself on the biblical affirmation that the man and the woman form but one flesh and appealing to a Vietnamese proverb, de Rhodes says:

> Furthermore, God did not give the man two or three wives but only one, because they became one and not many flesh, as Adam prophetically affirmed. The Vietnamese themselves say: "The husband and the wife give one another their bones and flesh." Just as the man has a right to the body of the woman, so that as long as he lives, she may not attach herself to another man, so the woman has a right to the body of the man, so that as long as she lives, he may not take another woman. In this respect, the man and the woman are equal, according to God's command, carried out in Adam and Eve at the beginning of the world, and followed later on, at least in the first age of the world, until the deluge, by those who observed God's law.[58]

As we have seen in chapter 3, it is this teaching on monogamy that earned de Rhodes the Lord of Tonkin's wrath. It undermined the moral code and the social and even political-economic organization of seventeenth-century Vietnam. As de Rhodes warns us at the end of his *Cathechismus*, it is the doctrine that presents the greatest challenge to Vietnamese catechumens. And it is of great interest that de Rhodes attempts to ground it not only on the basis of Scripture but also of Vietnamese popular wisdom.

THE IMMORTALITY OF THE SOUL

According to Vietnamese anthropology, humans have three *hon* (superior souls) and seven (for the man) or nine (for the woman) *phach* or *via* (inferior souls). The three *hon*, deriving from the *yang* principle, are immortal, whereas the *phach* or *via*, deriving from the *yin* principle, perish at death. To translate the Christian concept of "soul," de Rhodes avoids the words *phach* or *via*, since they are perishable. Rather he uses the word *hon* and prefixes it with another word *linh*, meaning powerful and spiritual.

But de Rhodes does not discuss whether humans have three *linh hon*, as Vietnamese anthropology maintains. He does, however, speak of the tripartite distinction of vegetative, sensitive, and rational functions, as is done in Thomistic philosophy.[59] What concerns him is defending the immortality of the soul, a

---

58. *Cathechismus*, 77–78.
59. See *Cathechismus*, 45–46.

task made relatively easy by the fact that it is already affirmed by Vietnamese philosophy.[60] However, what is interesting is the way in which de Rhodes goes about proving the immortality of the soul. Of course, he makes use of a well-worn argument which consists in showing that certain operations of the soul are independent of the body. This independence indicates that the soul is immaterial and therefore survives death.[61] Like Matteo Ricci, de Rhodes also invokes the fact that we do not fear the bodies of dead animals whereas we have a natural fear of human corpses. This phenomenon intimates that the souls of animals are perishable and that those of humans are immortal.[62]

Whereas these arguments for the immortality of the soul are not derived specifically from the Vietnamese culture, others show that de Rhodes is consciously attempting to make this doctrine understandable to the Vietnamese audience by appealing to Vietnamese beliefs and practices. First, he shows that the Buddhist teaching on the transmigration of souls, with which most Vietnamese are familiar, affirms the immortality of the soul, since a dead soul cannot transmigrate.[63] Second, he invokes the Vietnamese practice of conducting lavish funerals for the deceased, which indicates a belief in their survival. Third, and most important, de Rhodes appeals to the Vietnamese practice of ancestor worship which presupposes the survival of the dead ancestors.[64]

Whether these arguments are philosophically convincing is debatable, but there can be no doubt about de Rhodes's intention to inculturate the Christian teaching on the immortality of the soul into the Vietnamese culture.

THE FALL AND ITS CONSEQUENCES

In accord with tradition, in his narrative of the fall of the first parents and of the entrance of evil into human history, de Rhodes lays the blame on Eve whom he regards as the weaker sex. For de Rhodes, Eve committed four strategic mistakes in her encounter with the wily snake. First, she wandered alone in the garden without the protection of her husband. Had she been with him, the devil, de Rhodes assures us, would have never dared to approach her. This teaches women, says he, never to go anywhere without their husbands so as not to be deceived. Second, she gazed at the forbidden fruit and admired its beauty and deliciousness. This warns us not to look at nor admire that which we are

---

60. See *Cathechismus*, 6: "...human beings are composed of two elements: body and soul. The body comes from the parents; it has bones, blood, and flesh that are corruptible. The soul, on the contrary, is spiritual, incorruptible, and immortal; it does not come from the parents but from a superior principle." Also on p. 36: "Lastly, the third kind of creatures are composed of body and spirit [*linh thieng*]. These are human beings who are corruptible and mortal on account of their bodies, and incorruptible and immortal on account of their spirits which are rational souls [*linh hon*]."

61. See *Cathechismus*, 118: "Furthermore, the principal operations of the human soul do not depend on the body, for example, the operations of the intellect and the will, which the soul exercises even in an aging and weakened body, and indeed a soul separated from its body exercises them better."

62. See *Cathechismus*, 128–32.

63. See *Cathechismus*, 116–17.

64. See *Cathechismus*, 118–20.

not allowed to desire. Third, she engaged in conversation with the snake rather than running to her husband and reporting to him its insidious suggestions. This teaches women never to talk to strangers, especially when they are alone. Fourth, she doubted the truth of God's command and God's threat of certain death if she disobeyed God. This teaches us never to doubt God's word and to believe that God does not deceive and cannot be deceived.[65]

Perhaps we will chuckle in amusement at de Rhodes's overconfidence in the man's moral superiority and his ability to protect the woman from spiritual dangers. Despite his affirmation that the woman is equal to the man in the obligation of monogamy, de Rhodes was simply a child of his time in his sexist view of the relationship between the man and the woman.

The consequences of the fall for humanity, de Rhodes points out, include the loss of innocence, symbolized by feeling of shame at nudity, and "the death of the immortal soul, that is, the loss of grace and of the original justice... [and] the death of the body by the separation of the soul from the body."[66]

BAPTISM OF CHILDREN AND THE THEOLOGY OF RELIGIONS

This loss of grace and the enmity with God as the results of the first fall (original sin) are the lot of all human beings. For this reason de Rhodes insists on the necessity of baptism for infants:

> That is why we all are born sullied by original sin, even the little babies still deprived of the use of reason who nevertheless contracted original sin before their birth. They themselves require a remedy which would remove this sin so as not to be deprived of heavenly happiness if per chance they should die before the use of reason.... Therefore, utmost care must be taken to baptize the babies, even those of pagans, who are on the point of death before the use of reason, and indeed with prudence we should baptize them, even without the knowledge and against the will of the parents, when they are on the point of death, before they breathe their last. This work of mercy is more meritorious than distributing innumerable treasures to the poor.[67]

No doubt, de Rhodes's pastoral policy with regard to the baptism of dying babies, "even without the knowledge and against the will of the parents," no longer appears to us wise and necessary, given our different understanding of original sin and of the possibility of salvation apart from actual baptism. With a new understanding of the necessity of baptism, we no longer consider pedobaptism a work of mercy "more meritorious than distributing innumerable treasures to the poor." Nevertheless, we should not fail to note that it is this profound concern for the salvation of all, including babies, that was the driving

---

65. See *Cathechismus*, 85–87.
66. *Cathechismus*, 75.
67. *Cathechismus*, 92–93.

force of de Rhodes's and many other missionaries' unstinting labors and heroic sacrifices for the sake of the Gospel.

Connected with this interpretation of original sin and the necessity of baptism is de Rhodes's theology of religions. As we have seen in chapter 3, despite his appreciation of some positive elements in the Vietnamese religions, in particular Confucianism, de Rhodes consistently regards non-Christian religions, which he calls "sects," as nothing but rank idolatries and superstitions. We have noted how his understanding of these religions, especially their doctrines, is severely deficient. Had he possessed, like Ricci, a more accurate understanding of these religious traditions, he might perhaps have exhibited a more sympathetic attitude toward them.

Even had this been the case, however, it would still be highly unlikely that de Rhodes would depart from what has been termed the "exclusivist" theology of religions. Indeed, for him Christianity is not "the law of the Portuguese." Rather,

> The holy law of the Lord of heaven is a light greater and older than the light of the sun itself. For example, when the suns sends its rays on a kingdom, it illuminates it, though the other kingdoms on which it has not sent its rays still remain in darkness. Nevertheless, no one would say that the sun belongs to that kingdom upon which it sends its rays first, because the sun is common to the whole world and exists before the kingdom it illuminates. Similarly, the holy law of God, though it has appeared to other kingdoms first, should not be seen as belonging to this or that kingdom, but as the holy law of God, the Lord of all things. It is a law nobler and older than any kingdom whatsoever.[68]

The universality of Christianity could not have been more explicitly affirmed. This universality, for de Rhodes, is based not on considerations of the sociopolitical, economic, and military power of the West but on the role of Jesus Christ as the unique and exclusive mediator and redeemer. Hence, de Rhodes would be opposed to any "inclusivist" theology of religions which maintains that though Jesus is the mediator, there might be other mediators dependent upon him. Much less would de Rhodes be open to the "pluralist" thesis that Jesus is one mediator among many others.[69]

Of course, the exclusivist theology of religions is being abandoned by the majority of theologians today, and de Rhodes's stance is no longer justifiable on biblical and theological grounds. But it would be an unpardonable anachronism to reproach de Rhodes for his rigoristic view. It would be difficult if not

---

68. *Cathechismus*, 25–26.

69. For a discussion of contemporary theologies of religions, see Peter C. Phan, "Are There Other 'Saviors' for Other Peoples? A Discussion of the Problem of the Universal Significance and Uniqueness of Jesus the Christ," in *Christianity and the Wider Ecumenism*, ed. Peter C. Phan (New York: Paragon House, 1990), 163–80; idem, "The Claim of Uniqueness and Universality in Interreligious Dialogue," *Indian Theological Studies* 31, no. 1 (1994): 44–66; idem, "Christian Mission in Contemporary Theology," *Indian Theological Studies* 31, no. 4 (1994): 297–347.

impossible for him, in the climate of post-Tridentine theology, to hold any other theology of religions than the one he actually puts forward in *Cathechismus*. That today we can hold a more positive view of the salvific value of non-Christian religions is only made possible by a number of momentous developments in the doctrines of divine revelation, of the universal presence of Christ's grace in the world through his Spirit, and of such traditional teachings as *extra ecclesiam nulla salus*. Such doctrinal developments were of course not available to de Rhodes in the seventeenth century.

THE TRINITY: THE MYSTERY OF SALVATION

One of de Rhodes's catechetical principles, as we have seen in the last chapter, specifies on the one hand that the mystery of the Trinity should not be expounded to catechumens before their religions have been shown to be erroneous, and on the other hand that it should be explained before teaching about Jesus Christ, and not at the end of catechesis. Furthermore, de Rhodes noted that in his catechetical experience he had not encountered objections on the part of pagans against the mystery of the Trinity, despite its incomprehensibility.

ONE GOD IN THREE PERSONS

De Rhodes's exposition of the Trinity is quite traditional, indeed, essentially Augustinian-Thomistic. He insists on the one divine essence and the trinity of persons equal in infinity, eternity, immensity, wisdom, power, goodness, and justice. He explains the origin of the Son as generation by the Father (without the need of a mother, he adds) in the Father's act of self-knowledge. Using the analogy of looking in the mirror, he says that God the Father contemplates himself in his essence as in a mirror, thus producing a perfect image of himself to whom he necessarily communicates his essence. The origin of the Spirit de Rhodes explains by using Augustine's model of the eternal and mutual love between the Father and the Son.

Just how traditional de Rhodes's trinitarian theology is, both in conceptualization and language, is revealed by the following terse summary of the doctrine of the Trinity to which he asks the catechumens to give their wholehearted consent before receiving baptism:

> God is one in God's essence and trine in God's persons, Father, Son, and Holy Spirit, such that the Father is truly God, the Son is truly God, and the Holy Spirit is truly God. They are, however, not three gods, but these three persons are the one true God, all-powerful, creator of heaven and the earth and all things, visible and invisible. The Father, proceeding from no one, is true God and true Father because he alone, without any other person, generates his Son to whom he communicates all his divine essence

by a true and ineffable generation. The Son is also true God and true Son, generated without a mother by the eternal Father by a true generation, consubstantial, equal, coeternal with the Father. The Holy Spirit is also true God, true and eternal love, proceeding from the Father and the Son, by whom the Father and the Son love each other ineffably from all eternity, communicating eternally to the Holy Spirit their divine essence. There are, therefore, three divine persons really distinct, but these three persons are not three gods, but are one true God.[70]

After reading this highly abstract summary of the doctrine of the Trinity, to which the catechumens were asked to give a firm assent, one can sympathize with their bewilderment. Indeed, de Rhodes makes no attempt at expressing this central mystery of the Christian faith with images drawn from the native culture.[71] The greatest contribution of de Rhodes's trinitarian theology consists not in his novel insights into the mystery of the Trinity but in the vocabularies he coins to express the Christian doctrine. The two key words are of course "nature" and "person." For "nature," de Rhodes uses the Sino-Vietnamese word *tinh*, which has its origin in the Confucian doctrine of *tinh* as the will of God. What God wills is our "nature."

The word "person" is much more difficult to render. There is no equivalent Vietnamese word for it. De Rhodes chooses the word *ngoi*. Literally, *ngoi* means throne, as in such expressions as *ngoi vua* (the throne of the king) or *ngoi chua* (the throne of the lord). It conveys sovereignty and honor as well as distinction of persons. Thus, de Rhodes uses the expression *Duc Chua Troi Ba Ngoi*, literally, the noble Lord of heaven on three thrones. Today, the Vietnamese still use the words coined by de Rhodes: *mot tinh* (one nature) and *ba ngoi* (three persons).[72] Though *ngoi* indicates well the distinction of persons, it does not imply equality necessarily. Consequently, de Rhodes adds that the three *ngoi* are equal among themselves: "The Father is God, the Son is God, and the *Spirito Sancto* is God. Yet there are not three gods. The three persons are only one God, only one Lord, so much as that eternity, immensity, wisdom, power, infinite goodness, and infinite justice, and everything that is infinite, are equally in the Father, the Son, and the *Spirito Sancto*."[73]

---

70. *Cathechismus*, 307–9. De Rhodes is aware that this explanation far exceeds the grasp of his hearers (and one may add, of most Christians). He therefore hastens to add: "If all this surpasses our intelligence, we must nonetheless believe it firmly, because God has revealed thus about Godself" (309). It seems that de Rhodes confuses the reality of the Trinity (to which we adhere with faith) with a particular explanation of the internal relations among the divine persons (a theological interpretation that may or may not command our total agreement).

71. There was an attempt at using the notion of three *hon* to explain the three persons of the Trinity. See Giovanni Filippo de Marini's manuscript contained in *ARSI, JS* 80, f. 35r–38v. But this analogy was not adopted since there is much obscurity in the Vietnamese notion of three *hon*. Perhaps the intention was not to draw analogies between the three divine persons and the three *hon*, but to justify the number three.

72. As we have seen in chap. 4, in *Cathechismus* de Rhodes keeps the foreign terms for the Trinity: *Sanctissima Trinitas, Trinidade, Sanctissima Trinidade.*

73. *Cathechismus*, 136–37.

As for the Father, de Rhodes uses the expression *Duc Cha* (the noble Father), and once *Duc Chua Deus Cha;*[74] for the Son, *Duc Con* (the noble Son);[75] and for the Holy Spirit, de Rhodes does not give the Vietnamese translation but leaves the Latin or Portuguese expression untranslated.[76]

De Rhodes completes his exposition of the trinitarian mystery by insisting on its salvific nature and its incomprehensibility. To explain that the Trinity is a mystery of salvation, he shows the intimate link between the trinitarian doctrine and baptism, saying that if in baptism there is no mention of the Trinity, there will be no forgiveness of sins and conferral of grace. And to illustrate the incomprehensibility of the Trinity, he tells the famous story of Augustine's meeting with a child who tries to fill a hole with the water of the ocean. De Rhodes concludes his explanation with an exhortation: "Let us, who walk in the footsteps of this saint, believe firmly the divine revelations, though they are obscure and above our intellect, so that having believed them on this earth, we may contemplate with clarity in the age to come."[77]

THE TRINITY AS THE MYSTERY OF SALVATION

It is admirable that in his catechesis to unsophisticated Vietnamese de Rhodes does not shy away from broaching such a difficult subject as the Trinity, especially in view of the daunting challenge of finding and even coining appropriate Vietnamese terms to express it, such as Trinity, essence, person, generation, consubstantiality, Word, Holy Spirit, and so on.[78] Whatever deficiencies de Rhodes's trinitarian exposition might have, his terminological achievements alone represent a permanent and groundbreaking contribution to both the Vietnamese language and Vietnamese theology.

De Rhodes's trinitarian theology follows the Western tradition of beginning with the unity of the divine essence and then making use of psychological analogies to illustrate the trinity of persons. While such an approach has its distinctive strengths, especially in eschewing the danger of tritheism, nevertheless contemporary theology of the Trinity prefers to takes its point of departure from the self-communication of the Trinity in history (the "economic Trinity") to preserve its character as the mystery of salvation.

De Rhodes himself is profoundly conscious of the salvific nature of the trinitarian mystery. In order to avoid giving the impression that the doctrine of the Trinity is a collection of apparently paradoxical and abstract propositions, irrelevant for Christian life, de Rhodes himself, as we have pointed out above,

---

74. *Cathechismus*, 265. Today, the Vietnamese use the expression *Duc Chua Cha*, literally, noble Lord Father, for God the Father, since *Duc Cha* is used as a title for a bishop.

75. Contemporary Vietnamese adds the word *Chua: Duc Chua Con*, literally, noble Lord Son.

76. Contemporary Vietnamese uses *Duc Chua Thanh Than*, literally, noble Lord Holy Spirit.

77. *Cathechismus*, 143.

78. In contrast, in his catechism (in the Latin version) Michele Ruggieri proposes that the exposition of the doctrine of the Trinity be omitted because it requires too much time and research to make it understandable to the catechumens.

attempts to highlight that the mystery of the Trinity was revealed to us "so that we may obtain grace, that is, friendship with God in this life"[79] by linking it to baptism. This is perhaps the greatest merit of de Rhodes's exposition. By expounding the Trinity at the beginning of the second stage of his catechesis (Fifth Day) rather than at its end, as others have suggested, he wants to impress at once upon his catechumens that the Trinity stands at the center of their new life in faith. Of course, much more could have been said about the practical import of the trinitarian mystery for Christian living, e.g., in the life of grace, in the church, and in the sacraments. It is regrettable that de Rhodes has not done so, but at least he has pointed us in the right direction.

JESUS CHRIST: THE LORD AND KING

In his reflections on catechetical methodology, de Rhodes notes that in his experience, contrary to the mystery of the Trinity, that of the Word made flesh has aroused much difficulty among his hearers. To the Vietnamese mind, the Incarnation seems to be at odds with God's spirituality, eternity, immortality, and omnipotence. To make it credible to the pagans, de Rhodes says, a triple strategy must be followed: (1) highlighting the cosmic miracles that occurred at Christ's death, (2) fostering devotion to the suffering Christ, and (3) connecting Christ's passion with his resurrection.[80] Keeping these methodological directives in mind we will expound and evaluate de Rhodes's christology.

THE INCARNATION OF THE SON OF GOD

Unlike his trinitarian theology, de Rhodes's christology is not constructed on metaphysical concepts but is what might be called a narrative theology. True, de Rhodes will use such notions as hypostatic union, for which he coins an ingenious Vietnamese circumlocution.[81] However, his christology is almost entirely made up of well-selected stories from the New Testament "contemplated" in the manner of *The Spiritual Exercises*. Thus, he begins his exposition of the Incarnation with stories of the birth of Mary and her parents Joachim and Ann, the annunciation, the conception, the visitation, the birth at Bethlehem, the angels, the shepherds, and the Magi.[82]

---

79. *Cathechismus*, 140.

80. See *Histoire du Royaume*, 177–78.

81. As we have shown in the last chapter, hypostatic union is rendered with a lengthy paraphrase, "duc Chua Troi buoc lai va xac va linh hon ay cung ngoi thu hai," literally, the Lord of heaven binding his body and soul to the Second Person (see *Cathechismus*, 152).

82. See *Cathechismus*, 143–65. Regarding Mary, de Rhodes inserts within the christological narrative Christian beliefs about her divine motherhood, her perpetual virginity, and her mediating function in the history of redemption.

Of course, it is not a historical report that de Rhodes offers, though he firmly believes in the literal historicity of the events narrated by the New Testament. Rather, it is a theological and spiritual "meditation" of biblical and extrabiblical materials in which the persons, their words, and their actions are made alive to the catechumens to excite their faith in, love for, and imitation of Jesus. At the same time, through these stories de Rhodes wants to affirm the true humanity and true divinity of Jesus. It is here that he indulges in metaphysical language:

> At the very moment when the Blessed Virgin gave her answer which the whole human race was hoping for, she conceived her Son by the power of the Holy Spirit; from her most pure blood and in her womb, the all-powerful God formed and shaped a most perfect little human body, and at the same time, God created a rational soul, most perfect and endowed with all God's gifts. At the same instant, by the greatest miracle God has ever performed and should ever perform, this body and this soul were united by means of the indissoluble knot of hypostatic union to the person of the Son of God, so that at that same moment he is both true God and true man: true God because he is truly the only Son of God the Father and consubstantial to the Father, and true man because he is composed of a rational soul and human flesh and the true son of the Mother of God, the ever-virgin Mary.[83]

To further emphasize the absolute perfection of Jesus, de Rhodes, following the medieval tradition, asserts that at the moment of its creation the human soul of Jesus was "adorned with marvelous gifts thanks to the hypostatic union," and had "a clear vision of God" as well as "the knowledge of all future things and of many things that will never be."[84]

Another way to impress upon the catechumens the divinity of Jesus, in compensation for his humble human appearances, is to highlight the miraculous events surrounding his birth. Here de Rhodes's predilection for the miraculous knows no bounds. Not only does he point out the virgin birth, the apparition of the heavenly host, and the star guiding the Magi, events that are mentioned in the biblical text, but he also goes out of his way to arouse awe in the catechumens with such doubtful stories as Emperor Octavius Augustus's seeing a woman holding a child appear in the sun, the Chinese emperor Mingdi receiving during a dream an order to seek the true religion in the West, a fountain of oil flowing in Rome, and the appearance of three suns in the sky.[85] Such a tactic might have been effective in de Rhodes's days, but of course, it can no longer be pressed into service today.

---

83. *Cathechismus,* 151–52.
84. *Cathechismus,* 152–53.
85. See *Cathechismus,* 165–66.

JESUS' PUBLIC MINISTRY AND MIRACLES

De Rhodes's penchant for the miraculous is even more evident in his account of Jesus' public ministry. Indeed, the narrative reads like the Gospel of Mark, with one miracle pressing upon another in rapid succession. After a reference to Jesus' presentation in the temple and his hidden life in Nazareth in submission to Mary and Joseph, de Rhodes recounts a series of miracles judiciously chosen to inculcate a sense of the absolute divine power of Jesus.

Figuring prominently among these are the changing of water into wine at Cana, the multiplication of bread, the healing of the woman suffering from hemorrhage, the raising of the son of the widow of Nain, the healing of a man with a withered hand on the sabbath, the healing of the paralytic at the pool of Siloam, the healing of the man born blind, the transfiguration, and the raising of Lazarus.[86]

For de Rhodes, Jesus performed miracles to confirm the teaching he was giving and to show that he is truly all-powerful God:

> The Lord worked innumerable other miracles to prove the truth of his doctrine. He not only urged people to observe the divine law but also opened the way of the highest perfection, till then unknown to the world. But, above all, by his miracles he proved his divinity. Thus he revealed himself as the Lord of all things, in the air by commanding the winds, on the sea by calming the waves, among humans by healing innumerable diseases, sometimes by a mere contact, sometimes by a simple word. He also showed his power over the devils by calming them or by ordering them to leave the bodies of the possessed. All that he did, not like some holy persons who in order to perform miracles must have recourse to prayers and fasting. On the contrary, the Lord Jesus performed miracles by his mere power, having dominion over all created things, without any need of prayer, though, to give us an example, he sometimes had recourse to it.[87]

Of course, Jesus' miracles have an apologetic value, and de Rhodes is right to point it out. Furthermore, among people such as his Vietnamese catechumens who were at the mercy of the forces of nature and diseases and who had lived in fear of whimsical demons and spirits, the figure of Jesus as the all-powerful and benevolent thaumaturge is very attractive indeed. However, it is generally acknowledged today that miracles are above all signs of the coming of the Kingdom of God, demonstrating not so much God's power as God's love, especially for the poor, the downtrodden, the oppressed of the society. It is this aspect that is unfortunately not prominent in de Rhodes's presentation of Jesus' public ministry.

Moreover, in de Rhodes's christology, there is a curious absence, almost total, of Jesus' teaching on the Kingdom of God, especially in his parables. Going

---

86. See *Cathechismus*, 180–207.
87. *Cathechismus*, 187–88.

through the first six days of catechesis, de Rhodes's catechumens would know well what Jesus did but precious little of what he actually said. This is quite regrettable in view of the well-known love of the Vietnamese for proverbs and stories. No doubt, in his actual preaching and teaching, de Rhodes would make use of Jesus' parables; one can hardly say something about Jesus without having to mention his uncanny gift for storytelling and his skillful use of one-liners. But to judge solely from *Cathechismus,* this aspect of Jesus' ministry has not been given its due.

Lastly, it is very instructive to note what materials de Rhodes selects from the Gospels' account of Jesus' ministry. Clearly, he gives attention only to those elements that make Jesus' divinity and omnipotence shine out, and leaves aside events that might induce doubt about Jesus' divine nature.[88] We do not, for instance, hear about Jesus' triple temptation, his acknowledgment of ignorance, his emotional anguish, his tender affections, and his physical needs. Indeed, de Rhodes's portrait of Jesus is that of a Lord and King, all-powerful and all-knowing, under whose standard the catechumens are urged to rally, very much in the tradition of the Second Week of *The Spiritual Exercises.*[89] The danger of Docetism and Monophysitism lurks in the shadow of the Sixth Day of *Cathechismus.* Fortunately, it is counteracted by the figure of the Suffering Christ, the Man of Sorrows, painted with so much tenderness and devotion in the following day.

THE CRUCIFIED CHRIST AND THE RISEN JESUS IN GLORY

De Rhodes warns us that we should foster devotion and love for the Crucified Christ and never speak of Jesus' passion and death apart from his resurrection and glorification. That is exactly what he does during the Seventh Day.

Continuing his narrative christology de Rhodes recounts Jesus' entry into Jerusalem, his betrayal by Judas, the Last Supper, Jesus' arrest, the trial before Caiaphas and Pilate, the flagellation and the crowning with thorns, the way of the cross, the crucifixion, and the death of Jesus.[90] Then follows the famous prayer to the Crucified Jesus to which we have already referred several times.[91] This prayer is a concrete example of de Rhodes's putting into practice the second strategy of his christology, namely, fostering devotion to and love for the Crucified Jesus.

Several key themes recur throughout de Rhodes's account of Jesus' passion and death. First, Jesus freely accepts his passion and death; without his permission his enemies would have had no power over him. As he puts it in his

---

88. It is interesting that among the miracles de Rhodes narrates, several come from the Fourth Gospel which, as is well known, emphasizes the divine sovereignty and majesty of Jesus.

89. Of course, *The Spiritual Exercises* also strongly emphasizes the Christ who is poor and humiliated, but this aspect is not evident in Day Six of *Cathechismus.*

90. See *Cathechismus,* 208–33.

91. See *Cathechismus,* 233–38.

methodological reflections: "From all this the conclusion is drawn that if he died, it is because he chose to do so of his own free will and that he granted his murderers the power which he had to kill him, in order to redeem and save the human race."[92] Second, Jesus was totally innocent. His death was caused by the jealousy and hatred of the Jews.[93] Third, Jesus suffered and died in obedience to his Father. Fourth, Jesus' death offered a sufficient vicarious satisfaction for the sins of the world and brought salvation to all.

No doubt, all these statements, especially those regarding the expiatory character of Jesus' death, are part and parcel of medieval and post-Tridentine soteriology. But de Rhodes does not merely replicate it but puts a personal stamp upon it by making a threefold contribution. First, he reminds the catechumens that the man who had been born in time, was being subjected to all sorts of humiliation and pains, and finally died in ignominy on the cross, is at the same time the eternal and immortal King and Lord, crowned with power and glory. He does so by highlighting the many portentous events that occurred at Jesus' death such as, as he puts it, "nature recoiling from the crime committed against his person, the sun withdrawing its rays and refusing to shine upon the earth guilty of such an execrable sacrilege, the tombs opening up, the rocks bursting asunder, the earth shaking, and all the creatures experiencing pains at the death of their creator."[94]

Second, de Rhodes enriches traditional soteriology with reflections on its spiritual implications in the tradition of *The Spiritual Exercises.* What emerges from his contemplations is a loving and realistic portrait of the Man of Sorrows who freely and willingly suffered indescribable pains in the place of his fellow human beings in obedience to his Father. For this Man of Sorrows de Rhodes urges tender love and compassion on the part of the catechumens: "Consider this most noble prince, in the prime of life, his head bowed, wasted by you in a most ignominious death. And since you can give nothing in exchange for so many benefits, at least acknowledge his immense love for you, shed tears from the bottom of your heart, show your compassion and gratitude to him."[95]

Third, he links Jesus' passion and death intimately with his resurrection and glorification. Thus, on the same day (Day Seventh), he recounts both Jesus' death and his descent among the dead, his resurrection, his appearances, his ascension, and his sending of the Holy Spirit.[96]

---

92. See *Histoire du Royaume,* 178.

93. It is appropriate here to note that de Rhodes reflects much of the anti-Semitism of the Christian tradition, especially in his account of the hostility of the "Jews" toward Jesus and their responsibility for Jesus' death. It goes without saying that in contemporary catechesis, such anti-Semitism must be excised.

94. *Histoire du Royaume,* 177–78. Once again, de Rhodes's penchant for the miraculous went overboard. He mentioned not only the miraculous events mentioned by the Bible but also how Dionysius, "a pagan philosopher and famous mathematician," saw the miraculous eclipse in Egypt and later converted to Christianity; how at Jesus' death many rocks were split in Tuscany, Mount Alverna, and Campania; and how the soldier who pierced Jesus' side was healed of his blindness when drops of Jesus' water and blood touched his eyes (see *Cathechismus,* 227–32).

95. *Cathechismus,* 235.

96. See *Cathechismus,* 238–55.

With regard to Jesus' descent among the dead, de Rhodes follows medieval cosmology in describing the four levels of hell in their descending order: (1) the limbo of the Fathers, that is, those just persons who had died before Jesus' death; (2) the prison of children, that is, the abode of the children who have died with original sin; (3) purgatory, that is, the place where the just souls are paying penalties for their already forgiven sins; and (4) the hell of the damned. Jesus' soul united with his divinity, de Rhodes explains, and descended to the limbo of the Fathers to announce to them their salvation.

From there, on the third day after his death, in de Rhodes's vivid description, "when dawn had just begun, Jesus' most holy soul, surrounded by the souls of the just who had just been released from the prison of the limbo and by a great number of angels, approached the tomb and reunited with his holy body, raising it immediately, glorious and impassible."[97]

Jesus, then, according to de Rhodes, appeared first to his mother and then to his apostles. To the apostles, "eyewitnesses of the resurrection of the Lord Jesus," was given the charge of confirming the resurrection of Jesus with miracles, and many of them witnessed to it with their blood. De Rhodes also very briefly alluded to Jesus' founding of the church and his commissioning of Peter and the apostles: "He also made Peter his vicar on earth and promised that his successor in the church (whom we call Pope) would never be lacking until the consummation of the world. He gave many instructions regarding the government of the church and the administration of the sacraments. And he ordered the Good News, that is, the true law, to be preached to the whole world."[98]

In retelling the ascension, characteristically, de Rhodes cannot resist mentioning three "miracles": first, the traces of Jesus' feet were miraculously imprinted on the rock which he stepped on as he was lifted up; second, when a church was built on this rock, its dome could never be completed, thus leaving open the space through which Jesus ascended into heaven; and third, on the anniversary of Jesus' ascension, the whole of Mount Olivet was illuminated by a marvelous light during the night.[99]

De Rhodes's narrative christology concludes with the account of the Pentecost: "This miraculous coming of the Holy Spirit confirmed that the Lord Jesus truly resided in heaven where he had gone and was enjoying sovereign power. At the same time, in order to propagate the Christian faith throughout the world, the apostles and others received the gift of knowledge of things human and divine, a remarkable holiness, and other spiritual embellishments of the soul."[100]

Speaking to the Vietnamese catechumens de Rhodes was concerned to stress the reality of Jesus' resurrection. This event taxes their credulity to the limit. There is nothing in their history or culture that suggests its possibility. Of

---

97. *Cathechismus,* 243.
98. *Cathechismus,* 248.
99. See *Cathechismus,* 251–52.
100. *Cathechismus,* 253.

course, they believe that their deceased ancestors are alive among them and indeed continue to be burdened with the same physical needs as the living. That is why they offer sacrifices to them. But the ancestors are not thought to achieve the kind of corporeal existence, albeit transformed, as that of the risen Christ and to lead the kind of glorious and transcendent life as Jesus. At best, they are venerated by their descendants.

To achieve his goal, de Rhodes has chosen to emphasize the miraculous dimension of Jesus' resurrection and its apologetical value, that is, its confirmatory role of Jesus' ministry, teaching, and above all divinity. In this de Rhodes succeeds well, perhaps too well, by narrating miracles mentioned by not only biblical but also extrabiblical sources. His audience must have been profoundly awed by such stories and might have been brought to faith by them.

Contemporary theology, of course, does not neglect this apologetical function of Jesus' resurrection. However, given the fact that it is a transcendent event, in principle not available to objective and empirical verification, contemporary theologians tend to regard the events surrounding Jesus' resurrection (e.g., the empty tomb) less as a proof than as a sign inviting faith in the risen Christ. Furthermore, they are more concerned with spelling out the theological significance of Jesus' resurrection for the Trinity, for Jesus himself, for humanity and its future, and for the cosmos as such. This is not of course the place to develop such a theology of the resurrection. Suffice it to note that de Rhodes's exposition of Jesus' resurrection, valuable though it is, needs to be extended in this direction to achieve an adequate catechesis of the paschal mystery.

CHRISTIAN LIFE AS *IMITATIO CHRISTI*

The Eighth Day of *Cathechismus* opens with a discussion of what is referred to today as eschatology. De Rhodes says practically nothing about death and dying. He simply states the traditional teaching that immediately after death, each person is judged by God, and if a person is free from sin, he or she is immediately admitted to eternal happiness, and if marked by a mortal sin, he or she is immediately condemned to eternal hell.

De Rhodes then moves to present the universal judgment. He argues for its necessity beyond the individual judgment on three grounds. First, it manifests God's justice and providence. Since at the universal judgment all the deeds of each person, good and bad, will be known by all, all will understand why sometimes bad people are rewarded with material things, and why sometimes good people suffer in this life, the former because of some of their good deeds, the latter on account of some of their bad deeds. Thus, God's justice and providence are vindicated. Second, the general judgment manifests Christ's universal sovereignty and kingship: He will judge all people, those who have accepted him as well as those who have rejected him. Third, the universal judgment acts as a deterrent against evil: since all one's deeds will be made known at the universal judgment, a person may be prevented from committing sin by the sense of shame if he or she remembers that his or her evil actions, even if secret, will be made manifest to all.[101]

Using the traditional apocalyptic imagery, which he takes to be a realistic description of the end-time, de Rhodes depicts the end of the world and the final resurrection. After a series of cataclysmic events, the world is brought to a dramatic end, and a new heaven and a new earth will be ushered in.

The bodily resurrection is necessary, he tells us, "so that each will give an account of what he or she has done in the body, good as well as bad. That is why the bodies of the godless will rise hideous and fetid, miserable in all things. But the bodies of the just will be exceedingly beautiful and elegant, perfectly healthy and perfectly aged, in the measure of the age of fullness of the Lord Jesus."[102]

Then the angels will gather all human beings in the valley of Jehoshaphat before Christ the judge, his mother, and the apostles, and separate them into two groups. In graphic terms de Rhodes paints the scene of judgment, with Christ sentencing the wicked to final condemnation into hell and welcoming the just into the eternal beatitude in heaven.

> The exceedingly wise, just, and powerful judge, the Lord Jesus Christ, true King of kings and Lord of lords, upon returning to the heavenly fatherland with his angels and saints, will present to his all-powerful Father the glorious multitude of saints, each raised with his or her body. At once, on the order of this same God and Father, the Lord Jesus, just judge, will distribute to each thrones, insignia, and degrees of happiness, according to the merits of each and in conformity with the sentence he will render on each.[103]

De Rhodes's eschatological description reads like any other post-Tridentine treatise on the Last Things, though perhaps with less flight of fancy. Nevertheless, there is no doubt that it made a strong impression on the unsophisticated minds of seventeenth-century Vietnamese peasants.

It is to de Rhodes's credit that he does not try to exploit the fear of hell to enforce good behavior, though he does believe that a salutary fear of God is necessary.[104] On the contrary, he attempts to present the Ten Commandments in the light of the human person's ultimate end which is eternal communion in love with the Trinity. In this way de Rhodes is following *The Spiritual Exercises,* especially its "principle and foundation." Moral behavior is seen not as a matter

---

101. See *Cathechismus,* 262–66.
102. *Cathechismus,* 269.
103. *Cathechismus,* 275–76.
104. Indeed, in the questioning of the catechumens before baptism, among the five acts that he attempts to elicit from them, is the act of fear of God: "The second act is that of fear of God and of our Lord Jesus Christ whom we must fear above all things, who not only has the power of life and death in this life, but who, after putting one to death, can cast one's body and soul into hell, delivering the rebels and the disobedient to the eternal fires of hell to be burnt and to suffer eternally" (*Cathechismus,* 312–13).

of observing the laws or commandments but as a response to God's creative and redemptive love.

In words reminiscent of the choice between the banner of Christ and that of Satan, de Rhodes challenges his catechumens to choose between the two eternal destinies and the two ways leading to them: "I will show you that way, and if you are willing to follow it, you will escape the unimaginable torments of eternal misery which the damned, together with the devil, suffer eternally and will possess the indescribable happiness in eternity. Either of these two ends will necessarily happen to each of us, as is attested by the supreme and infallible divine truth. While the goodness of the supreme God permits you the time, choose the good and straight path, that is, during the present life of which we cannot promise ourselves the tomorrow."[105]

This "good and straight path," de Rhodes assures his hearers, is very simple: it is "the divine law taught at the beginning by God to Adam, and with him to the whole human race and rational creatures."[106] He then expounds the Ten Commandments, dividing them into two "tables": the first three dealing with our duties towards God, and the last seven with those towards our neighbors. It is not necessary to summarize here de Rhodes's explanations of the Ten Commandments. Suffice it to highlight three aspects of his presentation that have particular relevance for the Vietnamese. First, in explaining the first commandment, de Rhodes emphasizes the necessity of rejecting the idols and superstitions of the Vietnamese religions and of rendering worship, both external and internal, to the one true God.[107]

Second, in explaining the fourth commandment, de Rhodes underscores the obligation of "love, respect, obedience, and assistance" that we have toward our parents and superiors, including our "kings, princes, governors, teachers, and leaders." Of course, such admonitions strike a chord with his Vietnamese audience. However, de Rhodes is careful to point out that such filial devotion must be rendered to each superior "according to his rank" and "except in what is opposed to God's commandments."[108] These qualifications serve to proscribe the practice of ancestor worship which, as we have seen, was the core of the Vietnamese indigenous religion but which de Rhodes held to be superstitious.

Third, in speaking of the sixth commandment, de Rhodes takes advantage of the opportunity to reiterate his condemnation of polygamy and divorce: "A legitimate marriage is one of one man and one woman so that as long as one partner is alive, no other partner may be taken. Consequently, polygamy as well as divorce is contrary to the divine law."[109] As we have already seen, from their cultural and religious perspectives, some Vietnamese had difficulty in accepting

---

105. *Cathechismus,* 277–78.
106. *Cathechismus,* 278.
107. See *Cathechismus,* 280–87.
108. See *Cathechismus,* 293–97.
109. *Cathechismus,* 299–300.

monogamy. Though fully aware of this difficulty, de Rhodes nevertheless makes the rejection of polygamy a sine qua non condition for the reception of baptism.

Lest Christian morality appears as a list of do's and don'ts, and moral life a legalistic observance of the laws, de Rhodes explicitly states that the way to observe these commandments is to follow the example of Christ. Hence, *imitatio Christi* is the heart of Christian life: "The Lord Jesus came not to abolish the law but to perfect it, in order to teach us how to fulfill it by his divine example."[110] Furthermore, he insists on the priority of the human heart over external actions. Speaking of the cult to God, he says: "The worship of the divine majesty takes place above all in the heart and soul since the supreme and infinite God is spirit; as the true Teacher and Lord Jesus taught, it is necessary that those who worship God, worship God in spirit and truth."[111]

DE RHODES'S BAPTISMAL CATECHESIS:
HOW ADEQUATE IS ITS CONTENT?

It is not the purpose of the concluding section of this chapter to critique de Rhodes's theology in general. I have already indicated throughout this chapter, from the perspective of contemporary theology, possible lines of development in various areas which might lead to a fuller understanding of Christian faith. In so doing, however, one must be careful to avoid both unfairness and anachronism.

First, to be fair to de Rhodes, we must remember that he was no academic theologian concerned with expanding the boundaries of theological knowledge or with constructing a theological system. He was first and foremost a missionary and a catechist dedicated to the preaching of the Good News of salvation. If there is any originality in his theology, it consists not so much in novel theological insights as in his inculturation of the Christian faith and practice into the worldview and life of his Vietnamese audience. About de Rhodes's attempts at inculturation we will offer some reflections in the concluding chapter.

Second, we should not anachronistically judge de Rhodes's work by applying contemporary standards of scholarly excellence. For instance, in assessing his biblical exegesis, it would be wrong to use the tools of historical-critical method as the criteria of evaluation, though it is of course legitimate to point out that like his contemporaries, he had a literalistic understanding of the Bible. Similarly, it would be anachronistic to judge de Rhodes's understanding of non-Christian religions in light of contemporary theology of religions, though, again, it is quite legitimate to point out that his view of non-Christian religions, like that of his contemporaries, is exclusivistic.

With these caveats in mind, it is necessary and useful to ask whether de Rhodes's catechesis, as presented in *Cathechismus*, communicates wholly and

110. *Cathechismus*, 279–80.
111. *Cathechismus*, 284.

integrally the content of the Christian faith *as this should be known by catechu-mens*, even those of the seventeenth century. This is a legitimate question, since one of the fundamental principles of catechesis is that at every level it should convey the whole Christian faith (*totum*), though not everything of it (*totaliter*).

To evaluate *Cathechismus* from this standpoint, it is necessary to remember its full title: *Catechism for Those Who Want to Receive Baptism Divided into Eight Days*. It indicates the limitation of both its targeted audience (catechumens) and its duration (roughly a week). *Cathechismus* is therefore not an ordinary catechism like its European predecessors, which were directed primarily to Christians (e.g., those of Peter Canisius, Edmund Auger, the Council of Trent, and Robert Bellarmine), or the ones composed in Japan (e.g., those of Francis Xavier and Alessandro Valignano) and in China (e.g., those of Michele Ruggieri and Matteo Ricci), all of which de Rhodes most probably knew. Furthermore, *Cathechismus* was planned as a text to be used in eight days, and not as a scholarly treatise to be discussed in a leisurely manner by a Christian theologian and a pagan philosopher like Ricci's *The True Meaning of the Lord of Heaven*. *Cathechismus* is nothing more than a manual to prepare catechumens for baptism.

Even within these restrictions, *Cathechismus*, insofar as it constitutes a preparation for the Christian initiation, strikes us as seriously deficient precisely in the sacramental dimension. It presents in detail fundamental Christian truths concerning divine revelation, the Trinity, Christ, eschatology, and moral life. In passing, it also mentions Mary and the saints.[112] On the sacraments of initiation, however, de Rhodes is almost completely silent. To baptism as the goal of catechetical instruction, of course, he makes occasional references, especially with regard to the four kinds of people who normally should not be admitted to it.[113] But of baptism as a sacrament itself, there is no systematic explanation, except to say that for baptism to be valid, there must be mentioned faith in the Trinity.[114] With regard to the effects of baptism, which he calls "a sacred bath,"[115] de Rhodes merely says that it remits sins and confers grace.[116]

Nor did de Rhodes ever mention the sacrament of confirmation, the existence of which had been taught by the Council of Trent.[117] Perhaps this silence is excused by the fact that the administration of confirmation was reserved to

---

112. De Rhodes affirms the divine motherhood of Mary as well as her perpetual virginity (*ante partum, in partu,* and *post partum*). See *Cathechismus*, 160–61. With regard to devotion to Mary and the saints, de Rhodes distinguishes between *hyperduleia* for Mary and *duleia* for the saints whom he calls "the friends of God" (see *Cathechismus*, 285).

113. See *Cathechismus*, 318–19.

114. See *Cathechismus*, 140.

115. *Cathechismus*, 318.

116. See *Cathechismus*, 140: "Therefore, adults who receive baptism cannot obtain the remission of their sins unless they believe this mystery firmly as infallible and revealed by God. And those who administer baptism and do not believe this mystery as true while performing baptism, cannot forgive sins and confer grace, that is, friendship with God."

117. In this connection, it must be pointed out that *Cathechismus*'s exposition on the Holy Spirit is also rather thin.

bishops, and since no bishop was available in Vietnam when de Rhodes was catechizing, there would be no point in teaching about this sacrament.

But such an excuse does not apply in the case of the eucharist, the complete silence about which in *Cathechismus* is most perplexing and disappointing. It is very strange indeed that in his account of the Last Supper, de Rhodes mentions the washing of feet but does not breathe a word about the eucharist.[118] That the eucharist played a prominent role in the spiritual life of de Rhodes's Christians and that of de Rhodes himself is repeatedly testified by his two memoirs. We are told that the first Vietnamese Christians braved numerous dangers and bore many sacrifices to be able to attend the Mass. The issue therefore is not whether seventeenth-century Vietnamese Christians understood and lived the eucharist. Rather it is why in his *Cathechismus* de Rhodes did not consider the doctrine about the eucharist as something his catechumens should know before receiving baptism.[119]

Two factors might account for this anomalous silence. First, a practical reason: since *Cathechismus* was written for lay catechists who were allowed only to administer baptism, there was no need to mention the eucharist. Second, a theological reason: *Cathechismus* aims at preparing for baptism only, and it was not thought that baptism is part of the total process of Christian initiation of which the eucharist is the central element. Most probably catechesis on the eucharist was given *after* the reception of baptism, when de Rhodes could visit the communities which his catechists had formed and celebrate the eucharist for them.

Intrinsically connected with Christian initiation is the church. Of the church de Rhodes again speaks relatively little in *Cathechismus*. In recounting Jesus' activities after his resurrection, de Rhodes says: "He also made Peter his vicar on earth and promised that his successor in the church (whom we call Pope) would never be lacking until the consummation of the earth. He gave many instructions regarding the government of the church and the administration of the sacraments. And he ordered the Good News, that is, the true law, to be preached to the whole world."[120]

Again, before baptism, one of the questions asked of catechumens concerns the church: "Lastly, we must believe everything that is believed by the Catholic, Apostolic Church, which is the assembly of all the Christian faithful spread throughout the world under the sovereign ruler, the holy Pope in the nation of Rome, vicar of the Lord Jesus Christ, successor of Saint Peter. Do you believe that it is truly so?"[121]

---

118. One reason for this silence about the eucharist in de Rhodes's account of the Last Supper is that he is following the Fourth Gospel, which contains no story of Jesus' institution of the eucharist. On the other hand, he does recount the miracle of the multiplication of bread and fish (see *Cathechismus,* 183–85); however, he makes no allusions to the eucharist.

119. Note how de Rhodes concludes his *Cathechismus:* "All this in general is what must be taught before baptism for the greater glory of God" (319).

120. *Cathechismus,* 248.

121. *Cathechismus,* 312.

Of course, contemporary theology has a lot more to say about the nature and mission of the church than what de Rhodes's basically anti-Protestant ecclesiology offers in these brief statements. The point here is not to critique his theology of the church, but to note that his silence about the Christian initiation brings in its wake a relative silence about the church. Obviously, for a contemporary catechumenate, the church and the sacraments will play a far more prominent role than the one de Rhodes assigns to them in his *Cathechismus*.

In this chapter we have surveyed the theological message of *Cathechismus*. By and large, unsurprisingly, de Rhodes's theology represents the Roman Catholic, post-Tridentine theological tradition, especially in his doctrines of revelation, the Trinity, christology, and moral life. Except for some minor aspects, such as its theories of primitive revelation and the origins of Chinese religions, and his narrative approach to christology, de Rhodes's catechesis reflects the theology of his times and Ignatius's *Spiritual Exercises*. Whatever original contributions de Rhodes has made to theology and catechesis lie not in having formulated new insights or constructed a new systematization of old ideas but in his pioneering attempt at inculturating Christian faith and praxis into the culture and society of seventeenth-century Vietnam. On this issue some critical comments will be offered in the final chapter.

6

Catechesis and Inculturation

A Contemporary Assessment

While "catechesis" is an ancient word, "inculturation" is a recent coinage.[1] Despite its relative youth as a technical term, however, inculturation, as part of the theological method, is as old as Christian theology itself. If theology's fundamental task is to mediate, imaginatively and critically, between the Christian faith and the contemporary culture, then inculturation is an essential and unavoidable ingredient of the theological method.[2]

---

1. For the history of the term "inculturation," see Arij Roest Crollius, "What Is So New about Inculturation?" *Gregorianum* 59 (1978): 721–38, reissued in Arij Roest Crollius and Théoneste Nkeramihigo, eds., *Inculturation*, vol. 5 (Rome: Editrice Pontificia Università Gregoriana, 1984), 1–18; and Aylward Shorter, *Toward a Theology of Inculturation* (Maryknoll, N.Y.: Orbis Books, 1988), 3–16. In general, inculturation is distinguished from enculturation and acculturation. *Enculturation,* which is a sociological concept closely related to that of socialization, denotes the process whereby the individual is inserted into his or her culture through formal and informal teaching and learning. There is an analogy between this process and the insertion of the Christian faith in a new culture.

Acculturation is the encounter between two cultures or among cultures. Such an encounter is a dynamic and diachronic process and is unavoidable today, given the fact that the world has become a global village. Acculturation may lead to a mere juxtaposition of unassimilated cultural expressions by which the two cultures operate side by side, or to one culture being practiced in its integrity together with selected elements of another culture, or to both cultures being practiced together, thus producing a form of "double belonging." Acculturation may also lead to syncretism, by which elements of one culture are mixed with those of another so that one, if not both, loses its or their basic identity and structures.

There are, of course, parallels between this process of acculturation between two cultures and the process whereby the Christian faith enters into a new culture, with the same dangers of juxtaposition and syncretism. See Robert Schreiter, *Constructing Local Theologies* (Maryknoll, N.Y.: Orbis Books, 1985), 144–58.

2. Besides the term "inculturation," other terms have been used to describe this process of critical interaction and exchange between the Christian faith and cultures, such as *contextualization, indigenization, transposition,* and *incarnation.* There are some disadvantages in these terms. *Contextualization* seems to suggest that inculturation is the task of only missionary lands and not of the already well-established churches of the West, whereas such a task is an urgent necessity for the West as well as for other parts of the world. *Indigenization* or *localization* historically connotes the recruitment of local people for the priestly ministry or religious life. *Transposition* suffers from the suggestion that the foreign culture is merely an external thing to be transplanted into the native cultural soil. *Incarnation* encourages the false view that inculturation is a one-time and one-way affair, whereas it is an ongoing process affecting both the local culture and the church. To eschew these deficiencies, the neologism "inculturation" (recognized as such by Pope John Paul II) or better "interculturation" (recommended by

The question is therefore not whether theologians can do without inculturation but what *kind* of method of inculturation is being used in one's theology. This fact makes it imperative explicitly to acknowledge that, despite universalistic pretensions endemic to human thinking, one's theology is always local, that is, done from a particular standpoint, in a particular framework, with particular categories, in view of particular interests, and for a particular audience. This consciousness of the culture-conditioned character of all theologies, including that of the church magisterium, tradition, and Scripture, was sharpened by the rise of the historical consciousness in modernity, the discovery of cultures other than the Western, the end of colonialism, and Europe's loss of cultural, economic, and political hegemony.[3]

De Rhodes, of course, did not know the word "inculturation." He did not offer any theory of culture nor describe the dynamics of cultural formation, change, persistence, and integration.[4] But no doubt he was an inculturationist *avant la lettre.* Not only was he deeply aware of the differences between the Vietnamese culture and his own and of the need to adapt to the native culture, but he took great pains to acquaint himself with practically all aspects of Vietnamese life of his times, both in Tonkin and Cochinchina. He also designed and practiced a catechetical method specifically for the Vietnamese people.

DE RHODES AND THE 1659 INSTRUCTION
OF PROPAGANDA FIDE

To appreciate de Rhodes's work of inculturation during his missionary and catechetical labors, it would be helpful to review it in light of a little-known document which, though written after de Rhodes's mission in Vietnam, was the immediate result of his endeavors. As was mentioned in chapter 2, after his return to Rome from Macao, de Rhodes worked assiduously for the appointment of bishops in Vietnam. Largely as the result of his efforts, in May 1658 the Congregation of Propaganda Fide presented to Pope Alexander VII François Pallu and Pierre Lambert de la Motte as apostolic vicars for Tonkin and Cochinchina

---

Bishop Joseph Blomjous) is used. For a discussion of these terms, see Shorter, *Toward a Theology of Inculturation,* 10–16, 79–83; Peter Schineller, *A Handbook of Inculturation* (New York: Paulist Press, 1990), 14–27; and Gerald Arbuckle, *Earthing the Gospel: An Inculturation Handbook for the Pastoral Worker* (Maryknoll, N.Y.: Orbis Books, 1990), 17–20.

3. See Peter C. Phan, "Contemporary Theology and Inculturation in the United States," in William Cenkner, ed., *The Multicultural Church: A New Landscape in U.S. Theologies* (New York: Paulist Press, 1996), 109–30, 176–92.

4. For a discussion of the inculturation of Christianity, besides the works already cited, the following are very useful: Louis J. Luzbetak, *The Church and Cultures: New Perspectives in Missiological Anthropology* (Maryknoll, N.Y.: Orbis Books, 1988); Charles H. Kraft, *Christianity in Culture: A Study in Dynamic Biblical Theologizing in Cross-Cultural Perspective* (Maryknoll, N.Y.: Orbis Books, 1979); Anthony Bellagamba, *Mission and Ministry in the Global Church* (Maryknoll, N.Y.: Orbis Books, 1992); and Anthony J. Gittins, *Gifts and Strangers: Meeting the Challenge of Inculturation* (Maryknoll, N.Y.: Orbis Books, 1989).

respectively. Before their departure for the missions, the new apostolic vicars received specific instructions from the Congregation on how to conduct their missionary work.[5]

The bishops are instructed to observe four principles in their missions: first, to form an indigenous clergy from whom future priests and even bishops can be selected; second, to preserve a close union with Rome; third, to keep away from national politics; and fourth, to respect local cultures and customs and to adapt to them with prudence. It is not possible to quote the lengthy text in full here. Only passages relevant to the issue of inculturation, those dealing with the first and fourth principles, will be given:

> The main reason which induced the Sacred Congregation to send you as bishops to these regions is that with all possible ways and means you so form the youth as to make them capable of receiving the priesthood. You will then ordain them and assign them in those vast territories, each to his own region, with the mission to serve Christianity there with utmost diligence and under your direction. You must therefore always keep in mind this goal: to lead as many and as suitable candidates possible to the priesthood, to educate them, and to promote them in due course.
>
> If among those whom you have promoted there are some worthy of the episcopacy, you must not, under the strictest prohibition, elevate anyone of them to this high dignity, but first make known to the Sacred Congregation by letter their names, qualities, age, and whatever other useful information, such as where they could be consecrated, to which dioceses they could be appointed...
>
> Do not in any way attempt and do not on any pretext persuade these peoples to change their rites, customs, and mores unless these are clearly contrary to religion and good morals. For what could be more absurd than to bring France, Spain, Italy, or any other European country over to China? It is not these countries but faith that you must bring, the faith that does not reject or jeopardize the rites and customs of any people as long as these are not depraved, but rather desires to preserve and promote them. It is, as it were, written in the nature of all peoples that the customs of their country and especially their country itself should be esteemed and loved above anything else. Nothing causes more hatred and alienation than changing the customs of a country, especially those by which the memory of their ancestors is preserved. This is particularly so if these customs are abrogated and then replaced with those imported from your country. Never make comparisons between the customs of these peoples and those of Europe. On the contrary, be anxious to adapt yourself to them. Admire and praise whatever deserves praise. As to things that are not praiseworthy, they should not be extolled, as is done by

---

5. The text is found in *Collectanea Sacrae Congregationis de Propaganda Fide* (Rome, 1907), 1:42–43, and in Chappoulie I, 392–402.

flatterers. On the contrary, exercise prudence in either not passing judgment on them or in not condemning them rashly and exaggeratedly. As for what is evil, it should be dismissed with a nod of the head or by silence rather than by words, though without missing the opportunity, when people have become disposed to receive the truth, to uproot it without ostentation.[6]

From what we have said about de Rhodes's missionary strategies and catechetical method (chapters 3 and 4), it is clear that in his efforts at inculturation de Rhodes anticipated and fulfilled these directives beyond measure. To promote the indigenous clergy, he founded the organization of catechists from whom the first Vietnamese priests were later selected. He shared with his catechists the ministry of preaching and catechesis and made them ordinary ministers of baptism. To some of them he bestowed the honor of wearing clerical garbs to bolster their authority in the community. Not only did de Rhodes train a corps of leaders with religious vows but he also enabled ordinary Christians, including women, to assume positions of leadership in their communities.

Furthermore, de Rhodes went far beyond the recommendations of the Propaganda Fide regarding the rites, customs, and mores of the Vietnamese people. While rejecting rituals he considered superstitious (e.g., ancestor worship and the cult of Confucius) and social practices he regarded as immoral (e.g., polygamy), de Rhodes not only praised Vietnamese rituals (e.g., the *Nam Giao* sacrifice) but also gave a Christian meaning to some of the Vietnamese cultural, social, and religious practices (e.g., the signing of newborn babies with the sign of the cross). Moreover, he took over some of the Vietnamese practices and modified them in such a way as to make them legitimate from the Christian point of view (e.g., the swearing of the loyalty oath, the erection of a bamboo pole on New Year's Eve, the three-day celebration of Tet, Taoist magical arts, Confucian rites, and ancestor worship).

In addition, de Rhodes not only christianized Vietnamese customs but also, as we saw in chapter 3, Vietnamized Christian practices, especially Christian rituals. Thus, under his leadership, the Vietnamese Christians celebrated Christmas, the Purification of the Virgin, Palm Sunday, baptism, the sacrament of penance, and other pious practices (e.g., *ngam dung*) with original adaptations to the Vietnamese culture.

Beside liturgical adaptations, de Rhodes also made good use of Vietnamese proverbs and sayings to undergird his doctrinal and moral teachings. Most importantly, through his *Cathechismus* and his *Dictionarium*, he both perfected the Romanized script (which is now the national script) and introduced into the Vietnamese language theological terms, many of which are still in use today.

---

6. For the Latin text, see Chappoulie I, 396–400, *passim*. My translation.

DE RHODES AND CONTEMPORARY MODELS
OF INCULTURATION

While de Rhodes has undeniably more than fulfilled the directives of the 1659 Instruction of the Propaganda Fide, it will be of interest to assess his efforts of inculturation in mission and catechesis in the light of contemporary theologies of inculturation. In broad strokes, there are currently five models of inculturation or contextual theology.[7] Stephen Bevans suggests that four elements are involved in the inculturation of theology: on the one hand, the Gospel message and tradition, and on the other hand, culture and social change.[8] The five models differ among themselves according to the greater or lesser emphasis they place either on fidelity to the first two elements (Gospel message and tradition) or adaptation to the second two elements (culture and social change).

The first model, labeled the *translation model,* is the most conservative of the five. It stresses fidelity to the Christian message. It presupposes that all cultures, despite their diversities, possess the same basic structure and that divine revelation is primarily a communication of truths in propositional form. These truths or meanings, decoded from their culture-dependent expressions, constitute the supracultural gospel core that can be translated by functional or dynamic equivalence into the idioms and categories of other cultures. Theologizing in cross-cultural perspectives consists mainly in decontextualizing the Christian message from its Western cultural context and reconceptualizing it in the forms of other cultures.

At the opposite end of the spectrum is the *anthropological model.* It stresses identification with culture and social change. It views divine revelation not as a body of supracultural truths but as a process of God's self-communication taking place in each and every culture. Theologizing in cross-cultural perspectives is not translating a foreign gospel core into the language of another culture, but digging deep into the history and tradition of the native culture itself to discover God's grace already actively present therein and naming it in Christian terms. Its starting point is not the Gospel message but each culture, which is considered as the unique place of divine revelation and the locus of theology. Its primary practitioners are not professional theologians but ordinary people who are not yet contaminated by Western culture. This model makes extensive use of the

---

7. For a helpful presentation of these five models, see Stephen B. Bevans, *Models of Contextual Theology* (Maryknoll, N.Y.: Orbis Books, 1992).

8. To emphasize that culture is constantly changing, Bevans makes social change a factor distinct from culture. Others, e.g., Robert Schreiter, speak only of three elements in the inculturation of theology, namely, the Gospel message, the church, and culture. See his *Constructing Local Theologies,* 22–24. Furthermore, insofar as inculturation is conceived as a process, three poles are seen as interacting with each other in a hermeneutical circle: the Christian message, the situation, and the pastoral agent. See Schineller, *A Handbook of Inculturation,* 61–73. Gerald Arbuckle prefers to use the image of "earthing" for the process of inculturation in which the evangelizer, under the action of the Holy Spirit, is the sower, the Gospel is the seed, and culture is the earth. See his *Earthing the Gospel,* 2–4.

social sciences and interreligious dialogue to unveil the word of God present in each culture as the dormant seed to be brought to full growth.

The third model, termed the *praxis model,* privileges neither fidelity to the Christian identity nor identification with culture but sociopolitical and cultural transformation in the light of the Gospel message. Its starting point is neither the Gospel nor cultural analysis but praxis, that is, reflected-upon action and acted-upon reflection in light of a rereading of the Bible and Christian tradition. This circular and spiraling process of transformation of unjust structures and critical reflection on this transformative process is theologizing in a cross-cultural manner.

The fourth model, called the *synthetic model,* combines the best insights of the first three models. On the one hand, with the second and third models, it recognizes the role of culture in the formulation of the Christian message and the necessity of fostering social transformation in the light of the Christian message. Hence, it starts with a careful study of a particular culture to discover its basic system of symbols. On the other hand, with the first model, it stresses the need to maintain fidelity to the Christian tradition which it views as a series of local theologies and with which it remains in constant dialogue. In addition, it emphasizes the necessity for people of one culture to learn from other cultures. Hence, it holds both the uniqueness and complementarity of all cultures, since one's cultural identity is shaped by a dialogue between one's cultural traditions and those of other peoples. Such a dialogue between one's own culture (including popular religiosity) on the one hand and other peoples' cultures and previous local theologies on the other hand will produce mutually enriching results in all conversation partners. Only by synthesizing one's own cultural tradition, those of other peoples, and previous local theologies of the Christian tradition can a contextual theology be formulated.

The last model, called the *transcendental model,* approaches the issue of contextual theology, starting not from culture as such, but from the subject doing theology. The theologian is one who is converted — intellectually, emotionally, morally, and religiously — that is, a self-transcending subject who falls in love with God unrestrictedly. Though the emphasis is on the individual's personal conversion, such a subject is not an isolated person but a member of a particular cultural community. Furthermore, practitioners of this model are convinced that despite cultural differences, the human mind, driven by an irrepressible desire to know, operates in identical, transcultural ways. As Bernard Lonergan has shown, there is in human knowing an unrevisable and universal fourfold pattern of experiencing, understanding, judging, and deciding.[9] To the extent that a theologian carries out the theological task in authentic conversion in a particular cultural context, she or he, so this model claims, is doing genuine contextual theology.

---

9. See Bernard Lonergan, *Insight: A Study of Human Understanding* (New York: Philosophical Library, 1958), and *Method in Theology* (New York: Herder and Herder, 1972), esp. 6–20.

It is to be noted that these five models are not mutually exclusive and that a certain model may be more appropriate and effective than another in a particular context. It is this particular cultural context that will determine which model or combination of models is to be adopted in the process of inculturating the Christian faith. Thus, for example, in the initial contact between Christianity and the native culture, the translation model seems to be the most effective in making the Christian faith known and accepted until the local Christians reach the degree of intellectual and spiritual maturity to construct their own indigenous theology. Again, in countries marked by poverty and sociopolitical oppression, such as those of the Third World, the praxis model seems to be called for to construct a theology that serves the goal of liberation and social transformation. On the other hand, in places where indigenous cultures have been obliterated in favor of the hegemony of the Western cultures, such as many African countries, the anthropological model may be most appropriate in order to retrieve the lost and suppressed cultural traditions. Further, in situations of multicultural diversity such as those of North America and Asia, the transcendental model may be effective in creating a common ground upon which each ethnic group can construct its own theology. Finally, the synthetic model appears useful in all situations since it calls for a synthesis of one's own cultural traditions, those of other peoples, and previous local theologies of the Christian tradition in formulating an indigenous theology.

From what has been said about de Rhodes's missionary and catechetical method and strategies, it is clear that of the five models of contextual theology, that of translation was favored by de Rhodes. Indeed, it could not have been otherwise, since in the first encounter between Christianity and Vietnam, the urgent order of the day was to find equivalent expressions in Vietnamese for the terms and concepts used in Western theology. Not only did de Rhodes translate seventeenth-century Latin theology into Vietnamese, but in the process he also coined a new set of vocabularies and perfected the Romanized script to convey the truths of the Christian faith.

Moreover, it may be said that de Rhodes did not entirely neglect the synthetic model. As demanded by this method, he listened very carefully to the sociopolitical, cultural, and religious traditions of the people to whom he announced the Gospel. He took pains to familiarize himself with them and described them in surprisingly accurate details.

While predominantly negative in his judgment of their intrinsic worth, especially with regard to the Vietnamese religious traditions, de Rhodes made a judicious use of the Vietnamese cultural and even religious elements in composing his *Cathechismus*. He succeeded in establishing a dialogue in which there is a *mutual* enrichment between Christianity and the Vietnamese culture. Of course, de Rhodes's first and absolute loyalty was to what he took to be Christian truths, and his knowledge of the Vietnamese religions was far from comprehensive and accurate. Nevertheless, there can be no gainsaying the fact that de Rhodes recognized the necessity of learning the Vietnamese language and culture and using them in inculturating Christianity into Vietnam, as well as of bringing the Vietnamese traditions into line with the Christian faith.

It can also be argued that the transcendental model, which highlights the subject's integral conversion as the foundation for theologizing, was not foreign to de Rhodes. In the Ignatian tradition, he makes conversion to Christ the King the goal and cornerstone of his mission and catechesis. Though de Rhodes neither could nor did offer anything approaching a cognitional theory like that of Bernard Lonergan, he nevertheless made a radical and total conversion from the idols gathered under the banner of Satan to the true God as revealed by Jesus Christ the condition and basis for a new understanding of reality and a new way of life. Without this conversion it is, in de Rhodes's judgment, impossible to inculturate Christianity into Vietnam properly as well as to critique and reject the errors that, in his view, permeated Vietnamese religions.

Of the remaining two models of contextual theology, namely, the praxis and anthropological models, it must be said that they are remote from de Rhodes's theology of inculturation. His emphasis on conversion still retains the individualistic cast of post-Reformation theology that focuses on the salvation of the individual souls apart from the transformation of the sociopolitical and economic structures. Not surprisingly, de Rhodes's commentary on the decalogue, especially on the seventh commandment against theft, contemplates exclusively commutative justice, not distributive justice, and much less social justice. Furthermore, de Rhodes's starting point for theological reflection remains Christian doctrines and not praxis.

Similarly, de Rhodes's theology of revelation and religions does not allow him to acknowledge the presence of God and God's self-communication anywhere other than in Christianity. This exclusivistic theology goes against the grain of the anthropological model of inculturation which affirms the presence of God's grace already active in the history and traditions of the native culture and which views inculturation mainly as the process of naming the elements of the native culture in Christian terms.

This is said not by way of criticism of de Rhodes, which would be intolerably anachronistic, but simply to note that the two most popular and effective models of inculturation in contemporary theology, especially for the Third World, do not find a place in de Rhodes's theology. The absence of these two models of contextual theology, though to be expected in de Rhodes's post-Tridentine theology, implies that his missionary and catechetical method needs to be updated to achieve its full effectiveness in contemporary Vietnam.

The need of further development for de Rhodes's method of inculturation is rendered acute by a more adequate understanding of what constitutes culture and of the process of inculturation. There is a plethora of definitions of culture from the various standpoints of the social sciences. The following definition by the missionary anthropologist Louis Luzbetak serves our purposes well: "Culture is (1) a *plan* (2) consisting of a set of *norms, standards,* and associated *notions* and *beliefs* (3) for *coping* with the various demands of life,

(4) shared by *a social group*, (5) *learned* by the individual from the society, and (6) organized into a *dynamic* (7) *system* of control."[10]

Such a unique and comprehensive plan for living possessed by a particular society and composed of norms, standards, notions, and beliefs to be learned by the individual in the process of enculturation is made up of three levels. To quote Luzbetak again:

> (1) At the surface level are the individual building-blocks of culture, the meaningless *forms*, the "shapes," the signs or symbols minus their meaning, the *who, what, when, where, how*, and *what kind*. (2) The society relates such forms to one another through *function* to create a system of meanings (their immediate *whys*). (3) On the third and deepest level is the *basic psychology* (the underlying *whys* of a society; the starting points of thinking, reacting, and motivating; the fundamental premises, attitudes, and drives — the "mentality"). This inner logic on the third level of culture tends to give the middle-level relationships a general consistency and the whole culture a distinct character.[11]

Ideally, in the process of inculturation all the three levels of culture described above should be engaged in, if not simultaneously, at least ultimately. Inculturation is the process whereby the Christian faith is integrated into the culture of the people to whom the Good News is preached in such a way that *both* the faith is expressed in the elements of this culture and transforms it from within, *and* the culture in turn enriches and transforms the previous expressions of the Christian faith brought in from outside. Essential to inculturation is the *mutual* criticism and enrichment between the local culture and the Christian faith. Both expressions of faith and culture are transformed as the result of this process.

Strictly speaking, then, inculturation is a three-step trajectory of evangelization and missionary activity. In the first phase, foreign philosophical and theological categories, elaborated in the missionaries' culture, as well as foreign ecclesiastical structures and liturgico-sacramental rituals, are imported into the country to be evangelized. In this phase, the concern is to find in the local cultures what Luzbetak calls the "individual building-blocks of culture," "the signs and symbols," "the *who, what, when, where, how*, and *what kind*" that would be roughly equivalent to the Christian counterparts. Obviously, here *translation* is the chief means of adaptation. De Rhodes has made a brilliant and lasting contribution in this phase, as his *Dictionarium* eloquently testifies.

Then comes the stage of *acculturation* in which the Christian faith acquires certain elements of the host culture which, in its turn, adopts certain elements of the Christian faith and way of life. Such a mutual borrowing of concepts, symbols, myths, rituals, and organizational structures may bring about an enrichment of both the Christian faith and the host culture. However, often such

---

10. Luzbetak, *The Church and Cultures*, 156.
11. *The Church and Cultures*, 223.

a mutual borrowing still operates at a superficial level. Its basic strategy is that of adaptation or accommodation of the foreign religion to the local culture or vice versa. The Christian faith still remains a subculture within the host culture, and not infrequently a particular brand of Christianity, often a European one, exercises a dominant role on the local church.

Often acculturation may lead to either juxtaposition (elements of the Christian faith and those of one's culture are unassimilated and are allowed to operate side by side) or syncretism (the basic identity of both faith and culture is lost). At this level, at best the building blocks of culture are engaged in their immediate meanings or *whys,* that is, their functions, and the attempt consists in discovering their functional equivalences in Christianity.

At this level, too, de Rhodes has made significant contributions to the process of inculturating Christianity into Vietnam with his adoption of certain Vietnamese popular proverbs, religious beliefs, and ritual practices into Christian theology and life as well as with his insertion of some Christian beliefs and moral norms into the Vietnamese symbolic universe and ethos. In spite of all these remarkable achievements, there is no doubt that Latin theology, and more specifically, post-Tridentine theology still reigns supreme in de Rhodes's *Cathechismus,* both in its terminology and concepts.

There is still the third and deepest level of culture, which Luzbetak calls "basic psychology," to be engaged in. A better term for it might be the "comprehensive worldview" or the *Weltanschauung* of the native people. This worldview is embedded mainly in the people's *philosophy* and *religion(s).* Only when the people's philosophy and religion(s) are taken seriously as the locus of God's self-communication in grace, in spite of their possible defects and errors, can integral inculturation take place. This is the level of *inculturation* proper. Only when the local church has achieved sufficient autonomy from the "sending church," both intellectually and institutionally, and its members, both clerical and lay, have taken over the task of evangelizing not only individuals but their own culture as a whole, does inculturation, properly speaking, begin to take place.

At this stage, theological, liturgical, and ethical expressions of the Christian faith and the fundamental elements of the native culture are affected in their very foundations. As a result, new resources, besides Scripture and Western theological tradition, will be mined to develop a contextual theology (e.g., people's stories, sacred texts and practices of various religions, non-Christian monastic traditions, myths, folklore, symbols, poetry, songs, visual art, dance, etc.).[12]

---

12. For studies in the use of these resources, see the works of Choan-Seng Song, especially *Third-Eye Theology: Theology in Formation in Asian Settings* (Maryknoll, N.Y.: Orbis Books, 1979; rev. ed., 1990); *Tell Us Our Names: Story Theology from an Asian Perspective* (Maryknoll, N.Y.: Orbis, 1984); and *Theology from the Womb of Asia* (Maryknoll, N.Y.: Orbis Books, 1986). For an excellent anthology on the new hermeneutics, see R. S. Sugirtharajah, ed., *Voices from the Margin: Interpreting the Bible in the Third World* (Maryknoll, N.Y.: Orbis Books, 1991).

Furthermore, not only the historico-critical method (which retains its validity and usefulness in order to discover the world *behind* the text) but also a new hermeneutics must be used to discover the worlds *in* and *in front of* the texts of the Bible and tradition. Such a hermeneutics, given the current sociopolitical, economic, and religious situation of the Third World (Vietnam included), will require a starting point in praxis in favor of the people living in the underside of history and in interreligious dialogue.[13]

In other words, the anthropological and praxis models of contextual theology must be joined with the other models (translation, synthetic, and transcendental) to create an inculturated Christianity and Christian theology in Asia and in particular in Vietnam. In this process of inculturation, the Christian faith and the native culture will not simply be juxtaposed one alongside the other nor will they be fused into one another in a form of syncretism with the consequent loss of their own distinct identity and configuration.

On the contrary, each will preserve its own identity; each will challenge, critique, and correct the other from its own vantage point and traditions (and not simply the Christian faith unilaterally challenging and correcting the errors of the native culture, from a superior position, as de Rhodes and many others maintained). Each will enrich and develop the other (and not only the Christian faith one-sidedly uplifting and improving the native culture, again as de Rhodes thought).[14]

What will result from this process of inculturation is neither the old Christianity imported from outside nor the old culture of the indigenous people, both remaining in their previous condition or even in a "new and improved" version, but a *tertium quid* whose concrete contours are yet unknown and can be defined only negatively, that is, in contrast to the imported Christianity and the native culture. In rather general terms, it may be said that the new inculturated Christianity or Christian church will achieve four "selfs": self-government, self-

---

13. Aloysius Pieris has repeatedly argued that an authentic Asian theology must make use of two methods conjointly: social analysis and what he calls "introspection." With social analysis, Asian theology discovers the *poverty* of Asian religiousness, and with introspection, the *religiousness* of Asian poverty. For Pieris, the most appropriate form of inculturation of Christianity in Asia is not the Latin model of incarnation in a non-Christian *culture* nor the Greek model of assimilation of a non-Christian *philosophy* nor the North European model of accommodation to a non-Christian *religiousness*. Rather it is the monastic model of participation in a non-Christian *spirituality* which demands a *voluntary* poverty as a way of struggling against *imposed* poverty and oppression. See his *An Asian Theology of Liberation* (Maryknoll, N.Y.: Orbis Books, 1988) and *Love Meets Wisdom: A Christian Experience of Buddhism* (Maryknoll, N.Y.: Orbis Books, 1988).

14. Personally, I believe that a Vietnamese Christian theology will be founded on at least three major axes: first, on the threefold way (*tam tai dao*), that is, the way of heaven, the way of humanity, and the way of the earth (*thien dao, nhan dao, dia dao*) — in other words, the theoanthropocosmic way; second, on ancestor worship and family ethics, which form the heart of Vietnamese piety; and third, on liberative praxis, which has been the hallmark of the history of the Vietnamese people who, in succession, fought to regain their freedom from a thousand-year domination of the Chinese, one-hundred-year colonization of the French, twenty-five-year interference of the Soviets and the Americans, and now the oppressive Communist regime. For an attempt at a Vietnamese christology, see Peter C. Phan, "The Christ of Asia: An Essay on Jesus as the Eldest Son and Ancestor," *Studia Missionalia* 45 (1996): 25-55, and idem, "Jesus the Christ with an Asian Face," *Theological Studies* 57 (1996): 399–430.

support, self-propagation, and self-theologizing, while maintaining the unity and communion of faith and of all the churches.

It would be too much to expect de Rhodes, a missionary of the seventeenth century, to think of inculturation in these terms, let alone to set out to achieve it. However, what he has done in his mission and catechesis in Vietnam far surpassed what the official church of his times could have dreamed of, even in its most catholic moments.

Founder of the Vietnamese Christianity, perfector of the Vietnamese national script, author of the first Vietnamese theological work, and pioneer in catechesis for the Vietnamese people, de Rhodes has left a cultural and theological legacy for which the Christian Church in Vietnam and the Vietnamese people as a whole will be eternally grateful.

Bibliography for Part One

I. MANUSCRIPTS

Vatican Archives

Ep. ad Princip., vol. 65, ff. 153v–154v: Pope Alexander VIII's letter to the Christians of Tonkin, May 31, 1664.

Ep. ad Princip., vol. 73, ff. 288v–289v: Pope Innocent XI's letter to the king of Tonkin, September 20, 1679.

Ep. ad Princip., vol. 81, f. 225: Pope Innocent XII's letter to the priests, catechists, and Christians of Tonkin, January 15, 1697.

Archives of the Propaganda Fide

Miscellanee diverse, vol. 16, ff. 208–9: Letter of the Christians of Tonkin to Pope Urban VIII in 1630; translated from Chinese into Latin by Alexandre de Rhodes.

Miscellanee diverse, vol. 16, f. 78: Letter of the Christians of Cochinchina of July 15, 1640, to Pope Urban VIII, with the request that the Jesuit priests be allowed to administer the sacrament of confirmation; translated from Chinese into Latin by Alexandre de Rhodes.

Vatican Library

Fonds Barberini, vol. 158 (mss. orient.): Lord Trinh Trang's letter in Chinese of 1627 engraved on a large silver leaf and addressed to Jesuit Father Andrea Palmiero, visitor of the province of Japan and the vice-province of China.

Jesuit Archives of the Paris Province

Fonds Brotier, vol. 73, n. 136: Alexandre de Rhodes's letter of November 4, 1655, to the superior general Goswin Nickel from Isfahan.

Fonds Brotier, vol. 73, n. 138: Alexandre de Rhodes's letter of November 10, 1657, to the superior general Goswin Nickel from Isfahan.

Fonds Rybeyrete, n. 29: Aimé Chézaud's circular letter of November 11, 1660, from Isfahan on Alexandre de Rhodes's death in Isfahan on November 5, 1660.

Fonds Rybeyrete, n. 161: Alexandre de Rhodes's letter of May 20, 1658, to his Jesuit brother Georges from Isfahan.

Library of Ajuda (Lisbon)

Jesuitas na Asia, codex 49-V-31: Mission in Vietnam. First volume, ff. 1–24, 215–56. Beginning of the mission in Tonkin. Giuliano Baldinotti's travel to Tonkin in 1626. Mission in

Tonkin in 1627–30; report written by Alexandre de Rhodes. Annual report of December 1632 written by Gaspar do Amaral from Thang Long, Tonkin.

Jesuitas na Asia, codex 49-V-32: Mission in Vietnam. Second volume, ff. 289–307, 315–23, 469–70, 474. Alexandre de Rhodes's travels from Macao to Cochinchina. Report written by himself at Macassar on June 4, 1647. Baptismal formula adopted by Alexandre de Rhodes for the Vietnamese. Alexandre de Rhodes's letter of October 1651 from Rome to João Cabral, Jesuit provincial in Japan. Death of Fathers Felice Morelli and Francesco Montefusculi on March 21, 1651.

Real Academia de la Historia de Madrid

Jesuitas, bundle 21, fasc. 6, ff. 702–3: Mission in Tonkin, report written by Alexandre de Rhodes in Macao in May 1631.

Jesuitas, bundle 21bis, fasc. 16, ff. 31–38: Report on the catechists of Tonkin written by Gaspar do Amaral in Thang Long on March 25, 1637.

Jesuitas, bundle 21bis, fasc. 17, ff. 228–34: Report on the martyrdom of Andrew of Phu Yen written by Alexandre de Rhodes on August 1, 1644.

Library and Museum Calvet of Avignon

Manuscripts, vol. 2099, n. 38: Purchase of a pension of 42 crowns for Michel and Bernardin II de Rhodes from the community of Cavaillon in 1571.

Manuscripts, vol. 2098, n. 56: Renewal of the pension of 42 crowns made by the community of Cavaillon to the Jesuit High School at Avignon, grantee of Michel and Bernardin II de Rhodes, February 26, 1588.

Manuscripts, vol. 3243, ff. 36–45: Alexandre de Rhodes's ratification of the transaction between the Jesuit High School of Avignon and Françoise de Rafaélis, his mother, June 11, 1618.

Manuscripts, vol. 3975, f. 184: Receipt of Françoise de Rafaélis, mother of Alexandre de Rhodes, March 12, 1624.

Departmental Archives of Vaucluse

Sainte-Magdeleine, 1064–1635, GG 3: Baptismal record of the Sainte-Magdeleine parish in Avignon from 1064 to 1635. In this record are the dates of baptism of François de Rhodes and Hélène de Rhodes, Alexandre de Rhodes's younger brother and younger sister, respectively.

Series E, de Rhodes Family, n. 146: Proceedings of a lawsuit brought against Françoise de Rafaélis, mother of Alexandre de Rhodes at Avignon in 1636.

Vincenti 1582, ff. 147–158v: "Will of Mr. Bernardin de Rhodes, son of Jean, deceased, citizen of Avignon." Made at Avignon on November 10, 1601.

Vincenti 1587, ff. 259–275r: "Will of Nobleman Bernardin de Rhodes, son of Mr. Jean de Rhodes, deceased, citizen of Avignon." Made at Avignon on December 18, 1610.

Vincenti 1591, ff. 251–272r: "Will of Nobleman Bernardin de Rhodes, son of Mr. Jean de Rhodes, deceased, citizen of Avignon." Made at Avignon on July 26, 1615.

Vincenti 1591, ff. 272v–274r: Will of Suzanne de Rhodes, sister of Alexandre de Rhodes. Made at Avignon on July 28, 1615.

Archivum Romanum Societatis Jesu

Fondo Gesuitico, n. 732: Alexandre de Rhodes's letter, written in the fall of 1617, to the superior general Mutio Vitelleschi requesting to be sent to the missions.

Fondo Gesuitico, n. 734: Alexandre de Rhodes's letter of April 15, 1614, to the superior general Claudius Aquaviva requesting to be sent to the missions of China and Japan.

Fondo Gesuitico, n. 735: Alexandre de Rhodes's letter of May 15, 1617, to the superior general Mutio Vitelleschi requesting to be sent to the missions of China and Japan.

Jap.-Sin. 25, ff. 128–38: Catalogue of the Jesuits of the Japan province, prepared in December 1623.

Jap.-Sin. 25, ff. 229–262r: Catalogue of the Jesuits of the Japan province, prepared in 1691, 1697, 1699, and 1705.

Jap.-Sin. 68, f. 13: Alexandre de Rhodes's letter of June 1625 from Cochinchina to Nuno Mascarenhas, Assistant of Portugal.

Jap.-Sin. 68, f. 15: Manoel Fernandes's letter of July 2, 1625, from Hoi An (Faïfo) to father general.

Jap.-Sin. 68, f. 17: Gabriele de Mattos's letter of July 5, 1625, from Cochinchina to the superior general.

Jap.-Sin. 68, f. 28–29v: Francesco Buzomi's letter of July 13, 1626, from Cochinchina to the superior general.

Jap.-Sin. 69, ff. 95–140v: Alexandre de Rhodes's travels from 1640 to 1649, reported by himself in 1649.

Jap.-Sin. 70, ff. 1–8r: Annual report written by Father Br. Roboredo in Da Nang on April 14, 1641.

Jap.-Sin. 71, ff. 23–27r: Annual report written by Gaspar Luís in Macao on December 12, 1621, on the mission in Cochinchina.

Jap.-Sin. 71, ff. 56–71r: Annual report written by Gaspar Luís at Nuoc Man (Cochinchina) on January 1, 1626, on the mission in Cochinchina.

Jap.-Sin. 72, ff. 2–16v: Annual report written by João Roiz in Macao on November 20, 1621, on the mission in Cochinchina.

Jap.-Sin. 72, ff. 69–86r: Annual report written by António de Fontes at Hoi An on January 1, 1626.

Jap.-Sin. 73, ff. 56–64r: Annual report written by Gaspar Luís at Nuoc Man in May 1627.

Jap.-Sin. 80, ff. 13–14r: Letter of the Christians of Tonkin to the superior general Mutio Vitelleschi in 1630; translated from Chinese into Latin by Alexandre de Rhodes.

Jap.-Sin. 80, ff. 15–16v: Alexandre de Rhodes's letter of January 16, 1631, from Macao to Nuno Mascarenhas, Assistant of Portugal, on the mission in Tonkin.

Jap.-Sin. 80, f. 25: Felice Morelli's letter of April 30, 1645, from Tonkin to the superior general.

Jap.-Sin. 80, f. 32r: Felice Morelli's letter of May 30, 1945, from Tonkin to the superior general.

Jap.-Sin. 80, f. 34r: Gaspar do Amaral's letter of November 21, 1645, from Macao to the superior general.

Jap.-Sin. 80, ff. 35–38v: Baptismal formula adopted by Alexandre de Rhodes for the Vietnamese, approved in 1645 by 33 Jesuit fathers of whom one half were professors of theology. Document prepared in Macao and sent to Juan de Mattos, Assistant of Portugal.

Jap.-Sin. 80, ff. 45–47v: Instructions to the catechists of Tonkin (27 articles), written in 1647–48.

Jap.-Sin. 80, ff. 69v: Certificate given by Lord Trinh Tac to Felice Morelli on March 11, 1647, in which he adopted Morelli as his son. Portuguese translation of the Chinese original.

Jap.-Sin. 80, ff. 88–89v: Giovanni Filippo de Marini's letter of May 12, 1655, from Tonkin to Francisco de Tavora, Assistant of Portugal, on the baptismal formula adopted by Alexandre de Rhodes for the Vietnamese.

Jap.-Sin. 80, f. 96: Giovanni Filippo de Marini's letter of 1652 (?) from Tonkin to Giovanni-Luigi Confalonieri, Assistant of Italy, on the baptismal formula adopted by Alexandre de Rhodes for the Vietnamese.

Jap.-Sin. 80, ff. 103–118v: Baptismal formula adopted by Alexandre de Rhodes for the Vietnamese, defended by Metello Saccano. Document written in Macao on July 5, 1653.

Jap.-Sin. 80, f. 151r: Joseph Tissanier's letter of November 20, 1660, from Tonkin to Le Cazre, Assistant of France, in French.

Jap.-Sin. 80, f. 152r: Joseph Tissanier's letter of November 12, 1661, from Tonkin to Le Cazre, Assistant of France.

Jap.-Sin. 81, f. 246: Catechist Bento Thien's letter of October 25, 1659, from Tonkin to Giovanni Filippo de Marini. In Vietnamese with Romanized script.

Jap.-Sin. 81, f. 247: Catechist Igesico Van Tin's letter of September 12, 1659, from Tonkin to Giovanni Filippo de Marini. In Vietnamese with Romanized script.

Jap.-Sin. 81, ff. 254–259v: Short history of Vietnam written by Catechist Bento Thien and sent to Giovanni Filippo de Marini. In Vietnamese with Romanized script.

Jap.-Sin. 83 and 84, ff. 1–62v: History of Tonkin written by Alexandre de Rhodes in Macao in about 1636.

Jap.-Sin. 85, ff. 125–175v: Annual report written by Gaspar do Amaral in Tonkin on December 31, 1632, on the mission in Tonkin in 1632.

Jap.-Sin. 89, ff. 545–548v: The expression *dao Hoa-Lang* (religion of the Portuguese, i.e., Christianity) discussed by Isidore Lucion, September 30, 1712.

Rom. 172, f. 158v: Register of entrants into the novitiate of San Andrea in Rome in 1612.

II. WORKS BY ALEXANDRE DE RHODES, ARRANGED CHRONOLOGICALLY

de Rhodes, Alexandre. *Relazione de' felici successi della Santa Fede Predicata da Padri della Compagnia di Giesu nel regno di Tunchino, alla santità di N.S. PP. Innocenzio decimo. Di Alessandro de Rhodes avignonese.* Rome, 1650 (=*Relazione*).

———. *Dictionarium annamiticum, lusitanum, et latinum ope Sacrae Congregationis de Propaganda Fide in lucem editum ab Alexandro de Rhodes è Societate Jesu, ejusdemque Sacrae Congregationis Missionario Apostolico.* Rome, 1651 (=*Dictionarium*).

———. *Linguae annamiticae seu Tunchinensis brevis declaratio*, in *Dictionarium*, pp. 1–31. Rome, 1651 (=*Linguae annamiticae*).

———. *Cathechismus pro iis, qui volunt suscipere Baptismum, in Octo dies divisus. Phep giang tam ngay cho ke muan chiu phep rua toi, ma beao dao thanh duc Chua bloi. Ope Sacrae Congregationis de Propaganda Fide in lucem editus. Ab Alexandro de RHODES è Societate Jesu, ejusdemque Sacrae Congregationis Missionario Apostolico.* Rome, 1651 (=*Cathechismus*).

———. *Histoire du Royaume de Tunquin, et des grands progrez que la prédication de l'Evangile y a faits en la conversion des infidelles. Depuis l'année 1627, jusques à l'année 1646. Composée en latin par le R. P. Alexandre de Rhodes, de la Compagnie de Jesus. Et traduit en françois par le R. P. Henry Albi, de la mesme Compagnie.* Lyon, 1651 (=*Histoire du Royaume de Tunquin*).

———. *Tunchinensis historiae libri duo, quorum altero status temporalis hujus Regni, altero mirabiles evangelicae predicationis progressus referuntur. Coeptae per Patres Societatis Iesu, ab Anno 1627, ad Annum 1646. Authore P. Alexandro de Rhodes. Avenionensi, ejusdem Societatis Presbytero; Eorum quae hic narrantur teste oculato.* Lyon, 1652 (=*Tunchinensis historiae*).

————. *Relation des progrez de la Foy au Royaume de la Cochinchine vers les derniers quartiers du Levant. Envoiée au R. P. Général de la Compagnie de Jésus. Par le P. Alexandre de Rhodes employé aux Missions de ce païs.* Paris, 1652 (=*Relation des progrez*).

————. *La glorieuse mort d'André Catéchiste de la Cochinchine qui a le premier versé son sang pour la querelle de JESUS-CHRIST en cette nouvelle Eglise. Par le Père Alexandre de Rhodes, de la Compagnie de Jesus, qui a toujours este présent à toute cette Histoire.* Paris, 1653 (=*La glorieuse mort*).

————. *Divers voyages et missions du P. Alexandre de Rhodes en la Chine, & autres Royaumes de l'Orient. Avec son retour en Europe par la Perse & l'Arménie. Le tout divisé en trois parties.* Paris, 1653 (=*Divers voyages*).

————. *Sommaire des divers voyages, et Missions apostoliques, du R. P. Alexandre de Rhodes, de la Compagnie de Jesus, à la Chine, & autres Royaumes de l'Orient, avec son retour de la Chine à Rome. Depuis l'année 1618, jusques à l'année 1653.* Paris, 1653 (=*Sommaire*).

————. *Histoire de la vie et de la glorieuse mort, de cinq Pères de la Compagnie de Jésus, qui ont souffert dans le Japon. Avec trois Seculiers, en l'Année 1643. Par le R. P. Alexandre de Rhodes, de la Compagnie de Jésus.* Paris, 1653 (=*Histoire de la vie*).

————. *Relation de la Mission des Pères de la Compagnie de Jesus. Establie dans le Royaume de Perse. Par le R. P. Alexandre de Rhodes. Dressée & mise au jour par un père de la mesme Compagnie (Père Jacques de Machault).* Paris, 1659 (=*Relation de la mission*).

III. SELECTED WORKS CONSULTED

Baldinotti, Giuliano. "Relation du voyage fait au Royaume de Tunquin nouvellement découvert." In Gaspar Paes, *Histoire de ce qui s'est passé es Royaumes d'Éthiopie, en l'année 1626 jusqu'au mois de mars 1627. Et de la Chine, en l'année 1625 jusques en février de 1626. Avec une brève narration du voyage qui s'est fait au Royaume de Tunquim nouvellement découvert.* Paris, 1629.

Bernard-Maitre, Henri. "Le P. De Rhodes et les Missions d'Indochine (1615–1645)." In *Histoire universelle des Missions Catholiques: Les Missions modernes*, vol. II (Paris, 1957), 53–69.

————. "Viet-Nam–Iran. Le P. Alexandre de Rhodes: 1660–1960." *Études* (December 1960): 321–36.

Bettray, Johannes. *Die Akkommodationsmethode des P. Matteo Ricci S.I. in China.* Rome: Pontifica Universitas Gregoriana, 1955.

Bonifacy, Lt. Col. *Les débuts du Christianisme en Annam. Des origines au commencement du XVIIIè siècle.* Hanoi, 1930.

Bontinck, François. *La Lutte autour de la liturgie chinoise aux XVIIè et XVIIIè siècles.* Paris: Béatrice-Nauwelaerts, 1962.

Borri, Cristoforo. *Relation de la nouvelle Mission des Pères de la Compagnie de Jésus, au Royaume de la Cochinchine, Traduite de l'Italien du Père Christophe Borri, qui fuit un des premiers qui entrèrent en ce Royaume, par le Père Antoine de la Croix, de la mesme Compagnie.* Lille, 1631.

Boudet, Paul. "Le Père de Rhodes au Tonkin." *Cahier de la Société de Géographie de Hanoi XXXII* (1941): 3–6.

Bourgeois, R., Nguyen Van To, and Paul Boudet. "Alexandre de Rhodes, 1591–1660." *Indochine, hebdomadaire illustré* 41 (June 1941): 1–10.

Braido, Pietro. *Lineamenti di storia della catechesi e dei catechismi. Dal "tempo delle riforme" all' età degli imperialismi (1450–1870).* Turin: Editrice Elle Di Ci, 1991.

Brenier, Henri. "Le Père Alexandre de Rhodes. Un grand missionnaire provençal au XVIIè siècle." *Les Missions Catholiques* 74 (1942): 105–6, 119–21, 134–38, 151–53, 172–73.

Brucker, Joseph. *La Compagnie de Jésus: Esquisse de son institut et de son histoire (1521–1773)*. Paris: Beauchesne, 1919.

Cadière, Léopold. "Cha Alexandre de Rhodes tim duoc tieng annam ma goi ten Dang Tao-Hoa." *Sacerdos indosinensis* (1927): 47–55.

———. *Croyances et pratiques religieuses des Vietnamiens*. Vol. I. Hanoi: Imprimerie d'Extrême-Orient, 1944. Vol. II. Paris: École Française d'Extrême-Orient, 1955. Vol. III. Paris: École Française d'Extrême-Orient, 1956.

———. "Les Européens qui ont vu le Vieux-Huê, le Père de Rhodes." *BAVH* II (July–September 1915): 231–49.

———. "Iconographie du P. De Rhodes." *BAVH* XXV (1938): 27–61.

———. "Le P. A. de Rhodes: chronologie et itinéraires." *Extrême-Asie* (1927): 113–26.

———. "Le titre divin en annamite. Etude de terminologie chrétienne." *Revue d'Histoire des Missions* (December 1931). Supplément au numéro de Décembre, 1–27.

Cardim, António Francisco, and Francesco Barreto. *Relation de ce qui s'est passé depuis quelques années, jusques à l'an 1644 au Japon, à la Cochinchine, au Malabar, en l'Isle de Ceilan, & en plusieurs autres Isles & Royaume de l'Orient compris sous le nom des Provinces du Japon & du Malabar, de la Compagnie de Jésus. Divisée en deux Parties selon ces deux Provinces*. Paris, 1646.

Chappoulie, Henri. *Aux origines d'une Eglise. Rome et les Missions d'Indochine au XVIIè siècle*, 2 vols. Paris: Bloud et Gay, 1943, 1948.

Do Quang Chinh. "Les adaptations culturelles d'Alexandre de Rhodes." *Études interdisciplinaires sur le Vietnam*, vol. 1, no. 2 (1974): 115–43.

———. "La mission au Viet-Nam 1624–30 et 1640–45 d'Alexandre de Rhodes, S.J. avignonnais." Diss., Sorbonne, 1969.

Favre, Pierre-François. *Lettres édifiantes et curieuses sur la visite apostolique de M. de La-Baume, évêque d'Halicarnasse à la Cochinchine en l'année 1740. Où l'on voit les Voyages et les Travaux de ce zélé Prélat, la conduite des Missionnaires Jésuites & de quelques Autres, avec des nouvelles Observations etc. Pour servir de continuation aux Mémoires Historiques du R. P. Norbert Capucin: Par M. Favre, prêtre Suisse, Protonotaire Apostolique & Provisiteur de la même Visite*. Venice, 1746.

Gaide, Dr. L. "Note sur une noble figure avignonnaise: le Père jésuite Alexandre de Rhodes, le premier missionnaire français qui ait séjourné en Indo-Chine." *Mémoire de l'Accadémie de Vaucluse* 34 (1934): 199–212.

———. "Quelques renseignements sur la famille du P. Alexandre de Rhodes." *BAVH* (July–December 1927): 225–28.

"Un Géant. Alexandre de Rhodes." *Missi* (1961): 147–73.

Huonder, A. "P. Alexander de Rhodes, S.J., und die Gründung des Pariser Seminars der auswärtigen Missionen." *Zeitschrift für Missionswissenschaft* III (1913): 258–61.

Launay, Adrien. *Histoire de la Mission de Cochinchine (1658–1823). Documents Historiques*. Vol. I. Paris, 1920.

Machault, Jacques. *Relation des Missions des Pères de la Compagnie de Jésus, dans les Indes Orientales. Où l'on verra l'estat présent de la Religion Chrestienne & plusieurs belles curiositez de ces Contrées*. Paris, 1659.

Marillier, André. "Le catéchisme d'Alexandre de Rhodes." *Bulletin de la Société des Missions-Étrangères de Paris* (1961): 327–49.

Marini, Giovanni Filippo de. *Relation nouvelle et curieuse des Royaumes de Tunquin et de Lao. Contenant une description exacte de leur Origine, Grandeur, Estendue, de leurs Richesses, & de leurs Forces; des Moeurs, & du naturel de leurs Habitants; de la fertilité, & des Rivières qui les arrosent de tous costez, & de plusieurs autres particularitez utiles & nécessaires pour l'Histoire, & la Géographie, Ensemble la Magnificence de la Cour des Roys de Tunquin, & des Cérémonies qu'on observe à leurs Enterrements. Traduite de l'Italien du P. Mariny Romain.* Paris, 1666.

Minamiki, George. *The Chinese Rites Controversy from Its Beginning to Modern Times.* Chicago: Loyola University Press, 1985.

Nguyen Chi Thiet. "Le Catéchisme du Père Alexandre de Rhodes et l'âme vietnamienne." Diss., Pontificia Universitas Urbaniana, 1970.

Nguyen Huu Trong. *Les origines du clergé vietnamien.* Saigon: Ra Khoi, 1959.

Nguyen Huy Lai. *La tradition religieuse, spirituelle et sociale au Vietnam.* Paris: Beauchesne, 1981.

Nguyen Khac Xuyen. "Le Catéchisme en langue vietnamienne romanisée du P. Alexandre de Rhodes." Diss., Pontificia Universitas Gregoriana, 1956.

———. "L'écriture vietnamienne romanisée du XVIIe siècle jusqu'à la fin du XIXè siècle." *Bulletin de l'Institut de Recherches Historiques* (1961): 137–41.

———. "Le Père Alexandre de Rhodes et la Romanisation de la langue vietnamienne." *Bulletin de l'Institut de Recherches Historiques* (1961): 108–12.

———. "Le Père de Rhodes et l'édition de ses oeuvres." *Bulletin de l'Institut de Recherches Historiques* (1961): 195–96.

Otto, Josef. "Alexander von Rhodes S.J. Apostel von Annam und Vorkämpfer der neuen Missionshierarchie." *Die Katholischen Missionen* 56 (1928): 6–13; 45–50; 69–77.

Pfister, Louis. *Notices biographiques et bibliographiques sur les Jésuites de l'ancienne Mission de Chine (1552–1773).* Shanghai, 1932–34.

Pham Dinh Khiem. "La société vietnamienne au XVIIè siècle sous les yeux d'Alexandre de Rhodes." *Bulletin de l'Institut de Recherches Historiques* (1961): 69–74.

Poncet, C. A. "Le voyage du P. Alexandre de Rhodes de Cua Bang à Hanoi en 1627." *BAVH* XXIX (1942): 261–82.

Raguin, Yves. "Le P. Alexandre de Rhodes né en Avignon le 15 mars 1591 mort à Isphan le 5 novembre 1660. Cochinchin–Chine–Tonkin–Perse. Une méthode missionnaire." *Jésuites missionnaires* V (1940): 156–60.

Ricci, Matteo. *The True Meaning of the Lord of Heaven.* Translated, with introduction and notes, by Douglas Lancashire and Peter Hu Kuo-chen. St. Louis: Institute of Jesuit Sources, 1985.

Saccano, Metello. *Relation des progrez de la Foy au Royaume de la Cochinchine és années 1646 & 1647. Envoiée au R. P. Général de la Compagnie de Jésus. Par le P. Metelle Saccano Religioeux de la mesme Compagnie, employé aux Missions de ces païs.* Paris, 1653.

Seffer, J. "Le Catéchisme d'Alexandre de Rhodes." *Les Missions Catholiques* V (1955): 115–20.

Tan Phat, Placide. "Méthodes de catéchèse et de conversion du Père Alexandre de Rhodes." Diss., Institut Catholique de Paris, 1963.

Tissanier, Joseph. *Relation du voyage du P. Joseph Tissanier de la Compagnie de Jésus. Depuis la France, jusqu'au Royaume de Tunquin. Avec ce qui s'est passé de plus mémorable dans cette Mission, durant les années 1658, 1659, & 1660.* Paris, 1663.

Torralba, Edouard. "La date de naissance du Père de Rhodes, 15 mars 1591, est-elle exacte?" *Bulletin de la Société des Études Indochinoises* 35 (1960): 683–89.

Vu Khanh Tuong. "Les Missions jésuites avant les Missions-Étrangères au Viet-Nam (1615–1665)." Diss., Institut Catholique de Paris, 1956.

Part Two

THE *CATHECHISMUS* OF ALEXANDRE DE RHODES, S.J.

CATHECHISMVS

Pro ijs, qui volunt suscipere

BAPTISMVM

In Octo dies diuisus.

Phép giảng tám ngày cho kẻ muẩn chịu phép rửa
tọi, ma ḅěào đạo thánh đức Chúa blời

Ope Sacræ Congregationis de Propaganda Fide
in lucem editus

Ab Alexandro de Rhodes è Societate IESV,
eiusdemque Sacræ Congregationis
Missionario Apostolico.

ROMÆ, Typis Sacræ Congregationis de Propaganda Fide
Superiorum permissu.

Figure 4. Title page of the *Cathechismus* of Alexandre de Rhodes.

CATECHISM
for those who want to receive
BAPTISM
divided into eight days

Published under the Auspices of
the Sacred Congregation of the Propaganda Fide

by Alexandre de Rhodes of the Society of Jesus
and Apostolic Missionary
of this Sacred Congregation

Gosswinus Nickel Societatis Iesu Vicarius Generalis.

Cum Catechismum Latinum et Tunchinensem a P. Alexandro de Rhodes nostrae Societatis Sacerdote conscriptum, aliquot nostri Theologi recognoverit, et in lucem edi posse probaverint, facultatem facimus ut typis mandetur si ita videbitur iis ad quos spectat; cuius rei gratia has littereas manu nostra subscriptas, sigilloque nostro minitas, damus Romae 8 Julii 1651.

Gosswinus Nickel

Imprimatur: F. Vincentius Cepola Mag. et Socius R. P. Magistri Sacri Palatii Apostolici.

NOTE

It is to be noted that *Cathechismus* is divided not into chapters but into "days." All the chapter titles and paragraph titles are added by the translator, and are not found in the original.

The First Day

The Purpose of Our Precarious Life:
Reason, the Soul, and God

PRECARIOUSNESS OF THE PRESENT LIFE

Let us humbly ask the excellent Lord of heaven to help us understand well the way of the Lord. To do so we must consider that no one in this world lives a long life; there are indeed not too many who would live to seventy or eighty years of age. Let us therefore look for the way to live a long life, that is, to live eternally.[1] This task is incumbent upon a gentleman.[2] All the other ways of this world, though apt to bring us riches and honors, are not able to prevent us from becoming a miserable, ungentlemanly person in the afterlife.[3] We should not therefore learn the way of the Lord in order to obtain riches and honors in this world, since the benefits of the holy way of the Lord of heaven concern the afterlife.[4] People of this world know well what is good and bad for the present life but are ignorant of the means to pass from this world through death to the joy and happiness in the next life.

---

1. In an effective move in inculturation de Rhodes presents Christianity as the answer to the Vietnamese quest for longevity which he interprets as a quest for eternal life.

2. De Rhodes uses the expression *quan tu,* in Chinese *chün-tzu.* Literally "son of a ruler" and variously translated as gentleman, superior man, princely man, wise man, the word connotes not only superiority of birth but also and above all superiority of character and behavior. It represents the ideal person in Confucian philosophy, that is, the person who practices virtue (*te*) or goodness (*jen*). Here de Rhodes uses the word to refer to the truly wise person. For Confucius's notion of the *chün-tzu,* see *The Analects* IV, 5, 24; VIII, 6; XIV, 29; XV, 17; XVI, 10; XIX, 21.

3. The opposite of *quan tu* is *tieu nhan,* here translated as "ungentlemanly." One of the marks of *tieu nhan* is acting for material gains, against which de Rhodes immediately warns the catechumens.

4. De Rhodes never uses the word "religion" to refer to Christianity. Rather he employs the Sino-Vietnamese word *dao* and the purely Vietnamese word *dang* or *duong* which mean "way and law." The Vietnamese terms suggest that religion is not a set of doctrines to be believed but primarily a way of life. The Latin text uses the word *lex* to translate the Vietnamese *dao* and *dang.* This word is acceptable only if it does not imply legalism as if Christianity were essentially a set of rules to be followed. I will translate *dao* with "way," "law," and "religion" interchangeably.

BODY AND SOUL; SUPERIORITY OF THE SOUL OVER THE BODY

To know this means it is necessary to realize that human beings are composed of two elements: body and soul. The body comes from the parents; it has bones, blood, and flesh that are corruptible. The soul, on the contrary, is spiritual, incorruptible, and immortal; it does not come from the parents but from a superior principle.[5] The soul is like the master of the house, the body is like a servant or domestic help and must obey the soul like its master. Would it not be improper and contrary to reason if the servant or domestic help commands and the master obeys?

Let us consider whether one should take care of the servant or the master first. Of course, it is only right that one should take care of the master first, and then of the servant. Plowing rice fields, doing commerce and the like are the occupations of the body. Among farmers there are some who store abundant grain in their barns, and yet upon leaving this world, they cannot take with them even a handful of it. Others serve the court and wait upon the king and are made mandarins, but when their souls are separated from their bodies, they have to leave everything behind, bringing with them nothing. As the proverb says, "At birth, one cannot bring a cent to the world; at death, one cannot take a cent away."[6] Since this is something no one in this world can avoid, let us learn the sacred way to the next life, so that we may. live eternally.

To understand this point clearly, remember the common Vietnamese proverb of yours: "Life is a journey, death a return."[7] However, you must know that there are two dwellings in the afterlife: the one is good, the other bad; the one is above, the other below; the one is paradise, the other hell. Indeed, in heaven there is paradise: whoever reaches there enjoys eternal happiness.

SEEKING THE CREATOR OF ALL THINGS

To obtain this happiness, one must first of all ask who produces the heaven which covers us, who produces the earth which supports us, who produces all the things which nourish us. Ask to find, find to worship, that is the way of merit.

In this country, whoever wishes to become a mandarin, must serve and wait upon the king; whoever wishes to be free from penalties, must pay common taxes. Whoever enters into the service of a rebel or robs or declares himself a

---

5. De Rhodes coins the word *linh hon* to translate "soul." According to Vietnamese anthropology, the man has three *hon* and seven *via* or *phach*, whereas the woman has three *hon* and nine *via* or *phach*. De Rhodes adds the word *linh*, meaning spiritual and powerful, to the word *hon*. Sometimes he uses three words, *linh hon thieng*, meaning spiritual and powerful soul.

6. The proverb reads: "Khi sinh ra chang co dem mot dong ma lai; khi chet cung chang co cam mot dong ma di." De Rhodes's clever use of Vietnamese proverbs is one effective way to make Christian teachings acceptable to his audience.

7. De Rhodes quotes the proverb in both the Vietnamese and the Sino-Vietnamese forms: "Song the gui, chet thi ve" and "Sinh la ki da, tu la qui da," respectively.

mandarin, is liable to punishment by the king. Whoever lives in the kingdom must inquire who the king is so as to render him homage.[8] How much more should all in this world find out who is the true lord and the creator of heaven and the earth and all things in order to adore him.

It is incumbent upon us to discover who is the creator of all things in order to worship him rightly.[9] Only in this way can we go to paradise and obtain infinite happiness.[10] But if instead of finding out who is the true lord and worshiping him, one worships and prays to the demon, one is like someone who while living in this kingdom enters into the service of a rebel. Whoever worships the Lord of heaven rightly, will be granted to enter paradise to be with the Lord of heaven.[11] Whoever worships the demon will be with the demon.[12] But where is the demon? Without doubt the demon is in hell which is his home. Where is hell?[13] It is in the center of the earth, the prison the Lord of heaven has made to punish evil people.[14] It is popularly called *am phu,* and rightly so, because it is a place of darkness and obscurity. Don't imagine that down in hell there are commerce, rice fields, plowing and sowing as in this world. In the prisons of this world where the guilty are punished by kings, what is there but chains, shackles, rods, and the like? And those who are detained there, can they do what they please? So much less can those who are in the prison of hell; there they suffer the fire of sulphur for ever, condemned to infinite pains, without hope of ever escaping from them.

That is why we must learn the way, because the way is the way to the true country. The way that leads downward is easy: eating and drinking, living a dissolute life, doing the works of the body. The way that leads upward is difficult:

---

8. These examples are very well chosen to appeal to the experiences of the audience.

9. Throughout his work de Rhodes insists on the intimate connection between doctrine and practice. Belief in God must lead to the worship of God.

10. For paradise de Rhodes uses the word *thien dang* (the heavenly way or the way leading to heaven).

11. One of the greatest contributions of de Rhodes to the Vietnamese theological vocabulary is his use of the expression *Duc Chua Troi Dat* to refer to God. The earliest missionaries transliterated the Latin *Deus* into Vietnamese (*Chua Deu*). The disadvantage of this transliteration is that it does not convey the meaning of who God is. Furthermore, the Vietnamese might be led to think that the Christian God is some being other than the God they have worshiped in their religion (whom they call *Ong Troi,* Mr. Heaven). In a meeting of Jesuits in 1626 in Cochinchina, in which de Rhodes participated, it was decided to use the Chinese word *Thien Chu* (Master of Heaven). After long reflection, de Rhodes coined a new Vietnamese expression for God: *Duc Chua Troi Dat.* The particle *Duc* means "noble" and is used as a title. *Chua* means "lord." *Troi* (or *Bloi*) means "heaven." *Dat* means "earth." Thus, the full expression for God means "the noble Lord of heaven and earth." Sometimes the expression is shortened to *Duc Chua Troi* (the noble Lord of heaven), *Chua Troi Dat* (Lord of heaven and earth), *Chua Troi* (Lord of heaven), *Duc Chua* (the noble Lord). With this expression de Rhodes connects the Christian notion of God with the Vietnamese religion focused on "Mr. Heaven," a magnificent feat of inculturation, and preserves the idea of divine sovereignty and majesty.

12. De Rhodes combines two Vietnamese words *ma* and *qui* to translate devil. *Ma* refer to the (benevolent) souls of the dead, and *qui* to the malevolent ones.

13. De Rhodes uses three expressions for hell: *dia nguc* (prison at the center of the earth), *hoa nguc* (prison of fire), and *am phu* (place of darkness). The last expression is often used in Buddhist and Taoist literature.

14. De Rhodes expresses the popular opinion of his time regarding the location of hell.

218 *The* Cathechismus *of Alexandre de Rhodes, S.J.*

living a good and upright life, being primarily concerned about the affairs of the soul.

CONFORMITY OF THE TRUE RELIGION WITH REASON

Therefore, the true law is the law of reason, the law of right order.[15] If our actions conform to reason, we earn merit; if they are contrary to reason, we fall into sin. There is a Vietnamese proverb which says: "The horns of the buffalo are tied with solid ropes, the hearts of humans are drawn by solid reasons."[16]

If there had been established in Vietnam a law conformable to reason, there would have been no need to search for it with great pains elsewhere, in far-off countries. However, there commonly are among the Vietnamese two parts of law or religion. One is to worship heaven as the principle of all things; the other is to accord the idol the first place.[17]

HEAVEN ACCORDING TO THE CHINESE

Let us now consider heaven; later we will consider the idol. The Chinese have a proverb: "Heaven covers, the earth supports."[18] Heaven, therefore, is the house, while the earth is its foundation. Now, every house must have a builder and a master. Heaven, then, must have a lord and a creator. There is another Chinese expression: "Since the creation of heaven and the establishment of the earth...."[19] There are people who worship heaven, make vows to heaven, say that heaven judges, and attribute to heaven the power over life and death. Is it not stated in the book of Confucius, whom the Chinese recognize as a saint,[20] that "a woman by the name of Oa puts a stone on her head and repairs heaven"?[21] All the more must there be a creator of heaven.

Of course, in order to have a palace or a house, we must have an architect to make them. Anyone who is born has a father and a mother. Similarly, for heaven and the earth to exist, there must be a lord and creator who makes them. Suppose there were no one to create this heaven and this earth, who would maintain this heaven and the earth and this world so that we may dwell

---

15. This is one of de Rhodes's fundamental principles. It underlies his attempt to prove the truth of Christianity in the first four days of catechesis.

16. The proverb reads in Sino-Vietnamese: "Kien thang kha ke nguu giac, ly ngu nang phuc nhan tam."

17. De Rhodes accurately describes the Vietnamese indigenous religion as consisting in the worship of *Ong Troi* (Mr. Heaven). Indeed, a Vietnamese theology must takes this worship as its focus.

18. The proverb reads in Sino-Vietnamese, "Thien phu dia tai," and in Vietnamese, "Troi che dat cho."

19. The proverb reads in Sino-Vietnamese, "Tu tao thien lop dia," and in Vietnamese, "Xua dung troi dat."

20. De Rhodes uses the word *thanh* to translate saint. Another expression is *thanh hien* (holy and kind), which is the title given to Confucius. De Rhodes will dispute that Confucius deserves to be called saint.

21. According to legend, *Nu thi Oa*, a sister of Fu Hsi, an ancient king of China, made colorful stones to repair the sky as a sign of love and respect for heaven.

in them and have life? There is, therefore, a creator and lord of heaven and the earth and all things.

There are some who say: "If we do not venerate heaven, and heaven strikes us with thunder and lightning, how can we escape?" This fear is groundless, since heaven cannot strike us. Only the Lord of heaven can do that. Others say: "The cannons destroy the city." Actually, the cannons cannot destroy anything by themselves. One can lie in front of the mouth of the cannon and yet have nothing to fear, unless somebody injects the powder and the iron ball and then fires the cannon. People seem to have been misled to honor and adore heaven by a Chinese character. The Chinese character for heaven, *thien,* is composed of two words, namely, *nhat* (one) and *dai* (great).[22] Together they mean "the great one." But who is the great one except the Creator and Lord who makes heaven, the earth and all things? He is the Great One whom the whole humankind must worship and venerate, as right reason dictates. Heaven as a dwelling does not know anything, and it is not reasonable to worship it.

There are some who say: "Heaven covers us, the earth protects us, why should we not adore them?" Suppose you enter a house and see that things to eat and drink have been prepared and laid out. After you have eaten and drunk and rested, to whom do you give thanks, to the house or to the master of the house, even though you do not see him? Would it not be foolish to give thanks to the house and not to its master? The same thing applies to heaven and the earth. If someone adores heaven, that person would not only appear incapable of reason but is also ignorant of astronomy. If someone uses the expression "Heaven be adored!" perhaps it should be interpreted reasonably as an abbreviation. As when someone says, "This great house orders this or that," the great house should be understood to mean the master of that great house, namely, the king, who commands this or that.

Suppose someone, upon hearing the name of the great house, invokes the house itself and ignores its master, saying, "I pay homage to the four walls of this house and ask to be made a mandarin"; will he receive an office in this way? The house is one thing, its master is another. Similarly, heaven is one thing, the Lord of heaven is another. As the house is a thing without life and intelligence, so heaven is a material thing, without reason and intelligence. We should therefore neither worship heaven nor adore it. Rather we should both worship the Lord of heaven and adore him. Therefore, when people say in common parlance, "Heaven be adored!" there is lacking the word "Lord," which must be added. Henceforth, we must say: "I adore the Lord of heaven who is Lord above all things."[23]

---

22. De Rhodes might have taken this etymology from Matteo Ricci. See *The True Meaning of the Lord of Heaven,* translated, with introduction and notes by Douglas Lancashire and Peter Hu Kuo-chen (St. Louis: Institute of Jesuit Sources, 1985), 127. Henceforth, *True Meaning.* This etymological analysis has recently been shown to be erroneous.

23. In this way de Rhodes corrects a common ambiguity in the Vietnamese language in which the word *troi* can mean both sky (the material heaven) and Heaven (Mr. Heaven).

If it is not reasonable to adore heaven, so much less is it to adore the earth, which we tread with our feet and upon which we throw all our refuse. Furthermore, with iron plows we open up the earth as we please, with shovels we dig wells and holes in it as we please, but the earth does not complain, because it is inanimate and insensate. Therefore we must not adore the earth. Rather we must adore the one true Lord of heaven and earth who creates them.[24]

As for idols, should we worship and adore them? Now the idols came much later than the earth. Indeed, the Buddha, who is the chief of Chinese idols, was born three thousand years after the creation of the world. Consequently, we have to treat first of all God the creator and source of all things, next the origin of heaven and the earth and all things, and lastly the events of history until the birth of the Buddha. We now have to ask: Should one worship the Buddha? If this worship is according to reason, then it should be done; if not, not.[25]

THREE DEGREES OF HONOR

Now it must be noted that there are three grades of superiors or fathers who require commensurate veneration and reverence from us.[26] The lowest grade is composed of the father and mother who give birth to our bodies; the middle grade of the king who governs our country; lastly, the highest grade of the Lord of heaven and earth, the true Lord above all things.

Our life and existence depends on these three grades of superiors. From our father and mother, our bodies receive their origin through generation, though not our souls. We are indebted to our mothers for conceiving us, bearing us in their wombs for nine months and ten days, giving birth to us in great pains, and nursing and feeding us for three years. Sometimes a mother would take food from her own mouth to feed her child; sometimes she would eat the bitter part and save the sweet portion for her child; sometimes she would lie on a wet place and spare the dry spot for her child. The father, after having generated his child, worries about raising him or her. Sometimes he rises early, with little sleep, works at this and that job, runs here and there, looking for the wherewithal to support his children. Hence, it is according to reason that children show their parents filial piety; those who fail to show them respect and obedience are guilty of serious sin.[27]

The king is called the father of the whole nation and his subjects. Without him, the country cannot remain in peace, since the role of the king is to govern so that the people can live in peace and order. On the one hand, the king has

24. Here de Rhodes might have been influenced by Matteo Ricci who had already argued that neither the material heaven nor the earth should be worshiped. See *True Meaning*, 127–28.

25. De Rhodes refutes the worship of idols and of the Buddha only in passing here. A systematic critique of various non-Christian religions will be given only on the Fourth Day, in accord with de Rhodes's catechetical method.

26. De Rhodes might have taken this idea from Ricci. See *The True Meaning of Heaven*, 433.

27. This moving description of parental love must have struck a chord with the Vietnamese audience whose first duty is filial piety toward their parents.

to defend the country from external enemies lest they destroy the country and harm the people. On the other hand, the king has to take care that within his kingdom high dignitaries are in harmony with one another and the populace remain in loving and friendly relations with each other. Were there not a king to rule the nation, even for a day, without doubt many disorders would arise to disturb the peace of the people. Mandarins in a kingdom must assist the king in governing the country; the populace lend their support by paying taxes. Therefore, everyone who lives in the country is bound to honor the king; whoever joins the cause of the rebel deserves great punishment.[28]

Lastly, there remains the supreme Father and Lord of all things, who creates and preserves heaven and the earth and all things. Who, endowed with reason, would be foolish enough to doubt that we owe him worship above everything? At the beginning, when there were not yet heaven and earth, when there was nothing at all, God is there alone, sufficient unto himself. Then God created heaven and the earth and everything in this world. In heaven, he created the sun, the moon, and the stars to give us light, because without light we cannot survive. On this lower part, he created birds and animals, flowers and fruits, trees and vegetables to feed us. He also produced wood, water, fire, wind, and all the elements for our use. For, if there were not rain and sunshine, how can we live? Therefore, heaven, the earth, and all things in this world owe their origin to the infinitely good and great Lord of heaven.

WORSHIP OF THE LORD OF HEAVEN AND EARTH

Consequently, for everything we must render thanks and the highest worship to the highest Father and Giver of all good things.

Some, little versed in the Chinese letters and books, claim that there is nothing prescribed in the Chinese books except the worship of heaven. They are dead wrong. Indeed, in the books both of Confucius and of others, there is expressly prescribed the worship of the Supreme Ruler. This expression, of course, must be understood to mean the Lord of heaven, king of all things and king of all kings. And even if there were in the Chinese books no mention of the Lord, creator of all things, it does not matter. There is indeed in our hearts a light by which we know, as we should, that there is this supreme Father, creator of all things, so that all things may be.

THE *NAM GIAO* SACRIFICE

That is why at the beginning of the year, the king of Tonkin proceeds out of the gate, in great pomp, in the company of all the high mandarins and military officers and the entire people, to offer the sacrifice to the Supreme Ruler.

---

28. This affirmation of the duties of the citizen toward the king and the country will serve as an effective defense against charges that Christians betray their country.

When the king has completed his sacrifice to the Supreme Lord of heaven or the Supreme Ruler, the mandarins and the nobility and the entire people make their public obeisance to the king. Then everyone goes home and renders honor to the father, the mother, and the ancestors.

Thus, it is apparent that the Vietnamese, following their reason, venerate three different kinds of father, even though they have not recognized clearly that the Supreme Father is the Supreme Ruler, to whom, in the presence of the mandarins and the nobility, the king of Vietnam offers the sacrifice in the name of his subjects. These, in accompanying their king in his sacrifice, also worship in their silence, together with their king, the Supreme Ruler who is the Great Father of all things, even though they do not know him.[29]

After the completion of the sacrifice to the Supreme Ruler, the nobility and the mandarins and the entire people venerate the king by prostrating themselves before him according to the Vietnamese customs. In so doing they venerate the king as the second father of the country.

Lastly, when everyone comes home and venerates the father, the mother, and the ancestors, each, following his or her reason and nature, venerates the third and lowest degree of fatherhood.

THREE DEGREES OF REWARD AND PUNISHMENT

As there are three degrees of fatherhood which nature makes us recognize, so there are three kinds of reward and punishment. If a father has generated a good son, obedient to his orders, he will reward him by giving him his possessions. But if he has generated an obstinate son, disobedient to his orders, he will punish him by beating him with a stick. And if the son is incorrigible, the father will send him away and deprive him of his inheritance. However, parents cannot bestow public offices to their good and obedient children nor can they beat their disobedient children to death; were they to do so, they would be guilty of a crime.

On the contrary, the king can not only reward his obedient subjects with money and other goods as the parents, and even by giving houses and lands more abundantly than the parents, but also can grant honors and public offices according to each one's merits. Those who rebel and break the laws of the country, the king can punish not only by taking away their possessions but also by imposing death.

As to the Supreme Father, Creator and Lord of all things, he is the Supreme Judge. To those who observe his law, God gives not only material rewards in this world but also eternal recompenses in the future life. Those who do not worship God the Father but the demon and other things, God will punish in

---

29. Here de Rhodes uses two other names for God: *thuong phu* (the supreme Father) and *thuong de* (the supreme King; Chinese: *Shang-ti*).

this life by taking away their material possessions, their health, and even their lives. Furthermore, he will send them to hell to punish them with eternal pains.

THE HOLY WAY OF GOD

If in the past you have not known the true Lord of heaven and earth and have not worshiped God rightly, there is now a light shining upon you, as the way of the Lord is being announced. Those who preach the way are like town criers sent by God himself so that you may escape eternal punishments and obtain everlasting recompenses. Do not say that this law is the law of the Portuguese. The holy law of the Lord of heaven is a light greater and older than the light of the sun itself. For example, when the sun sends its rays on a kingdom, it illuminates it, though the other kingdoms on which it has not sent its rays still remain in darkness. Nevertheless, no one would say that the sun belongs to that kingdom upon which it sends its rays first, because the sun is common to the whole world and exists before the kingdom it illuminates. Similarly, the holy law of God, though it has appeared to other kingdoms first, should not be seen as belonging to this or that kingdom, but as the holy law of God, the Lord of all things. It is a law nobler and older than any kingdom whatsoever.[30]

Now that this holy law of God has enlightened Vietnam, let no one among you close the spiritual eyes of your heart and soul. Rather, with all your heart and strength embrace the way that is in conformity with reason. Detest and renounce the darkness of your errors and the blindness of your sins you have committed so far. Receive this law with your whole heart, rendering thanks to the Creator and Lord for the light of the new law, though it is more ancient than the heavens. And so that the Lord God may enlighten you in the future, prostrate yourselves before him to adore and pray to him.[31]

---

30. This is an attempt to reject the charge that Christianity is a religion of the West or of Portugal and to affirm the catholicity of the Christian faith.

31. Typically, de Rhodes combines religious instruction with prayer.

The Second Day

Knowledge of the True God, Creator and Remunerator

Praise be to God! Yesterday we said that one should not adore heaven, because it is a house without intelligence; that one should not adore the earth, because it is a foundation without soul. However, it is conformable to reason to worship the Lord of heaven and earth, the creator of heaven and earth, just as it is reasonable to show filial piety towards our fathers and mothers because they gave birth to us and to demonstrate respect and honor to the king and the mandarins who govern the country.

We know our fathers and mothers well, and even the king, since we see them with our bodily eyes. As to the creator of heaven and earth, even though our bodily eyes cannot see him, we must know him nonetheless in order to worship him rightly. It is now necessary to explain who is this true Lord of heaven and earth, where he is, and where he originates from.

The Lord of Heaven, the First Origin of All Things

Beginning with the last point, let us say that the true Lord of heaven and earth is not created by anyone, since the Lord of heaven is the first root of all things.[1] If he had been made by another being, he would not be the first root of all things. Take as an example a beautiful and tall tree, with large and leafy branches, and loaded with delicious fruits. If it is asked where its leafy branches come from, we will say: from the root. The same answer is given with regard to its fruits and leaves. If it is asked whether its root comes from another root, we will reply that all the elements of the tree come from its root, and that if this root comes from another root, then it would not be the first root of this beautiful tree.

The same thing applies to the Lord of heaven. He is the first root and cause

---

1. The Latin translation of the Vietnamese expression "coi re dau lam moi su" as "rerum omnium creatarum prima causa efficiens" is too abstract and inaccurate. The Vietnamese literally means: "the head (*dau*), trunk (*coi*), and root (*re*) making everything (*lam moi su*)." This expression makes the example de Rhodes subsequently gives more meaningful.

of all things, because heaven, the earth, and all things originate from the Lord of heaven. There is no other origin and root besides the Lord of heaven. If there were, the Lord of heaven would not be the first cause. If there were another prior cause, it may be asked if it still has another prior cause, and so it goes on infinitely, which is repugnant to reason. We must therefore stop at this first root and cause of all things who is the true creator of heaven and the earth and all things.

REFUTATION OF FALSE BELIEFS ABOUT THE LORD OF HEAVEN

Some have asked if the Lord of heaven is the same as *Muc moi*.[2] Now, since the Lord of heaven is not a human being, whereas *Muc moi* is said to be a human being by the books of this false sect, then *Muc moi* cannot in any way be the creator and Lord of heaven.

The same thing should be said about *Nguc hoang* who also is said by the books of the same false sect to be the nephew of Lao-tzu.[3] Furthermore, these books mention his father and mother. Hence, he cannot be the true Lord of heaven.

Even if all the kings and lords are added to the entire human race, they cannot touch a single star in heaven with their fingers; a fortiori, how can they create the stars? But why do I speak of creating a new star? Not even a single living ant can they make! Therefore, no human being can be the true Lord of heaven who creates all things. On the contrary, the entire human race itself owes its existence to a creator, no less than heaven itself. Hence, no human being can be the first cause of all things. On the contrary, there must be a first cause by whom humans are created in order that they can receive their being from it.

Furthermore, if there were humans who had created heaven and earth, they should be adored and worshiped. However, nowhere in the Chinese books is there prescribed a cult for them.[4] In the whole of Vietnam there has been no pagoda or temple destined for their worship. There are, of course, pagodas for the worship of the Buddha and other idols, but even in their books, these are said to begin their existence long after the creation of heaven and earth.

As to the question of whether a cult should be rendered to idols, we will discuss later, after we have talked of the creation of heaven and earth. If this cult is in accord with reason, it should be rendered; if not, not.[5]

---

2. This figure is said to have been mentioned by the Taoist books. De Rhodes's basic argument is that since this figure as well as the following ones are believed to have a temporal beginning, they cannot be identified with the Lord of heaven and earth who is without beginning.

3. *Nguc hoang* literally means the king of hell.

4. The appeal to the Chinese classics carries probative weight with the Vietnamese audience.

5. The necessity of a true religion to be conformable to reason is repeated again and again. Here we have a terse formulation of this key principle of de Rhodes's theology.

As to the claim that a certain person named *Ban co* created heaven and earth, what we have said about *Muc moi* and *Nguc hoang* applies to him as well.[6]

Others, who understand well that heaven and earth are not created by any human being, imagine a kind of corporeal substance with neither life nor intelligence which they call *Thai cuc* from which two other substances proceed which they call *am* and *duong*.[7] The former is earth, the latter heaven. But is it reasonable to hold that something material, without life and intelligence, can create something as perfect as heaven and all the things that move in it?

THE LORD OF HEAVEN AND EARTH AS SUPREME ARCHITECT

Would you not consider someone as a liar if he tells you that a magnificent palace, with rooms, and courts and comfortable dwellings, decorated with innumerable paintings, was created by chance by a blowing wind? Of course, in order to come to existence, such a palace requires a talented architect who would conceive it first in his mind and form an idea of it within himself, before he builds it outside with the greatest care. So much more would heaven and earth require a maker endowed with an infinite intelligence who forms a perfect idea of everything in heaven and earth and is possessed of an infinite power to accomplish such a great work.

Therefore, *Thai cuc*, which is without life and intelligence, is incapable of creating heaven and earth. The Chinese books are right in not prescribing a cult to *Thai cuc* since it is without life and intelligence, but they go against reason in saying that this *Thai cuc*, which has neither life nor intelligence, is the creator of heaven and earth.

THE TRUE CREATOR

Who is then the supreme cause and artisan of heaven, the earth, and all things? It is reported that once upon a time, a king posed this question to a philosopher,[8] who asked for a day to think over his answer. After a day had passed, he asked for another two days to think further. After the two days, asked by the king, the philosopher begged for another four days. The king then said: "You are making fun of me; you keep asking for delay and do not answer my question." The philosopher replies: "Far from me the audacity to make fun of you, Sire. The answer to your question is so difficult that the more I reflect

---

6. *Ban co* is understood by de Rhodes to be a human person and therefore cannot be the creator. In fact, in Taoism there is the myth that the world is created from the corpse of *P'an-ku* who emerged from the original egglike lump.

7. *Thai cuc* is the Vietnamese word for *T'ai-chi*. De Rhodes takes it to be a kind of corporeal substance without intelligence and without life from which two other substances proceed, *am* (*yin*) and *duong* (*yang*). Hence, he asks, how can something without intelligence and without life be the creator of heaven and earth? It is clear that the subtleties of Taoist metaphysics elude de Rhodes.

8. De Rhodes uses the word *quan tu* to refer to the philosopher.

on it, the more I understand that there is still more to think about; that is why I beg for further delay."[9]

This non-Christian philosopher is like someone who, contemplating the immensity of the ocean, sees it better the more he moves away from the beach. We, however, assisted by the Lord of heaven, will dare to say something about who the supreme Lord, the noble artisan of heaven and the earth and all things, is.[10]

GOD AND GOD'S THREE KINDS OF CREATURES

First of all, we affirm that there is as it were a light in the human heart which manifests the existence of God, since without God as creator, lord, and the first cause and original source, nothing of this entire world would exist.

Secondly, we affirm that among the things the Lord of heaven produces, there are three kinds of creatures. The first kind consists of purely material and corporeal things with no spirit whatsoever. They are corruptible beings which have a beginning and an end. Such are heaven, earth, water, wind, fire, and all things composed of the last four elements. For example, trees, birds, and all the animals on land or in the air or in the water, and all other insensate and inanimate things fall in this category. This is the lowest kind of creature which will have an end, just as they had a beginning.

The second kind consists of beings with a spiritual nature, without any material or corporeal admixture, which are sublime, intelligent, and absolutely incorruptible. Though having a beginning, they will never have an end but rather will endure forever. Such are the nine choirs of angels,[11] innumerable heavenly citizens whom God has placed at the head of corporeal creatures to carry out the will of God in all things. They are endowed with the highest intelligence and free will so that, by subjecting themselves to the Lord God, they may obtain eternal happiness. We will speak of these incorporeal spirits again later.[12]

Lastly, the third kind of creatures are composed of body and spirit. These are human beings who are corruptible and mortal on account of their bodies, and incorruptible and immortal on account of their spirits which are rational souls. They have a beginning but no end.

Such are the three kinds of things created by God from which as from three degrees we have to ascend to their creator, the sovereign Lord. In these creatures as in a mirror we see the attributes of God's infinite perfection.

---

9. This same story is related by Ricci. See *True Meaning*, 91.

10. De Rhodes uses the expression *duc Tho ca*, literally, the noble supreme Artisan, to refer to God as creator.

11. To translate the word "angel" de Rhodes coins the word *thien than*, composed of two words, *thien* (heaven) and *than* (spirit). The existence of angels poses no problem for the Vietnamese. According to Vietnamese cosmology, the world is populated with spirits and human life is constantly influenced by them. Sacrifices are offered to these spirits to obtain their favors.

12. See Day Three in which de Rhodes narrates the creation of the universe.

THE INFINITE POWER OF GOD THE CREATOR:
CREATION FROM NOTHING

Indeed, even though the supreme Lord of heaven is not included among these three kinds of beings but is infinitely more perfect than they, nevertheless, from the first kind of beings which are corporeal such as heaven, the earth, and all corruptible things, we deduce clearly the existence of their omnipotent creator. Through his infinite power and by himself, without the help of anyone, God makes the great machine of the world from nothing.[13] If we compare this infinite power with the power of all the kings of this world, past, present, and future, the latter should be called non-power rather than power at all. Is there ever a king of this world, even the most powerful, who can make from nothing even a tiny little house?

To build even the smallest house, one must first of all prepare all the things necessary without which it is impossible to build. Now the Lord of heaven and earth created all the visible things without using preexisting matter, for nothing can exist which has not received its being from him as from the first cause. This first cause must then have in itself an infinite perfection and an infinite essence corresponding to the infinite power with which it creates all things out of nothing.

That this power is infinite is also clear from the fact that it does not use the assistance of anyone to make the universe. However powerful they are, those who undertake the construction of a great palace require not only preexisting matter but also the help of many workers; without them, they cannot accomplish their project. Similarly, the most brilliant architect, planning the construction of a splendid palace, however wonderful a picture of it he has formed within his mind, will not be able to build such a palace without the assistance of numerous workers who make his interior vision an external reality. God alone, when God plans to make something and conceives it most perfectly in himself, can, without the assistance of anyone, create this entire universe, which proves that God's power is infinite.

Furthermore, an architect, however capable, if he is planning a masterpiece, is not able to bring it about without much time. On the contrary, the Lord of heaven, the supreme architect of this visible world, brings all things into being by a simple act of his efficacious will. The Lord of heaven spoke, and everything was made; he commanded, and everything was created. Which proves without doubt the infinite power of God who creates everything in an instant.

Lastly, an architect, once he has produced his work, no longer influences it in any way. His work will remain even if, after having completed it, he dies. On the contrary, God the creator of all things, creates them in such a way that they depend on him in order to continue their existence no less than when they were first created. Consequently, just as they would never have begun to exist without God's concourse at the first creation, so they will return immediately to

---

13. De Rhodes conveys here the idea of creation *ex nihilo.*

nothingness unless the Lord of heaven acts continuously to preserve them. They depend on God much more than light depends on the sun, not only in the first moment of production of light but also throughout its preservation.

Moreover, God influences continuously not only in order to conserve all things; God's concourse is also required for all actions and operations, both internal and external, of all things. Without divine concourse, not a leaf can fall from the tree by itself. Indeed, as God's infinite power is the first cause of the powers of all creatures, so when any of these powers does anything, even the smallest act, it cannot do it without the concourse and action of that supreme cause.

GOD'S INFINITE PERFECTIONS

God, the sovereign Lord, creator and conserver of all things, shines with the sun that shines, warms with the fire that warms, refreshes with the air that refreshes, fecundates with the soil that fecundates, produces with the earth that produces. God acts continuously with all other things so that we cannot move our hands, our feet, and our eyes without the perpetual concourse of this first cause. This God does with such ease and calm as if he did nothing at all, and this is true even if he had created out of nothing millions of other worlds. God does each action with such wisdom and perfection as if he were engaged in a single action, though in each moment he is doing an infinite number of actions. In this way God's infinite power and wisdom are made manifest because they are neither tired nor perturbed by so numerous, so varied, and so continuous actions by which God is present to all things in every moment.

From the infinite power and infinite wisdom of the first cause it is necessary to conclude to its infinite divinity and infinite essence which are (to our way of saying) the root of the infinite attributes of the Lord of heaven. Indeed, how can God's essence be finite if he has an infinite power and an infinite wisdom?

Furthermore, from the infiniteness of God's essence one concludes also to God's infinite duration or eternity, without beginning and without end. In fact, an infinite essence requires a duration proportionate to it, that is, without beginning in going backwards, and without end in going forwards. Consequently, before there was heaven, before there was the earth, before there was anything at all, that is, before all ages, there is eternally God, the first cause of all causes, needing nothing besides himself, perfectly happy in himself, containing in himself all this infinite happiness which he possesses before the world ever existed, and which he would possess were no creature ever to come into being.

Nevertheless, because God's goodness is no less infinite than God's essence and eternal divinity, and because goodness communicates itself (*bonum est diffusivum sui*),[14] God wanted to create not only this visible and corporeal world

---

14. De Rhodes translates this Latin principle into Vietnamese: "Su lanh nao hay thong su minh cung ke khac."

which, by its finite existence and its almost innumerable activities, participates in the infinite existence and action of the first cause. It is as it were God's visible imprint. But the divine goodness also wanted to communicate itself to reasonable creatures who not only possess existence but also become participants in the divine beatitude.

That is why the Lord of heaven creates the angelic species, called *angeli*,[15] totally without bodies, that is, completely spiritual, capable of friendship with God, called *gratia*,[16] and of *gloria*,[17] that is, capable of seeing God himself in order to participate in God's beatitude. By creating these beings the divine goodness manifests itself more clearly than by creating the visible world and all the purely material creatures which are capable of neither friendship with God nor God's beatitude. Indeed, although the Lord of heaven is sufficient unto himself and needs no creature to be perfectly happy, nevertheless, because goodness tends to communicate itself, God wanted to create a purely spiritual and intelligent creature capable of friendship, that is, *gratia*, with God and of *gloria*, that is, eternal beatitude.

HUMAN BEINGS AND THEIR DESTINIES: GOD'S GOODNESS AND JUSTICE

Lastly, the Lord of heaven added the third kind of being, composed of body and spirit, that is, the human race, which is as it were the summary of all creatures. In fact, humans possess being or existence like inanimate things, vegetative life like plants and trees, sensitive life like animals, and rational life like angels, capable of *gratia*, that is, friendship with God and *gloria*, that is, eternal beatitude like the angels themselves.

To humans, however, the infinitely good Lord of heaven gives the span of this life to merit eternal beatitude. Here is the condition: if during this present life, they do the will of God, they will obtain beatitude in the next life; on the other hand, if they do not obey God's will and do not observe God's orders, unless they repent in this life, they will be tormented by eternal punishments. Here both divine goodness and justice are manifested: infinite goodness and mercy, because humans are elevated to such a dignity as to participate in the divine nature, which they are able to do if they obey divine orders; infinite justice, because those who obey God's commands are given an eternal reward, that is, eternal happiness in heaven together with all good things and the vision of God.

---

15. It is interesting that here de Rhodes gives the Latin expression, even though earlier he has used the Vietnamese expression *thien than*.

16. Even though here de Rhodes gives the Latin word *gratia*, he also translates it accurately with the Vietnamese word *nghia*. This word means friendship, friendly relations, loving relations between friends, spouses, parents and children. Contemporary Vietnamese words for grace are *on nghia* (literally, gratuitous friendly relation) and the Sino-Vietnamese *thanh sung* (literally, holy gift).

17. De Rhodes does not translate the word *gloria*, but paraphrases it as seeing God's face and sharing in God's joy and beatitude.

But those who rebel against God and disobey his commands are inflicted with eternal punishments.

Therefore, we should not be surprised if in this brief life God sometimes tests good people, denying them the perishable goods of this world, and sometimes grants an abundance of these goods to evil people who rebel against him. Furthermore, God sometimes inflicts good people with many calamities in this life, and allows evil people to prosper. This we see in the life of St. Lazarus, who was a poor man, and a rich man, who was evil. Lazarus suffered poverty and calamities in this life, but has been enjoying unspeakable happiness for over sixteen hundred years and will enjoy such happiness eternally in heaven. The rich man, on the other hand, enjoyed material goods for but a moment in this life, but has been suffering eternal punishments and the fire of hell for over sixteen hundred years, and will be tortured like that eternally, without hope of escape nor even of death.[18]

GOD THE REMUNERATOR

Sometimes divine justice punishes evil people in this life in order to bring them to repentance and to make sure that impious people do not deny divine providence in human affairs. Sometimes the Lord of heaven also grants good people material goods in this life to attract to him, by the hope of these goods, those who are still too weak in faith and then raises them to love the eternal goods of the soul.

From these considerations we have some understanding of the afterlife: Since many good people are in this life weighed down by poverty and calamities, and on the other hand, impious people enjoy in this world prosperity and riches, often to an advanced age, it follows that there must be an afterlife in which the supreme Lord of all things, who is most upright and just, will grant good people the eternal happiness they deserve and chastise evil people with eternal punishments according to their sins.

This is what is commonly affirmed everywhere and by your Vietnamese books and ancient tradition: "Sinh ki da, tu qui da," that is, "life is a journey, death a return." Indeed, for good and faithful servants of God, death is but a passage from this valley of miseries to the heavenly home in which they will be rewarded by the Lord of heaven, the creator of all things, with eternal life and eternal happiness. For evil people, however, death is a passage to eternal sufferings with which God the utmost just judge punishes them in hell by means of eternal death. Just as God is supremely good and merciful to good people, God is also supremely just towards the wicked.

---

18. Obviously de Rhodes takes Lazarus and the Rich Man as historical personages; hence, he calculates the duration of their respective happiness and punishment up to his time.

GOD'S ATTRIBUTES AND OUR ATTITUDES TOWARD THEM

These attributes of the sovereign creator of all things, Lord of heaven, the earth, and all things are made known to us not only by God's revelation in his book but also by natural reason impressed in our hearts by God.[19] God is infinite in essence, eternal in duration, immense in presence, most wise in counsel, omnipotent in action, all-good and generous in communication, most just and inscrutable in judgment.[20] To God's infinite spiritual essence we owe worship and adoration, first in our spiritual souls which derive their existence from God alone. It is in spirit that God desires to be adored and worshiped, being infinite spirit, the first origin and the last end of ourselves and of all things. From this internal adoration and worship must proceed the external adoration by the body so as to be pleasing to the Lord of heaven.

Because the Lord of heaven is present everywhere, we must worship him everywhere. We must always remember that God sees us everywhere. Whatever we dare not do in the presence of kings of this world or in public, let us dare not do it in the presence of the Lord of heaven.

From God's eternal life and infinite duration, without beginning and without end, let us remember this: deriving our life from God, source of all life, we cannot hope to have a long life except in God who is the source of life. It is foolish in our desire for a long life to ask our deceased parents to give it to us, who could not themselves prolong their own lives.[21] Nor should we hope from God, the supreme source of all life, only bodily life and health; rather, we must first of all pray for the life of the soul, that is, friendship with God or *gratia*. If we maintain friendship with God until the end of our ephemeral life, God will grant us eternal life and endless beatitude with him in heaven.

We should also venerate the infinite wisdom of the Lord of heaven, the origin of all things, believing that nothing can be hidden from his eyes, not even our thoughts and the affections of our hearts. Everything is known to God: the present, the past, and the future; absolutely nothing can be hidden from God. No one can deceive God nor does God deceive anyone, since God is infallible truth. We venerate therefore God's supreme wisdom if we believe God's words and if we submit our minds totally to God's infinite wisdom and knowledge. We also venerate the infinite knowledge of the Divine Majesty to whom everything is naked and open, if we unceasingly and respectfully direct our eyes to God, remembering that God watches over us and scrutinizes our actions, internal as well as external, as if there were nothing else to be seen in the world. This consideration, frequently renewed and firmly held, will engender in us a great

---

19. Here is another fundamental principle of de Rhodes's theology: that besides human reason there is also divine revelation to give us knowledge of divine things.

20. With great originality de Rhodes connects God's various infinite perfections with the corresponding attitudes that are required on our part. De Rhodes offers here a profoundly theocentric spirituality which prevents his presentation of God's attributes from being a dry and abstract metaphysical treatise.

21. De Rhodes is obliquely attacking certain aspects of Vietnamese ancestor worship. A full-scale critique of ancestor worship will be given in Day Four.

respect for the Divine Majesty and prevent us from doing anything offensive in the eyes of God.

If, on the one hand, we consider the infinite power of the Lord of heaven by whom we live, move, and have our being, and if we consider that we cannot move even our feet without God's assistance, we will acquire humility and contempt for ourselves, seeing clearly that we are not capable of anything by ourselves, and that without God's continuous action, we will be reduced to nothingness. This is true of our natural existence which the Lord of heaven gratuitously grants to us, without any merit on our part. Much more so is this true of our supernatural being, of *gratia,* by which we are elevated by God's infinite mercy to participate in God's nature by *gratia.* In fact, without God's special assistance, we cannot have *gratia* which sanctifies our souls, nor can we persevere in *gratia,* that is, in the friendship with God, until the end of our lives, without God's continuous assistance.[22]

If, on the other hand, we consider well that the omnipotence of the Supreme Deity is always ready to assist us, not only in insignificant matters of this world but also in serious matters of the *gratia* of the afterlife, we will acquire courage and hope in God's infinite power, so that nothing is impossible for us because of God who strengthens us.

If we consider well that the goodness and love of the Sovereign Deity is infinite, with which God loves us before the creation of the world, and that in God's preestablished time God communicates himself to us, by creating us in his image and likeness, which God gives to our souls, and by restoring and perfecting this image by means of *gratia* or friendship with him, if we consider all things well, our hearts will be filled with a great love and gratitude for the Lord of heaven. How can we not love God's infinite love by which he loves us first, without any merit of ours, while we were still miserable little creatures?

LOVE OF GOD AND OBSERVANCE OF GOD'S COMMANDMENTS

And because true love is not shown by clever words but by great works, and as the infinitely good God has deigned to instruct us, true love is shown by keeping God's commandments perfectly. Therefore, to respond with at least a measure of gratitude to such goodness, let us resolve to keep God's commandments fully, with God's help, without which we can do nothing.

Lastly, when we consider the perfect equity of the sovereign creator of all things and incorruptible judge, who renders to each according to his or her merits or demerits, to the good people eternal beatitude in heaven, and to the wicked eternal sufferings in hell, we will be inspired to implore the supreme judge, as long as he is still willing to relent, to forgive the innumerable sins of our past, repenting with all our strength for having offended the Divine Majesty

---

22. There are here strong echoes of Ignatius of Loyola's teachings on the majesty of God and our humility before the Divine Majesty.

and for having earned his wrath, and resolving to mend our ways from now on according to the norms of God's will and his commandments, with confidence that God's infinite mercy will forgive those who ask for forgiveness and do penance.

Let what we have said so far about the knowledge of God on the basis of natural reason suffice.[23]

---

23. Once again de Rhodes reiterates his catechetical method of confining himself at this stage to what human reason can discover about God.

The Third Day

Creation of the Universe and the Fall of Humanity

Yesterday we have explained briefly that from all eternity, before there was heaven, before there was the earth, before there was anything at all, there already is a spiritual substance, infinite, eternal, immense, endowed with infinite intelligence, infinite power, infinite goodness, infinite equity, and infinite justice. This infinite substance, called *Deus*,[1] the true Lord of heaven, though needing no one, perfectly self-sufficient, lacking nothing to be perfectly happy and totally complete in himself, nevertheless has willed, in God's free and infinite will, to create, by God's infinite power, all things out of nothing in which they lay from all eternity. At the preestablished time, God made heaven, the earth, and all things of this world.

CREATION IN SIX DAYS

Though God could have created together in an instant by the one act of his all-powerful will all these things and innumerable other worlds more perfect than this, which God has freely left in the darkness of nothingness, all the things God wanted to create, God created them in six days, to show both that God freely created them and that the things God made on each of these days are not self-sufficient by themselves.

On the first day God created the empyreal heaven[2] as the most happy and perpetual dwelling place for his saints whom God has elected and the earth which was still a confused mass surrounded by waters on all sides. At that time all things were still enveloped in darkness, so God created material light to make material beings visible. The Lord of heaven also created spiritual light, that is, purely spiritual and intellectual substances which not only distinguish clearly and perfectly all the creatures and all the natures and their properties but also can be made capable by God through *gratia* of seeing God's face (though

---

1. Sometimes de Rhodes uses the Latin *Deus* preceded by *Chua* (lord) instead of the more familiar *Duc Chua Troi*.

2. This empyreal heaven is distinct from the material sky; it is the abode of the angels and the saints.

235

no spiritual being can see it by its natural power). If these spiritual creatures are perfectly submissive to their creator, they will merit that eternal beatitude.[3]

THE NINE CHOIRS OF ANGELS

The sovereign Artisan and Lord of all things therefore created nine choirs of angels, each of which has innumerable angels.[4] It may be concluded from this that from the lowest choir of angels the Lord of all things has assigned to each human being an angel whose task is to protect us throughout our lives, from the day of our birth to that of our death. It follows that among this lowest choir of angels, there are as many angels as people in the entire world. Some saints have said that the higher the choir, the more it has angels. Hence, the army of the Lord of heaven, who is king above all kings, is unspeakably numerous.

The angels' wisdom is such that they knew at the very moment of their creation all natural things. However, with regard to supernatural and divine mysteries, they receive a new light from God, so that the highest three choirs receive the light directly from the supreme King, to whom they attend unceasingly, and communicate it to the three middle choirs, who in turn transmit to the three lowest choirs the light they receive from the three highest choirs. In this way, all the choirs, illuminated either directly by the supreme King or indirectly by the higher choirs, execute with diligence the will of the sovereign Lord. The power and effectiveness of the angels are such that even just one angel is capable of moving the entire heaven and all the stars in it, each of which is far larger than the terrestrial globe. Though from the beginning of the world till now, during thousands of years, they have been working, without a break, at this task, they have never been tired, nor will they ever be tired, even until the end of the world. What else can I say? One single angel, at God's command, struck the entire army of Assyria and in one night killed 185,000 men, with ease and without fatigue.

Thus the Lord of heaven, the sovereign Lord of the angels and of all things has divided the angels into nine choirs or nine armies of his soldiers. The three highest choirs attend unceasingly to the supreme King in his heavenly court and do not as a rule descend to the earth or do so only rarely, for serious and important business; otherwise, they apply themselves constantly to praising God. The three middle choirs are in charge of the movement and influence of all the skies, the sun, the moon, the planets, and the fixed stars as well as of the preservation of the elements and other kinds of beings for the good of the universe. Lastly, the three lowest choirs look after the well-being of the inferior beings of this world. The highest angels of these choirs take care of the kingdoms assigned to them and of their prosperity; to the angels next in rank is given the care of

---

3. De Rhodes is referring of course to the angels.

4. For his angelology de Rhodes is indebted to his professor at the Roman College, Del Bufalo de' Cancellieri, who wrote *De substantia, natura angelorum* (Rome, 1622). Of course, this angelology is inspired in its turn by Pseudo-Dionysius's *Celestial Hierarchies*.

kings and princes so that these may administer their kingdoms well. The lowest angels, finally, watch over human beings, one angel for each person. Moreover, the angels of the lowest three choirs also direct the lights and inspiration of the divine Spirit on behalf of those who receive from God eternal salvation as their heritage.[5]

Now, someone may ask, with so many spirits, so noble, so wise, and so powerful, to watch over the universe, why is it that so many evils, so many sins, so many pains befall hapless mortals? Why is it that so many wars and disorders occur if so many angels of peace watch over the peace and well-being of humans?

To answer this question, it must be remembered that all reasonable and intelligent creatures are created by God, the sovereign maker of all things, in such a way that they have the freedom to choose to do good or evil. This power of choice has also been given to these pure spirits so that by submitting themselves to the sovereign King and Lord in the freedom of their choice and will, they may obtain eternal beatitude and be eternally confirmed in *gratia* or friendship with God; those who rebel, however, will be delivered to eternal sufferings according to their sins.

LUCIFER AND MICHAEL THE ARCHANGEL

Although all these very noble spirits have obtained at the very moment of their creation *gratia* of the supreme Father and sovereign Lord, nevertheless, later an angel called Lucifer, whom the supreme King had appointed prince of all the angels, considered how he possessed great gifts and perfections. Growing vain in his thoughts, he puffed up against his King and creator and wanted to sit as an equal and be similar to the Most High. Furthermore, as head of the angels he instigated them to the same rebellion so violently that one third of them defected from the supreme King. The other two-thirds of the angels, however, remained faithful in the friendship with their supreme King, without consenting in any way to the evil invitation of Lucifer. On the contrary, they resisted it with all their strength.

That is why, when the Lord of all things saw that Lucifer puffed up with his partisans and raised a war in heaven, he immediately created hell in the center of the earth and put there an eternal fire to burn the rebellious angels. At the same time, he made the angel Michael, who had remained faithful, the leader of the heavenly army and ordered him to chase rebellious Lucifer and his followers out of heaven and to throw Lucifer, leader of the impious revolt, and his main companions in the rebellion into hell to be delivered to eternal punishments.

At once Saint Michael, following the order of the sovereign King, and with his faithful companions, the holy angels, turned their arms, which are the Lord's

---

5. This presentation of the nine choirs of angels, each with an appointed task, and all divided in orderly hierarchy, must have mightily impressed the Vietnamese whose cosmology presents a bewildering multitude of uncontrollable spirits.

word, against the rebels, saying: "Who is like God? Who is this Lucifer who wants to be equal to our sovereign creator and Lord?" Immediately, Lucifer, turned into the devil and called Satan, fell like lightning with his companions from heaven down into the Tartar.

Some of them, however, were allowed by God the sovereign Judge to remain in the air until the end of the world. These devils are the tempters who seduce humans to all sorts of impiety; from them originate all false sects, lies, perjuries, enmities, quarrels, impurities, killings, stealings, and finally all the sins which humans committed under their seduction. Thus, the supreme creator of all things, in his exceedingly mysterious but exceedingly just decisions, permitted that good comes out of evil rather than allowing nothing to exist at all.

Thus, on the first day, that is, at the beginning of time, God created heaven and earth, paradise and hell. And God placed in paradise all the holy and faithful angels, and granted them *gloria,* that is, eternal happiness and clear vision of God's face. On the contrary, God delivered the rebels to eternal sufferings and marked them with everlasting shame. Thus, God, the sovereign judge, will judge humans in the same way: God will give eternal rewards to those who imitate the good angels and submit themselves perfectly to God, the supreme Lord; on the contrary, God will condemn to eternal pains with Satan those who rebel and imitate the demons.

CREATION OF THE MATERIAL UNIVERSE

On the second day, God created the visible heaven which we call *firmamentum,* whereas on the first day God created the higher or empyrean heaven, invisible to our eyes, dwelling of the blessed angels and palace of the supreme creator of all things.

Scripture says that God ordered the visible heaven to separate the waters that are above from the waters that are below. Indeed, the Lord of heaven filled the whole space between the terrestrial globe and the empyrean heaven with the waters which we may call the great chaos. God placed the visible firmament in the middle of these waters, with, in the opinion of some, the larger part of the waters located above the firmament, and the remaining part located beneath the firmament and covering the entire terrestrial globe. We may say that it is from these lower waters and from their more subtle parts that the Lord of heaven makes air and fire. These two elements cover the space between the firmament and the waters (which at that time still covered the whole terrestrial globe). According to some, all this should be called heaven, because Scripture calls the birds that fly in heaven birds of the air.

It is to be noted that the first, second, and third days, the three days preceding the formation of the sun, were separated by the light which God made on the first day and which divided day and night by a circular movement.

On the third day, as the waters still covered the entire globe which thereby was not habitable to humans, the supreme creator commanded the waters to gather together and to leave a part of the earth dry and habitable to humans. Thus, the seas were made which are the gathering of waters.

Next, the supreme Lord commanded that the earth produce trees, plants, herbs, and other vegetation for the use of humans and animals which would be created a few days later. At once, the earth, upon God's order, without having previously received any seed, brought forth trees loaded with ripe fruits, other plants, and vegetables. On the same day the Lord of heaven produced a paradise of delights, a magnificent garden, always cool with a perpetual spring season, never with the discomfort of excessive cold or heat, where the trees are covered with ripe fruits throughout the year.

On the fourth day the sovereign creator furnished the firmament. He made the sun, the movement of which constitutes day, to govern the day, and the moon to govern the night. God also made beautiful stars not only to decorate the firmament but also to promote through their qualities the well-being of the universe in the lower regions.

On the fifth day the Lord of heaven commanded that different kinds of birds come out of the waters, and they immediately flew into the air. Also, different kinds of fish were made which lived in the waters and dwelt there as inhabitants. Both birds and fish were to multiply according to their species.

On the sixth day the supreme creator of all things made different species of animals and reptiles to come out of the earth and gave them the capacity to reproduce their own kind until the end of the world.

THE CREATION OF HUMANITY

On the same day God decided to create humans according to God's image and likeness as a summary of all God's work and as the highest glory of the universe. God formed out of the earth a perfect human body, of about thirty years of age, and breathed on its face a breath of life, that is, a reasonable soul which God created out of nothing, and infused it into this already formed body. Thus, the man became a living being, in the image and likeness of God, his creator. He was endowed not only with knowledge and natural virtues at the very moment of creation but was also raised to *gratia*, that is, friendship with God, endowed with numerous supernatural gifts in order to obtain with the blessed angels the supernatural end of eternal beatitude.

In addition, the man received dominion over all living beings, on earth, in the air, and in the waters so that all of them would obey the man according to their natural instinct given by the creator himself. To each of them the man gave a name appropriate to its nature. And each has the name by which Adam called it. In order that the man could lead a happier life, God brought him to the garden of delights. There, among the other fruit trees, was the tree of life whose fruits were such that if eaten, they would restore youth and vigor to an old man.

However, the sovereign Lord wanted to test the man's faithfulness by not putting under his power, in the garden of delights, the tree of knowledge of good and evil. God forbade him to eat of its fruits, though God did give him the permission to eat of all the other fruits which were in paradise. Furthermore, God threatened him, saying: "You will die on the day you eat the fruit."

This death must be understood as referring in the first place to the death of the immortal soul, that is, the loss of *gratia* and of the original justice which would occur immediately after the fall. In the second place, it refers to the death of the body by the separation of the soul from the body, with innumerable other evils preceding, accompanying, or following these two kinds of death.

When Adam heard this order of the Lord his creator, threatening him with the death of the body and the soul, together with innumerable other evils, which would pass on to his posterity, with the loss of *gratia* and of the friendship with the Lord of heaven, were he to disobey his sovereign Lord, he submitted himself with all his heart to his creator, saying: "I bow down before you, Lord of heaven. I did not exist before; created by you from nothing just a while ago, I owe all my being to you, Lord. You have given me so many and so holy gifts, both internal and external. I want and desire nothing but that which pleases you, my supreme benefactor. Therefore, I am ready to obey whatever order you, my supreme Lord and benefactor, give. Indeed, what would it cost me if I abstain from eating the fruit of only this tree!"[6]

THE CREATION OF EVE:
RELATIONSHIP BETWEEN MAN AND WOMAN

At this point Adam had not had a companion. The Lord of heaven made him fall into a deep sleep, and while he was sleeping, God extracted one of his ribs and replaced it with flesh. From this rib God made a woman, roughly of the same age as Adam, and infused into her a rational soul. Adam awoke from his sleep, and upon seeing his companion, he exclaimed: "This bone now is from my bones, and this flesh is from my flesh. That is why the man will leave his father and mother and will attach himself to his wife, and the two of them will become one flesh."[7] Adam said all this under the prophetic spirit.

It is necessary to note with the holy doctors that the Lord of heaven did not make the woman from the bone of Adam's head, because the head of the woman is the man, and she must obey him. Though she may, should he err, admonish him gently, she may not inveigh against him, because she is subjected to him and is not his head. But God did not make the woman from the man's feet either, but from his rib, because the man should not treat his wife like a slave, but love her like a companion.[8]

---

6. Clearly, there is no biblical basis for de Rhodes's description of Adam's response to God's command. What de Rhodes intends to do with this imaginary response is to encourage the catechumens to adopt an obedient attitude toward God's law.

7. De Rhodes departs from Genesis in attributing to Adam the words, "That is why the man will leave his father and mother and will attach to his wife, and the two of them will become one flesh." His intention is to defend monogamy on the basis of Adam's prophetic utterance.

8. De Rhodes's statement about the man being the head of the woman and about her duty of obedi-

AGAINST POLYGAMY

Furthermore, the Lord of heaven did not give the man two or three wives but only one, because they became one and not many flesh, as Adam prophetically affirmed.[9] The Vietnamese themselves say: "The husband and the wife give one another their bones and flesh."[10] Just as the man has a right to the body of the woman, so that as long as he lives, she may not attach herself to another man, so the woman has a right to the body of the man, so that as long as she lives, he may not take another woman. In this respect, the man and the woman are equal, according to God's command which was carried out in Adam and Eve at the beginning of the world, and followed later on, at least in the first age of the world until the deluge, by those who observed God's law, as we will see later with Noah and his children, and after the deluge.

THE SABBATH AND WORSHIP OF GOD

Thus in six days the sovereign author of the whole world completed his work and it is said that on the seventh day God rested from his labor because on the seventh day God did not undertake any new work and did not create any new creature. God blessed the seventh day and sanctified it. Therefore, Adam and his wife dedicated that day to the worship of the supreme Deity to thank him for the innumerable benefits they had received. From the origins of the world until now, the true worshipers of Deity have exactly kept this observance, holding the seventh day as sacred and reserved for the worship of the sovereign creator of all things.

After six days in which they devote themselves to servile occupations that concern food and the clothing of the body such as agriculture, commerce, iron-works, and the like, they cease from them for one day to devote themselves to the worship of the supreme Deity and to render thanks for so many benefits they receive at each moment from the sovereign creator of all things. And though they praise the exceedingly good and great God and thank God with all their strength, they will remain quite unequal to the benefits they have received from God.

THE EARTHLY PARADISE

Our first parents dwelt therefore in this paradise of delights, in a great rest and peace of soul as well as body. All the animals on the earth, in the air, and in

---

ence to him would have gone over well with the Vietnamese men in the seventeenth century. However, de Rhodes's exhortation that the man should treat his wife not "like a slave, but love her like a companion" would have been a serious and unexpected challenge to them!

9. This is the first time de Rhodes provides a theological argument against the practice of polygamy. For many Vietnamese men in the seventeenth century the rejection of polygamy was one of the most difficult obstacles to their conversion to Christianity.

10. De Rhodes skillfully attempts to defend monogamy on the basis of a Vietnamese proverb which reads: "Hai vo chong gui xuong gui thit nhau."

the water so submitted to them that they all obeyed the man at his mere signal. If Adam called the lion out of the forest, he would come out at once, feeling by a natural instinct the dominion that the sovereign Lord had given to Adam. If Adam called a fish from the bottom of the sea, it would immediately swim to him. If he ordered a bird to come from the air, it would fly docilely to him.

In that garden, there was neither heat nor cold to bother our first parents; on the contrary, they enjoyed a perpetual spring and continuously splendid weather.

Moreover, what is more important, their flesh was so submissive to their spirit that the latter did not experience any rebellion; and all their senses, both internal and external, were so subjected to the rule of reason that they did not contradict it in anything. And our first parents could transmit to their children and grandchildren all the things they possessed in addition to the friendship with the Lord of heaven, without any fear of death. Furthermore, when they or their descendants decided in their own time to enjoy eternal beatitude, God would have taken them into heaven, in their bodies and souls, without passing through death.

TEMPTATION AND THE FALL OF EVE

But the wicked and perverse devil was jealous of such a great happiness of humans. The hatred that he could not direct against God himself, he turned against the lovable image of God. He tried his best to break it, all the more because he knew that the seats in heaven that he and his companions had lost would be, according to God's disposition, occupied by humans. In his pride, he said: "Will I allow that humans, made of dust, obtain this seat of supreme happiness which I have lost, while I, pure spirit, reside in hell, afflicted with extreme sufferings? I will make them, too, fall with me into eternal ruin by disobeying God!"

The clever devil saw that the man was more prudent and would not easily accept his temptation. Hence, he preferred to tempt the woman who was weaker; once the woman was conquered, the man would himself fall from the state of happiness into misery.

The wicked devil looked for opportune occasions when the woman would be alone, far away from her husband, in order to deceive her more easily. Adam had made known to Eve God's command, under pain of death, not to eat the fruit of the tree of the knowledge of good and evil. Later, as Eve was taking a stroll alone in the garden of delights and was looking with curiosity at the forbidden fruit, she praised its beauty to the eye and its deliciousness to the taste, though she dared not touch it.

Nevertheless, she gave the devil an opportunity for temptation. The latter entered into a snake and began asking her: "This fruit is so good, why don't you eat it?" Foolishly, she replied: "God has forbidden, lest perhaps we should die." She seemed to doubt that she would die were she to eat it. This doubt opened the door for the lie and seduction of the tempter. At once the devil contradicted the words of God: "You will not die at all; on the contrary, God knows that the day you eat its fruit, your eyes will open and you will be like the gods, knowing good and evil." With impudence the devil accused the Lord of heaven, the supreme Deity, of envy as if the Lord of heaven did not want humans to have the knowledge of good and evil, forbidding them to eat the fruit of this tree so as to become like the Lord of heaven, with the knowledge of good and evil.

The woman listened to the words of the devil in the form of the astute snake, and rejecting the order of God, extended her hand toward the forbidden fruit and thus deceived, ate it. Her errors were many. First, she abandoned her husband and took a stroll by herself in the garden. Had she been with her husband, the devil would never have dared to approach her. May this example teach women not to go around alone, without their faithful companions, to escape deceivers.

Next, she contemplated the fruit of the forbidden tree, admiring in her heart its beauty to the eye and deliciousness to the taste, thus providing the devil with an occasion to tempt her. From this we all should learn not to look at nor admire that which we are not allowed to desire.

She committed a third mistake by exchanging words with the devil hidden in the snake. Upon hearing the voice of the snake, she should have run away, looked for her husband, related to him the poisonous suggestions of the snake, and made no reply to it so as to avoid deception. But because she had replied thoughtlessly, she was easily deceived. This serves as a lesson to women not to enter ready conversation with strangers, especially when they are alone, so as not to be deceived.

Moreover, the woman sinned most grievously by doubting the order and the death threat that God had formally announced. Eve said: "Lest perhaps we should die." This doubt gave the devil the opportunity to lie and to deny absolutely that such a death penalty would come, saying to her: "You will not die at all." This teaches us not to hesitate at all and to doubt God's words so as not to sin grievously. God, indeed, who knows all things before they ever come to be, cannot be deceived by anyone nor deceive anyone because God is supreme and infinite Truth and Goodness. Rather we must extinguish the darts of fire that the enemy shoots at us by taking up the spiritual shield of faith, and strengthened by faith resist him.

I will not speak of the woman's inordinate desire to know in believing what the devil told her: "You will be like the gods." Her desire to know rather than her desire to taste the fruit seems to have led her to sin, since there were not lacking in the garden other fruits much more precious, especially those of the tree of life which was in the middle of paradise and which our first parents were allowed to taste as they might wish, as well as all other fruits. The only fruit forbidden by the Lord of heaven was that of the tree of knowledge of good and evil.

The Fall of Adam

Moreover, the woman did not content herself with eating the forbidden fruit. She induced her husband to the same sin. The devil had not dared to approach Adam directly by himself, though it was he that the devil had especially wanted to make fall, in order to corrupt as it were in the head the whole mass of the human race. That is why he induced the woman to offer the forbidden fruit to her husband.

Adam, upon seeing his companion, whom he loved above all else, already corrupted for having eaten the forbidden fruit, did not reprove her as he should have; rather he followed her example and ate the fruit offered by his wife. Not that Adam was deceived; he knew perfectly well that if he ate the fruit, he would break God's command and lose *gratia*, that is, friendship with the Lord of heaven together with the original justice for himself as well as for the whole human race.

By his sin Adam incurred the death of the body and the soul with innumerable evils which he himself and all his descendants would have to suffer. His excessive love for his companion led him, knowingly and voluntarily, to so great and so many ills, and it was perhaps in order not to sadden his companion that he did not hesitate to transgress the divine order and to eat the fruit forbidden by God.

Consequences of the Fall

Immediately after their sin, our first parents began to be ashamed of their nudity, and to cover themselves they sewed together fig leaves. Upon hearing God's voice as God strolled in paradise, they took fright and hid in the middle of paradise. (Evidently, the Lord of heaven had taken a visible form to reproach them.) But how could they hide from and escape the eye of God who sees all things exceedingly clearly? The Lord of heaven therefore called Adam and said to him: "Where are you?" Adam, terrified by his own sin, replied: "My Lord God, I heard your voice in paradise and I was afraid because I was naked and I hid myself." The Lord of heaven asked him in return: "Who told you that you were naked? You must have eaten of the tree of which I had ordered you not to eat!" For when our first parents still had the friendship with the Lord of heaven, they were not ashamed though they were naked. But after their sin, feeling the revolt of their flesh, they became ashamed of their nudity.

The Lord of heaven spoke to Adam about his sin so that he could simply confess it and obtain forgiveness for it more easily. However, he chose to shift his sin onto the woman, and indirectly onto the Lord of heaven himself: "My Lord of heaven, the woman whom you had given me for a companion gave me the fruit of the tree and I ate it." Thus spoke Adam as if he should not have kept the command of God and rejected the counsels of the woman. This is all the more blameworthy since he himself had not been tempted but had knowingly and freely eaten the fruit of death.

Then the Lord of heaven also questioned the woman: "Why did you do that?" She answered: "My Lord of heaven, the snake deceived me and I ate it." It was as if she wanted to disown her sin and blame it on the snake, whereas the Lord of heaven wanted her to recognize her guilt for having eaten the forbidden fruit and then given it to her husband to eat. Nevertheless, the good Lord was already preparing the remedy for the human race so miserably fallen.

The Lord of heaven got angry first with the snake, or rather with the devil hidden in the form of the snake: "I will put an enmity between you and the woman, between your descendants and her posterity, and she will crush your head." With these words, the Lord of heaven predicted the fall of the devil brought about by the savior of the world born of the woman. It was only after this that the Lord of heaven announced to our parents the various pains they would have to suffer, they and all their descendants, and lastly, death, which all would have to undergo because of Adam's sin.

It is for this reason that God chased them out of the garden of delights without any hope of returning to it. In this way they would not be able to eat of the fruit of the tree of life and thus avoid the death of the body.

ORIGINAL SIN AND BAPTISM OF INFANTS

That is why we all are born sullied by original sin, even the little babies still deprived of the use of reason, who nevertheless contracted original sin before their birth.[11] That is why every infant must receive baptism[12] to remove this sin so as not to be deprived of the heavenly happiness for ever should they per chance die before the use of reason. On the other hand, if any one of them is touched by death after having validly received baptism, he or she will enjoy eternal beatitude in the company of the blessed angels.

Therefore, utmost care should be taken to baptize the babies, even those of pagans, who are on the point of death before the use of reason, and indeed with prudence we should baptize them, even without the knowledge and against the will of their parents, when they are on the point of death, before they breathe their last.[13] This work of mercy is more meritorious than distributing innumerable treasures to the poor.

---

11. De Rhodes translates "original sin" with the Vietnamese expression *toi to tong*, literally, sin of the first parents (this expression is still in use today), or *toi to ne truyen cho*, that is, sin transmitted by the original ancestors.

12. De Rhodes translates "baptism" with the Vietnamese expression *phep rua toi*, literally, powerful ritual of washing sins away. This expression is still in use today.

13. This pastoral policy of de Rhodes regarding the baptism of infants was understandable in the context of seventeenth-century theology of original sin. Of course, contemporary theology of grace and original sin makes the baptism of dying infants, especially against the will of their parents, less urgent.

The Fourth Day

The History of Humanity – The Patriarchs – Oriental Religions

Adam, cast out of paradise after his sin, though he began to do penance for it, immediately felt how many ills his sin had inflicted upon himself and his descendants. If, as far as his guilt is concerned, he had received forgiveness for his sin from the divine mercy, he still earned his bread by the sweat of his brow. And Eve received as her punishment the pains of childbirth.

Cain and Abel

What is worse, she witnessed such a great rebellion in her firstborn son that he did not spare even his brother Abel whom he killed out of jealousy. Abel offered his pious worship to the Lord of heaven and God accepted his sacrifices. Cain, on the contrary, was impious and displeased God. He was jealous of his younger brother and killed him. That is why he wandered upon the earth, and begot children similar to himself, impious and rebellious against the Lord of heaven and preoccupied with worldly affairs alone. They introduced polygamy into the world, musical instruments, and weaponry.[1]

Descendants of Seth

Adam begot a third son whom he named Seth. He taught him and his descendants to worship the Lord of heaven with piety. That is why Seth's children were called children of God, among whom there was Enoch, who was so agreeable to God that God lifted him up, not to be seen again. Whereas the other patriarchs had died a long time ago, only Enoch, for more than four thousand years, is still among the living, preserved by God in a secret place. Later, at the

---

1. It is interesting that de Rhodes traces the practice of polygamy to evil Cain's descendants. In fact, it is said that one of Cain's descendants, Lamech, "took two wives" (Genesis 4:19). One of Lamech's children, Jubal, "was the ancestor of all who play the lyre and the pipe" (4:21) and another "the ancestor of all who forge instruments of bronze and iron" (4:22).

coming of the end of the world, he too will die, in conformity with the holy divine law.[2] Although before the flood, some patriarchs had reached nine hundred years of age, like Adam who was 930 years old, none reached a thousand years, except Enoch who, as we have said, is still alive and is already more than four thousand years old. Methuselah, son of Enoch, who surpassed the other patriarchs in age, was 960 years old. Thus he lived with Adam for more than two hundred years and could receive directly from him information on how God created this world and transmit it not only to Noah, his grandson, but also before the flood to the latter's three sons. Indeed, he lived until the coming of the flood and died in the same year when the flood happened.[3]

Since the children of God, that is, the descendants of Seth, had taken wives among the daughters of men, that is, the impious descendants of Cain, their morals began to corrupt, so that, except Noah and his family, all were corrupted and incurred the wrath of the supreme God who decided to destroy them, except Noah and his family, with a universal flood.

NOAH AND THE FLOOD

God ordered Noah to build an ark large enough to save his family, that is, Noah, his wife, his three sons, their wives, and to save all the animals, birds, and reptiles on the earth to preserve their species. Of the pure animals and birds, there were saved seven of each species, from which, immediately after the flood, Noah took some to offer a sacrifice of thanks to God. Of the impure animals, he had to take two of each species, male and female.

During the roughly hundred years which Noah took to build his ark, he warned others of the impending flood in order to incite them to repentance for their sins. But they ridiculed Noah as a fool and indulged in sins and excesses. When under the command of the Lord of heaven, as the deluge approached, all the animals, reptiles, and birds entered the ark, Noah also entered it with his family. The Lord closed the door from the outside, and rain fell upon the earth without interruption for forty days and forty nights. The waters covered not only the surface of the earth but also the high mountains so that the level of the waters surpassed their tops by fifteen cubits.

Outside of the ark, the animals and the birds that had the spirit of life and all humans died, except Noah and those who were with him in the ark carried above the waters. The waters covered the earth during 150 days. God then remembered Noah and all those who were with him in the ark; then the waters began to diminish little by little on the earth. The flood had begun on the

---

2. De Rhodes takes the Genesis account of the patriarchs as a historically accurate report. With regard to Enoch (Genesis 5:24), he understands him still to be alive, and hence his calculation of Enoch's age.

3. De Rhodes's retelling of the patriarchs' enormously long lives has two purposes: first, to impress the Vietnamese, whose concept of happiness includes longevity; and second, to establish continuity in God's revelation from Adam to Abraham.

twenty-seventh day of the second month of the six hundredth year of Noah's life. On the twenty-seventh day of the seventh month, the ark rested on the mountains of Armenia. On the first day of the tenth month, the tops of the mountains appeared. Noah opened the window which he had taken care to make in the ark and sent out a raven who did not come back until the waters had dried off from the earth. After the raven Noah sent out a dove which, having found nowhere to alight and perch, returned to the ark. After waiting for another seven days, Noah again sent the dove out of the ark. It returned to him in the evening carrying in its bill an olive branch with green leaves. Noah understood that the waters no longer covered the earth.

Nevertheless, he waited seven more days and released the dove once more, which did not come back to him. It was on the first day of the first month of the six hundred and first year of his life that, the waters having receded on the earth, Noah opened the roof of the ark and looked and saw that the surface of the earth was dry. However he did not dare to come out of the ark without being first admonished to do so by God. He waited in the ark until the twenty-seventh day of the second month, roughly two months. Then the Lord of heaven spoke to Noah and ordered him to come out, him, his wife, and those who were with him, as well as the animals, the birds, and the reptiles.

Noah's Sacrifice

After coming out of the ark, Noah built an altar to the Lord of heaven and, taking from every clean animal and every clean bird, he offered a burnt offering to God. The Lord of heaven was pleased with this burnt offering and smelled its sweet odor. He made a covenant with all the flesh that no universal flood would ever occur again, saying: "When I cover the sky with clouds, my bow will appear in the clouds, and I will remember my covenant with you and each living soul that animates the flesh; there will not be another universal flood to destroy all living flesh."

Noah lived 350 years more after the flood, so that the total of his age was 650. From Noah's three sons, Shem, Ham, and Japheth, the human race multiplied while he was still alive, and all people spoke only one and the same language.

By the order of the Lord, Noah urged his children and grandchildren to spread throughout the earth in order to fill it.

The Tower of Babel

When Noah's many children and grandchildren came from the East into the land called Shinar, they exhorted one another to build a city and a tower with the top reaching heaven, to make a name for themselves before they would scatter throughout the earth. While they were engaged in this project, God confused their language so that one could not understand what another said. They abandoned the work they had begun; the ruins of this attempted tower still exist today in the land called Babylon, which means confusion.

Thus the children of Adam spread throughout the earth during the life of Noah, who very probably kept for himself the first language, that is, *hebraea*.[4] This language and the true cult of God he left to his son Shem. Before the flood, for almost a hundred years Shem had had conversations with his great grandfather Methuselah who had had conversations with Adam. Shem himself lived until the times of Abraham and his son Isaac. Furthermore, since Abraham was born about three hundred years after the flood and since Noah survived the flood by 350 years, Abraham could receive the tradition of the divine law either from Shem or from Noah himself. He kept it for his family and transmitted it as well as the *hebraea* language to the entire kingdom of Judea of which Abraham was the ancestor. The other kingdoms lost the *hebraea* language in the confusion of the languages as well as the tradition of the divine law, and as a result degenerated into false sects.[5]

THE CHINESE AND THEIR FALSE SECTS

After the confusion of the languages came the kingdom of the Chinese, from whom the Vietnamese received their religious sects. Because the Chinese, after the confusion of the languages, lost the language in which the true way was found, and because they had no books in which the true way was contained, they were divided into different false ways, just like those who have lost the true way are dispersed in many ways that are all false.[6]

The Chinese were divided into three main false ways, without counting many other less important but equally false ones. The first religion is that of the literati called *Nho*; the second is that of those who worship demons and perform sorcery, called *Dao*; the third is that of idolaters, called *But*.[7]

THE BUDDHA AND BUDDHISM

Let us begin with the last one, which had its origin in India; its falsehood will be apparent from its origin itself. About three thousand years after the creation of the world and more than one thousand years after the confusion of lan-

---

4. De Rhodes leaves this word untranslated. The contemporary Vietnamese word for Israel is *Do Thai*.

5. De Rhodes might have derived the notion that the Hebrew language was the preserver of authentic divine revelation from Augustine's *City of God*, bk. XVI.

6. After having shown by rational arguments the existence and the nature of God and by historical arguments the existence of true divine revelation among the Hebrews, de Rhodes now proceeds to the *pars destruens* of his catechesis by demonstrating the errors of the Chinese and Vietnamese religions.

7. De Rhodes cannot be expected to present an objective and accurate account of these three religions and their philosophical doctrines. Rather he is describing these religions as he saw them practiced at the popular level. His basic intention is apologetic, that is, to demonstrate the errors of these religions and the superiority of Christianity.

guages, there was in India a king named Tinh Phan.[8] His son had a penetrating intelligence but was very proud. First of all, the son married the daughter of a nearby king with whom he had only one child, a daughter.[9] Against the will of his wife, he withdrew by himself into the wood, because he was given to magical practices, either to win admiration from people or to have freer dealings with demons. Among the many demons who taught him, there were *Alala* and *Calala.* He himself was seated between the two who taught him that there is no God and gave him the name of *Thich Ca.*[10]

When he wanted to teach others this impious doctrine, so contrary to natural reason, they all abandoned him. Seeing this, he began, with the demons as his teachers, to teach another way filled with false stories in order to retain his disciples. He taught them the false doctrine of reincarnation, and at the same time taught the people the worship of idols, among whom he placed himself as their head, as if he were the creator and lord of heaven and earth. Using the name of heaven and earth he deceived the people. He himself had a human body, but the other idols were represented with hands and feet, flesh and bones, as both male and female, even with genitals.

Those who were more advanced in his impious doctrine were forbidden to divulge it to the public. By means of his falsehoods and magical practices he made the people so foolish as to adopt the worship of idols, promising those who worship idols that they, though they may be of the lowest social rank in this world, will be born again as children of kings in the transmigration of souls. As to his closest disciples, he led them to the abyss of atheism, holding that nothingness is the origin of all things, and that at death all things return to nothingness as to their ultimate end.

The doctrine of Buddhism has thus two ways: the first is called the external way and consists in the worship of idols with its innumerable false tales and magical chants which are used to induce people to worship idols and commit numerous sins. The second is called the internal way, which is much worse and consists in denying a deity, the creator of this world, removing the brake against all kinds of sin. Followers of the poison of the second way are much worse than those of the first. That is why Confucius, whom the Chinese regard as the greatest teacher, calls in his books the worship of idols the doctrine of savages.[11]

BUDDHISM IN CHINA

How could this barbarous cult of idols, you will ask, have spread among the Chinese, since it originated among the Indians whom the Chinese regard as uncouth? The answer is that the Chinese are indeed much more civilized than the Indian tribes, with regard to the sciences, the soul, and the care of the

---

8. This is the Vietnamese transliteration of *Siddhartha.*
9. The Buddhist texts speak of a son rather than a daughter.
10. *Thich Ca* is the Vietnamese word for Buddha.
11. Like Ricci, de Rhodes shares the Confucianists' contempt for Buddhism.

body. First of all, regarding the sciences, the Indians are quite ignorant. As far as the care of the body is concerned, they go about naked most of the time or barely dressed. For daily meals, they are so boorish that they do not make use of plates or bowls but only fig leaves; they use their hands to pick up foods, even liquid ones.

Now Confucius had announced in his books that one must look for the Saint in the West. A Chinese king, by the name of Han Minh, who had read Confucius, is said to have received from God the order to seek the true religion from the Great West. He selected one of the first mandarins of his kingdom for this task. After a long voyage of many months, the mandarin came to India, which was for the Chinese situated in the West. But he had not made even half of the trip to the Great West. Broken by fatigue and by the difficulties of the journey, he did not want to go further; he therefore asked if there was there, in India, a religion he could bring back to the Chinese king. He was given the impious religion of Thich Ca. He received it with joy, and upon his return, presented it to the king, telling him, not without lie, that he had brought the religion back from the Great West.

The king, trusting his envoy, received the religion without examining whether he was telling the truth, and at once began worshiping the idols and to have temples built for them. The ignorant people followed the king's example and accepted the impious cult of the idols. The literati and the learned scholars in general despised this cult, though some of them, to please the king, began rendering an external cult to the idols while despising it in their hearts, and together with their master Confucius called it the way of the barbarians.[12]

Worshipers of the idols were so demented that they thought that Thich Ca was the creator of heaven and earth, though it is apparent from his books that heaven and earth had existed well before him. Other idolaters say that the creator of heaven and earth is a fictitious being whom they call *Ban co;* they do not render him any worship nor have temples built in his honor, but worship only Thich Ca who is impious.

LAO TZU AND TAOISM

The second religion among the Chinese is that of a certain Lao Tzu. His followers regard him as the creator of heaven and earth though it is clear from the books of the Chinese that heaven and earth had been made several thousand years before him. This religion venerates demons and consists mainly in sorcery; it does not render Lao Tzu any cult and is wrapped in thickest obscurity. There is a saying of Lao Tzu in which it is affirmed: "Tao, that is, the law or the way, has made one; one has made two; two has made three; three, lastly, has made

---

12. This story of Emperor Minh De (Chinese: Mingdi, of the Ming dynasty, 58–77 C.E.) had been told by Ricci in *True Meaning,* 453–54.

everything."[13] If asked where Tao comes from, followers of this religion would answer: "From nothingness and emptiness; the great Tao or the great law has no other principle."[14] Of the origin of all things they know nothing else. They make emptiness and nothingness the first principle of all things. Now, is it not absurd that emptiness or nothingness creates something?[15] Ignorant of the true creator of all things and sovereign Lord, they worship demons, and trapped by numerous sorceries, they are miserably deceived by demons.

CONFUCIUS AND CONFUCIANISM

Lastly, the third religion of the Chinese is called *dao nho,* that is, the religion of the literati. They render a cult to Confucius because they have received from him certain books as well as some political principles by which the kingdom of the Chinese is administered. That is why the Chinese render a supreme cult to Confucius whom they call the saint or the good *par excellence.*[16] But they are wrong in speaking thus. Either Confucius knew this supreme creator and Lord of all things, source and origin of all holiness and goodness, or he did not. If he knew, he should have told his disciples, since he was a master, so that they might render an appropriate cult. Because he did not do so, he could be neither good nor holy but rather perverse and evil, because he deprived others of a most necessary knowledge. But if he did not know the supreme God, principle and source of all goodness and holiness, how could he have been holy and good?

Consequently, there is no reason to call him a saint, much less to pay him the honors due to the Lord of heaven alone, or to invoke him in order to obtain this or that, since all things should be asked and received from the sovereign Lord of all things alone.

At most one could and should pay Confucius the homage and reverence due to teachers during their lifetime and not go beyond the norms of politeness.[17] To honor him by bowing one's head to the ground, as the Chinese are wont to do for their teachers during their lifetime, is the same as our custom of taking off one's hat and bowing to our teachers.

In the presence of people who are pagan (such as those who adore Confucius as their god), no reverence should be done without first explaining to them clearly that this reverence is not done to Confucius as to a god but only as a

---

13. De Rhodes gives the Sino-Vietnamese formula: "Dao sinh nhat, nhat sinh nhi, nhi sinh tam, tam sinh van vat."

14. De Rhodes gives the Sino-Vietnamese expression: "Hu vo tu nhien chi dai dao."

15. De Rhodes takes "nonbeing" (*hu vo* in Sino-Vietnamese, and *wu* in Chinese) to mean absolute nonexistence (hence the absurdity he sees in holding nonbeing to be the creator), whereas in Taoism *wu* is not the opposite of being but that original being which exists before the appearance of all differentiations and multiplicities. Consequently, Tao is referred to as *p'o,* or the "uncarved block" which precedes the emergence of the myriad things.

16. The title for Confucius is *thanh hien,* literally, holy and kind.

17. The Latin text uses the expression *cultum politicum,* which is the standard way of describing the cult of Confucius to make it legitimate to Christians. The Vietnamese simply says that the cult should not go beyond the norms of politeness of this world (*la phep le ve the nay, cho lich su ma thoi*).

teacher from whom one has received writings and political guidance. Otherwise, it would be a sin to show reverence to Confucius in front of someone without this explanation. The pagans would think that Christians render him a cult as to a god, if a preliminary explanation is not given, and the pagans would thereby be confirmed in their error.

There is, however, almost no one who dares to make this protestation in public so as to avert the pagans from their error. Hence, we urge most vigorously that such reverence to Confucius be omitted, lest it become a trap for someone.[18]

In this same religion of the literati, the pagans have the habit of adoring heaven as a god; this error was spread among the populace, but it has been refuted above, at the beginning of this catechism, on the first day.

Many other errors have derived from these three religions[19] as from poisoned sources, but it is unnecessary to refute them one by one. Suffice it to know what their sources are in order to perceive their falsehood.

REFUTATION OF THE DOCTRINE OF REINCARNATION

Just as in cutting down a sterile and dangerous tree one also cuts down all its branches, so once the dark and mendacious Thich Ca is knocked down, from whom came all the other tales about idols, these also crumble. What he teaches regarding the transmigration of souls in his external way is ridiculous. How can one not remember this former life if one were there for some time before the present one? It is therefore a pure invention of Thich Ca, who also expressly teaches in his books that there is no difference between the souls of plants, trees, and humans. He declares that the human soul is as mortal as the vegetative and sensitive souls. But subsequently he contradicts himself when he teaches the transmigration of reasonable souls into other bodies. For, if in his opinion the human soul is as mortal as those of beasts and trees, how can it transmigrate into other bodies? If the human soul dies together with its body at death, how can it animate other bodies?

Furthermore, this transmigration is contrary to common sense and to the proverb found both among the Chinese and the Vietnamese, namely, "life is a journey, death is a return."[20] If this imaginary transmigration exists, our souls would always be on a journey, now in this body, later in another.[21]

---

18. De Rhodes imposes a stricter pastoral policy with regard to the cult of Confucius than most of his Jesuit confreres in China.

19. De Rhodes uses the common Sino-Vietnamese expression *tam giao*, literally, "three religions," to refer to the three religions imported to Vietnam from China.

20. This proverb (*Sinh ki da, tu qui da*) is cited several times to stress the fact that life is a return to its source, that is, the Lord of heaven, and that Christianity is the true way leading back to this source.

21. De Rhodes might have been influenced by Ricci in his refutation of reincarnation. Both argue that we have no memory of alleged former lives and that the soul is immaterial. See *True Meaning*, 239–57.

The Immortality of the Human Soul

But it would be much worse to affirm that the human soul is mortal, as Thich Ca himself has said in his internal way, because, as we have argued above, he contradicts himself. Besides opening the door to all kinds of vices, this nefarious teaching expressly goes against the common tendency of the rational soul to leave behind a memory of itself after this life, as is evidenced by our desire for a magnificent tomb and by our wish to transmit to posterity our outstanding achievements.

Furthermore, the principal operations of the human soul do not depend on the body, for example, the operations of the intellect and the will, which the soul exercises even in an aging and weakened body. This shows that these faculties do not depend on the body, and indeed a soul separated from its body exercises them better.

Lastly, why do people, guided by nature, commonly take care of their parents after their death? Why do Vietnamese celebrate with so much devotion the anniversary of the death of their ancestors? Why do they go to such expense to prepare banquets for the dead and other marks of deference to their parents after their death?[22]

If indeed the soul dies with its body, all the care for the dead would be in vain. Although irrational animals, guided by nature, take care of their offspring, and although birds, to feed and raise their little ones, build tiny nets with such meticulousness and ingenuity, since offspring need the help of their parents, nevertheless, no animal species, even the most intelligent, takes care of the remains of its parents after their death, because the souls of all animals die together with their bodies and no longer need the help of their offspring.

The Lord of heaven does nothing in vain. Hence, God has not placed in animals a concern for their dead parents, since there is nothing left to be concerned about. On the contrary, humans, instructed by nature itself, take care of their deceased parents with the same solicitude as that with which parents take care of their living children. From this one must acknowledge that the Lord of heaven himself teaches us that, even after this life, our parents survive, since they still need our services. Therefore, our soul lives on after being separated from the body. By itself and by its nature, it is immortal; no natural agent can destroy it after its separation from the body.

Proper Cult of Ancestors
in Vietnamese Indigenous Religion

However, it must be acknowledged that our soul, after being separated from the body, being spiritual, no longer needs food, clothing, or other material

---

22. This is a skillful use of a Vietnamese custom to defend the immortality of the human soul. It must have been very well received by the Vietnamese audience.

things of this kind. Hence, the Vietnamese err grievously when they offer meals to the souls of the dead. Our souls are too noble to use this sort of food. In so doing the Vietnamese gravely offend their parents, even more gravely than if they were to feed their living parents, when they come to visit, with hay or other animal feed.

Giving material foods to our spiritual souls is more disrespectful than giving hay or other animal feed to living humans. The Vietnamese would show a greater disrespect, even mockery, to their deceased parents when they use paper to make houses, clothing, pieces of money, and other utensils as offerings to them. No man in his right mind would offer these things to a living person, even the poorest, for his or her use.

How would the Vietnamese dare to offer to their deceased parents these imaginary things for their use? You may say: By being burned, these things become something else. Indeed, you hit the nail on the head: by being burned, they become partly flames and partly ashes. But then, which part do you send to your parents? If it is ashes that you send, how can they live well amidst ashes? How can they be dressed properly and cleanly with ashes? If it is flames that you send, then indeed you are sending them flames, because these works of error and sin which you perform and which you learned from your parents are like flames to increase the sufferings of your deceased parents.[23]

Just as the joy of the saints in heaven increases when the good teachings they have given are put into practice by their disciples after their death, so also those who have given and practiced perverse teachings suffer more pains and torments in the other life, even if they are dead, on account of the new sins of those they have taught.

Therefore, those children who offer their parents these imaginary objects by burning them, truly send them flames of fire, because when they engage in such perverse practices which they have learned from their deceased parents, they increase their pains and sufferings in the other life, not counting their children's own sins for which, unless they repent in time, they will be punished in the next life.

Consequently, these erroneous acts and false honors should be avoided, for they are nothing but offenses and mockeries against the parents and increase their pains. We will teach you what kind of honors you should render to your deceased parents when we treat the honors that the law of the Lord of heaven prescribes we should render to our parents both living and dead.

ABRAHAM AND THE TRUE WAY REVEALED TO THE HEBREWS

Whereas the Chinese and all other kingdoms lost the tradition of the true way and sank, by the ruse of the devil, into different false religions, only the

---

23. De Rhodes makes effective use of irony and sarcasm to criticize certain practices of the Vietnamese ancestor worship.

Jewish nation kept the law of the supreme creator of all things as well as the *hebraea* language.

Abraham, the first parent of the Jewish race, received the true way directly from the Lord of heaven himself to whom he was very dear because of his holiness. God appeared to him often and often talked to him as to a friend, teaching him many mysteries. But Abraham could also have had Shem, Noah's son, as teacher, since he spent many years with him when the latter was still alive. Shem received the true law not only from his father Noah but also from his great grandfather Methuselah with whom he lived for a long time before the flood. Methuselah in turn received it directly from Adam himself with whom he lived for a long time, as we have pointed out above.

Thus, Abraham, through Shem and Methuselah, received from Adam the tradition of the true way; he transmitted it to his son Isaac whom he begot at the age of ninety-nine from Sarah who was already in her nineties and sterile. Abraham received the promise from God that in the future, from among Isaac's descendants, the Lord would come into the world to redeem the entire human race.

About a thousand years later, the same promise was made by God to David, king of the nation of Judea, who was pleasing to God, and then to other holy prophets, until the Lord of heaven would come into the world to redeem this world. During this time, the other nations lay in the darkness of infidelity, particularly the great empire of the Chinese. The various false religions, which we have enumerated and refuted, precipitated the Chinese into the abyss of atheism, which is so contrary to the light of reason, and generally made them deny the immortality of the rational soul.

THE IMMORTALITY OF THE SOUL
AFFIRMED BY BOTH REASON AND REVELATION

The true law, however, which recognizes the sovereign Lord, creator of all things, first root and last end, not only in virtue of divine revelation but also by the light of natural reason, teaches that the human soul is spiritual and immortal. The Lord of heaven, the creator of all things, is necessarily just. But God's justice could not be perfectly safeguarded if there is not after this life another in which the good are rewarded and the wicked punished. Indeed, there are many just and holy persons who live in poverty and contempt till old age, or even suffer diseases and die young, often oppressed by evil and dishonest people to death; and they bear all this with patience and remain good. On the contrary, we often see the wicked arrive at prosperity and enjoy riches and the comforts of life till a very advanced age, though they commit many evil deeds and are charged with horrible crimes.

There must therefore be another life in which the good receive the crowns and rewards owed to their virtues, and where the wicked are consigned by the supreme judge and Lord of all things to pains and punishments according to what they deserve.

This is what happened at one time to Lazarus, as we have already noted, the holy poor beggar covered with sores who, bearing during this brief life all the trials with patience and virtue, has been enjoying eternal happiness for more than sixteen hundred years and will possess eternally the beatitude of glory. On the contrary, the rich hedonist who lived in luxuries was buried into hell immediately after his death on account of the many sins he had committed. He has been consigned to unquenchable fires for more than sixteen hundred years and will be eternally tormented with no hope whatsoever of escape. Such is the infinite justice of God, just as everything in God is infinite.

ANOTHER PROOF FOR THE IMMORTALITY OF THE SOUL

To those who are so obtuse that from what we have said have not yet grasped the immortality of the soul we may pose this question: Why is there in us all a natural disposition such that persons who are most dear to us, with whom we have shared intimate conversations and meals during their lifetime, give us, immediately after their death, such fear and terror that we cannot without fear stay near them? Why do we have fear? It is because their separated souls, as nature teaches us, provoke this terror in us. Here is an evident sign, given by nature itself, of the survival of the human soul after death; the relationship which it continues to keep with the body makes us fear the latter even after its death.

On the contrary, we fear wild animals such as lions, tigers, and wolves if they are alive, and nature makes us run away from them. But once they are killed, we do not fear them any more. Even little children would seize their sharp teeth and their nails to play with them. Nature makes us understand that nothing in them survives that is to be feared; that souls die with their bodies.

If a house has an owner, even if he is away, people would instinctively refrain from ransacking it for fear of being caught and punished by the owner. But if the house is totally abandoned and without owner, anyone would pillage it freely and without fear, because it has no owner. Similarly, although we naturally fear and run away from wild animals if they are alive, we would tear up their bodies without fear if they are dead, because their souls perish with their bodies and there survives in them no owner to be feared.[24]

Nature teaches us to fear the bodies of deceased humans because their souls, being the mistresses of these corpses, fill us with fear by their survival. Thus, nature makes us understand that the human soul survives the body at death. As a consequence, it is immortal. No natural agent can corrupt or destroy the soul separated from the body. Only the Lord of heaven, who has created it from nothing and conserves it in its existence by a sort of continuous creation, would

---

24. This argument for the immortality of the soul based on the fear of the dead has been put forward by Ricci. See *True Meaning*, 161–65.

be able to destroy it, if God so chooses, by refusing it this creative concourse. This, however, the Lord of heaven would never do, as revelation tells us. But God will give the good eternal rewards in heaven, and the wicked God will punish with eternal pains in hell.

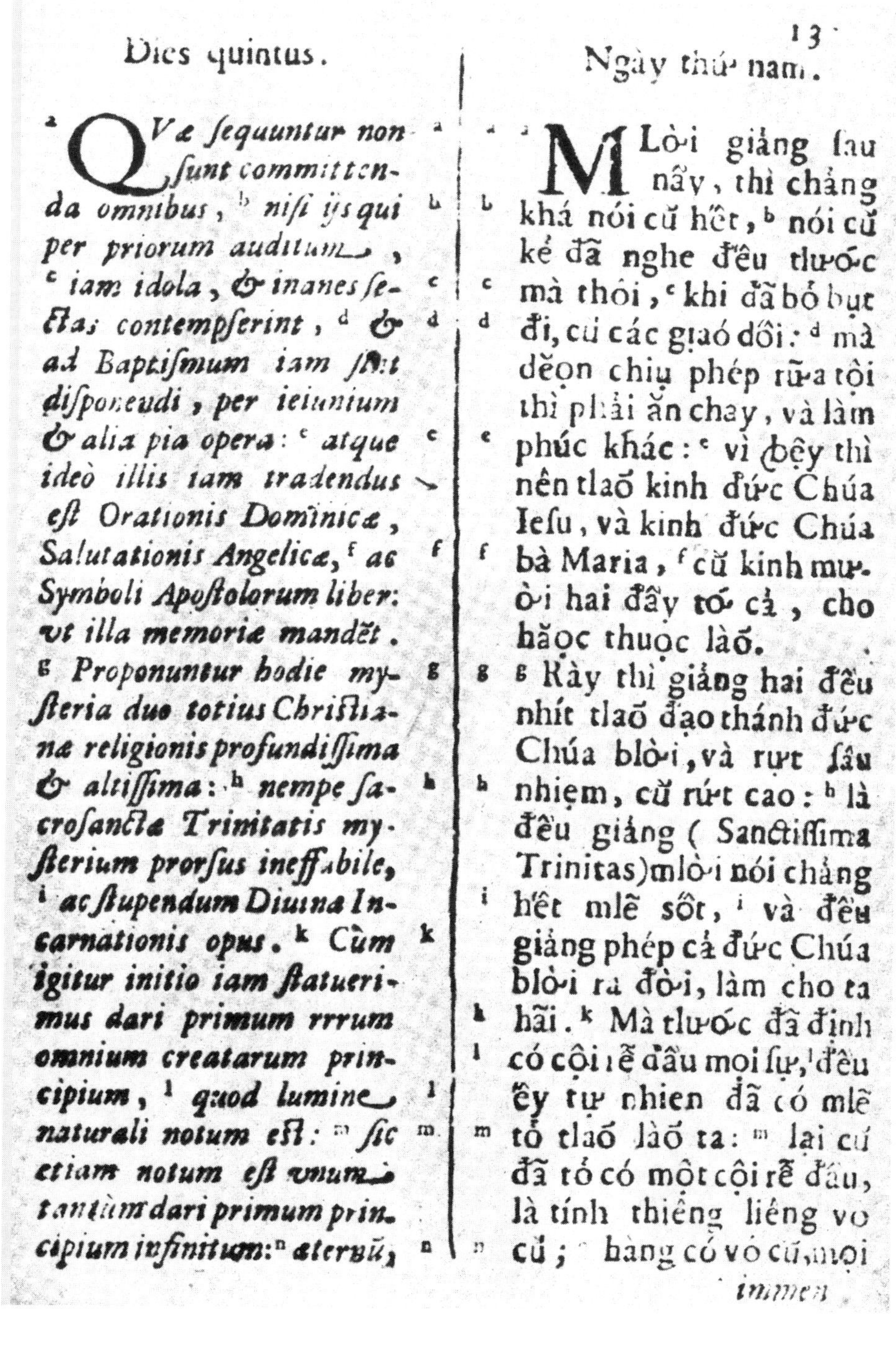

QVæ sequuntur non
sunt committen-
da omnibus, nisi ijs qui
per priorum auditum,
iam idola, & inanes se-
Etas contempserint, &
ad Baptismum iam sint
disponendi, per ieiunium
& alia pia opera: atque
ideò illis iam tradendus
est Orationis Dominicæ,
Salutationis Angelicæ, ac
Symboli Apostolorum liber:
vt illa memoriæ mandēt.
Proponuntur hodie my-
steria duo totius Christia-
næ religionis profundissima
& altissima: nempe sa-
crosanctæ Trinitatis my-
sterium prorsus ineffabile,
ac stupendum Diuinæ In-
carnationis opus. Cùm
igitur initio iam statueri-
mus dari primum rrrum
omnium creatarum prin-
cipium, quod lumine
naturali notum est: sic
etiam notum est vnum
tantùm dari primum prin-
cipium infinitum: æternu,

MLời giảng sau
nầy, thì chẳng
khá nói cử hết, nói cử
kẻ đã nghe đều tlước
mà thói, khi đã bỏ bụt
đi, cử các giaó dối: mà
dẽon chiụ phép rửa tội
thì phải ăn chay, và làm
phúc khác: vì bệy thì
nên tlaổ kinh đức Chúa
Iesu, và kinh đức Chúa
bà Maria, cử kinh mư-
ời hai đầy tớ cả, cho
hãoc thuộc lảo.
Rày thì giảng hai đều
nhít tlaổ đạo thánh đức
Chúa blời, và rựt sầu
nhiệm, cử rứt cao: là
đều giảng (Sanctissima
Trinitas)mlời nói chẳng
hết mlẽ sốt, và đều
giảng phép cả đức Chúa
blời ra đời, làm cho ta
hãi. Mà tlước đã định
có cội rẽ đầu moi sự, đều
ẩy tự nhiên đã có mlẽ
tổ tlaổ lảo ta: lại cử
đã tỏ có một cội rẽ đầu,
là tính thiêng liếng vo
cử; hàng có vô cử, moi

immen

Figure 5. Sample page from the *Cathechismus* of Alexandre de Rhodes.

The Fifth Day

The Trinity – The Incarnation – Mary

What follows should not be expounded to all but only to those who, having heard what has been said above, have already despised idols and false religions and are prepared to receive baptism by fasting and other works of piety. At this stage, they may be given the Our Lord's Prayer, the Hail Mary, and the Apostles' Creed to learn by heart.[1]

On this day we will expound the two most profound and sublime mysteries of the Christian religion, namely, the ineffable mystery of *sanctissima Trinitas*[2] and the stupendous work of divine incarnation.[3]

GOD KNOWN THROUGH THE LIGHT OF REASON AND THE LIGHT OF FAITH

We have established at the beginning that there exists a first root of all created things, knowable by the light of natural reason. It is similarly known that there exists a single first principle, infinite, eternal, immense, all-powerful, omniscient, containing in itself all goodness and perfection, incomprehensible, such that nothing more perfect can be conceived.[4] But God's incomprehensible essence and attributes are such that no created intellect can grasp them unless it is elevated by God with a supernatural light.

---

1. At this point we come to the second stage of de Rhodes's catechesis. It presupposes that the catechumens have already renounced their former religions and have decided to accept the Christian faith. Whereas the first stage of de Rhodes's catechesis makes uses of natural reason to convince the catechumens of the existence of the true Lord of heaven, the second will rely on the light of revelation to explain the mysteries of the Christian faith.

2. One of the most difficult tasks facing de Rhodes was finding appropriate Vietnamese words for Christian terms. Here he retains the Latin term *sanctissima Trinitas*. Other variations include: *Santissima Trindade* and *Santissima Trinitate*. We will comment on de Rhodes's Vietnamese words as they appear in the text.

3. De Rhodes translates "incarnation" with a circumlocution: "Duc Chua Troi ra doi cuu the," literally, the Lord of heaven (*Duc Chua Troi*) came out into the world (*ra doi*) to redeem the world (*cuu the*). There are today two Sino-Vietnamese expressions for incarnation: *giang sinh* (descend from heaven and to be born) and *giang the* (descend from heaven into the world).

4. This phrase calls to mind St. Anselm's definition of God as "quod nihil maius cogitari nequit."

This light is twofold. The first is the light of faith by which the Lord of heaven reveals himself and divine matters to us in this life through his words. Although knowledge through this light is still obscure, it surpasses all natural reason and is very certain, founded as it is on the witness of the Lord of heaven as absolute truth. This first truth cannot be deceived by anyone because it knows all things, nor does it deceive anyone because it is at the same time supreme goodness which cannot lie.

The second light is called the light of *gloria;* the created intellect, elevated and enlightened by it, sees the face of the Lord of heaven clearly, as it is. This light is given only to the blessed in eternal happiness. When the king of China resided quietly in his royal palace, no one outside the court could see him. Much less can one see the King of kings as he is, without coming first to his heavenly court in the beatitude of the age to come.

For us to obtain this light of *gloria,* the merciful God gives us in this life the supernatural light of faith; through it we assent firmly and unchangeably to God's revelation to the saints in the *Ecclesia Catholica,*[5] and through the church to us. Going forward thus in this world by the light of faith, we will finally arrive at the eternal happiness in order to see clearly by the light of *gloria* that which we have firmly believed in this life.

We must therefore hold as true whatever the light of faith teaches us, not doubting any mystery, even though human reason cannot comprehend it. Furthermore, we must be certain of whatever is revealed by God and proposed by the holy *Ecclesia* as if we see it with our own eyes. Indeed, our eyes can be deceived or hallucinate, but the Word of God can in no way be deceived or deceive.

THE MOST HOLY TRINITY

The first and principal mystery to which we must give our firm assent concerns the Lord of heaven himself:[6] Although God's essence is one, God is trine in persons.[7] Thus God is called *Sanctissima Trinidade,* that is, Father, Son, and *Spiritus Sanctus.* The Father is God,[8] the Son is also God,[9] and the *Spirito*

---

5. De Rhodes never translates the words *ecclesia* and *ecclesia catholica,* though he explains them by saying that the church is the "assembly of the saints." Contemporary Vietnamese uses *hoi thanh* (holy assembly) and the Sino-Vietnamese *giao hoi* (religious assembly) to translate "church."

6. Against some of his fellow missionaries, de Rhodes insists that the exposition of the mystery of the Trinity should not be delayed until the time of baptism. Rather, according to him, catechesis on the Christian mysteries must begin with it. There are two reasons for this: First, logically, the doctrine of the incarnation presupposes that of the Trinity; and second, this is the order followed by the creed.

7. De Rhodes uses *tinh* for nature, and *ngoi* for person. *Tinh* is a Sino-Vietnamese term meaning essence or character. *Ngoi* means royal throne. The idea of three thrones as applied to the trinitarian persons indicates both distinction and majesty. Contemporary Vietnamese still uses de Rhodes's terminology to summarize the doctrine of the divine uni-trinity: *mot tinh* (one nature) *ba ngoi* (three thrones).

8. De Rhodes uses *Duc Cha* (noble father) for the first divine person. Today the word *Chua* is added, *Duc Chua Cha* (the noble lord father), since *Duc Cha* is now used to translate "bishop."

9. De Rhodes uses *Duc Con* (noble son) for the second divine person. Today the word *Chua* is added: *Duc Chua Con* (the noble lord son).

Sancto is also God.[10] Yet there are not three gods. The three persons are only one God, only one Lord, so much so that eternity, immensity, wisdom, power, infinite goodness, and infinite justice, and everything that is infinite, are equally in the Father, the Son, and the *Spirito Sancto*. For there is only one essence and majesty of the Father, the Son, and the *Spirito Sancto*, though the three persons are distinct from each other. Indeed, God the Father is truly Father because he generates the Son eternally; and God the Son is truly Son because he proceeds from the Father by eternal generation; and God the *Spirito Sancto* is truly *Spirito Sancto* because he proceeds from the mutual love of the Father and the Son.

As God the Father from all eternity knows himself and understands himself perfectly, he produces his own image or infinite Word and communicates to him his whole essence, so that he is equal to the Father and is truly Son. However, when you hear of Son, do not think that there is need of a mother, as in human generation. God the Father is truly spirit, perfectly pure, who generates his perfect image from himself alone and by his intellect, without anything material. We can take an imperfect example of a very clean mirror in which we produce the perfect image of our face, with all our features represented. Similarly, God the Father, contemplating himself in his essence as in a splendid mirror, produces the most perfect image of himself and communicates necessarily all his essence to it. This image is the eternal Word of God, truly Son of God, consubstantial to the Father, coeternal, true God like the Father.

Just as the Father loves the Son with an eternal love, so the Son loves his Father. This mutual infinite love between the Father and the Son is called *Spiritu Sancto*. He is truly God proceeding from the Father and the Son, because the Father and the Son communicate their entire nature to the *Spiritu Sancto*. Therefore, the *Spiritu Sancto* is the one true God, consubstantial and coeternal with the Father and the Son. Such is the *Sanctissima Trinidade*, that is, the Father, the Son, and the *Spiritu Sancto*, God truly one in his essence, and truly three in his persons, original source, root, first principle, and last end of all created things.

THE TRINITY AND BAPTISM

This first mystery the Lord of heaven himself has in truth revealed to the saints, and through them God has proposed it for our belief so that we may obtain *gratia*, that is, friendship with God in this life. Therefore, adults who receive baptism cannot obtain the remission of their sins unless they believe this mystery firmly as infallible and revealed by God. And those who administer baptism and do not believe this mystery to be true while performing baptism, cannot forgive sins and confer the *gratia*, that is, friendship with God.

---

10. De Rhodes does not coin a Vietnamese name for the third divine person. He uses *Spiritus Sanctus* twice, *Spirito Sancto* 16 times, and *Spirito Santo* 10 times. He prefixes these terms with the honorific *Duc* (noble).

INCOMPREHENSIBILITY OF THE TRINITARIAN MYSTERY

It is sufficient to believe this mystery without further disquisitions; for in this life our intellect is so weak that it is incapable of grasping itself or the soul which are finite, much less the infinite essence and properties of the Lord of heaven.

In the past a saint, by the name of Augustine, composed twenty-four books on the ineffable mystery of the holy Trinity. One day, as he was strolling on a beach and reflecting on this divine mystery, seeking ways to expound it more clearly, he saw an angel under the appearance of a child sitting on the beach, digging a small hole and filling it with the water he collected from the sea with a small shell. The saint asked him: "Little child, what are you doing?" The angel replied that he was drawing water from the sea and pouring it into the hole to empty the sea. Then the saint said to the angel whom he took to be a child: "Don't you see that the hole is too small to contain the immense ocean?" The angel then replied, smiling: "Your tiny intellect, how can it contain the infinite and incomprehensible mystery of the blessed *Trinidade?*" Thereupon, the child disappeared and the saint realized that it was not a child, despite the appearances, but a holy angel sent by God to teach him that we should not scrutinize with curiosity that which is above the capacity of our intellect, the inscrutable mysteries of divinity. Rather we should believe them with humble veneration in this life where we walk by faith until the day when the dawn of eternity shines upon us and by the light of *gloria* we will see clearly in heaven the *Sanctissima Trinidade* as it is.[11]

This is what Saint Augustine has done, and for more than a thousand years, he has been enjoying this *gloria*, that is, the clear vision of the *Sanctissima Trinidade*. Let us, who walk in the footsteps of this saint, believe firmly the divine revelations, though they are obscure and above our intellect, so that having believed them on this earth, we may contemplate them with clarity in the age to come.

THE INCARNATION

The second ineffable mystery is that of divine incarnation, that is, of God's coming into this world to redeem us.[12] After the omnipotent God had created humans in God's image and likeness and had ennobled them with his *gratia* and friendship, they, though innocent, fell miserably into sin through the jealousy

---

11. This story has been narrated by Ricci in *True Meaning*, 91.

12. De Rhodes tells us that in his experiences of teaching pagans, he has found that no one objected to the mystery of the Trinity but many had difficulty with that of the Incarnation. Since God is an absolute mystery, it is easy to accept the Trinity as a mystery. On the other hand, it is difficult to reconcile the fact that God is eternal, omnipotent, spiritual with the assertion that God has been made temporal, weak, and bodily. One of the ways to overcome this contradiction is, de Rhodes suggests, to emphasize the miraculous events which occurred during Jesus' birth and passion.

of the devil. As a result, Adam and all his descendants merited not only bodily death but also eternal damnation, having offended God by violating God's command.

In his mercy the Lord of heaven decided to give by himself the remedy to heal the human race, and at the preestablished time, he deigned to assume human nature, as he had promised before through the prophets. To accomplish this sublime work, God chose the kingdom of the Jews, who alone in the world professed the holy way of God; and in this kingdom the Lord of heaven promised to king and prophet David that he would be born of his descendants.

The Birth of the Ever-Virgin Mary, the Mother of God

About a thousand years elapsed since this promise. In the kingdom of Judea there lived a couple, advanced in age and pleasing to God, named Joachim and Anna, of the house of David. Although faithful observers of the divine law, they had no children, and the priests despised them when, according to the law, they brought their offerings to the Temple. This brought them no small suffering. Nevertheless, they entrusted themselves entirely to God's will, and persevered in prayer.

The Lord of heaven, good and merciful, hearkened to the prayers of these holy spouses. He chose these saints to give birth to a holy daughter from whom the redeemer would come into this world. God sent a holy angel to announce to them the good news that they would give birth to a daughter more pleasing to God than all the things God has created, even more than the angels. The Lord of heaven chose to take flesh from her who is at the same time truly the mother of God and a virgin. Her name would be Mary.

After receiving this happy message, the spouses in their humility gave thanks to God with all their strength and they gave birth to a daughter, a flower of virginity, conceived, according to the teaching of many doctors, without the sin that Adam transmitted,[13] because God, who would come into the world to restore the human race, had chosen her as his mother before the ages. Thus was born to them the most blessed Mary, ever-virgin, the future mother of God. At the age of three, she was presented to God in the Temple by her pious parents, and when she arrived at the age of reason, she consecrated herself totally to God, even with the vow of perpetual virginity. She remained in the Temple with other virgins, outshining them in all kinds of virtues, and she stayed there until she was fourteen.

While other virgins at that age would be given in marriage, the Blessed Virgin was, by the will of God, entrusted to a very holy and noble man named Joseph, also of the house of David, although he was poor and was a carpenter by trade.

Before the Blessed Virgin conceived the Lord of heaven and gave birth to

---

13. The Immaculate Conception, defended by such theologians as Duns Scotus, did not become a dogma until 1854 when it was defined by Pius IX.

him, God gave her a husband as similar to her as possible, himself keeping perpetual virginity, so that he might be the guardian and the faithful witness to the virginity of his immaculate spouse. Another purpose was to prevent the Blessed Virgin, soon made pregnant by divine power, from being stoned to death by the Jews if she appeared pregnant without a husband. An additional reason was so that during the travels she would have to undertake abroad among the pagans, the Sovereign Lady[14] might be protected by her just husband. The final reason was so that the fact of her childbirth might be hidden from the devil who would be led to believe that it was that of a married woman, and not of a virgin.

The Blessed Virgin, brought to Nazareth by her holy husband Joseph, spent her days and nights in prayers, ceaselessly sending to heaven sighs and groanings, according to the customs of her ancestors, asking for the redeemer of the human race fallen into sin, all the more so because she knew, from the books of the prophets which she read continuously, that the time of the coming of our redemption was near.

THE ANNUNCIATION

One night, the Blessed Virgin happened to read the prophecy which said: "The Virgin will conceive and will bear a son called Emmanuel." Kindled with a desire to know and serve this virgin, she prayed to God with more vigor and fervor that God would deign to come.

The blessed angels in heaven also desired the same thing and implored God to redeem the human race. The merciful Lord of heaven, having thoughts of peace, decided to send the archangel Gabriel, one of the seven preeminent princes, to the Blessed Virgin Mary to announce to her that God had chosen her to be a helper in the realization of the mystery of the redemption of humanity.[15]

Since God the Father so loved the world that he decreed to give his only Son for the redemption of the world, the Son of God would take the human nature in a person in order to carry out this divine plan. The Blessed Virgin was chosen by the *Sanctissima Trindade* to be the true mother of God, and the only Son of God, true God, would have to take flesh from her flesh.

Saint Gabriel received with joy the mission he was assigned, and immediately flew from heaven to the little house of the Blessed Virgin Mary. He greeted her humbly, using the words he had received from the Lord of heaven: "Hail, full of *gratia,* the Lord is with you, blessed are you among women." Hearing this greeting full of such high praises, the Virgin Lady, full of humility, was afraid, and asked herself silently what the greeting meant. Then the angel answered her: "Lady Mary, do not be afraid, because you have found *gratia* with God

---

14. De Rhodes uses the title *Duc Chua Ba* (the noble lady sovereign) for Mary. Today, the shortened title (*Duc Ba*) is used. This last title was used for the principal wife of the king's son or for one of the king's wives.

15. The Latin text uses the word *mediatrix* whereas the Vietnamese text simply says: "to be a helper in the realization of the mystery of the redemption of humanity."

and are pleasing to God. You will conceive and bear a son to whom you will give the name of Jesus. He will be great and will be called Son of the Most High, and his reign will have no end."

At these words, the most wise Virgin became more afraid, and adducing the vow of virginity she had taken as a child, said: "How can this be, since I do not know a man?" The angel explained to her and affirmed that it would be the work of the *Spirito Sancto*, who far from taking away her virginity would strengthen it because, he said, "nothing is impossible with God." Indeed, it would not be appropriate that a virgin mother would give birth to anyone other than God; nor would it be appropriate that God would be born of anyone other than a virgin. Hearing these words, the Blessed Virgin, collecting herself in deepest humility, accepted God's gift of being chosen to be the mother of God and answered: "Behold, I am the handmaid of the Lord. May it be done to me according to your word."

INCARNATION OF THE SON OF GOD

At the very moment when the Blessed Virgin gave this answer which the whole human race hoped for, she conceived her Son by the power of the *Spiritu Sancto*. From her most pure blood and in her womb, the all-powerful Lord of heaven formed and shaped a most perfect little human body, and at the same time, God created a rational soul, most perfect, and endowed with all God's gifts. At the same instant, by the greatest miracle God has ever performed and should ever perform, this body and this soul were united by means of an indissoluble knot to the person of the Son of God.[16] At that same moment he is both true God and true man: true God because he is truly the only Son of God the Father and consubstantial to the Father, and true man because he is composed of a rational soul and human flesh and the true son of the Mother of God, the ever-virgin Mary.

Nevertheless, there is only one *Christo*,[17] because true God and true man subsist in the unique second Person, the son of God. At the first moment of its creation, the blessed soul of *Iesu Christo* was adorned with marvelous gifts thanks to the hypostatic union.[18] It immediately had a clear vision of God, much more perfect than that which the angelic spirits and all the saints are destined to possess. This blessed soul also had the knowledge of all future things and of many things that will never be. All these gifts belong to the perfection of this exceedingly holy soul.

---

16. The Latin text uses the expression *unio hypostatica*. The Vietnamese text uses a circumlocution: "an indissoluble knot of the body and soul to the person of the Son of God."

17. De Rhodes transliterates this word rather than translating it.

18. The Latin text uses *unio hypostatica*. De Rhodes uses another circumlocution: "because it has been united to the Son of the Lord of heaven."

Jesus the Redeemer

In the first instant of his creation, the Lord *Iesu Christo* knew that God the Father had established him as the redeemer of the human race. Immediately he offered himself to suffer death for the salvation of humanity, with all the attendant pains and shame. To this soul endowed with a clear vision of God was due a totally impassible body, much more than cold is due to water and heat to fire. But, because he had to suffer for us, he miraculously forbade these gifts to rebound from his already blessed soul upon his body, so as not to impede his painful passion and death for our sake.

Although the superior part of his soul was already blessed, in this first instant most holy Jesus began to taste in the lower part of his soul the bitter chalice of his passion. Indeed, at once he foresaw and had before the eyes of his mind not only what he would have to suffer during his life until his bitter death but also all the sins that have been committed since the beginning of the world and those which will be committed until the end of the world, offending the divine majesty most grievously. All these things, made present to the eyes of his most holy spirit, caused the greatest pain to his most loving heart.

Furthermore, Jesus saw the sufferings of all his faithful servants and of the martyrs who would be tortured by tyrants who persecute them out of hatred for the Lord of heaven as well as the almost infinite number of those who would fall into eternal death because they despise his holy love and merits.

How much these things pained the heart of the Lord Jesus even in his mother's womb, at the first instant of his incarnation, no mere creature can ever comprehend, just as no mere creature can ever comprehend the ardent love he had for God the Father whom humans offend with their impious sins as well as for people who will suffer so great evils both in body and soul.

The Visitation

The Lord Jesus, exercising his office of redeemer even in the womb of his virgin mother, urged his most holy mother to visit Saint Elizabeth, her cousin, already advanced in age but carrying in her womb John, who would later become the precursor of the Lord Jesus, but then still lying in the terrible darkness of the original sin transmitted by Adam. When the Virgin Mother, full of God, entered the house of Zachariah, and as soon as she greeted Elizabeth, John, though still enclosed in his mother's womb, leaped for joy. He recognized his redeemer God coming to him in the Virgin Mother's womb. Jesus at once delivered him from the stain of original sin, giving him at the first encounter his *gratia* and friendship. The blessed Virgin Mary, our Lady, remained with her cousin for three months, no doubt in order to help her because she was old and pregnant and to assist her in childbirth.

When the most holy Virgin returned home, it became clear that she was carrying in her womb the child she had conceived by the power of the *Spirito*

Sancto. Her holy husband Joseph was ignorant of the mystery, though he could not entertain any evil suspicion of the spouse whom he revered as most holy and for whom he had the greatest love and the deepest respect. Nevertheless, he feared that were he to remain with her, he would offend God and break the holy law. He decided to send her away secretly, though with the greatest pains, because there was so much resemblance between them in terms of behavior and virtues that their life together was purer than that of angels. This separation was extremely painful for him; nevertheless, sacrificing everything for the law of God, he was going to send his beloved spouse away.

As Saint Joseph was pondering over these thoughts, an angel appeared to him in a dream and chased the clouds away from his mind, unveiling to him all the mystery and saying to him on the part of God: "Joseph, son of David, do not be afraid to keep Mary your wife, because the child conceived in her womb came from the *Spirito Sancto.* She will bear a son and you are to name him Jesus, because he will save his people from their sins."

How much joy this happy and divine message brought to holy Joseph can be expressed only by the one who understands his immense love and respect for his most holy spouse. From that time on, such love and respect for her grew, all the more because Joseph regarded her not only as his beloved spouse, but also venerated her as the most holy Virgin Mother of God, considering himself unworthy to serve such a virgin and mother who one day will give birth to the Son of God.

THE BIRTH IN BETHLEHEM

During that time an edict was published by the emperor of Rome named Augustus Caesar ordering a census of the entire world under the rule of the Roman empire. This first census was carried out by Quirinius, governor of Syria, and everybody had to go to be enrolled, each in his or her own town. Saint Joseph went from Galilee, from his town of Nazareth, to Judea in the city of David called Bethlehem, because he was from the house and family of King David, to be enrolled with the most holy Virgin Mary, his wife made with child by the *Spirito Sancto.* Thus he showed an example of obedience even to secular princes, in legitimate matters.

While they were there, the time came for the Virgin Mother of God to have her child. She gave birth to her firstborn and only son; she wrapped him in swaddling clothes and laid him in a manger, because there was no room for them in the inn. Because they were poor and because many rich people had come to the same place to be enrolled, the most comfortable lodgings had been booked by the wealthy.

The Son of God was placed in a manger to teach us to despise the vanity of the world. While he was infinitely rich, he made himself poor, in order to enrich us with his infinite riches rather than with his poverty.

THE TRIPLE VIRGINITY OF MARY

Many miraculous things shone out at the birth of the Lord Jesus. First, he wanted to be born of a perpetual virgin who was at once virgin and mother. She was a virgin before giving birth to her son, a virgin while giving birth, and a virgin after giving birth. For the Son of God at his birth in the flesh did not destroy the integrity of his most holy mother but perfected it. Just as the ray of sunlight penetrates a crystal and illumines it without breaking it, so this divine ray, infinitely more brilliant than a ray of sunlight, coming out of his mother's womb, did not break the gateway of her virginity but perfected and confirmed it, because all-powerful God, creator of all things, had wanted to be born of a virgin mother without the seed of any man.

Just as at the beginning of the world, God commanded the earth to produce, without any seed, green grass, and so it happened, so also the all-powerful creator of all things and of all species ordered that the Virgin conceive without any seed and give birth to God his Son without damage to her virginal integrity. Thus, the most holy Mary Mother of God is a virgin before, during, and after parturition, and she who remained intact after parturition did not experience any pain during parturition. Furthermore, immediately after giving birth, she adored the one she had just brought into the world, because she gave birth to her progenitor and the first creator of all things.

ANGELS, SHEPHERDS, AND THE MAGI

The second miraculous event is that immediately after the birth of the Lord, the whole heavenly court, that is, all the blessed spirits, came down to the blessed manger. When they saw the divine infant wrapped in swaddling clothes and placed in the manger, they acknowledged him as their Lord and humbly worshiped him.

One of these blessed spirits announced this great joy to the shepherds who were keeping the night watch over their flocks. He told them that the savior of the world, the Lord *Christo,* had been born at Bethlehem, the city of David, and gave them this sign: "You will find an infant wrapped in swaddling clothes and lying in the manger." At the same time, a multitude of the heavenly host joined the angel; they began praising God, saying: "Glory to God in the highest, and peace on earth to people of good will." The shepherds went to Bethlehem and found what the angel had told them.

The third miracle at the time of our Lord Jesus Christ's birth was that a new star appeared to three kings in the East; by this star they came to know that the Lord Christ, the new king of the Jews, had been born. Upon their arrival in Jerusalem, the capital of the nation of Judea, all three of them, who were kings in the East, posed the question: "Where was the new king of Judea born whose star we had seen in the East?" To which the leaders of the priests replied:

"God was born in Bethlehem of Judea, so it was announced by God in the prophetic books."

When the three kings set out for Bethlehem, behold, the star which they had seen in the East preceded them and stopped over the place where the infant had just been born.

At the sight of the star, the kings rejoiced greatly, and on entering the house, they found the child God with Mary his mother. They prostrated themselves and adored him. Then they opened their treasures, kings as they were, and offered the newborn king of the Jews gold, incense, and myrrh: gold as offering to a king; incense to the true God; and myrrh, which preserves the body from putrefaction after death, to a mortal man.

OTHER MIRACULOUS EVENTS

At the same time, it is reported that Octavianus Augustus, the emperor of the Romans, saw a woman appear in the sun itself carrying her child in her arms. Augustus worshiped the child as if he acknowledged him as his Lord, and as long as he lived, he never dared call himself lord anymore.

We have told you above the story of the king of the Chinese who was warned in a dream to look for the true law in the Great West. This happened, I believe, at the time of the birth of the Lord Jesus Christ, the true lawgiver and only teacher.[19]

I will pass over other miraculous events that occurred on that day, such as the fountain of oil that flowed in Rome, the memory of which still exists today. It is also said that three suns were seen as well as other things which the supreme creator of the world and Lord of all things wanted to make in order to manifest his mercy, which he exercised in the midst of the earth by being born into the world. This God did in order to achieve the salvation of humanity so that all humans, abandoning their false and diabolical religions, might return to God to worship him with piety and adore him alone, visible in his human nature, though invisible in his divine essence.[20]

DEVOTION TO THE TRINITY AND TO MARY

At this point, we should show a beautiful image of the Blessed Virgin Mary carrying her infant son Jesus, our Lord, so that people may adore him humbly by bowing their heads to the ground. First, a triple adoration should be made to the three divine persons in the one divine essence, thus confessing the mystery of the divine Trinity by this external adoration. The knees should be bent only once, to confess the one divine essence. The head should be bowed to the

---

19. De Rhodes's chronology is quite off the mark, since Mingdi ruled from 58 to 77 C.E.

20. De Rhodes's predilection for the miraculous shows itself here as well as in his later narrative of Jesus' passion and death. The point of the miracles is to emphasize the fact the humble child Jesus is truly the Son of the Lord of heaven.

ground three times, demonstrating our adoration to the three divine persons, imploring each of them to forgive our sins. The head should be bowed to the ground once more to render reverence and adoration to the Lord Jesus Christ, man and mediator, humbly asking him to make us worthy to receive the fruits of his abundant redemption and to forgive all our sins.

Lastly, reverence should be shown to the Blessed Virgin by bowing the head to the ground once, though we know that the Blessed Virgin is not God, but because she is the mother of God, all-powerful over her son, we hope to obtain pardon for our sins through her holy intercession.[21]

THE CULT OF IMAGES

Here we should give the catechumens this warning: In former times, before the birth of God, as God was totally invisible, a cult without images was rendered to God. From the time he was made a visible man, was seen on earth, and has lived among humans, we represent God with images, paintings, sculptures, and so forth. But when we kneel, adore, or pray before the images of the Lord Jesus Christ or of the saints, our mind must be directed to the one who is represented by the image and adore or venerate the saint who is there represented.

---

21. The use of prostration in prayer is a wonderful example of how de Rhodes makes use of local customs to express Christian truths. At the same time it illustrates well the connection de Rhodes establishes between religious teaching and worship.

The Sixth Day

The Hidden Life and Public Ministry of Jesus

After having proposed for belief the ineffable mysteries of the one God in three persons and the divine incarnation, which exceed by far the ability of every created intellect, it is necessary now to see, according to our ability, why the Son of God, true God, has deigned to unite his human nature so intimately to his person,[1] so that the invisible and immortal Lord of heaven became truly visible and mortal.

THREE EVIL CONSEQUENCES OF THE FALL

There are three main evils that attack the human race as the result of the original sin: first, the inclination to evil; second, ignorance of the right path leading to eternal life; and third, the penalty of death, not only temporal but also eternal, which makes humans into eternal slaves of the devil in hell.

Against these three evils the Lord Jesus, true God and true man, who is also the heavenly doctor, wanted to bring three remedies. That is why on the eighth day after his birth, he took the most holy name of Jesus, not without shedding his blood, assuming thus the name and office of Savior.

This inclination to evil, by which we are as it were driven to vices, the Lord Jesus wanted to conquer by the virtues and examples of his holy life. During the thirty-three years he lived among humans and dealt with them, he showed us marvelous humility and obedience toward God his Father. To his Father's holy will he offered himself entirely when he was presented in the Temple by his holy mother. He was also submissive to his mother, the Blessed Virgin Mary, and to her husband, Saint Joseph, until he was thirty. For thirty years he wanted to be subjected to them even though he was the infinite Wisdom of God. He chose to be subjected to humans in order to give us during so many years a remarkable example of obedience and humility.

---

1. Again, the Latin text uses the expression *unio hypostatica* as the equivalent of the Vietnamese circumlocution of "binding the human nature intimately to the divine person."

The Child Jesus in the Temple

Once, however, when he was twelve, our Lord Jesus Christ, according to a particular disposition of the Eternal Father, remained in the Temple, without the knowledge of his parents, in order to teach people about the long-awaited Lord of heaven descending into the world to redeem humanity. Forty days after his holy birth, when he was presented in the Temple by his mother, according to the ritual God prescribed to the Jews, he had already been publicly acknowledged and announced by old Simeon, a holy man to whom the *Spiritu Sancto* had revealed that he would not die before having seen the *Christum Domini*,[2] that is, the Lord of heaven coming into the world to redeem sinners. This good old man took the child Jesus in his arms and gave thanks to God: "Now, Lord of heaven, you may let your servant die in peace, as you have said to me, because my eyes have seen the savior you have given us and have destined to be exposed to the sight of all peoples, to be the light shining on all nations and the glory of Israel, your people." He also foretold many other things that would happen to the child God.

However, the Lord Jesus himself wanted to show clearly to the Jewish masters[3] that the time of the long-awaited divine redeemer had arrived. Everyone, even the most wise among the Jews, was astonished by his teaching and his answers. Thus, they could easily, if they wanted, recognize him when the time of his manifestation came.

After three days his holy mother found him in the Temple among the teachers. His pious mother was looking for him with love and said: "My son, why have you done this to us?" The Lord Jesus replied: "Mother, why were you looking for me? Did you not know that I must do the things of my Father?" By his example the Lord Jesus showed us that we must follow the will of the heavenly Father, even if this demands that we withdraw from our parents according to the flesh.

Jesus' Submission to Mary and Joseph at Nazareth

Nevertheless, from that time until the thirty-third year of his holy life, he was so submissive to his blessed Virgin Mother and to her most holy husband Joseph that he was thought to be a carpenter apprentice to the latter till that age. Furthermore, he served them in domestic chores because he came not to be served but to serve. He deemed nothing contemptible and unworthy of his divine status, except sin. He therefore never did anything sinful, and no lie was ever found or could be found on his lips.

We must therefore imitate the Lord Jesus in not running away from or avoiding lowly occupations by means of excuses. Rather we must embrace them to

---

2. It is interesting that de Rhodes has not translated the word *Domini* as though *Christus Domini* forms one single title of Jesus.

3. De Rhodes uses the word *quan tu* (gentleman) to refer to the Jewish teachers of the law.

imitate the Lord Jesus more faithfully and to avoid laziness, the origin of all evil and sin. Let us shrink from all sins and lies as the vilest things unworthy of a person endowed with reason and made in the image of God. In this way we follow in the footsteps of the Lord Jesus who came in visible flesh to draw us to him by means of the cords of his charity and his sweetest love. He will break our chains and the bad inclination to evil we have acquired since our birth as a result of original sin.

Jesus' Preaching of the Law of Grace

To heal our ignorance, the second evil we suffer, the Lord Jesus, the divine doctor, at the age of thirty, began teaching what he had practiced. At the beginning of his preaching, to prepare people to receive the seed of his divine Word, he invited them to repent of their sins, saying: "Repent, the kingdom of God is near."

Saint John the Baptist, chosen to be the precursor of the Lord, bore witness to the Word of God and showed to the Jews Jesus Christ, true Son of God, and savior of the world. At the beginning of his preaching, he also exhorted people to repentance, saying: "Produce fruits worthy of penance."

Among the disciples the Lord Jesus had with him he chose twelve whom he called *Apostolo*[4] with whom he continually conversed, forming them in a special manner in order to leave them behind as teachers of the entire world.

The Lord Jesus himself proclaimed a law called *Evangelio*, that is, good news,[5] which does not abolish the old law given to the holy ancestors but perfects it. Indeed, three times did the sovereign author of all things give humans the holy law. First, when God impressed in human hearts the natural law so that they may immediately distinguish right from wrong, good from evil. Natural reason and the light of God's face are etched in our hearts so that if we do not walk on the right path we will be inexcusable, as the Lord said to Cain in former times: "If you have done well, will you not receive good things? But if you have done evil, your sin will be immediately at your door."

However, because the light of reason was badly darkened by sins, not only original but also personal, people could hardly distinguish false from true, wrong from right. Consequently, the Lord of heaven gave to Moses, his friend, and through him, to the Jewish people, the written law which contains the Ten Commandments or the decalogue of which we will speak later. It was the second publication of the divine law.

But because this carnal people, though they were not ignorant of the law of God, failed to keep it, the divine Teacher, Jesus Christ our Lord, came to promulgate himself the law of *gratia,* establishing friendship with us. With this law the holy Teacher and Lord not only taught us the way to eternal life but also

---

4. Elsewhere de Rhodes translates "apostles" with *day to ca,* literally, great servants. See *Cathechismus,* 177.

5. The Vietnamese word is *Tin lanh.* Today this expression is used to refer to Protestantism.

with *gratia* and the divine assistance which he merited, he gave us the necessary strength to keep it. That is why this law is called the law of *gratia*.

JESUS' MIRACLES

To lead people to believe his divine word, the Lord Jesus performed many miracles, confirming the holy law he taught. To the blind he restored sight; to the deaf, hearing; to the lame, straight walk; to the sick, health; and even to the dead, life. He also performed many other marvelous deeds during the three years in which he taught his doctrine. Thus he proved that he was a true man, living among men and women, and like a man, ate, drank, worked, and lived among us the human life he had assumed. Furthermore, he also proved that he was truly God, changing at will the natural laws of this world as the true Lord of all things.

THE TRANSFORMATION OF WATER INTO WINE AT THE WEDDING OF CANA

The first miracle that the Lord Jesus deigned to perform occurred at Cana in Galilee. Invited to a wedding with his mother, the holy Virgin Mary, and with his disciples, he saw that the guests would lack wine which was being served according to the customs of that country. The holy Virgin Mary warned him that they were running out of wine; she also told the servants to do whatever the Lord would order them. Though she seemed to have been rebuffed by her most loving son when he told her: "Woman, what is there between you and me?" she urged the servants to do whatever the Lord would tell them.

Then the most holy Lord Jesus ordered the jars to be filled with water. When the servants filled six rather big jars with water up to the brim, he ordered them to draw the water and serve it to the guests. Immediately, this water, on the order of the Lord, was changed into excellent wine, so much so that the guests were astonished, especially the headwaiter, who did not know where the wine came from. The servants, however, knew because it was they who had drawn the water. Seeing this miracle, the disciples of the Lord were confirmed in their faith, and they believed in him.

Because the Lord Jesus performed numerous miracles, preached the good news of the kingdom of heaven, and because he had the words of eternal life, all people hung on his divine words, so that everywhere he went a crowd followed to listen to him and to be healed of their sicknesses.

THE MIRACULOUS CATCH OF FISH

Once, when there was a large crowd on the shore, he climbed on the boat of Peter, the first of his disciples, to teach. Afterwards, he ordered Peter to put out into deep water to catch fish. Peter answered: "Master, we have worked hard

all night and have caught nothing. But at your command, I will lower the nets."
And soon he caught such a great number of fish that the nets were tearing. He
signaled to his companions on the other boats to come to help him, and the two
boats were filled with fish. Seeing this, Peter said to the Lord: "Depart from me,
Lord, for I am a sinful man." The catch of the fish filled him with astonishment.
But the Lord, full of goodness, said: "Do not be afraid, Peter, from now on you
will be catching people." When they had brought their boats to the shore, they
followed the Lord.

The Multiplication of Bread

Another time, a large crowd followed the Lord Jesus out of the cities into
the desert to listen to him. The hour was late and they had nothing to eat. The
merciful Lord said: "I have pity on the crowd, because they have nothing to eat;
if I send them away hungry, they will collapse on the way." He then asked his
disciples: "How many loaves do you have?" They answered: "There is a boy
here who has five loaves and two fish. But what good are these for so many?"
Nevertheless, the good Lord ordered everybody to sit down on the grass, and
giving thanks to the eternal Father, he divided the loaves and the fish, gave them
to his disciples who distributed them to the crowds. They all ate and were filled.
So that nothing would be lost, the Lord gave the order to collect the fragments,
and twelve baskets were filled with them. Those who ate were five thousand,
not counting women and children.

From these miracles we learn that to those who look for heavenly beatitude,
which is the kingdom of God and the virtues leading to it, there lacks nothing
that is necessary to maintain this life; rather there will be a superabundance of
it. The last miracle shows that almsgiving does not diminish but augments the
earthly resources. Before the alms were given to the crowd, there were only five
loaves and two fish, barely enough to fill a basket. After the almsgiving and
distribution, there were twelve baskets filled with fragments.

The Healing of a Hemorrhaging Woman

Another time the Lord Jesus was pressed around by the crowd who was
following him. Coming up behind him was a woman who was sick with a hemorrhage for twelve years and had spent all her possessions on doctors without
getting cured. She approached the Lord Jesus with great faith and touched the
tassel on his cloak. She said to herself: "If only I touch the tassel on his cloak,
I will be cured." At once, she was healed of her illness. Although the crowd
was pressing around him, the Lord Jesus looked for the one who had touched
him. In fact, he felt a power had come out of him that cured the woman who
came to him with faith. She confessed with trepidation that she had touched
him. But the Lord gently replied to her: "My daughter, have trust, your faith

has saved you." This story teaches us to come to the Lord with faith to be healed of our diseases.

THE RAISING OF THE DAUGHTER OF A SYNAGOGUE LEADER

At the same period, the daughter of a synagogue official, aged twelve, had died in her father's house. The Lord Jesus entered the house, took her hand, and said to her: "Little girl, arise." At once, the young girl got up as easily as if she had only slept. The Lord Jesus was the lord of life and death, and he could wake whomever he wanted from death as easily as from sleep.

THE RAISING OF THE SON OF A WIDOW AT NAIN

Thus, at the gate of the city of Nain, he raised from death a young man, the only son of his mother, whom people were carrying out for burial. As the Lord saw his mother, a widow, accompany her son in tears for the burial, together with a large crowd of the city, he was touched with pity and said to her: "Do not weep." Then he touched the coffin and said: "Young man, I tell you, arise!" At once, the dead man got up, sat, and began to speak. The Lord gave him back to his mother.

THE APOLOGETICAL VALUE OF MIRACLES

The Lord worked innumerable other miracles to prove the truth of his doctrine. He not only urged people to observe the divine law but also opened the way of the highest perfection, till then unknown to the world. But, above all, by his miracles he proved his divinity. Thus he revealed himself as the Lord of all things, in the air by commanding the winds, on the sea by calming the waves, among humans by healing innumerable diseases, sometimes by a mere contact, sometimes by a simple word. He also showed his power over the devils by calming them or by ordering them to leave the bodies of the possessed.

All that he did, not like some holy persons who in order to perform miracles must have recourse to prayers and fasting. On the contrary, the Lord Jesus performed miracles by his mere power, having dominion over all created things, without any need of prayer, though, to give us an example, he sometimes had recourse to it.[6]

Not only did the Lord work these miracles but he also gave his disciples the power to perform them, just as a sovereign king not only exercises power over his subjects but also communicates his power to the magistrates.

Furthermore, the Lord Jesus made his divinity plain by penetrating and discerning the intimate thoughts of people as if these were their faces. He de-

---

6. Clearly, for de Rhodes, miracles have the predominantly apologetic value of confirming Jesus' teaching and demonstrate his divinity. The function of miracles as signs of the rule of God is left unstressed.

nounced evil when it was still hidden in the hearts as easily as the external bad deed. His adversaries tried in vain to plot against him to entrap him in both his word and deed, but he eluded their schemes with greatest ease.

Among the Jews the Lord had many and very skillful enemies, because their works were evil. These were called *Scribae* and *Pharisaei*.[7] On the contrary, the Lord's teaching was just and can easily be taught to all, even the lowest class of the society, and its denunciations of sins are very clear. Many powerful people hated the light the Lord projected in the holiness of his life as well as in his admirable doctrine because they were charged with various sins. As a result, people venerated him and abandoned the *Pharisaei* to follow him. This increased the jealousy of the *Scribae* and *Pharisaei* who sought to destroy the Lord's reputation in front of people by means of calumnies under the guise of piety and religion.

MIRACLES ON THE SABBATH

The Lord was engaged in teaching the people, especially on the sabbath, and often the sick came to him to be healed on that day. The Lord Jesus took pity on them and performed many healings even on the sabbath. Thus, there was a woman who had been miserably bent with sickness by the devil for eighteen years and could not look upwards. The Lord had mercy on her and healed her on the sabbath. He also healed a man with a withered hand on the sabbath. Those who hated the Lord Jesus murmured against him and even got angry against those poor people who had come to be healed on the sabbath.

Under the pretext of religion they said: "There are six days when work is permitted; come on those days to be cured, not on the sabbath when work is forbidden." But the good and kind Lord rejected their sham piety and also in order to heal their spirits, said: "If your cattle and buffaloes[8] fall into a hole on the sabbath, won't you pull them out? And don't you untie them to lead them out for watering? Why do you get angry if I untie on the sabbath this daughter of Abraham whom Satan has bound for eighteen years?" As they could not reply, they were all the more consumed by jealousy. But the people rejoiced exceedingly for the great deeds he had done.

HEALING OF A PARALYTIC

There was in Jerusalem a pool with five porticoes where a large number of ill, blind, and infirm people lay, waiting for the water to stir. In fact, an angel of the Lord would come down from heaven and stir the water. The first person

---

7. Like his contemporaries, de Rhodes has a very negative opinion of the Pharisees and the Jews in general, here as well as in his account of Jesus' passion.

8. The Vietnamese expression is *trau bo*, literally, buffaloes and cattle, a nice reference to the Vietnamese custom of using buffaloes rather than cows and bulls to plow the field.

to come down into the pool after the stirring of the water would be healed immediately of whatever ailment he or she was afflicted with.

One day, out of goodness, the Lord Jesus visited this spot where the sick were. There he saw a paralytic who had been ill for thirty-eight years. The good Lord asked him: "Do you want to be well?" He answered: "Sir, I have no one to help me get into the water after it is stirred. Because I am paralyzed, someone else would reach the water before me, so I could not get healed for a long time." The merciful Lord Jesus, moved with pity, said to him: "Rise, take up your bed, and go home." Fortified by the life-giving words of the Lord, the poor man got well at once, stood up briskly, and with his strength regained, picked up his bed as the Lord commanded him, and walked home. Now that day was a sabbath.

Those evil men who were jealous of Jesus, seeing the man carry his bed on the sabbath, remonstrated with him bitterly for not observing the sabbath. Wishing to defend himself against the unjust reproaches, he said that he had received the order from the one who had healed him with his word. They asked him who was the man who did not observe the sabbath. But the man who had been healed did not know that it was the Lord himself, because once his deed was done, he vanished from the crowd. The Lord did not in fact seek his own glory. As a result, the man who had been cured did not identify Jesus to those who despised him.

Later the Lord met him and warned him not to sin anymore, lest something worse would happen to him, indicating thereby that bodily infirmities and pains befall us often because of our sins. Then the man who had been healed told the Jews that it was the Lord Jesus who cured him. This, by the instigation of the devil, made them all the more jealous of the Lord whom they should have venerated on account of his many wonderful miracles and virtues.

HEALING OF A MAN BORN BLIND

The Lord Jesus wanted to work another great miracle on the sabbath, and if they wished, those envious people could have recognized clearly the divine power in the Lord. But they were blinded by envy and jealousy. There was then a blind man by birth, well known to all. Seeing him, his disciples asked the Lord: "Who sinned, this man or his parents, that he was born blind?" With kindness, the Lord replied: "Neither he nor his parents sinned; it is so that the works of God might be made visible in him." Spitting on the ground, the Lord Jesus made clay, smeared it on the eyes of the man born blind, and ordered him to go wash in the Pool of Siloam (which means Sent). Obeying promptly, the blind man went there, washed, and at once recovered his sight.

Some people, noticing that the man they had known as blind could now see, were astonished. Others said that it was someone who looked like him, and not the man born blind. But the blind man said: "It's me, the man born blind!" They took him to the teachers of the Jews called the *Pharisaei*, who asked him whether he was born blind and how now he could see. The good blind man recounted faithfully what had happened to him, how the Lord Jesus had made clay, smeared it on his eyes, and ordered him to go wash his eyes in the Pool of Siloam. "I went there," he said, "I washed, and now I see."

These jealous men did not believe that he was born blind until they summoned his parents and asked them: "Is this man your son, was he born blind, and how is he now able to see?" His parents answered with candor: "Yes, he is indeed our son, and he was born blind." But because they were afraid of offending those teachers, they said: "But how he now can see, we do not know. Ask him yourself, since he is of age; he will tell you what has happened to him." They, therefore, recalled the man who had been blind and said to him, "Give God the praise. We know that this man is a sinner," in an attempt to ruin the Lord's reputation with lies. But the man who had been blind replied: "Whether he is a sinner, I do not know. One thing I do know is that I was blind and now I see." They said to him: "What has he done? How did he open your eyes?" He answered them: "I told you already and you have heard me. Do you want to hear the story again? Do you want to be his disciples too?"

Then the *Pharisaei* cursed him and said: "You are his disciple, we are the disciples of Moses. We know that God spoke to Moses, but we do not know where that man is from." The man answered them: "This is what is so amazing, that you do not know where he is from, yet he opened people's eyes. We know that God does not listen to sinners but to those who honor God and do God's will. It is unheard of that anyone ever opened the eyes of a person born blind. If this man were not from God, he would not be able to do anything." They answered and said to him, blaming him for pride: "You were born totally in sin, and you want to teach us!" Then they threw him out. They could not refute the clear argument by which he demonstrated that from such a remarkable miracle it must be deduced that the Lord Jesus came from God. They did not want to confess this truth because of their excessive blindness and unheard-of jealousy.

When the good Lord Jesus learned that they had thrown him out, he found him and said: "Do you believe in the Son of God?" He answered: "Who is he, Lord, that I may believe in him?" "You have seen him, and the one speaking with you is he." Then he said: "I do believe, Lord," and falling to his feet, worshiped him. Jesus said: "I came into this world for judgment, so that those who do not see might see, and those who see might become blind."

Indeed, those who, humbly acknowledging their ignorance, submit themselves to the divine will, God will enlighten and help to walk in the way of the commandments so as to reach enlightenment and eternal life. Those who in their pride rely on their own wisdom and refuse to accept the Word of God, will fall into many sins; they become blind and finally fall into the precipice of eternal death. Thus, the *Pharisaei,* impious and proud as they were, refusing to accept the light of the Lord Jesus manifested by so many great miracles, became blind and finally fell into the ruin of eternal damnation.

The *Pharisaei* and the *Scribae* sought ways to kill the Lord Jesus, but the time which the Lord Jesus had established to give his life for our salvation had not yet arrived. He worked such miracles as manifested his divinity clearly, but they did not prevent his most holy passion from happening which he desired ardently.

He returned therefore from Judea to Galilee so that his time might be fulfilled. Every day he taught his doctrine with increasing clarity, moving through towns and villages, and worked innumerable miracles.

THE TRANSFIGURATION

He also wanted to show to some of his disciples a little of his glory. On his way up a mountain called Tabor, he allowed only three of his disciples whom he loved the most to accompany him. Then he was transfigured in front of them. His face shone like the sun and his clothes became white as snow. Moses and Elijah appeared and conversed with him about the death he was going to suffer in Jerusalem. Peter, one of the disciples, seeing the glory of the Lord Jesus, cried out with joy, "It is good that we are here," and at once, the voice of the Lord of heaven was heard among the clouds: "This is my beloved Son, with whom I am well pleased; listen to him."

When the disciples heard this voice, they were very much afraid and fell prostrate. When the Lord bade them to arise, they saw no one else but Jesus alone who ordered them not to tell anyone about this vision until the Lord has been raised from the dead. He did not want anything to prevent his passion which he ardently desired for our salvation. Furthermore, he severely rebuked Peter, his beloved disciple, who tried to dissuade him from accepting suffering and death.

THE RAISING OF LAZARUS

When the time came which the Lord Jesus had decreed to die for our salvation, he returned to Judea. The occasion was that Lazarus, an important personage and a dear friend of the Lord's, had died during his absence. He decided to raise him from the dead, though he had been in the tomb for four days, so that his enemies would be totally inexcusable if, having seen and heard about such a miracle, they still would not believe in him.

When the Lord arrived, Mary and Martha, the sisters of Lazarus, were weeping and said: "Lord, if you had been here, our brother would not have died." Weeping with them, the Lord went to the tomb. When the tomb was opened, there was a stench. Both his sisters and many other Jews who had come to comfort the sisters were there. Some of them said: "Could not the one who opened the eyes of the blind man have done something so that this man would not have died?"

Then, the Lord Jesus lifted his eyes to heaven and said: "Father, I thank you for hearing me. I know that you always hear me, but because of the crowd here I have said this, that they believe that you sent me." After he had said this, he cried out in a loud voice: "Lazarus, come out!" At once the dead man came out, his hands and feet tied with burial bands and his face covered with a cloth. Jesus told them: "Untie him and let him go." Many of the Jews who had come to console his sisters Martha and Mary and who had witnessed what Jesus had done, believed in him.

PLOT TO KILL JESUS

After such a great miracle as the resurrection of Lazarus, who had been dead for four days, performed by the Lord Jesus, it would stand to reason that his enemies would convert to the Lord. But the priests and the *Pharisaei,* hearing about such an evident sign of his divinity, gathered together and said: "What are we going to do? This man is performing many signs. If we leave him alone, all will believe in him, and the Romans will come and destroy our city and our nation." One of them, Caiaphas, who was high priest that year, said to them: "You know nothing, nor do you consider that it is better that one man should die instead of the people, so that the whole nation may not perish." He did not say this on his own, but since he was high priest for that year, he prophesied that the Lord Jesus was going to die for the nation, and not only for the nation, but also to gather into one the dispersed children of God.

From that day on, they plotted to kill Jesus. Jesus, waiting for his day of triumph, no longer walked about in public among the Jews. Rather he withdrew to the region near the desert, to a town called Ephraim, and there he remained with his disciples, waiting for the solemn day of Passover which had been fixed for his passion.

And as the enemies of the Lord saw that many of the Jews had come to believe in Jesus because of Lazarus whom the Lord had so marvelously raised from the dead, they plotted to kill Lazarus too. Their blindness and malice had reached such a point that they thought that by killing him they could take away from the Lord the power to raise him a second time from the dead.

Meanwhile let us detest the hard-heartedness of the Jews, let us adore the Lord, and let us embrace ardently in our minds his divine teaching in order to be enlightened now, and to obtain eternal life later.

The Seventh Day

*The Passion, Death, Resurrection, and Ascension of Jesus –
Pentecost and the Church*

JESUS' TRIUMPHANT ENTRANCE INTO JERUSALEM

When the time fixed by the Lord of heaven came for the only Son of God,
the Lord Jesus, to suffer the most painful death for our salvation in order to
show how fully and freely he executed his Father's command, he wanted to
make a triumphant entry into the city of Jerusalem where he had to suffer most
painfully. As Jesus made his entry, the whole city turned out. The Jews spread
palm branches and even their clothes along the roads Jesus was passing, ac-
claiming him king of Israel and saying: "Blessed is he who comes in the name
of the Lord!" In great state the Lord was brought to the Temple, to the deepest
distress for the *Scribae* and the *Pharisaei* who during this time were plotting his
death, and by engaging in this crime, were serving the most holy Redeemer.

JUDAS'S BETRAYAL

Impious Judas, the son of perdition, who was a thief and could not steal
from the perfumed oil which Mary Magdalene had poured on the head of the
reclining Lord, in order to recoup what he thought he had lost, agreed to deliver
his own Master and Lord to his enemies if they would pay him thirty pieces of
silver, the equivalent of our nine or ten pieces of gold. He would betray the
Lord quietly, without the presence of the crowds. But how could he hide this
from the Lord who knew everything?

THE LAST SUPPER

In the course of the last supper, which he wanted to eat with his disciples, on
the eve of his passion, the Lord washed the feet of everybody, including those
of Judas himself, the traitor. In so doing he showed him the treason he was
plotting in order to turn him away from such an enormous crime. But Judas's

hardened heart despised all the warnings and rushed headlong to his perdition. The devil was already the master of his heart, and he went out.[1]

Jesus' Agony and Capture

The good Lord, after consoling his disciples upon whom he showered numerous and unusual marks of affection during the last supper, left for the place where he knew Judas would soon arrive with soldiers to arrest him. While waiting, the Lord Jesus was so anguished that he sweated blood so abundantly that it ran on the ground. He thus showed us the agony he suffered because of our sins, and how much we should be smitten with sorrow and pain for our sins, when the afflictions of the Lord Jesus for the sins of others were so violent.

When Judas arrived at the head of the impious band of people, he dared to kiss the Lord with his sacrilegious lips. But the good Lord did not refuse his kiss and said: "My friend, why did you come here? Judas, by a kiss, you deliver the Son of Man." But the impudent fellow returned to his henchmen to whom he had given a signal: "The man I shall kiss is the one; arrest him and lead him away with care."

However, if the Lord had not freely delivered himself, no created force would have been able to hold him. The Lord Jesus walked toward his enemies and said: "Whom are you looking for?" They replied: "Jesus the Nazarean." Jesus told them: "It is I." As soon as the Lord Jesus had pronounced these words, all the Lord's enemies fell backwards. They would not have been able to get up had not the good Lord asked them again whom they were looking for and allowed them to stand up. And they would not have been able to arrest him had he not delivered himself to them, forbidding them to touch any of his disciples.[2]

Saint Peter, upon seeing these godless men throw themselves on the Lord as ferocious wolves on a sweet little lamb, could not bear the sight. He drew out his sword, struck one of them, and cut one of his ears. The good Lord forbade Saint Peter to use the sword, made him put it back in its scabbard, and said to the ungodly men who had already seized him: "Wait a moment!" He then healed the ear of the impious man, returning good for evil. After they had seized him, they still could not hold him, since he did not let himself be held until he had healed the ear. Once he had healed it just by touching, he gave himself up again to them and said: "Now is your hour and that of the power of darkness."

Jesus before Caiaphas

After arresting the Lord Jesus, they brought him to the high priest named Caiaphas. It was he who had counseled the Jews to kill the Lord. Caiaphas

---

1. It is noteworthy that in his account of the Last Supper, de Rhodes did not mention the institution of the Eucharist. The reason may be that he is following the Johannine Gospel exclusively.

2. To soften the scandal of the death of the Son of God, de Rhodes recommends that catechesis highlights the freedom with which Jesus accepted his death.

questioned the Lord on his teaching and his disciples. The Lord answered him with deepest humility and sincerity: "Why do you question me? I have spoken publicly in the synagogues. Question those who have heard me." When the Lord had given this wise answer, one of the servants, with great impiety, lifted his arm to slap the Lord, saying: "Is this the way you answer the high priest?"

But the exceedingly good Lord, bearing this injury with great gentleness, did not want to keep silent lest he appeared to have lacked respect for the high priest. He answered with greatest humility: "If I have spoken wrongly, show me what I have said wrongly; but if I have spoken rightly, why do you strike me?"

Many false witnesses testified against the Lord Jesus, but their testimonies do not agree with one another. The purity of the Lord's life as well as his innocence were so great, so well known to all, that his adversaries could not accuse him of anything containing even a shadow of sin.

Very early the next morning they brought Jesus to their council. The high priest by the name of Caiaphas said to him: "I beseech you, by the living God: tell us if you are the *Christo,* the Son of the Blessed God!" The Lord Jesus answered clearly that he was the *Christo,* the Son of the living God, whom they would see at the end of the world come with great majesty on the clouds of heaven. At once, the godless high priest accused the most holy Lord, whom he should have venerated as his true Lord, of blasphemy. Feigning sorrow, he tore his robes and declared with utmost impiety that the author of all life deserved death, and all the others, birds of a feather, concurred in the death sentence.

JESUS BEFORE PILATE AND HEROD

With common agreement they brought the innocent Lord as someone deserving death to the governor of the kingdom, Pontius Pilate, who administered the kingdom of the Jews in the place of the Roman emperor.

Pilate knew very well that the Lord had not done anything wrong and that he had been delivered to him out of envy; so he tried different ways to free him from an unjust death. He handed the case over to Herod to rid himself of it. As Herod sent the Lord Jesus back to him, Pilate proposed to the crowd that the Lord, rather than Barabbas, a criminal, be freed. Pilate proposed to the crowd to release Barabbas with the hope that they would refuse him, the criminal, and choose instead Jesus, the innocent, and in this way save the Lord Jesus from death. But instigated by the evil priests, the inept Jewish crowd, who had received from the Lord so many good things and who just a few days earlier had acclaimed him king of the Jews, now preferred the criminal homicide Barabbas and demanded atrocious death on the cross for the innocent Lord.

FLAGELLATION OF JESUS AND HIS CROWNING WITH THORNS

Pilate attempted another barbarous way to save the Lord from death. With much cruelty he delivered the Lord to the soldiers to be whipped, hoping to satisfy the godless Jews and make them renounce their demand for the Lord's death. The soldiers carried out the flogging with extreme cruelty. The Jewish custom for flagellation was not to go over and even not to reach forty lashes. But in the Lord's case, they multiplied them atrociously, up to more than five thousand. Had the Lord not borne this flagellation with divine strength and had he not miraculously prevented his death, without doubt he would have ended his life under these atrocious lashes. He wanted, however, to suffer all that because of our innumerable sins.

Like wild beasts, the soldiers were not satisfied with this savagery against the Lord Jesus, an innocent lamb. Instigated by the devil, they concocted another invention. They took very long and sharp thorns, wove them into a crown, and placed it on the Lord's head. These thorns caused seventy-two wounds on his divine head. Then the godless soldiers took an old scarlet cloak, wrapped it around the Lord, put a reed in his hand, and then, kneeling before him, mocked him, saying: "Hail, King of the Jews!" They spat on him and struck his divine head with the reed, causing these sharp thorns to pierce it, so that the most gentle Lord suffered both a pain and an insult to which nothing can be compared.

Seeing the Lord Jesus in such a miserable state, Pilate thought that the sight of him would pacify his enemies. He made the Lord come out, wearing the crown of thorns and the red cloak, and said, "Behold, the man," that is, here is the man who you say pretends to be your king, in so miserable a condition that he does not look even human. But the Jews, ever violent against the Lord and more cruel than wild beasts, demanded with more vigor that he be crucified.

Pilate saw that he had nothing more to do for these evil people, and as the crowd got more agitated, he washed his hands in the sight of the crowd, saying: "I am innocent of this man's blood. Look to it yourselves." The Jews shouted: "His blood be upon us and upon our children." Pilate's wife sent him a message: "Have nothing to do with that righteous man. I suffered much in a dream today because of him." That is why Pilate was looking for a way of wresting the Lord Jesus away from the rage of the Jews and from death.

The Jews understood what Pilate was trying to do, and to bend the judge away from righteousness, they threatened him with the anger of Caesar, saying: "If you release him, you are not a friend of Caesar; everyone who makes himself a king, opposes Caesar." These words carried such a weight with the unjust judge that he sided with the Jews. At once he delivered the innocent Lord to their will, like a sweet little lamb to the rage of cruel wolves.

JESUS CARRYING THE CROSS

The Lord Jesus did not want to say even a word in defense of himself so as not to prevent in any way his passion and death which he would suffer according to the will of his eternal Father. Although the governor admired this silence and was convinced of the innocence of the Lord Jesus, nevertheless he committed a gross injustice by delivering him to his enemies to be put to death. They stripped the scarlet cloak off the Lord Jesus and made him put his clothes back on so that everybody could recognize him on his way toward the place of punishment.

Then they placed a heavy *crux*[3] on the Lord's shoulders, already torn by the recent atrocious flogging, so that he would have to climb, thus loaded, up to the mount of Calvary where he would be crucified.

When they saw the Lord Jesus about to succumb under the heavy *crux*, and fearing that the Lord might die on the way before being nailed to the *crux*, they took hold of a certain Simon, a Cyrenean, who was passing by, and made him help the Lord carry the *crux*.

On this mournful road, as the Lord Jesus was walking filled with anguish, covered with sweat and blood because of the crown of thorns he was wearing on his head, a certain pious woman, named Veronica, took pity on him, fetched a cloth, folded it in two, and cleaned his divine face. At once, the suffering face of the Lord appeared miraculously on the two halves of the cloth, one of which has been piously kept in the greatest church in Rome and the other in Genoa until this day. Clearly it was a divine miracle, both because the image is more lifelike than any painter could have produced and because the face of the Lord was not painted on the cloth with any colors except that of the cloth itself.

THE CRUCIFIXION

When the Lord Jesus reached the mount of Calvary, outside of the gate of Jerusalem, they stripped him of his clothes. It is said that at this place of Calvary the head of Adam, the first father of the human race, was buried. It was there that our Lord Jesus Christ, Son of God, true God and innocent man, at the age of thirty-three and three months, at noon on the twenty-fifth day of March, was nailed hands and feet to the *crux*, was lifted on, and died for our sins. Thus was fulfilled the prophetic word of David, pronounced a thousand years earlier: "They have pierced my hands and my feet. They have counted all my bones."

The Lord Jesus, subjected to such insults, not only did not rebel and take revenge on his enemies, as he had the power, but also prayed for them to God his Father, saying: "Father, forgive them, because they know not what they do."

In ancient times, Isaiah, under the prophetic influence of the *Spirito Sancto*, foreseeing the crucifixion of the Lord, said in chapter 53: "He has neither form nor beauty. We have seen him despised, the last of humans, knowing infirmities, and his face was as though hidden. Truly, he has borne our sicknesses and he has carried our sufferings, and we ourselves looked upon him like a leper, smitten by God and humiliated. But he was wounded because of our iniquities, he was crushed because of our crimes, upon him was the chastisement that brought

---

3. For unknown reasons de Rhodes did not translate this word, which he could have easily done. Contemporary Vietnamese uses *thanh gia* (holy cross) and the Sino-Vietnamese *thap gia* (the Chinese character for the number ten in the form of the cross).

us peace, and by his stripes we were healed. Like a lamb led to the slaughter or like a sheep before the shearers, he was silent and opened not his mouth. And he was counted among the criminals. He himself carried the sins of many and he prayed for transgressors."

THE GOOD THIEF

In order that this prophecy be fulfilled, the Lord wanted to be crucified between two thieves, one on his right, the other on his left. That one on his left blasphemed against him, saying: "If you are the Christ, save yourself and us!" The other on his right, named Dismas, rebuked his companion: "Have you no fear of God, you who are condemned to the same punishment? And indeed, we have been condemned justly, for we received the sentence we deserved; but this man has done nothing wrong." Then turning to Jesus, he said: "Lord, remember me when you come into your kingdom." The Lord replied to him with great kindness: "Today you will be with me in paradise."

Pilate had an inscription written in *Hebreo, Greco, Latino* which read: "Jesus of Nazareth, the King of the Jews." The Jews did not like this inscription, which indicated the cause of the Lord's death. They wanted the inscription to read: "He said: 'I am the King of the Jews'." But because the Lord of heaven had ordained this inscription, he did not permit the least modification to be made, and therefore, although the Jews applied much pressure, Pilate replied: "What I have written, I have written."

The soldiers who crucified the Lord Jesus divided his clothes among themselves. When they took his tunic, which was seamless, they said: "Let us not tear it, but cast lots for it to see whose it will be." This seamless tunic has been preserved at Trier until this day. According to the tradition of this city, this seamless tunic was made by the Virgin Mother for the Lord Jesus when he was still a child. He wore it all the time so that it grew little by little to fit his size.

MIRACLES AT THE SIXTH HOUR

At the sixth hour, darkness came over the whole earth until the ninth hour. To understand the greatness of this miracle, it is necessary to note that the sun never undergoes an eclipse if the moon is not located between the earth and it. By being in-between, the moon prevents the rays of the sun from reaching us. That is why a solar eclipse happens only with the new moon, that is, on the thirtieth or the first day of the month. At full moon, the earth is between the sun and the moon diametrically opposite to each other. Then the moon cannot prevent the rays of the sun from reaching the earth. Because the Lord Jesus was nailed to the *crux* during the Passover celebrations, which took place only at full moon, it was by a divine miracle that a solar eclipse occurred. At this moment, the moon found itself opposite to the meridian line of the sun and was hidden by the earth. It suddenly turned, moved up to the meridian line of the sun and immediately came to a standstill under the sun, and eclipsed it, not only for certain regions as was normal, but for the entire world. Thus dense darkness was everywhere, which never would happen again.[4]

The eclipse lasted for three full hours, as long as the Savior was suffering alive on the *crux,* as if the lights of heaven, though inanimate, were ashamed of shining on such a crime of the Jews and such a humiliation of the Son of God, creator of all things.

When Dionysius, a pagan gentleman and a famous mathematician, saw at Hieropolis in Egypt this unheard-of miracle since the beginning of the world, he cried out, struck by the strangeness of the event: "Either the God of nature suffers or the machine of nature is out of order." When several years later, in Athens, he heard Paul, one of the apostles of the Lord, speak of the Christian way, of the passion of the Lord Jesus, and of the miracles accompanying it, in particular of this strange solar eclipse, Dionysius realized that it had happened on the day and at the hour of the eclipse he observed at Hieropolis. Thereupon he embraced the Christian truth which he received from Saint Paul himself.

THE DEATH OF JESUS

At the ninth hour, the Lord Jesus cried out: "Father, into your hands I commend my spirit." Then, bowing his head, he breathed his last. To these men endowed with reason but godless and enraged against the Lord of all things, inanimate creatures, at least, showed at the hour of his death signs of affliction and mourning. The veil of the Temple was torn in two from top to bottom; the earth was shaken; and it is said that in many countries, more than one city was swallowed up by the earth. Rocks were split: it is reported that even today many large fissures from top to bottom can be seen not only on Mount Calvary but also in many other places, in particular in Tuscany, a province of Italy, on Mount Alverna, and on Promontory Gaieta in Campania. Tombs were opened, and many saints were raised from the dead.[5]

At the foot of the *crux* of the Lord Jesus stood his deeply anguished mother, the Virgin Mary. She witnessed all this, her soul so afflicted with incredible pain at the death of her only and beloved son that she was almost lifeless.

Then the cruel soldiers came to break the legs of the two thieves. But when they came to the Lord Jesus, seeing that he was already dead, they did not break his legs, so that the Scripture which says, "Not a bone of him will be broken," might be fulfilled.

One of the soldiers, however, thrust his lance into Jesus' side, and immediately blood and water flowed out, some of which touched his eyes. Saint Gregory of Nazianzus wrote that till then his eyes were bleary and almost blind;

---

4. De Rhodes puts to good use his astronomical knowledge, not only here but also on many other occasions during his mission in Vietnam.

5. De Rhodes's heavy use of the miraculous elements to prove the divinity of Jesus is again evident throughout his narrative of Jesus' passion and death.

at once he recovered the sight of both body and soul. Acknowledging the Lord, whom he had pierced with his lance with such impiety, he was struck with a deep sorrow, begged for forgiveness, and obtained such a pardon that he later became a saint. The centurion, hearing the Lord's loud cry as he breathed his last, said: "Truly this man was the Son of God!" The crowd who was there, at the sight of the earthquake and of everything that had happened, went away in repentance, beating their breasts.

DEVOTION TO THE CRUCIFIED JESUS

At this point it would be appropriate to display some beautiful representation of the Lord Christ on the *crux*, if possible with candles and incense, and to address those present with the following words or words to this effect:

You who are present here, lift the eyes of your spirit and contemplate the Lord Jesus Christ nailed to the *crux* and lifeless, as if before your very eyes. He is the one the Lord of heaven has promised who would reopen the doors of paradise which had been closed in former times by our first parents.

He is the one whose coming as the redeemer of the human race the Lord of heaven announced to the patriarchs and prophets. He is the one who, though by nature impassible God, wanted to become for us passible man, who, after showing us the way of eternal salvation and confirming with greatest miracles the doctrine he preached, opened for us the way to eternal life, offering his Father satisfaction for our sins by shedding his blood and accepting his ignominious death. He is the unique redeemer and savior of humanity, without whose assistance no one can gain the salvation of his soul.

That is why we desire that he be known by all and we preach him to all people as long as our strength allows us. And you, therefore, if you have any understanding and if you have not been deaf to what we have been saying so far, recognize the immense goodness of your redeemer. Though needing nothing from humans, he has given himself up for our salvation, he the true Lord of heaven and earth. In order to redeem his ungrateful servants, he wanted to suffer pains, torments, shame, and atrocious punishment.

Look at the Lord of heaven, your redeemer, hung upon the *crux* for your sake, all his members torn. Consider his innocent hands, which had worked so many miracles, streaming with blood; see his holy feet, which were exhausted in search for your eternal salvation, pierced by horrible nails. Observe the divine side pierced by the cruel lance; look at this supremely elegant face covered with blood and spit, and gaze upon this forehead one time so serene and now bloodied by a crown of thorns.

Consider this most noble prince, in the prime of life, his head bowed, wasted by you in a most ignominious death. And since you can give nothing in exchange for so many benefits, at least acknowledge his immense love for you, shed tears from the bottom of your heart, show your compassion and gratitude toward him.

Look, even those who persecuted him were saddened by his death and beat their breasts; the dead rose to suffer with the dying Jesus; even inanimate things gave unusual signs of sorrow at the demise of the Lord.

And you who are endowed with reason, you for whom the Savior was hung on the tree, will you be as hard as iron, and not burst into tears and groanings? Will you not be inflamed by love and gratitude for such a great love? Speak thus to the good Lord, loving Savior, who was hung on the *crux* for your sake: "Hail, my King and my good Savior! You alone pitied my errors, obeying your eternal Father till death, and death on the *crux*. I give you thanks with all my strength, and yet so little, for your so many exhausting labors and sufferings for my salvation. With all my heart I am sorry for having until now, godless and ungrateful, offended your infinite majesty; I am sorry for not having until now served you as I should; from the bottom of my heart I am sorry for having obeyed your enemies.

"Would that I had never offended you, O my most beloved Lord, but because the past is no longer in my power, I am firmly resolved to serve you in the future with all my heart and obey your commandments with all my strength until I depart from this world. I also renounce all the vain idols and all the diabolical religions I have foolishly adhered to till now; and you, my true God, who suffered and died on the *crux*, I adore you and bless you for ever and ever. Amen."

DESCENT INTO HELL

When the Lord Christ died on the *crux*, of course not as God but as man, his most holy soul was separated from his body. But both his soul and his body remained united to the divine person of the Son, since the Son of God never left that which he had assumed. As the one who draws the sword out of the scabbard holds in his right hand the sword and in his left hand the scabbard, so the second divine person, the person of Jesus Christ, withdrawing his soul from his body, kept both his most holy soul and his most holy body hypostatically united, without ever losing them.

But at his death, as his body was still hung on the *crux*, his blessed soul descended into hell.[6] Now there are four regions in hell. The lowest of all is that of the devil and his angels. In this region are the eternal fire and eternal torments with which the demons and the souls of the damned are punished; the

---

6. De Rhodes translates "hell" with the Sino-Vietnamese word *dia nguc*, literally, the prison of the earth.

worms that eat their entrails will never die, and the fires that burn them will never be extinguished.

Above this region are the fires of purgatory where the souls of the just who have not yet fully expiated for their forgiven sins in this life are purified.[7] The third is the prison for children who depart from this life with original sin; they are enclosed in darkness without suffering the pains of fire or other torments; they have committed no actual sin but have only the original sin contracted through Adam. The fourth region is called *limbo*, that is, the prison where the souls of all the just from the creation of the world until the most precious death of the Lord Jesus were detained. Though they were free from sin, they were in this subterranean place as if in detention until our Savior, the Lord Jesus Christ, fully satisfied for all the sins by his most precious death and by his divine blood.

The most holy soul of our Lord Jesus, as soon as it was separated from its body, descended into this fourth region of hell, the highest; it went there, surrounded by the army of angels. His most holy soul was, as we have said, united to its divinity; therefore, when it penetrated into the *limbo*, not only did it fill it with heavenly light and incredible joy, but also, lifting up all the just who were there to the blessed vision of divinity, it gave them at that moment the happiness and glory of paradise. That is what happened to the soul of the good thief arriving there a little later, according to the promise the Lord Jesus had given him on the *crux:* "Today you will be with me in paradise." This region of hell, then, began to be paradise.

THE BURIAL

The holy body of the Lord Jesus was still hung on the *crux,* separated from his soul but not from his divinity. When evening came, one of the disciples of our Lord Jesus, by the name of Joseph, chief of a ten-man guard, asked Pilate for Jesus' sacred body. He removed it from the *crux* in the presence of the Virgin Mother, other pious women, and one or two disciples of the Lord Jesus. He wrapped it in a shroud and laid it in his own tomb, still new, which had been hewn out of a rock and in which no one had yet been buried. Then he rolled a huge stone in front of the tomb.

Next, those who were learned in the law assembled before Pilate and said: "Sir, we recall that this seducer, when still alive, had said: 'After three days I will rise up.' Give orders, then, that the grave be secured until the third day, lest his disciples come and steal him and say to the people: 'He has been raised from the dead'." Pilate replied: "You have your own guard; go guard it as best as you can." So they went, closed the tomb securely, fixed a seal upon it, and set the guard.

---

7. For "purgatory" de Rhodes uses *lua giai toi,* literally, fire that absolves sins.

THE RESURRECTION

On the third day after the holy death of the Lord Jesus Christ (the day on which the Lord had often foretold that he would rise from the dead), when dawn had just begun, his most holy soul, surrounded by the souls of the just who had been released from the prison of the *limbo* and by a great number of angels, approached the tomb and reunited with his most holy body, raising it immediately, glorious and impassible.

He who had raised others back to life by his mere word and by his order, could he not raise himself from the dead by his divine power? He did so by the greatest of miracles, so easily that it rather seemed he had awakened from sleep. Upon his resurrection, he came out of the tomb, the stone that had been placed at the door of the tomb remaining unmoved and the seal intact. Perhaps the guards had seen the miracle and were dazed. At once, there was a big earthquake. Indeed, the angel of the Lord, whose apparition was like lightning, came down from heaven and testified that the Lord Jesus Christ had been raised. The guards were so terrified that they fell back like dead men.

Some of them then informed the scholars of the law and the *Pharisaei* of all that had happened. These took counsel with the leaders of the Jews and gave the guards a large sum of money, telling them: "You are to say: 'While we were asleep, his disciples came by night and stole him'." Some of the guards took the money and did as they had been told.

However, Longinus, who had been led by the miracles accompanying the death of the Lord Christ to recognize his divinity and whose faith had been confirmed by his miracle-filled resurrection, could not be seduced by the *Pharisaei*. Despite their shouts, retorts, and even death threats, Longinus preached the resurrection of the Lord Christ and his divinity, converted many people to the faith, and as a result, suffered death and received the crown of martyrdom.

THE APPARITIONS

The Lord Jesus raised from the dead appeared in all his glory first of all to the Virgin his mother who had been crushed by unspeakable sorrows at the atrocious death of her only and beloved son. He gladdened her with a heavenly consolation proportionate to her sorrows. Then he sent the angels to bear witness to his true resurrection as he had foretold.

Lastly, during forty days, he appeared risen to his apostles as well as to other disciples. He appeared to them in groups of two, ten, or more than five hundred, who were eyewitnesses to the resurrection of the Lord Jesus Christ, with the highest and irrefutable authority. Indeed, their authority was confirmed by the Lord of heaven, both with the great holiness of their lives and with their great miracles, in order to confirm the faith, especially the faith in the resurrection of the Lord Christ. Furthermore, almost all of them became martyrs for this truth and thus confirmed it with the signature of their blood.

We must add the witness of the saints who came out alive from their tombs after the resurrection of the Lord Christ and appeared to many in Jerusalem, testifying that the redeemer had been truly raised from the dead. All this is more than abundant to establish the faith.

FOUNDATION OF THE CHURCH

The Lord Christ, raised from the dead, having accomplished the work of redemption of the human race which his Father had entrusted him, could have returned at once to the Father in heaven. Nevertheless, he wanted to remain for forty days on earth, first in order to console his holy mother, the apostles, and the other disciples, for a number of days equal to the forty hours during which, according to the Jewish calculation, they were grieved by his death (indeed, he remained dead for this period of time).

Secondly, he wanted to do a lot of good for the human race during these days. During this time he confirmed all the believers in their faith; he taught his apostles; he explained many secrets contained in the sacred books; above all, he made his followers understand that it was necessary that the Christ should suffer death and rise from the dead on the third day, and that penance and the forgiveness of sins should be preached in his name to all peoples.

He also made Peter his vicar on earth and promised that his successor in the *Ecclesia* (whom we call *Papa*) would never be lacking until the consummation of the world.

He gave many instructions regarding the government of the *Ecclesia* and the administration of the *Sacramento*.[8] And he ordered that the Good News, that is, the true way, be preached to the whole world, saying: "All power in heaven and on earth has been given to me. Go, therefore, and make disciples of all nations, baptizing them in the name of the Father, and of the Son, and of the Holy Spirit, teaching them to observe all that I have commanded you." And in order that they might carry out this task more easily and effectively, he gave them the power of working many miracles.

THE ASCENSION

When the day for him to ascend to heaven arrived, intuiting the sadness that his absence would cause his apostles and other disciples, he consoled them with much affection. He promised them that he would watch over them from above and that in his place another teacher and consoler, the *Spirito Sancto*, would come a few days later.

He led his disciples out of Jerusalem and departed for Mount Olivet. He said goodbye to the Virgin Mother and the others with tender and loving words;

---

8. De Rhodes left untranslated the word "sacrament." Today, the Sino-Vietnamese word *bi tich*, literally, mysterious sign, is used.

then he raised his hands and blessed them. And as they all were looking on, he began to be lifted up and was brought to heaven in solemn procession and glorious triumph, accompanied by the souls of the saints who had come out of *limbo* and the whole army of angels. The gates of heaven, closed until this day because of the sins of humanity, were opened to the Redeemer. He himself, in his glorious ascension to the highest heaven, was received by God the Father in the heavenly court amidst such exaltation and joy of all that no tongue can express and no human mind can conceive.

However, the Virgin Mother and the others were astonished, their eyes fixed on heaven. And, behold, two angels stood beside them under human appearances, their garments resplendent. They said: "Men of Galilee, why are you standing there looking at the sky? This Jesus who has been taken up from you into heaven will return in the same way as you have seen him going into heaven."

So that signs attesting the Lord's ascension may reach us also, a divine miracle caused the traces of his feet to be marvelously imprinted on the rock which the Redeemer stepped on as he was being lifted up. The Christians began to scratch this rock to get relics from it. Nevertheless, even till this day, the sacred footprints have remained intact throughout the centuries.

On this subject we must also report the following fact. Once, in memory of the Lord's ascension, Christians were building a small church with a canopy above the sacred footprints. Try as they might with all their skills and efforts, they could not cover the canopy, whereas the rest of the building was easily completed. Doubtless, this is so that the path on which Christ ascended would remain always clear, from the sacred footprints to the highest heaven. Furthermore, every year on the day Christians celebrated the anniversary of the Ascension, the whole of Mount Olivet was illuminated by a marvelous light during the night.

PENTECOST

After the Lord Christ had ascended into heaven, the apostles and the other disciples, together with the Virgin Mother and other pious women, altogether about 120, returned to Jerusalem, entered the room where the Lord, before bidding them goodbye, had eaten the *coena* with his disciples, and remained together in prayer, as the Lord had commanded.

On the tenth day after the Ascension, the fiftieth after the Resurrection, at the third hour according to the Jewish time, that is, about three hours before noon, suddenly there came from the sky a noise like a strong wind, and it filled the entire house where they were staying. They saw tongues as of fire appear and come to rest on each one of them separately, and they were all filled with the *Spirito Sancto*. This miraculous coming of the *Spirito Sancto* confirmed that the Lord Jesus truly resided in heaven where he had gone and was enjoying sovereign power.

At the same time, in order to propagate the Christian faith throughout the world, the apostles and others received the gift of knowledge of things human and divine, a remarkable holiness, and other spiritual embellishments of the soul. Thus, as soon as they had received this *Spiritu Sancto,* they came out in front of the people and began, the apostles first, to evangelize and speak to a very large crowd in different languages, as the *Spiritu Sancto* enabled them.

There were then in Jerusalem Jews coming from all nations under heaven. As news of this spread, a huge number of them gathered and were stupefied, because each one heard them speak in his own language of the marvels of God. Saint Peter stood up with the Eleven apostles and said: "Jews! Know that what God has of old foretold through the prophet Joel has been fulfilled: I will pour out my *spirito* upon all flesh. Your sons and your daughters shall prophesy, your young men shall see visions, your old men shall dream dreams. Israelites! Listen to these words. Jesus of Nazareth, a man commended to you by God with mighty deeds, wonders, and miracles which God worked through him in your midst, this man you have killed, delivering him into the hands of evil men. But God raised him from the dead, according to the words of the prophets, of this we are witnesses. Exalted to the heavens by the power of God, and having received from God his Father the promise of the *Spirito Sancto,* he it is who has poured it forth, as you have both seen and heard." Hearing Saint Peter, the Jews repented in their hearts; instructed by him and the other apostles, three thousand people were baptized on that day.

MISSION TO THE WHOLE WORLD

Then the apostles and other disciples began spreading the Christian religion not only in Jerusalem and the kingdom of Judea but also in the principal regions of the earth. The Lord assisted them, and according to his promises, confirmed their preaching with miracles. By means of these things the effects of the Lord's passion were little by little recognized, and at the same time, in the weakness of the world, in so many sufferings, shame, and even death itself which the Lord had undergone, divine power shone forth by a glorious triumph over its enemies, sin, and the devil.

DE RHODES'S MISSION IN VIETNAM

And we too, the smallest servants of the Lord Jesus Christ, we have come here in the kingdom of Annam, to preach the good news and to propose to all faith in our Lord, so that all may receive the forgiveness of their sins during the time of mercy, before the coming of the day of bitter justice and vengeance, as it has happened to the Jews.

Indeed, our Redeemer delivered himself into the hands of the Jews in order to accomplish the work of our redemption and, as Saint Leo has said, he gave himself up, freely and voluntarily, into the hands of the godless who, while committing their own crime, were serving the Redeemer.

THE PUNISHMENTS OF THE JEWS; DESTRUCTION OF JERUSALEM

Because this crime of the Jews was the most atrocious since the creation of the world, it should not pass without receiving even in this life its punishment, as the Lord of heaven had once foretold through Daniel. After predicting that the Lord Jesus would be put to death by the Jews, he added: "They will not be his people, the people who would reject him; and their end shall be devastation, and after the end of the war, devastation has been decreed."

The Lord Jesus himself, when he came up to Jerusalem shortly before his passion, foresaw that he would be crucified on the *crux* there by the most grievous crime of the Jews. He wept over Jerusalem and said: "The days will come when your enemies will surround you with trenches and will press you on all sides, and they will destroy you entirely, you and your children who are in your bosom; and they will not leave a stone on another stone, because you have not recognized the time of your visitation."

It is true that as he was crucified on the *crux*, Jesus Christ prayed to God his Father for the Jews who were persecuting him very cruelly so that each one of them might receive the fruit of this most holy prayer, repent of such a crime, and convert to God. In fact, several of them did. They were given forty years to do repentance; then came the time of divine vengeance. In the course of a war, Jerusalem was taken by the Romans and destroyed from top to bottom, as the Lord had predicted.

Josephus, one of the principal leaders of the Jews and opponents of Rome, has described this destruction of Jerusalem in seven books and the whole history of this war.[9] He wrote that among the many misfortunes that happened during the siege of Jerusalem, there was such a terrible famine that, besides a great number who died on every side during this war, about twelve thousand people perished in a matter of a few days. He wrote: "Everybody ate what they could find; they gathered for food that which even the most impure beasts would look at with horror. There was an incredible and horrible story of a hungry mother who was suckling her child; she killed it with her own hands, cooked it, and ate it." Josephus also reports that a great multitude of people were killed at war; their number, together with other dead, would amount to eleven thousand. The prisoners of this war against Jerusalem were eighty-seven thousand.

The same Josephus records various strange happenings that marked such a great calamity, and affirms that it was divine vengeance against the evil Jews. The following fact confirms this opinion. Those among them who had received

---

9. De Rhodes is referring to Flavius Josephus's *History of the Jewish War.* For an English translation, see *The Jewish War,* trans. G. A. Williamson (London: Penguin Classics, 1959).

the Christian law were admonished by God and could escape to the city of Pella and avoid such terrible evils.

Appeal to the Vietnamese

Now, too, those of you in this country who, responding to the counsels of divine goodness, receive the faith and submit themselves to the law of God, will place themselves in safety and will escape the future wrath which will come with the eternal calamity. On the other hand, those who contradict the Good News or who, despising the divine counsels, refuse to receive the sweet law of God, will see the coming of the days of a bitter death and judgment, followed by eternal death much more terrible than the disaster of the Jews, of which we will speak in what follows.[10]

Devotion to the Risen Christ

For now let us adore the Lord Jesus seated on the high throne of heaven. Let us ask him pardon for our lives spent in iniquities and at the same time the grace to serve him with all our hearts in the future, rejecting all superstitions and other sins of our past lives.

Here we should present a beautiful picture of the Lord Christ holding the globe in his hands, so that all may adore the Lord Jesus as the true Lord and the sovereign king of heaven and earth.

---

10. De Rhodes is referring to God's judgment after death.

The Eighth Day

Eschatology – The Decalogue – Preparation for Baptism

At the moment someone dies, the Lord of heaven brings a judgment on his or her condition. Those who are not guilty of any sin are admitted at once to eternal happiness; on the contrary, those who die with a grave or mortal sin will immediately have their souls cast into hell, there to suffer eternal fires.

GENERAL JUDGMENT

Nevertheless, at a time whose coming God alone knows, there will be a universal judgment of all people. God has revealed this to the ancient prophets, and the Lord Christ himself often foretold that he would be the judge of this judgment. There are many reasons why the Lord of heaven has decided to hold this universal judgment.

First, because the universal judgment is appropriate to God's glory and to the manifestation of God's justice and providence. Indeed, it often happens that good people are crushed by poverty and adversity, despised and tormented by many, afflicted with diseases and infirmities. On the contrary, evil people enjoy riches, honors, pleasures, and receive preferential treatment in this world. Given these facts, those who are ignorant of the sublime and hidden dispositions of the Lord of heaven and who do not understand the secrets of God, are often bewildered.

Also, it is not rare that someone, forgetful of the weakness of his judgment, is not afraid, in rashness and audacity, of indicting the exceedingly just providence of God. That is why, in order to reveal the disposition of Providence in the government of the human race, all the actions of all people will be laid bare before all at the universal judgment. In this way all will recognize how the Lord of heaven has disposed of all things with justice proportionate of each person's deeds.

On the one hand, the iniquities of the godless deserve the eternal torments of hell; on the other hand, no one is so evil as not to have done some good deeds. Now, the reward for these good deeds cannot be given in hell where there is no consolation whatsoever. Since no good deed should go unrewarded, the providence of God recompenses these good deeds of the wicked with successes in this life. Furthermore, since in this life good people and even saints commit at least venial faults, God punishes them with temporal adversities and pains in this life, so that at their death they may be purer and may be admitted to the heavenly glory more speedily. In addition, by bearing these adversities, they can earn a greater collection of merits and thus increase their happiness. So that all may recognize how this and other things have been disposed most wisely by God, at the universal judgment, all the deeds of all people will be unveiled, and the conduct of divine Providence will be manifested before the human race.

In the second place, because the Lord Christ humiliated himself to death, and death on the *crux*, God the Father has exalted him, establishing him Lord and Judge of all. Thus, he who has been judged most unjustly by men will exercise the supreme judgment on all humanity, and all will freely venerate him or fear him in spite of themselves.

In the third place, it often happens that people, inflamed by the desire to sin, will be deterred from sinning by the feeling of shame if they realize that others will see their actions or that these will not remain secret for long. That is why the Lord God has fixed the day of universal judgment and declared that it will happen, so that those whom the fear of God does not refrain from sinning, will at least be deterred by shame when they realize that all their sins, even the most secret, will be laid bare before all. There are many other reasons for this universal judgment, but let these three suffice.

THE END OF THE WORLD

God has left us uncertain about the time when this universal judgment will take place, just as it is uncertain how long this world will last. Nevertheless, it is certain that the universal judgment will occur at the end of this world. Indeed, it is certain that this world will have an end, at least with regard to the cycle of birth and death in their present mode. For all people will die and the generation of things will cease, as God has often attested in Scripture. As Saint Peter has said, we are awaiting, according to God's promise, new heavens and a new earth. We should not look for reasons for this other than the will of God on whom alone depend the duration and preservation of the world.

The Lord of heaven has not wanted to declare to humans the time of this judgment so that they may live with greater circumspection, not knowing how soon they will appear before the tribunal of God. The Lord Christ has said: "Be ready, because the Son of Man will come at the hour you do not expect." However, our Savior has made known that certain things will happen before the time of the universal judgment. The Christian way will have first spread throughout the earth, as it is happening now, little by little. He has revealed many forerunning signs, saying: "Nation will arise against nation, kingdom against kingdom; there will be pestilences, famines, and earthquakes. All these are the beginning of the pains. Immediately after the tribulations of those days, the sun will be darkened, and the moon will not give its light, and the stars will fall from the sky, and the powers of the heavens will be shaken. All the peoples of the earth will weep. After all these things, fire will come down from the heavens and burn the face of the whole earth, and no one will survive."[1]

THE FINAL RESURRECTION

Then all men and women who have ever lived from the time of Adam to the consummation of the world will rise, each in his or her body, all on the same day. This the Lord of heaven will do as easily as waking up someone from sleep, because God is all-powerful. And because this universal judgment must take place, especially in order to manifest divine justice and providence, it is appropriate that the bodies, whose deeds must be judged, rise. The judgment must take place so that each will give an account of what he or she has done in the body, good as well as evil.

That is why the bodies of the godless will rise hideous and fetid, miserable in all things. But the bodies of the just will be exceedingly beautiful and elegant, perfectly healthy and perfectly aged, in the measure of the age of fullness of the Lord Jesus. They will be subtle, able to penetrate all bodies. They will be luminous with a light similar to sunlight, but without hurting the eyes, which will enjoy it. They will be impassible; not only will they not die anymore but also they will not be subjected to pains and necessities. They will be agile; like the spirits, they will be able to go wherever they wish in an instant.

When the resurrection of all humans is completed, there will appear in heaven the holy *crux* on which the Savior was hung for our sake. This holy *crux* will be shown so that the Jews who have crucified the Lord of majesty recognize their unjust decision, and accused by this wood, acknowledge their fault. It is also so that all the sinners may be confounded for not having, through their own fault, received the fruit of redemption by the *crux*. Similarly, the sight of this saving wood will rejoice the just.

THE COMING OF CHRIST IN THE COMPANY OF HIS MOTHER AND THE SAINTS

Then our Lord Jesus Christ, surrounded by legions of angels and the souls of the saints and accompanied by the holy Virgin Mother, will come with such power and majesty that have never been seen among humans nor can be imagined by human minds.

This universal judgment will take place in the valley of Jehoshaphat near Jerusalem, where the Savior was crucified on the *crux,* condemned for the

---

1. De Rhodes of course assumes that these apocalyptic signs will actually occur at the end of time.

human race by an unjust sentence. That is why he will appear in the heavens, above this valley, seated in the clouds on a holy and splendid throne. The assistants of the divine judge will be first of all the apostles to whom he has promised: "I tell you, you who have followed me, when the Son of Man is seated on this throne of his majesty, you will sit on twelve thrones to judge the twelve tribes of Israel." There will be other saints who in their search for perfection had followed the examples of Christ the Lord.

Then a multitude of angels, sent by Christ the judge into the universe, will gather in a blinking of an eye from the four corners of the world all people before the judge, separating them into two groups, and placing the just on the right of the judge and the evil on his left. Then divine power will not only enable each one to see everything he or she has done during his or her life, both good and evil, as if it were present, but also to see the deeds of all others, as if they were written on their foreheads.

What will then be the joy of the just for having done good and kept the law of God! What will be the regret of the reprobates for their evil deeds! What sorrow, but already too late, for having refused to submit oneself to the law of God! What opprobrium for them to see their crimes spread out in front of thousands of people!

When all humans and angels have seen clearly the deeds, both good and evil, of each, Christ the judge will determine for the just, according to the number and greatness of their merits, corresponding degrees of happiness and glory. He will also pronounce for the wicked, according to the number and gravity of their sins, the depth of their sufferings. And all this with such wisdom and justice that all will see that nothing better or more just can be established.

Then the judge will turn toward the just, who are on his right, and will tell them with a happy face and with loving words: "Come, you who are blessed by my Father. Inherit the kingdom prepared for you from the foundation of the world." Turning next to the wicked who are on his left, he will say with a severe face and with words full of righteous indignation: "Depart from me, you accursed, into the eternal fire prepared for the devil and his angels."

HEAVEN AND HELL

When Christ the supreme judge has pronounced this just and irrevocable sentence, the angels will at once begin to ascend, carrying the holy *crux* with them, in the order in which they descended from the heavens. All the heavenly legions follow them with incredible jubilation. Christ the Lord, together with the Virgin Mary and the immense multitude of saints, will enter the heavens, in a solemn and majestic procession, a true divine triumph.

During this time, the earth will open up into a vast abyss down to the bottom of hell, and those who have been condemned to eternal punishments will be compelled to descend into it, pushed by the demons if they resist. They will turn their eyes to look at the triumph of the just, but dazzled by their exceedingly great light, they will be blinded. They watch the blessed ascend to their eternal happiness, while they themselves, by their own fault, are cast down into the eternal sufferings of hell. They could have easily avoided these sufferings had they been willing to submit themselves to the divine law by following their right reason. They will weep bitterly, groan, and burst with envy and rage. When all of them have entered, the abyss of the earth will close, and these wretched souls will be shut up for all eternity in this horrible and deadly prison. They will be tormented by the eternal fire with the devil and his angels, without any hope of ever coming out.

The exceedingly wise, just, and powerful judge, the Lord Jesus Christ, true King of kings and Lord of lords, upon returning to the heavenly fatherland with his angels and saints, will present to his all-powerful Father the glorious multitude of saints, each raised with his or her body. At once, on the order of this same God and Father, the Lord Jesus, just judge, will distribute to each thrones, insignia, and degrees of happiness, according to the merits of each and in conformity with the sentence he will render on each.

All the blessed, without exception, will abound in both their souls and their bodies with such a great joy that there is nothing left for them to desire. They will enjoy this glory for all eternity, without any danger or fear of ever losing this unspeakable happiness. Each one of these blessed, even the smallest one, will have such majesty and wealth that were all the kings of the earth to combine their riches together to make a throne, they would not be able to match the excellence and majesty of the smallest throne of the blessed.

DE RHODES'S MISSION

On the order of our Lord Jesus Christ, the King of kings, I have come here to bring you the good news and to invite you all in his name to receive these supreme joys of the blessed. I will show the way, and if you are willing to follow it, you will escape the unimaginable torments of eternal misery which the damned, together with the devil, suffer eternally, and you will possess the undescribable happiness in eternity.

Either of these two ends will necessarily happen to each of us, as is attested by the supreme and infallible divine truth. While the goodness of the supreme God permits you the time, choose the good and straight path, that is, during the present life of which we cannot promise ourselves the tomorrow.

If you are wise, grasp at once the divine ladder which I will show you. By climbing it, you will certainly reach the eternal joys of heaven; God himself promises it. And you will escape the eternal pains of hell. Who among you can live with eternal fires?

This path is very simple. It is the divine law taught at the beginning by God to Adam, and with him, to the whole human race and rational creatures. God himself will teach us how to walk on this path on our two feet. Avoid evil and do good. Follow what is conformable to reason and run away from what leads you away from the path of right reason.[2]

THE TEN COMMANDMENTS

Although this light of the face of God was sealed on us, it has been considerably darkened by sins. Therefore, the good Lord, more than two thousand years after the creation of the world, deigned to inscribe on two stone tablets his law which is contained in the Ten Commandments. This law God gave to God's servant Moses, so that Moses himself would teach to the Jewish people, who were then the people of God.

But because this carnal people no longer observed the divine law properly, the Lord of heaven sent his Son Jesus Christ to teach the divine law and to give us, by God's *gratia,* the strength to observe it. The Lord Jesus came not to abolish the law but to perfect it, in order to give us his divine example in fulfilling it.

There are then ten commandments of God. If we observe them, they are like a sure ladder to reach eternal happiness in the heavenly kingdom. God has given two tables of these divine precepts. The first table teaches us how we must honor God in the heart, by word, and by deed. These are the first three commandments of the first table.

WORSHIP OF THE LORD OF HEAVEN AND OUR ATTITUDES TOWARD HIM

The first commandment prescribes us to adore the one and only God, first of all by believing in God. The one who comes near God must believe, for without faith it is impossible to be pleasing God. We must believe everything that God has revealed and all that God proposes to our belief through the *Ecclesia Catholica.* For God is the First Truth who cannot be deceived because God knows all things, even before they come to be, and cannot deceive anyone because God is supreme goodness.

On the contrary, we should not believe the false religions, which are the inventions of the devil to lead humans to perdition. Consequently, we must fear the Lord of heaven above all things, because we believe God can send both our soul and our body into hell.

Although we must, as we will say shortly, fear and honor kings, princes, and their governors, we must fear and honor God above them all and more than them all. The Lord of heaven is the Lord of all things and therefore of all human beings; on God depends our welfare, both temporal and eternal.

The one who fears God thus above everything, should fear neither idols nor

---

2. Once again, de Rhodes emphasizes that not only Christian doctrine but also Christian morality are conformable to right reason. It is the conformity of Christian morality to reason, de Rhodes tells us, that makes many Vietnamese Confucian scholars and Buddhist monks accept the Christian faith.

demons that are in them, since none of them can, without the permission or order of God, harm us or even take away a single hair of ours.

That is why we must also hope in God above all things, both because God is all-powerful and because God is our loving Father who has loved us so much as to deliver his own Son to death to be our remedy and to forgive our sins. If the Lord of heaven has not spared his own Son but has delivered him for us, while we were still his enemies, how much more, once reconciled, will we not be saved by God from his anger? We must therefore first of all hope from the divine goodness for the unfailing forgiveness of our sins, if we take these remedies in the way God himself intends.

Once the remission of our sins is obtained, we must hope from the divine mercy for the final perseverance which opens for us the way to eternal beatitude. We must, of course, hope for it by our merits through the divine mercy, but also from the *gratia* of God which precedes, follows, and applies us to good works.

Next, we must also hope for temporal goods, life, health, and other goods of this world insofar as they are necessary and useful for us to possess eternal life in the next age.

Above all, this precept enjoins upon us a sincere love for the good Lord of heaven, whom we must love with all our heart and above all things. God is altogether worthy of all our love for God's sake, having loved us first and filled us, even without our merits, with so many benefits. That is why we must love God who is infinitely great and good more than ourselves, more than our parents, our children, our own life, ready to lose all things to preserve God's friendship and good will, and to suffer all things rather than offend God.

INTERNAL AND EXTERNAL CULT

The worship of the Lord of heaven takes place above all in the heart and soul since the supreme and infinite God is spirit. As the true Teacher and Lord Jesus Christ has taught, it is necessary that those who worship God, worship him in spirit and truth. But because we receive our bodies from God, we also owe God an external cult, building temples and altars to worship and adore God.

Granted that we should adore God above all things, but why is it not allowed, some may ask, to worship the idols under God? For example, in a kingdom, we honor the king or the supreme monarch above everyone else, but we also honor under him other chiefs and magistrates; the king does not forbid it, he even commands it. Indeed, this goes to show that we must not only render God the supreme cult called *latria* but also render a certain interior cult called *duleia* to the saints who are God's friends through whom we pray for divine gifts. The Sovereign Lady, in particular, we must venerate less than God but more than all the other saints, with a cult called *hyperduleia*.[3] Through her in-

---

3. These distinctions are very helpful since in Vietnamese the word *kinh tho* (venerate and adore) is used both for the adoration of God and the veneration of human beings, especially the ancestors.

tercession and that of the other saints, we must hope from the divine goodness many benefits of which we would justly be deprived because of our demerits and sins. But because of the merits of the saints, intimate friends of the divine goodness, God is moved and in his mercy grants us these benefits.

The Worship of Idols

Idols are nothing but demons, sworn enemies of the divine majesty. The gods of the pagans are demons or creations of the demons who cannot move God in our favor but rather drive God to a just punishment against us. Hence, we must reject all these creations and these lies to be able to adore God rightly and make God favorable to us. Those who honor a rebel or deserter no doubt earn the king's anger for themselves.

Consequently, we must absolutely reject all superstitious cult, and venerate and adore the one true God with all our heart, with all our soul, and with all our strength. This is the first commandment of God.

The Swearing of Oaths

The second commandment prescribes us not to offend God with our tongue by swearing by God's name in vain. For an oath in the name of God or of divine things not to be a sin, there are three conditions: truth, justice, and necessity. To swear for a falsehood is always a mortal sin. We would offend the divine majesty seriously if we call God in witness of a falsehood, even in matters of little importance. It would make the Lord of heaven a liar or an accomplice in a lie, which is without doubt a grave offense. If the oath is made against justice in serious matters, it would be a serious sin; in slight matters, generally, it would not be a serious sin. If there is no necessity, most often it is a slight sin, provided the oath is true and just.

We must faithfully fulfill the vows made to the Lord of heaven so as not to offend the divine majesty. It would be better not to make vows at all than to make them and not keep them. Similarly, making a promise to whomever and confirming it with an oath, and not fulfilling it, is to despise the divine majesty. To swear by the idols or by the demons rebellious to the divine majesty is a grave offense against God. Making a vow to them or making a promise in their honor is a serious sin.

We must lead the pagans, when they swear by their false gods whom they fear, to allow us to swear by the true God whom we acknowledge as the Lord of life and death.[4] But we must prefer any loss whatsoever, either of our mate-

---

4. This advice was very useful for the Vietnamese in the seventeenth century since many of them, being soldiers, had to swear a loyalty oath to the lord. On one occasion, one Christian soldier asked and was allowed to swear his loyalty oath in Christian terms. Once, de Rhodes himself had to swear his loyalty to Lord Trinh Trang; he did so in Christian terms.

rial possessions or of our own life, to swearing an oath in which we appear to invoke the false gods or to acknowledge them as lords of life and death.

As well, we must rather suffer death itself than deny God or the Christian way, even on our lips. Our Savior says: "Everyone who acknowledges me before others, I will acknowledge before my Father; but everyone who denies me before others, I will deny before the angels of God."

Holy Days

The third commandment, the last in the table concerning honoring God, orders us to sanctify the feast days. On these days, which we call feast days, we must dedicate ourselves in a special manner to the worship and veneration of God. It stands to reason that we must celebrate certain feast days to honor in a special way the many great benefits of the divine goodness.

On these days we must refrain from manual labor, which has to do with our corruptible body, in order to be able to devote ourselves more freely and more intensely to the worship of God and to the affairs of our soul. That is why the holy *Ecclesia* or the sovereign pastors in the *Ecclesia* who watch over us have imposed a certain number of days of this sort, especially the Day of the Lord. We devote six days to our bodies and to the things of the body, during which we should always offer something to God and to the soul, at least in the morning before we go to work and in the evening when we come home. But the day which we call the Lord's Day we rightly consecrate especially to God to honor on that day more particularly the divine majesty and to celebrate with gratitude the benefits received from the divine goodness.

Just as the sovereign creator of all things created everything in six days and rested from his work on the seventh, let us work on six days and let us avoid laziness, the origin of all evils. But on the seventh day, or rather the first day (for the seventh day, formerly a feast day, has been changed; the day which Christians observe nowadays as a feast day is the Lord's Day when the Lord Jesus was raised from the dead), let us abandon all works that concern the body and devote ourselves better to divine worship and the salvation of our souls. The same thing should be said about the other feast days contained in the calendar according to the precepts of the *Ecclesia*.

The Second Table: Love of Neighbor

The second table of the divine law teaches us how we must act toward our neighbor, that is, all people. It contains seven commandments which are summarized in this one commandment of love toward the neighbor: "You will love your neighbor as yourself." That is, whatever we wish others do for us, let us do for them; and whatever you do not wish others do to you, do not do it to them. Indeed, we must wish our neighbors well, love them not only in word but also in deed and in truth, not to harm them in any way, in their persons, their honor, their possessions, by deed, word, or even interior desire, even if not carried out in action. This is all that is contained in the seven commandments of the second table.

Duties toward Superiors and Parents

The fourth commandment, called in Scripture the first in the promise, teaches us to show our parents the honor that is due to them. Under parents we should include all our superiors. By honor we understand four things: love, respect, obedience, and assistance. Love, by wishing them and asking God to give them not evil but all goods. Respect, by submitting ourselves to them and not offending them in word and in deed. Obedience, by doing what they order rightly, above all if it is useful for our eternal salvation. And, assistance, by providing them with all that they need, especially during their old age and illness. Should they need spiritual assistance, because they do not yet know God or deviate from the path of eternal salvation, we must apply ourselves with greater fervor since the salvation of the soul is more important than that of the body.

To this commandment are also attached honor, respect, obedience that are due to kings, princes, governors, teachers, and leaders, each according to his rank. Not obeying these persons in what they command according to right reason or offending them is a sin against the divine law. It is a very serious crime to rebel against one's sovereign. The reason why we must obey our superiors is not only that we must show them gratitude for their beneficences and the care they take of us, but also that in honoring their persons we honor the Lord of heaven from whom the source of all dominion, all power derives. Consequently, we must obey in conscience, because of God from whom we expect reward for this obedience and whose punishment we fear for our disobedience.

We must know that we must obey our parents and other superiors in all things except in what is opposed to God's commandments. It is better to obey God than humans. First, because the Lord of heaven is by far higher and more venerable; secondly, because divine vengeance is far more terrible than that of humans. The latter can punish us by depriving us of material possessions or life, but God, in addition to these, can deliver us to eternal punishments. Third, though we owe a lot to our parents and our sovereigns, we owe much more to the sovereign Father of all, the Lord of lords, without whom the former have nothing to give us. The benefits of God are infinite in number and immense in greatness, especially when this divine majesty has borne for our sake (which no one has done) so many insults and sufferings and shed for us his blood of inestimable price and given his life.

It is to be noted that this commandment, which enjoins children and subjects to obey their parents and sovereigns, also enjoins the latter to counsel their children and subjects according to their conditions, to care for them, to correct their vices. In this way, the sovereigns protect the rights and the common good of all, and the parents teach their children good morals, especially those affecting eternal salvation.

Lastly, in this commandment are included all our neighbors. We must do good to all, helping them in their needs, both spiritual and material, as we would like them to assist us. On the day of the last judgment we will be asked to give an account on this point in particular, because the Lord Jesus will reward us for the good we did to others as if it had been done to himself, and he will punish us for refusing to come to the aid of our neighbors in their necessities as if we had refused it to himself.

HOMICIDE AND MURDER

The fifth commandment, which says, "Thou shalt not kill," prohibits homicide but not the killing of other animals.[5] Because the Lord God created all living beings and all bodily things for humans and gave them the right to take living beings for their use, killing them is not a sin (unless they belong to someone else, since killing them against the wish of their owner is contrary to the seventh commandment of which we will speak shortly).

But because the Lord of heaven did not make human for human but for himself and in his image and likeness, killing a human person is a very grave sin, against God himself. Just as when someone kills a servant of a prince, he is deemed to offend the prince himself grievously.

This same commandment forbids mutilating, striking, and harming the body of the neighbor. Just as it is forbidden to kill a human person because he is a servant of God, so, for the same reason, it is forbidden to do him harm. Nevertheless, princes, governors, and judges may chastise criminals and inflict them with a just punishment. Since all power derives from God, those who hold from God a just power are deemed to have the right to punish evil people with justice, even with death, to prevent their wickedness from spreading further and to deter others by these punishments from committing the same crimes.

SEXUAL ACTS OUTSIDE MARRIAGE

The sixth commandment prohibits every carnal act outside a legitimate marriage. Because these acts have been instituted for the sake of the begetting of children and their legitimate education, this act is licit only if it can issue in a legitimate offspring; much less is it permitted if no offspring can issue.

A legitimate marriage is one of one man and one woman so that as long as one partner is alive, no other partner may be taken. Consequently, polygamy as well as divorce is contrary to the divine law. Indeed, at the beginning, it was not so, as the Lord Jesus himself has taught with his own divine mouth. In fact,

---

5. There is here a polemic against the Buddhist prohibition to kill all life, because of the belief in reincarnation.

at the beginning, God gave Adam only one woman, Eve, and he remained with her until his death, for 930 years.

STEALING

The seventh commandment prohibits all usurpation of the goods belonging to another against his or her will. Thus, theft, which is taking things without the knowledge of their owner; robbery, which is stealing done with violence; fraud, which is done in business or contracts; and finally, all damages such as the killing of an ox or a horse of someone, burning his house, all acts of this kind are contrary to this commandment.

It is also necessary to know that it is a sin not only taking the possessions of another, as we have just said, but also unjustly keeping a good against the will of its owner or without his knowledge (which is but a continuation of theft). Thus, sins of this sort, as long as the damage caused has not been repaired as much as possible, are not forgiven.

LYING AND BEARING FALSE WITNESS

The eighth commandment, which says, "Thou shalt not bear false witness against your neighbor," prohibits harming the reputation and good name of another. It is possible to harm the reputation of another in three ways. First, by bearing false witness against someone in the court of law, which is a very serious sin, because it is contrary to justice, charity, and the common good. Second, by falsely accusing someone of a crime outside the court of law, which is also a grave sin, according to the gravity of the accusation and the quality of the person accused. Third, by uncovering a hidden crime, because no one would like to see one's faults divulged in public. In virtue of this commandment we are forbidden to offend our neighbor in words or in all other ways.

Finally, we must know that the one who has harmed the reputation of some-one must repair it, as if he had taken a material good. Normally, people, especially if they belong to the nobility, experience more pain when their reputation is harmed than when their possessions are taken. If someone has borne false witness in the court of law which has caused a damage, he or she must repair the damage in addition to the reputation.

ILLICIT DESIRES

Before speaking of the last two commandments, which say, "Thou shalt not covet the wife of your neighbor; thou shalt not covet the possessions of an-other," let us make this observation. Whenever the divine law forbids a deed, it also forbids the willing of this action. Thus, since it is forbidden to lie, it is also never permitted to decide in one's heart to lie. For the root of sin lies in the will, such that, if the free will does not consent to an action forbidden by the divine law, there is no sin.

Thus, if a mad person who cannot make use of free will does something contrary to the commandments of God, he or she is not guilty of sin. On the contrary, someone who can exercise judgment and decides, for instance, to kill someone, even if he does not actually kill that person, has already violated the commandment of God who sees the intimate thoughts of the heart and forbids even the willing to sin.

SINS OF DESIRE

This said, although the will to act against any commandment whatever is a sin, nevertheless, the coveting both of the wife and the goods of the neighbor is expressly prohibited by a special commandment, because the fallen nature of humans inclines them to these two sins more than to the others. No one, or rarely does anyone, kills a person for the sake of killing, or perjures for the sake of perjury. On the contrary, it is the desire for the goods or the wife of another which incites people to commit theft or adultery. That is why a special commandment forbids these two desires.

Although the ninth commandment prohibits all carnal desire, it is the desire for the wife of another that is singled out, because adultery, in addition to being a sin of lust, is also a grave injustice against the other partner.

The tenth commandment forbids the desire for the goods of another, which can be done in two ways. First, by desiring to take them by force; secondly, by just desiring to possess these goods or other things of this kind. The first desire is that which is properly forbidden by this commandment. But we must also avoid the second, because many evils arise from too great a desire for riches.

Such are the Ten Commandments of the divine law or the ten steps by which we climb without fail to the eternal beatitude of heaven. If anyone breaks just one of these steps, he will without doubt fall into eternal perdition, unless he repents in time.

All these commandments are summarized in two. The first is: "You shall love the Lord, your God, with all your heart, with all your soul, and with all your strength." The second: "You shall love your neighbor as yourself." In these two commandments are contained all the divine law. The one who keeps it will live eternally; the one who neglects it, will be struck with eternal death.

PRACTICAL ADVICE

Anyone who has listened to the entire catechism up to this point and has any doubt can express it either in public or in private, as he or she prefers. If the doubt concerns one's wife or wives, it would be better to hear him in private, and a decision made with him about what he has to do. The baptism will have to be postponed until he has done what has been decided. Experience teaches us that if these promises are not carried out before baptism, it would be very difficult to break these chains of the devil after baptism.

When all have expressed their doubts, we prepare them for receiving baptism by the following acts. Because these acts are supernatural, they must pray to the good God on their knees by reciting the Our Father and the Hail Mary. They must ask for the intercession of the Blessed Virgin Mary, the Mother of God, so that these acts may be performed well and that the catechumens be disposed to receive *gratia,* that is, friendship with God, in baptism.

Each one must answer the questions with the mouth and the heart. As they answer to the questions in all modesty with their mouths, let them indicate their consent in their hearts by crossing their arms on their breasts.

ACT OF FAITH

The first act is that of faith by which they believe the infallible truth of God who can neither be deceived nor deceive us. God reveals to us and proposes to us through the *Ecclesia* first that God is a spiritual being, infinite, eternal, immense, exceedingly wise, exceedingly powerful, exceedingly good, better than whom nothing can be imagined, first principle and ultimate end of all things.

God is unique in God's essence and trine in God's persons, Father, Son and *Spirito Sancto,* such that the Father is truly God, the Son is truly God, the *Spirito Sancto* is truly God. They are, however, not three gods, but these three persons are the one true God, all-powerful, creator of heaven and the earth and all things, visible and invisible. The Father, proceeding from no one, is true God and true Father because from all eternity he alone, without any other person, generates his Son to whom he communicates all his divine essence by a true and ineffable generation. The Son is also true God and true Son, generated without a mother by the eternal Father by a true generation, consubstantial, equal, coeternal with the Father. The *Spirito Sancto* is also true God, true and eternal love, proceeding from the Father and the Son, by whom the Father and the Son love each other ineffably from all eternity, communicating eternally to the *Spirito Sancto* all their divine essence.

There are, therefore, three divine persons really distinct, but these three persons are not three gods, but are one true God. If all this surpasses your intelligence, we must believe it nonetheless firmly, because the Lord of heaven has revealed thus about himself. Do you believe this with all your heart? Each one must truly respond and say: "I do truly believe so."

We must also believe that this true God, one in essence and trine in persons, is our first principle and our last end, who gives eternal rewards to the good and eternal punishments to the wicked. Do you believe this?

A: I do truly believe that it is so.

We must also believe that the only and true Son of God, our Lord Jesus Christ, has taken human nature for our eternal salvation and is made true man by the power of the *Spirito Sancto,* truly conceived and born of the Blessed

Virgin Mary who was virgin before parturition, virgin during parturition, and virgin after parturition, such that the Lord Jesus is truly God, born of the eternal Father without a mother before the ages, and truly man, born in time of the Virgin Mary without a father. Do you believe that it is so?

A: I do firmly believe so.

Next, we must believe that this same our Lord Jesus Christ, true God and true man, who has committed no sin, was crucified for our sins, died on the *crux* to free us from sins and eternal death. Although he is impassible and immortal in his divine form, in his human form he has truly suffered and died for us. Do you believe that it is truly so?

A: I do firmly believe that it is so.

Furthermore, we must believe that this same Our Lord Jesus Christ, after he had freely, of his own will, separated his soul from his body and truly died, was raised from the dead by his own power on the third day, and after several apparitions to his disciples, on the fortieth day after his resurrection, ascended into heaven in an admirable manner under the eyes of his disciples, and is reigning alive in the heavens and has all power in the heavens and on the earth, and at the end of the world, will come in glory to judge the living and the dead. He will then give eternal recompense to the good, making their bodies and souls eternally happy. Similarly, he will chastise the wicked with eternal punishments, delivering both their bodies and their souls to the eternal fires of hell. Do you believe that it is so?

A: I do firmly believe that it is so.

Lastly, we must believe everything that is believed by the *Ecclesia Catholica Apostolica*, which is the assembly of all the Christian faithful spread throughout the world under the sovereign ruler, the *Papa* in the nation of Rome, vicar of the Lord Jesus Christ, successor of Saint Peter. Do you believe that it is truly so?

A: I do truly believe that it is so.

ACT OF FEAR

The second act is that of fear of God and of our Lord Jesus Christ whom we must fear above all things, who not only has the power of life and death in this life, but who, after putting one to death, can cast one's body and soul into hell, delivering the rebels and the disobedient to the eternal fires of hell to be burnt and to suffer eternally. Do you thus fear the Lord Jesus above all things?

A: I do fear him thus above all things.

ACT OF HOPE

The third act is that of hope, which makes us hope, by the merits of Jesus Christ, our Lord and Savior, and by the divine mercy which he has promised, for the forgiveness of all our sins, if we take all the means which he has most mercifully given us. These are true penance, the reception of the *sacramento* which our Lord Jesus has commanded and which it is in our power to receive in time. Do you hope for the remission of your sins in this way?

A: I do hope for it in this way.

Furthermore, we must hope from the divine mercy, by the merits of Jesus Christ our Lord, for eternal life which will be given to us, with God's assistance and by the promise of God, if we cooperate with God. Do you hope that eternal life will be given you in this way?

A: I do hope that eternal life will be given me in this way.

Lastly, we must hope, from the divine goodness which has promised thus, for all the temporal goods which are necessary for us to live this life in such manner as to obtain eternal life. But above all, we must hope from the mercy of God the help of divine *gratia* by the merits of Christ, so as to be able to keep the divine law until the end of our life. Do you hope for all these things from the divine mercy?

A: I do hope for them and have confidence in this manner.

ACT OF LOVE

The fourth act is that of love for God above all things, because the Lord of heaven is infinitely perfect, good, containing in himself all goodness perfectly, and thus is worthy of all love. Do you love God, the supreme Good, above all that which is lovable?

A: I do love God in this way.

But because true love does not consist in words but in deeds, and because the Lord Jesus Christ has said, "If anyone loves me, let him keep my commandments," the proof of love is shown in deeds. If we love God, we must have the firm resolve to keep all God's commandments, with God's help, until the end of our lives. Do you have this resolve?

A: I do have this resolve.

ACT OF SORROW

The fifth act is that of the heart's sorrow for sins and the detestation of them above all things that are detestable, because they offend God, more lovable than all things, whom we should have loved above all things for so many reasons, and from whom we have received so many and so great benefits. Above all, it is because this God has been made man for our sake, and because God has borne so many sufferings on the *crux,* until death, for our sins. Therefore, we must have our hearts crushed with pain for having offended the divine goodness, whom we should have honored, in such a horrible manner by our sins.

Here, we should show again the picture of our Savior Jesus Christ hung on the *crux,* so that all may conceive sorrow in their hearts, open up their interior senses, and express externally whatever their spirit and feelings suggest.

Then we should ask them all if they truly are sorry above all things for having offended the infinite divine goodness.

A: I am sorry in this manner.

But because true repentance does not only weep over past sins but does not repeat again what we should weep over, we must take the resolution to suffer pains and adversities rather than offending the divine goodness again. Do you have this firm resolution?

A: I do have this firm resolution.

IMMEDIATE PREPARATION FOR BAPTISM

Now we must send everyone away so that each can weep in private over his or her sins, at least for one night. They must humbly ask the good God for the forgiveness of their sins, by the merits of the sacred passion and death of our Savior Jesus Christ and with the intercession of the Blessed Virgin Mary, Mother of God, and of all the saints. They must fast and pray so that, on the following day, they may approach, better prepared, the sacred bath of baptism.

Those to be baptized must be without any impediment, that is, having rejected all the idols, not only from their hearts but also from their houses which are the houses of the Lord. They must not wish ill to anyone, keep any rancor in their hearts, but must have forgiven all their enemies and repaired all damages. Husbands must have only one wife, the legitimate one, and married women must be the legitimate wives; otherwise they must ask for a certificate of repudiation before baptism. Finally, they must not have debts to be paid immediately.

These are the four kinds of people we must not as a rule admit to baptism before they have fulfilled what they promise. Experience has taught me that in these pagan countries, catechumens promise a lot to obtain baptism, but they tend not to keep their promises after reception of baptism, especially in matters regarding concubines.

That is in general what must be taught before baptism for the greater glory of God.

Index

Page numbers in italics refer to Part Two,
the *Cathechismus* of Alexandre de Rhodes, S.J.

FAITH AND CULTURES SERIES
An Orbis Series on Contextualizing Gospel and Church
General Editor: Robert J. Schreiter, C.PP.S.

The *Faith and Cultures Series* deals with questions that arise as Christian faith attempts to respond to its new global reality. For centuries Christianity and the church were identified with European cultures. Although the roots of Christian tradition lie deep in Semitic cultures and Africa, and although Asian influences on it are well documented, that original diversity was widely forgotten as the church took shape in the West.

Today, as the churches of the Americas, Asia, and Africa take their place alongside older churches of Mediterranean and North Atlantic cultures, they claim the right to express Christian faith in their own idioms, thought patterns, and cultures. To provide a forum for better understanding this process, the Orbis *Faith and Cultures Series* publishes books that illuminate the range of questions that arise from this global challenge.

Orbis and the *Faith and Cultures Series* General Editor invite the submission of manuscripts on relevant topics.

Also in the Series

Faces of Jesus in Africa, Robert J. Schreiter, C.PP.S., Editor
Hispanic Devotional Piety, C. Gilbert Romero
African Theology in Its Social Context, Bénézet Bujo
Models of Contextual Theology, Stephen B. Bevans, S.V.D.
Asian Faces of Jesus, R. S. Sugirtharajah, Editor
Evangelizing the Culture of Modernity, Hervé Carrier, S.J.
St. Martín de Porres: "The Little Stories" and the Semiotics of Culture, Alex García-Rivera
The Indian Face of God in Latin America, Manuel M. Marzal, S.J., Eugenio Maurer, S.J., Xavierio Albó, S.J., and Bartomeu Melià, S.J.
Towards an African Narrative Theology, Joseph Healy, M.M., and Donald Sybertz, M.M.
The New Catholicity, Robert Schreiter, C.PP.S
The Earth Is God's: A Theology of American Culture, William A. Dyrness